THE NEW HIGH YIELD BOND MARKET

Investment Opportunities, Strategies and Analysis

Jess Lederman
Michael P. Sullivan

PROBUS PUBLISHING COMPANY
Chicago, Illinois
Cambridge, England

ISBN 1-55738-436-3

Printed in the United States of America

BB

1 2 3 4 5 6 7 8 9 0

To the pioneers of the new high-yield market.

Table of Contents

Preface

During the last few years, the market for high-yield fixed-income securities has been almost entirely transformed. The speculative excesses of the 1980s—in the form of leveraged buyouts, recapitalizations and mergers and acquisitions—led to the bust of the 1990s. Defaults skyrocketed, spreads widened and the supply of credit for higher risk transactions was greatly curtailed. But the brokerage firms, banks, mutual funds, insurance companies, pension funds, and other investors who poured hundreds of billions of dollars into high-yield bonds in the last decade have not abandoned this market in favor of treasuries and AAA-rated debt.

The high-yield market has been reborn, but with a very different set of rules for playing the game.

The New High-Yield Bond Market: Investment Opportunities, Strategies and Analysis is the first book that addresses not only the new realities of the traditional high-yield market—the market for corporate debt—but also the alternative vehicles that investment managers and advisors are increasingly using to reduce risk without sacrificing return. The book's structure reflects this dual purpose. Part One focuses on the traditional market, but emphasizes the new opportunities and analytical techniques that have emerged in recent years. Section One, *Strategies and Analytical Techniques*, features chapters that discuss the future of high-yield corporates, analytical tools for merger and acquisition and HLT (highly leveraged transactions) deals, the use of financial ratios in evaluating transactions, the construction of tailored high-yield indexes, and the securitization of portfolios of high-yield debt.

Section Two, *Evaluating Corporate Bond Downgrades and Defaults*, examines the historical database of default experience, the techniques available for predicting future defaults, and the effect of default rate assumption on expected yield.

Section Three, *Opportunities and Pitfalls in Distressed Securities*, focuses on one of the fastest growing and least understood sectors of the high-yield market. Several case studies show how trading in distressed securities offers outstanding returns—and equally high risks. Other chapters look at different aspects of distressed securities, including approaches to selling troubled loans.

Part Two, *Alternative High-Yield Markets*, explores two of the most significant new markets that have emerged as investors look for ways to diversify their high-yield portfolios beyond corporate debt. Section One, *Opportunities in Sovereign Bonds*, analyzes the market for bonds issued by governments of developing nations. Section Two, *High-Yield Mortgage-Backed Securities*, shows how the trillion dollar mortgage- and asset-backed market has evolved three unique high-yield instruments: residuals, stripped securities, and subordinate securities.

— *Jess Lederman*

Contributing Authors

Kenneth J. Bock
Vice President
Morgan Stanley & Co.

Joyce Chang
Sovereign Assessment Group
Salomon Brothers

Michael A. Cherry
Merrill Lynch

Neil D. Dabney
Dabney/Resnick and Wagner, Inc.

Dirk W. Damrau
Sovereign Assessment Group
Salomon Brothers

Stephen H. D'Antonio
Vice President
Morgan Stanley & Co.

Jerome S. Fons
Moody's Investors Service

Mark R. Franklin
Corporate Bond Trading
Salomon Brothers

Martin S. Fridson, CFA
Merrill Lynch

Stuart C. Gilson
Harvard Business School

Lakhbir Hayre
Prudential Securities

Gail I. Hessol
Managing Director
Standard & Poor's

Kimberly L. Hirschman
Associate
Morgan Stanley & Co.

Randall C. Hoffman
Vice President
Morgan Stanley & Co.

Adrian Katz
Prudential Securities

Noel E.D. Kirnon
Associate Director
Moody's Investors Service

John G. Lonski
Senior Economist
Moody's Investors Service

Douglas J. Lucas
Assistant Vice President
Moody's Investors Service

Raymond W. McDaniel, Esq.
Managing Director
Moody's Investors Service

Errol Mustafa
Prudential Securities

Peter Niculescu
Vice President
Goldman Sachs

Vincent J. Palermo
Bond Portfolio Analysis
Salomon Brothers

Michael Pettis
Director
Emerging Countries Capital Markets
First Boston Corporation

Vincent Pica
Prudential Securities

John F.H. Purcell
Sovereign Assessment Group
Salomon Brothers

William B. Sacher
Associate Director
Bear Stearns & Co. Inc.

Darryl L. Schall
Dabney/Resnick and Wagner, Inc.

Michael C. Singer
R.D. Smith & Company, Inc.

Frank Torchen
Senior Vice President
General Electric Capital
and
Adjunct Professor
Pace University

Mitchell F. Vernick
Senior Group President
Heller Financial, Inc.

Rick Villaume
Prudential Securities

William F. Wallace
Managing Director
Morgan Stanley & Co.

Richard J. Watson
Vice President
Morgan Stanley & Co.

PART ONE:

HIGH YIELD CORPORATE DEBT

SECTION ONE:

STRATEGIES AND ANALYTICAL TECHNIQUES

Chapter One

The Future of the High Yield Bond Business*

by Martin S. Fridson, CFA
Merrill Lynch
and
Michael A. Cherry
Merrill Lynch

The default wave that began in 1989 did not kill the high yield bond market. Neither will deleveraging and debt repurchases. Mutual funds and (in time) insurance companies should have healthy appetites for noninvestment grade deals, as long as they are structured reasonably. The greater challenge may prove to be finding issuers that view noninvestment grade debt as the most attractive financing option.

Financial firms do surprisingly little forecasting of high yield bond supply and demand, considering their sizable allocation of resources to the area. In the mutual fund sector alone, there are 86 funds specializing in taxable noninvestment grade securities.[1] Portfolio managers report that upwards of 50 brokerage firms call on them to sell high yield obligations. On top of the large manpower commitments implied by

---

[1] *Source:* Investment Company Institute.

* Note: Laurie Allen, Ian Borsook and Mary Leming-Dennis provided valuable assistance in producing this study.

inventories in the $201 billion speculative grade market. As far as the publicly available evidence indicates, however, firms are making no commensurate effort in estimating future resource needs.

The disparity between the benefits of having reliable forecasts, on the one hand, and the limited efforts of financial services firms to make them, on the other, gives pause to would-be prophets. Perhaps those who have strong incentives to forecast have encountered serious obstacles. They may have concluded that the quality of information they could realistically hope to obtain would not justify the effort. This hypothesis is supported by two discoveries we made in the course of our study.

First, we found that we could estimate certain variables only by calculating them as small percentages of other numbers that seemed reasonably predictable. This meant that minor estimation errors could potentially produce wildly inaccurate results. For example, we determined that high yield mutual funds accounted for just 1.5% of financial assets of individuals. If projecting that rate into the future turned out to represent a "small" error of one percentage point, the misstatement of demand from the mutual fund sector would be 67%, i.e., 1% divided by 1.5%. Business planners' aversion to forecasting may be largely explained by similar instances in which small tolerances coincide with high sensitivities.

A second forecasting problem in high yield involves the market's historical propensity for major discontinuities. In 1983, for instance, new issue volume rose by 199% over the preceding year. The surge was not explained by growth in overall corporate bond issuance; the noninvestment grade slice of the pie leapt from 6% to 16%. An even greater discontinuity occurred in 1990, when high yield new issuance plummeted by 95% in volume terms and from 9% to less than 1% of total corporate issuance. Neither in 1983 nor in 1990 did related economic series foretell such radical shifts in noninvestment grade bond volume.

Based on the dual impediments of high sensitivity to small errors and chronic discontinuities, we have established two fundamental principles for the present forecast. First, we have deemphasized point estimates in favor of ranges and orders of magnitude. Second, we have distinguished between baseline supply/demand (premised on stable relationships among the relevant variables) and the very different figures that might result in the event of massive discontinuities. As a rule, managers should budget for the former and formulate contingency plans for the latter.

To organize our analysis, we have devised the simple supply/demand model shown in Figure 1.1. Note that over time, the two columns in Figure 1.1 must equate, even though dealers' capital may sop up temporary surpluses or fill temporary shortages (through inventory drawdowns or, if necessary, short sales). To illustrate, suppose that insurance companies decide (or are compelled) to reduce their high yield exposure. Dealer inventories can absorb the initial flurry of selling, but

Figure 1.1—Components of Supply and Demand

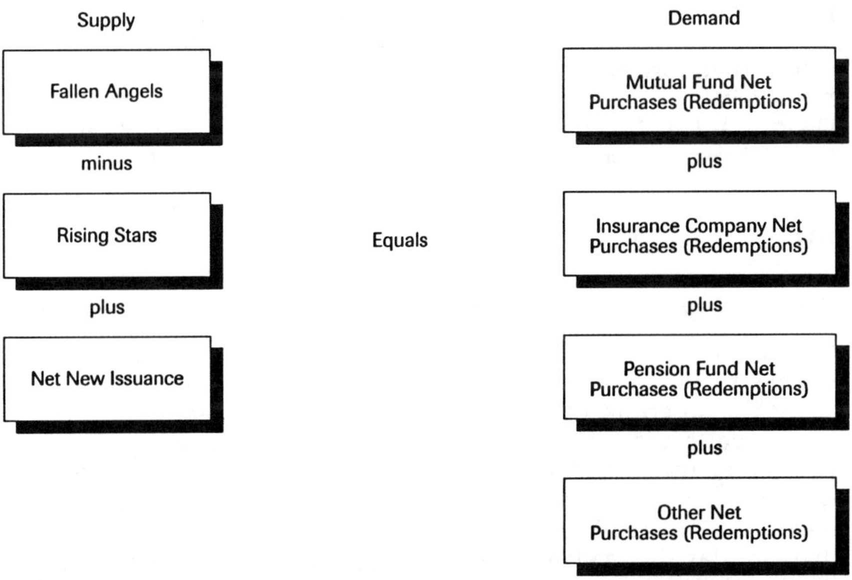

Note: This analysis defines "supply" and "demand" in "final" terms, i.e., in the sense of increasing or decreasing the amount of high yield assets outstanding. Refinancing of existing debt results in a purchase, but does not represent supply in our sense inasmuch as the new debt it creates is offset by retirement of old debt, so that the size of the high yield universe is not affected. Financing volume, in the investment banker's terms, is not identical to the demand we have set out to analyze.

In a similar vein, reinvestment of coupons is not a source of demand distinct from the categories illustrated above. Rather, the decision (on the part of a mutual fund shareholder, for example) to reinvest income is a residual of the individual's choice between saving and consuming. Recently, many insurance companies have elected not to reinvest their high yield income in the high yield sector, thereby effecting a reallocation of assets. Viewed in this light, the partial plowback of the $20 billion or so of annual coupon flow from nondefaulted, cash-paying high yield bonds is not quite the "guaranteed demand" source that it is cracked up to be.

before long the market-makers will reach their position limits. At that point, there are just a few ways for the market to get back into balance, some of which are rather improbable. For instance, cash inflows at the mutual funds might at that very moment generate purchases at prices at which insurance companies would be willing to liquidate. In a still more remarkable set of coincidences, an improving economic climate might shrink the high yield universe sufficiently (through upgradings) to offset the insurance company liquidations. The most likely scenario, though, would be a general price drop, resulting directly from the insurers' selling pressure. At that point, pension funds might be induced to increase their holdings, based on perceptions of an improved risk/reward ratio. Alternatively, corporate issuers might be the purchasers, motivated by opportunities to retire debt at deeper discounts than formerly.

The balance of this study will focus on quantifying the variables in Figure 1.1. Our timeframe will be the years 1992–1996, with an objective of forecasting an average annual rate over that period.

SUPPLY FACTORS

Fallen Angels and Rising Stars

One major factor that causes the size and composition of the noninvestment grade universe to change over time is the mobility of issuers along the spectrum of credit quality. In 1990 alone, $19.1 billion of investment grade corporate debt declined to Standard & Poor's speculative grade range, i.e., BB+ or lower. (Of this amount, an estimated 97% was in the nonconvertible category that comprises our current $201 billion tally of total high yield outstandings.) Bear in mind, though, that even as the "fallen angels" are expanding the high yield sector, the population is simultaneously being reduced by "rising stars." These are defined as issues that get upgraded to the investment grade level, i.e., BBB– or higher on Standard & Poor's scale.

Thanks to a study by Edward I. Altman and Duen Li Kao[2], we can forecast the average annual impact of rating changes on the size of the noninvestment grade universe, based on "rating drift." Altman and

---

2 Edward I. Altman and Duen Li Kao, "Examining and Modeling Corporate Bond Rating Drift" and "Corporate Bond Rating Drift: An Examination of Rating Agency Credit Quality Changes Over Time (Complete Appendices Only)," Working Papers, New York University Salomon Center, 1991.

Table 1.1—Five-Year "Production" of Fallen Angels

Standard & Poor's Rating	*Number of Issuers in Sample*	*Number in Sample Rated Below BBB at End of Period*	*Percentage of Fallen Angels*
AAA	450	1	0.2%
AA	1,048	16	1.5
A	1,429	39	2.7
BBB	514	65	12.6
Total	3,441	121	3.5%

Source: Edward I. Altman and Duen Li Kao.

Kao have tabulated the historical frequency and magnitude of downgrades and upgrades from specified Standard & Poor's rating levels. We consequently know, for example, the past probability of a bond beginning its life in the BBB category and being rated B three years later, or AA eight years later, or of remaining unchanged at BBB after ten years.

By extracting certain data from the Altman/Kao study, we can generate the analysis shown in Table 1.1. The figures indicate that for today's total universe of investment grade issues (rating categories AAA, AA, A and BBB, combined) some 3.5% are likely to be somewhere in the noninvestment grade range (BB, B, CCC, CC, C or D) five years hence.

Several technical problems arise in connection with projecting the 3.5% figure onto the present investment grade corporate universe. First of all, there is no assurance that the past will be indicative of the future, although we can derive some comfort from the length (20 years) of Altman and Kao's observation period. A second difficulty is that Altman and Kao base their figures on numbers of issues, whereas we are primarily interested in dollar volumes of downgradings. Some distortion could arise if small issues tended to be downgraded either more or less frequently than large issues. Furthermore, the mix of ratings within the investment grade universe may differ now or in the future from the mix of Altman and Kao's sample. Because Altman and Kao have found the frequency of decline to speculative grade to be higher in the lower rating categories, production of fallen angels should exceed 3.5% if the investment grade universe's ratings mix has deteriorated since the observation period of their study.

As a practical matter, though, attempting to adjust for all of these subtleties could create a false impression of precision in an inherently imprecise process. Keeping in mind our objective of determining ranges and orders of magnitude, we elected to concentrate our efforts on addressing only the most troubling technical problem associated with fallen angel projections, namely, the potential disparity between new and seasoned issues.

For reasons of feasibility in data collection and manipulation, Altman and Kao constructed their universe from issues that came to market during their observation period. Plainly, there is no assurance that their sample matched today's quality and maturity mix of outstanding issues, which is the proper base for estimating fallen angel production for the next five years.[3] Particularly of concern is the possibility that downgradings may accelerate as issues become more seasoned. In that case, a fallen angel production rate of 3.5% over five years (or an average of 0.7% annually) will understate the true rate on a sample partially composed of issues more than five years old. As it happens, though, an analysis of Altman and Kao's data, in the manner of Table 1.1 but extended over a ten-year horizon, produces a 5.2% (or a 0.5% annual) rate of decline to noninvestment grade status. In short, there is no evidence of acceleration of credit deterioration as investment grade issues age.

Splitting the difference between the five-year and ten-year mean annual rates produces the prediction that on average, 0.6% of today's $867 billion investment grade corporate market will fall to the speculative grade category in each of the next five years. Table 1.2 suggests that the resulting $5.2 billion figure is not out of line with actual experience during 1980–1990. The average volume of fallen angels (of which, by our estimate, 3% were convertibles) during that period was $9.4 billion, a figure swelled by leveraged transactions during the latter half of the 1980s. As in the past 11 years, the fallen angel production will undoubtedly fluctuate year-by-year in the future, in part because of variations in economic conditions.

The other side of the fallen angel coin is the upgrading of noninvestment grade issues to investment grade. This boon to bondholders usually comes about in one of three ways. First, if the rationale for the

---

[3] Taking an even more rigorous approach, the universe that will generate fallen angels during the next five years is not a static group, but rather will be supplemented by new issues and reduced by retirements. Making these additional refinements would rely heavily on arbitrary assumptions, however, so it is not clear that the effect would be to enhance the objectivity or precision of the forecast.

Table 1.2—Volume of Corporate Debt Downgraded to Noninvestment Grade 1980–1990 ($ Billions)

1980	$1.87
1981	1.71
1982	0.96
1983	4.80
1984	4.62
1985	2.95
1986	5.25
1987	21.37
1988	16.52
1989	23.76
1990	19.12

Note: Figures include small amounts of convertible bonds.
Source: Moody's Investors Service.

low rating involves weak operations, then an improvement either in industry conditions or in management's effectiveness can lead to an upgrading. Second, a highly leveraged company with solid operations may raise its rating by managing its balance sheet toward reduced reliance on debt. Finally, a speculative quality company may be acquired by an investment grade issuer and benefit from the latter's implicit or explicit support of its credit quality.

We can use the Altman and Kao rating drift data to forecast rising stars (Table 1.3), much as we did earlier for fallen angels. The resulting 13.6% production rate over five years implies that an average of 2.7% of noninvestment grade debt per year will be upgraded to investment grade. On the current base of $201 billion, this equates to $5.4 billion annually.[4] Rising stars, in short, should approximately cancel out fallen angels over time.

4 In contrast to our handling—in connection with fallen angels—of the possible disparity between Altman and Kao's new-issue-derived data and the universe of seasoned companies, we have made no adjustment to the five-year rising star figure. Altman and Kao show a sharp escalation in rising star production between Year 5 and Year 10, but we strongly suspect it is a function of "disappearance" of weaker issuers from the sample through defaults. Moreover, conservatism argues in favor of capping the rising star forecast at the five-year 13.6% number, given the absence of C- and D-rated issues in Altman and Kao's sample, as noted in Table 1.3.

Table 1.3—Five-Year "Production" of Rising Stars

Standard & Poor's Rating	*Number of Issuers in Sample*	*Number in Sample Rated Above BB at End of Period*	*Percentage of Rising Stars*
BB	103	29	28.1%
B	222	17	7.6
CCC	28	2	7.2
CC	1	0	0.0
C*	0	0	0.0
D*	0	0	0.0
Total	354	48	13.6%

Calculations are subject to rounding error.

Source: Edward I. Altman and Duen Li Kao.

* Altman and Kao based their data on new issues. During their observation period, no bond came to market with a C or D rating.

As a practical matter, though, a dollar of new fallen angel debt does not perfectly offset a dollar of new rising star debt. Many institutions that refrain from buying noninvestment grade bonds have no internal policies mandating the sale of securities that fall to the speculative grade category subsequent to purchase. Indeed, life insurance companies often hold on to their fallen angels to avoid realizing statutory losses, unless they believe principal repayment to be in danger. Accordingly, a significant portion of fallen angel debt tends to remain in investment grade portfolios until it exits the noninvestment grade sector either through retirement or via upgrading. Furthermore, many issues that fall only slightly below BBB never cheapen to yields high enough to entice high yield buyers.

In contrast, bonds that cross the investment grade frontier in the ascending direction are unlikely to stay in the hands of their existing holders. By the same logic that causes them to eschew Baa3/BB+ bonds yielding only about 200 basis points over Treasuries, noninvestment grade managers are inclined to take gains on bonds that rise to Baa3/BBB– or above. Their mandate is clearly to reinvest the proceeds at substantially higher rates.

This asymmetry between ownership patterns of fallen angels and rising stars implies that the net effect of rating changes over time will be a shrinkage in the "real" high yield universe. Market participants must therefore look to net new issuance to increase the available supply of paper.

Net New Issuance

In view of the volatile history of high yield new issue volume (Figure 1.2), no simple extrapolation from the past can have much validity. Had analysts extended a trendline from the early 1980s, they would have missed the surge to 1986's all-time peak of $32 billion, a discontinuity that reflected the coincident boom in mergers and acquisitions.

By the same token, the gradual decline in new issue volume during 1987–1989 gave no advance hint of the plunge to $1 billion in 1990. Historically grounded models for forecasting volume would have an-

Figure 1.2—High Yield New Issue Volume*
By Par Amount

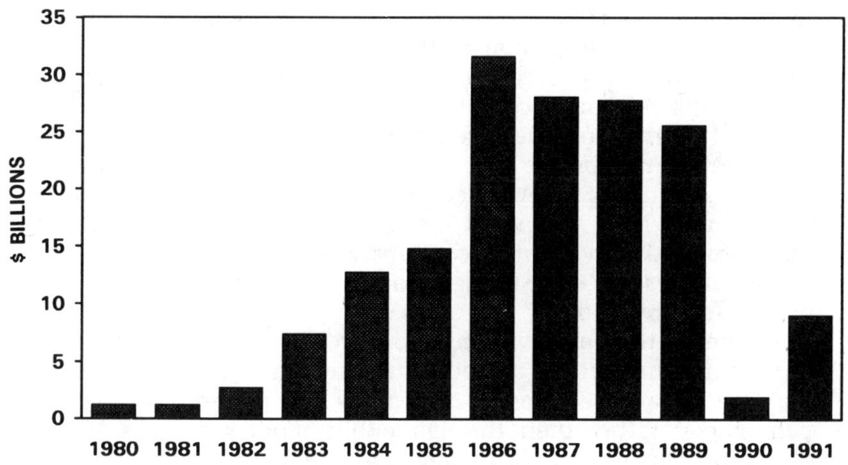

Source: Investment Dealers Digest.

* Includes public, nonconvertible corporate debt rated below investment grade by Moody's or Standard & Poor's.

ticipated neither Congress' 1989 banishment of savings and loan associations from the speculative grade market nor the massive withdrawals from high yield mutual funds during the Great Debacle of 1989–1990.

Looking forward, the new deal calendar would approximate $20 billion annually if existing issuers were simply to refund their outstanding public debt at maturity. (The average maturity of the $201 billion noninvestment grade market is roughly ten years.) Some speculative grade issuers, however, will instead choose to deleverage by letting their debt run off, preferring to fund themselves from internal sources or with equity. At many of the stronger noninvestment grade companies, projected growth in cash flow is such that financial leverage will drop sharply over the next few years through maturities and sinking funds, unless management deliberately offsets that tendency by buying in stock. Weaker credits, on the other hand, may have no choice; their debt will be converted to equity in order to keep (or bring) them out of bankruptcy.

Further eroding the outstanding amount of noninvestment grade debt is the currently heavy volume of corporate buybacks. Some of this is opportunistic; the repurchase of 14%-coupon debt at 80 cents on the dollar may simply represent a corporate treasurer's best use of $10 million of spare cash. Much of the buyback activity, however, reflects a more deeply rooted desire of companies to deleverage their balance sheets, reversing the fashion of the 1980s. In particular, a number of essentially conservative corporations converted to the leverage creed during the LBO boom, not out of conviction but out of fear of hostile takeovers. If the surest defense against raiders was a leveraged recapitalization, then corporate executives were willing to proclaim the doctrine of 1.1 times EBITDA coverage of cash interest, despite the gall in their mouths. Now that stock market values have caught up with or even surpassed private market valuations, however, many of these same managers are backsliding into the old-time religion of earnings and debt/equity ratios.

Whatever their motivations, noninvestment grade companies are currently retiring debt at a prodigious rate. Exact figures are impossible to obtain on a timely basis, since many repurchases are done in the open market rather than through public tenders or calls. The exact volume of debt retired via private transactions does not generally become known until the corporate buyers release their annual financial statements. Notwithstanding these impediments to data collection, we believe that $15 billion is a realistic estimate of the present level of annual aggregate high yield debt retirements, excluding maturities.

To some extent, primary activity will offset the shrinkage caused by debt retirement. Underwriters' efforts will face several formidable barriers, however.

To begin with, there is the already-mentioned trend of corporate deleveraging. The swing toward financial conservatism has been reinforced by a prolonged rally in stocks, which has greatly increased the attractiveness of equity financing. (In the five years ended September 30, 1991, the price-earnings ratio of the Standard & Poor's 500 Index rose from 16x to 20x.)

A second constraint on the issuance of public high yield debt is the availability of reasonable alternatives for borrowers in the form of bank or bank-like instruments. True, many U.S. commercial banks are constrained by stiff capital charges on highly leveraged transaction loans or limitations on the maturities of their assets. Investment banks, however, can craft senior obligations and place them privately with "prime funds" and assorted other domestic and foreign financial institutions. This financing option frees the borrower from the time-consuming public underwriting process.

At one time, many corporations were willing to forgo the ease of the private financing alternative and to pay up substantially in rate, all in the name of avoiding loan covenants they considered onerous. By the late 1980s, however, releveraging by successful LBO companies had reminded public high yield investors of the value of debt limitations and dividend restrictions. The noninvestment grade market's subsequent loss of liquidity undercut the argument that holding a marketable security adequately compensated lenders for an almost total sacrifice of covenant protection. Finally, in 1989–1990, a rash of defaults drove home to subordinated debtholders the importance of having meaningful rights to enforce when they sat down to negotiate with senior creditors and borrowers. These lessons have been reflected in increasingly tighter indentures on public high yield bonds. As a result, fewer companies than formerly view financial flexibility as a sufficient offset to public debt's cost disadvantage versus senior bank loans.

In light of the toughened covenants on speculative grade bonds, the "capital access" argument for the inevitability of high yield debt issuance provides cold comfort. Contrary to the tenets of high yield boosterism, emerging companies are not wholly dependent on the public debt market for their financing. Going forward, many small corporations will probably obtain capital from the same sources they tapped prior to the inception of modern high yield finance in 1977. These sources historically included banks, insurance companies, finance companies, venture capitalists and the public equity and convertible markets.[5] The traditional forms of funding for small companies had in common the characteristic of compensating investors in high-risk enterprises in ways (covenant protection or upside potential) that old-style high yield bonds did not.

To be sure, there is a large field of potential noninvestment grade issuers outside the category of small companies. For instance, investment banks remain saddled with something like $1.5 billion of bridge loans that had not yet been funded when the new issue market slammed shut in early 1990.[6] The resumption of public high yield financing activity in 1991 raised hopes among Wall Street firms of finally getting these obligations off their balance sheets.

A second group of potential issuers consists of companies that are overleveraged at present, but unwilling to dilute their shareholders to the extent necessary to re-equitize all the way back to investment grade. (Bear in mind that when a company floats new 12% par bonds to refinance depressed 15% debt, it increases the forward calendar without enlarging the outstanding amount of noninvestment grade paper. Such refinancing is a form of cannibalization, although it has the benign side-effect of raising the average credit quality of the high yield market.)

A related type of transaction is the "less-leveraged-buyout," or "LLBO." Imagine a billion-dollar company that overleveraged itself in 1988 and is now distressed, but owns a $100 million subsidiary that has steadily generated a high level of cash flow. To salvage something from the wreckage, the original equity participants (or, if the company is bankrupt, the creditors) may have no alternative to selling the "crown jewel" subsidiary. The most logical buyer in many such cases will be an investment grade corporation in a related business, but from time to time a financial buyer will get the inside track. Rather than doing an old-style LBO (ten times projected EBITDA, 90% debt financing, etc.) the purchaser will create a capital structure with enough eq-

---

5 Lending by banks and insurance companies, however, will probably remain constrained for some time by regulatory and market forces.

6 This rough estimate is derived from financial disclosures by the investment banks. Some of the houses are privately owned, however, and consequently do not reveal the data. Of the companies that do, moreover, a few lump their bridge loan commitments with other high yield debt exposure. Note as well that on September 18, 1991, one lending investment bank announced a plan to convert $510 million of bridge debt from one LBO (Sealy) to a combination of equity and $110 million of new notes. It is possible that much of the remainder of the bridge-loan-related potential issuance will disappear in similar fashion.

uity (say 30%) to avoid triggering a highly leveraged transaction designation by the banking regulators.

With some $48.3 billion of public and private corporate bonds currently in default,[7] the potential market for less-leveraged-buyouts is vast, in theory. Bear in mind, however, that the "crown jewels" described in our scenario represent small portions of the troubled companies that own them. Furthermore, with equities currently sporting hefty multiples, investors cannot generally acquire prize assets at prices cheap enough to produce extraordinary returns with leverage as low as 70:30. As a result, LLBO opportunities will probably be limited to situations in which the purchasers can enhance the value of the acquired assets through some means such as add-on acquisitions that create scale economies.[8]

Characterizing the opportunities for new-style buyouts as "limited" is not, however, equivalent to calling them "inconsequential." Figure 1.3 shows that LBOs are down but not out. At $4.1 billion (61 transactions) during 1991's first half, the buyout market continues to represent a potential, albeit much diminished, source of supply. With an estimated $10 billion-plus of investable funds at the disposal of LBO sponsors,[9] moreover, the capacity to create new transactions remains large. As in the emerging company sector, though, there are alternatives to public subordinated debt as financing mechanisms for LBOs. (One prominent buyout sponsor has, for many years, pointedly refused to use high yield bonds in its deals.)

Another group of companies that remains viable as high yield issuers are large, well-established public corporations that choose to be a little too leveraged to qualify for investment grade ratings. In control of their destiny through possession of stable, BB senior ratings, they will compare favorably both with fallen angels (which will be struggling to shore up operations) and with overleveraged buyout companies (which will be preoccupied with keeping their creditors at bay). Furthermore, the moderately leveraged corporations' public stock floats will assure them access to equity capital while also preserving their name recognition among investors. Unlike issuers that do not enjoy

---

7 *Source*: Bond Investors Association.

8 See Elizabeth A. Squeri, "Add-On Acquisitions Gain Favor in Uncertain Environment," *Buyouts* (September 11, 1991), pp. 1, 5. The author notes, "Financial buyers gain a competitive edge in bidding for add-ons because they can use the same strategic synergies available to corporate buyers."

9 *Source*: James Burke, president of Merrill Lynch Capital Partners. Quoted in Randall Smith, "Leveraged Buy-Out Funds Take a Back Seat Role in 1990s Deals," *Wall Street Journal* (September 11, 1991), p. C1.

Figure 1.3—Volume of Leveraged Buyouts

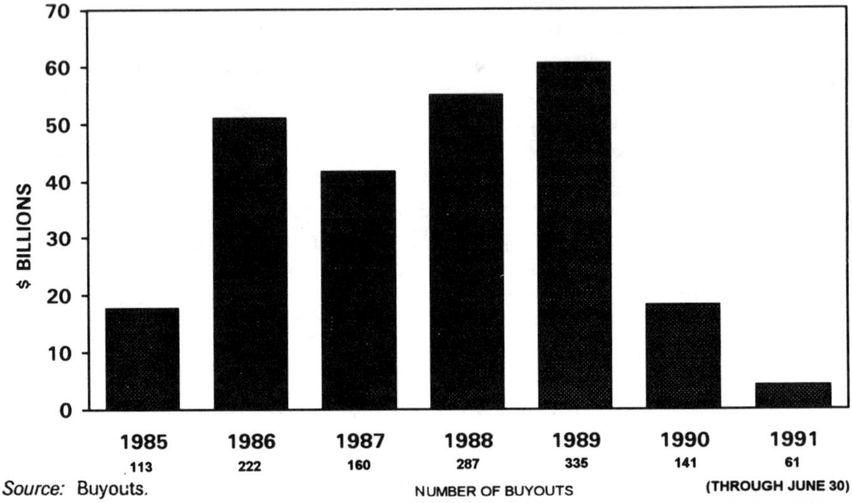

Source: Buyouts.

such advantages, these better-quality companies will probably be able to borrow in the public market without excessively severe covenants. This advantage should justify whatever premiums over senior bank debt they may be obliged to pay.

In years past, companies that fit this profile included Gulf & Western, Loews, Occidental Petroleum and Teledyne. Not coincidentally, perhaps, all four eventually rose to investment grade as their financial strategies changed. To some extent, their policy shifts were related to the fading popularity of diversified companies during the 1980s.

Today, a corporation is bucking the trend if it accepts noninvestment grade status despite an ability to capture a higher rating. Nevertheless, a few companies currently prefer to expand aggressively and would rather accept speculative grade ratings than severely dilute their shareholders. In recent years, examples have included GAF, Georgia-Pacific and some of the stronger cable television operators. Note that unlike their predecessors of the 1970s and 1980s, none of these companies could correctly be described as conglomerates.

Aside from this group, there may be some credible issuers in not-yet-identified growth industries of the 1990s. Casino and cellular communications financing, after all, arose during the 1980s largely because of regulatory and technological changes that were not necessarily foreseeable even a few years earlier. Like other classes of potential high yield borrowers, though, participants in dynamic growth industries will be able to select from an array of competing forms of financing. Better gifts of prophecy than we possess are needed to predict the share of this financing that the high yield market will capture.

More broadly, forecasting the new issuance potential is so dependent on bold assumptions that assigning a precise number to it could be reckless. It will be more beneficial to investors, we believe, if we now turn to the demand side of the equation. Gauging the capital market's appetite for noninvestment grade debt can help in estimating the extent to which potential supply will be translated into actual issuance. At the margin, an additional $100 million of investable cash in the hands of high yield managers may tilt the negotiation of terms of a particular financing toward moderately less restrictive covenants. One more borrower may thereby be induced to select public noninvestment grade debt over other funding options.

DEMAND FACTORS

Mutual Funds

High yield mutual funds grew exponentially during the mid-1980s. In 1984, when the Investment Company Institute first began tracking them as a distinct segment of its Bond and Income Funds group, the high yield funds had assets of $7.4 billion (Figure 1.4). By the end of 1988, that figure had surged to $33.4 billion, representing a 46% compounded annual growth rate.

While noninvestment grade funds were growing spectacularly in absolute terms, though, they were generally declining as a percentage of total Bond and Income Fund assets (Figure 1.5). Penetration of the overall bond fund market by high yield funds fell from 13.7% in 1984 to 8.8% in 1987, before a new burst of growth in 1988 raised high yield's share to 12.0%. Then, a vicious cycle of price declines and net share redemptions drove high yield penetration down to 5.8% by the end of 1990. In 1991, high yield fund assets rebounded from $18.9 billion to $24.5 billion, representing a recovery to 6.3% of the Bond and Income Funds total.

The volatile history depicted in Figures 1.4 and 1.5 hardly makes a case for projecting a rise in high yield funds' share of bond mutual fund investors' dollars. On the other hand, the positive trend observed in 1991 refutes any suggestion that lower-rated bond funds are disappearing from the scene. Based on an average penetration of 9.4% for

Figure 1.4—Total Assets of High Yield Bond Funds*
(As of December 31)

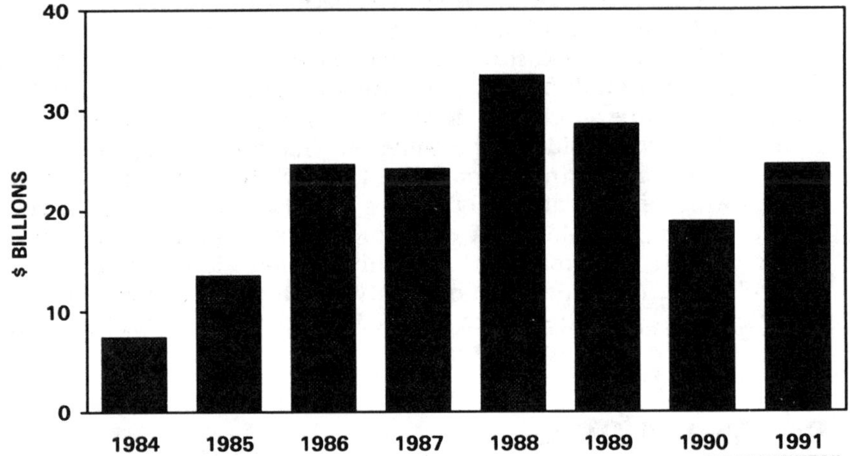

Source: Investment Company Institute.

* Total Assets = Market value of the portfolios held by the funds. The figure fluctuates both as a function of sales and redemptions of shares and as a consequence of price changes in the securities held by the funds.

Figure 1.5—High Yield Penetration—High Yield Mutual Fund Assets as a Percentage of Bond and Income Fund Assets
(As of December 31)

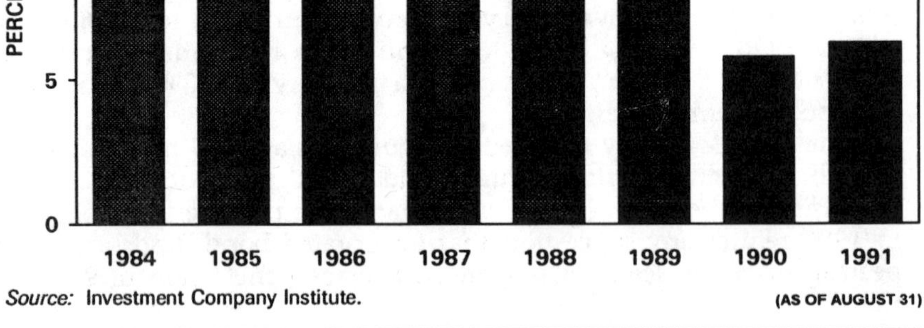

Source: Investment Company Institute.

the period shown in Figure 1.5, it seems reasonable to project high yield baseline demand by high yield mutual funds at 10% of the projected growth of all Bond and Income Funds.

Figure 1.6 shows a surge in Bond and Income Fund assets as a percentage of Equity, Bond and Income Fund assets between 1984 and 1986. Over that period, bond funds increased their penetration from 39.4% to 61.9%. The latter figure, however, was the high watermark for fixed income. Since 1986, Bond and Income Funds have settled into a range of 55% to 60% of Equity, Bond and Income Fund assets.

Figure 1.6—Bond Fund Penetration (A) Bond and Income Fund Assets as a Percentage of Equity, Bond and Income Fund Assets (As of December 31)

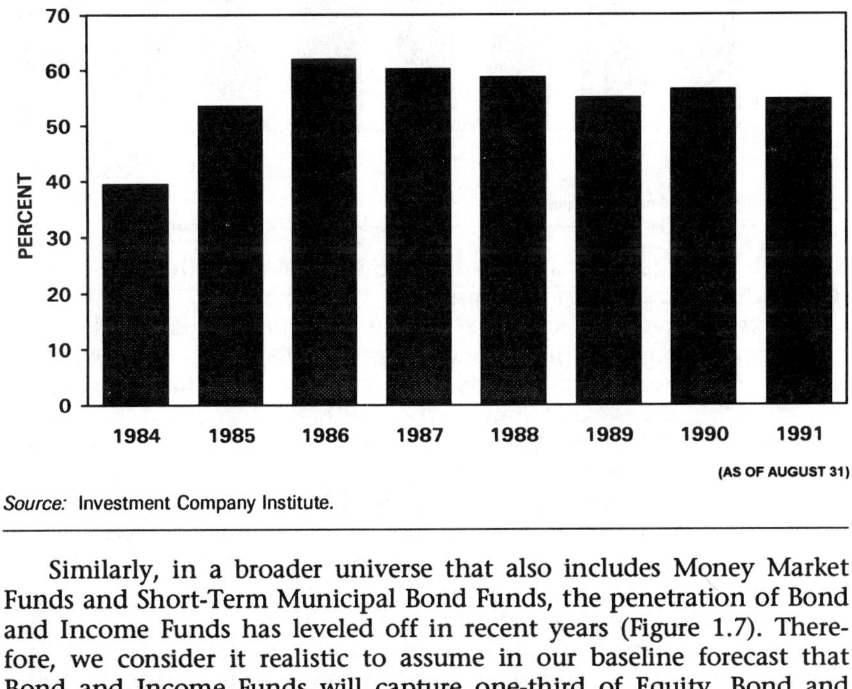

Source: Investment Company Institute.

Similarly, in a broader universe that also includes Money Market Funds and Short-Term Municipal Bond Funds, the penetration of Bond and Income Funds has leveled off in recent years (Figure 1.7). Therefore, we consider it realistic to assume in our baseline forecast that Bond and Income Funds will capture one-third of Equity, Bond and Income Fund asset growth over the next few years. Since we have already estimated high yield penetration at 10% of Bond and Income Fund asset growth, we can project High Yield Fund asset growth at 10% of one-third, or about 3%, of total mutual fund asset growth. This figure is close to the 1984–1990 mean penetration of all mutual funds

Figure 1.7—Bond Fund Penetration (B)—Bond and Income Fund Assets as a Percentage of Equity, Bond and Income, Money Market and Short-Term Municipal Bond Fund Assets (As of December 31)

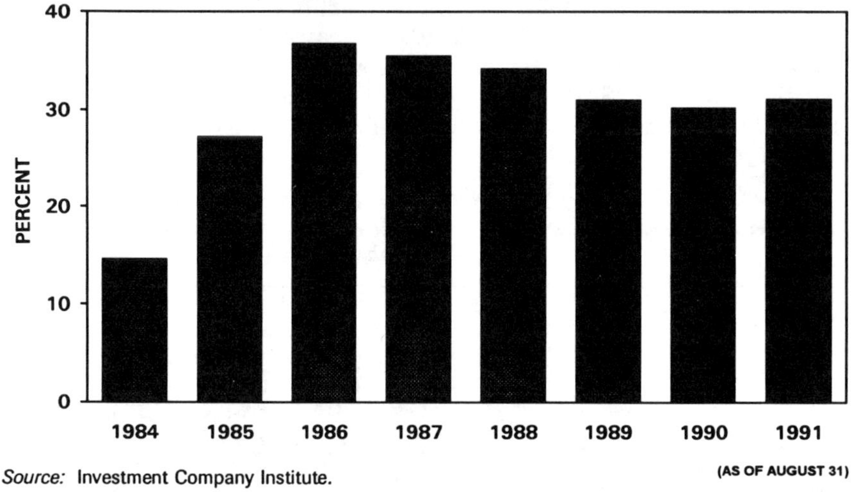

Source: Investment Company Institute.

by high yield funds, calculated without employing the intermediate penetration rates shown in Figures 1.5, 1.6 and 1.7.

Next we must determine a volume of total mutual fund growth upon which to project high yield's expected 3% penetration. As Figure 1.8 demonstrates, mutual funds captured a growing share of financial assets during the second half of the 1980s. Mutual Fund Shares as a percentage of Financial Assets of Individuals leapt from 1.70% at the end of 1984 to a high of 4.75% in 1987's second quarter. Since then, the ratio has essentially settled into the 4.0% to 4.5% range. The shift in savers' preferences toward mutual funds, in short, appears to be completed for now. Our baseline forecast is consequently a stable 4% of the growth in Financial Assets of Individuals.

Growth in individuals' financial assets, in turn, is influenced on a year-over-year basis by fluctuations in asset prices, as well as by the net dollars available to individuals for investment. The result is a fairly volatile annual series (Figure 1.9), including two years of negative growth. Over the full 1971–1990 period, though, the average annual increase was a healthy 9.81%. The 1971–1980 average figure (9.33%) came within 10% of the 10.30% recorded during 1981–1990, suggesting that over decade-long periods the growth of individuals' financial

Figure 1.8—Mutual Fund Penetration of Savings Mutual Fund Shares as a Percentage of Financial Assets of Individuals

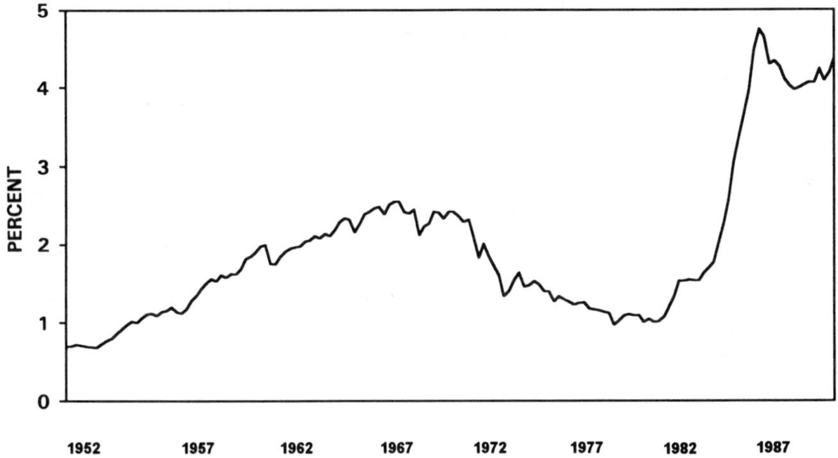

Source: Federal Reserve Board.

Figure 1.9—Financial Assets of Individuals Annual Changes (1971–1990)

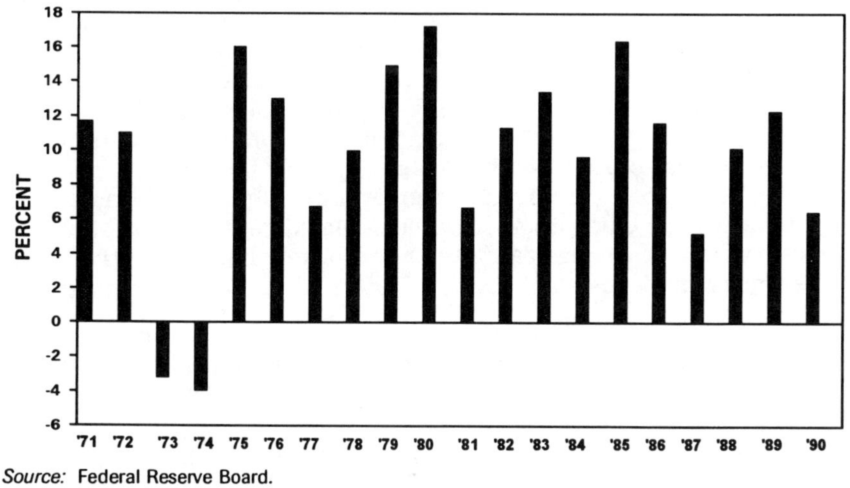

Source: Federal Reserve Board.

assets is reasonably stable. For our baseline forecast, we have chosen a round figure of 10%.

We next apply the 10% growth assumption to the $12.4 trillion of financial assets held by individuals at the end of 1990. The calculation produces a forecast of average annual demand by high yield mutual funds on the order of $1.7 billion during 1992–1996.[10]

Strictly speaking, we cannot assign that entire $1.7 billion of demand to the public noninvestment grade bond market. The high yield funds will probably continue to devote approximately 5% of their assets to cash, with small amounts also going into preferred stocks, investment grade bonds, private placements and sundry other instruments. By the same token, many mutual funds outside the high yield category will continue to devote minor portions of their assets to noninvestment grade bonds. Such holdings are currently about one-third as large as the high yield funds themselves, according to surveys conducted by Morningstar Inc. Netting out these out-of-category holdings, it is reasonable to forecast $2 billion of average annual demand for high yield bonds by the mutual fund sector as a whole.

Insurance Companies

During the 1980s insurance companies and mutual funds were the largest investors in high yield bonds. As the decade ended, however, insurance regulators became increasingly concerned about asset quality and consequently stiffened the reserving requirements on bonds rated below BBB. Few companies had worrisome concentrations in noninvestment grade securities, but the seizures of Executive Life and First Capital Holdings early in 1991 reinforced "junk bond" fears among agents and policy owners. Capitalizing on these anxieties, insurers that had low involvement in the noninvestment grade sector aimed heavy-hitting comparative advertising campaigns at competitors with above-average exposures. Faced with pressure from all sides, many insurance companies stopped putting new money into high yield bonds. Some went further, diverting their high-yield-related cash flow to other segments or, in a few cases, partially or completely liquidating their noninvestment grade assets.[11] During 1991's first half, ten major life

[10] Note that this figure is lower than the $2.4 billion of net inflows into high yield mutual funds during 1991's first nine months. We believe the market's record-setting price rebound during that period caused the cash influx to run above its long-term trend.

[11] For a more detailed discussion, see Martin S. Fridson, "Life Insurance Company Participation in High Yield—A 1991 Outlook," *Extra Credit* (January 1991), pp. 4–8.

insurers reduced their noninvestment grade exposure by an average of 26%, with single-company sales running as high as $800 million.[12]

Under present circumstances, a baseline forecast of net new demand for high yield bonds by the insurance industry would have to be very modest, perhaps even negative. The small saving grace is that net divestment is far from a certainty, barring further intensification of public concern about asset quality.[13] If companies wish to reduce noninvestment grade debt as a percentage of admitted assets, they can accomplish their goal simply by not reinvesting cash flow in the sector. Portions of their present high yield holdings would be retired through maturities, calls and buybacks, while other asset categories would grow.

Insurance companies could avoid disruptive dumping by simply declining to roll over their existing high yield assets. Still, the net effect would be a reduction of demand for noninvestment grade debt, relative to previous levels.

Our baseline forecast is somewhat more optimistic. Granted, the seizures of Executive Life, First Capital Holdings, Guarantee Security Life and Mutual Benefit Life will make consumers apprehensive about insurers' asset quality for a long time to come. The last-named company's problems, however, derived primarily from commercial real estate, rather than from high yield bonds. This underscores the reality that in the long run, portfolio quality is enhanced by diversification across asset classes, rather than by the concentration that can result from avoiding certain categories altogether. If, as time goes on, there is no repeat of the high yield sector's 1989–1990 turmoil, then insurance companies will not create marketing problems for themselves if they invest a modest percentage of their assets in noninvestment grade bonds.

In fact, many insurers will probably find it essential to enhance their portfolio yields by taking modest risk. The reason is that the growing consumer concern about the insurance industry's financial health has given AAA and AA carriers a competitive edge. To maintain their market share, A-rated companies will have to offer higher rates on annuities and guaranteed investment contracts. Controlled risk-taking, whether through noninvestment grade bonds, interest rate bets or

---

12 "Insurers Unload Junk Bonds," *New York Times* (September 19, 1991), p. D5.

13 High yield investors appear to be assuming that enlightened regulators will not force seized insurance companies to liquidate their holdings suddenly. Precipitous sales would hurt other companies' portfolios by depressing the market. Actions to date by state insurance commissions confirm that they are sensitive to such considerations.

equity investments, will be the only way for them to finance this price competition. Certainly, a low A-rated insurer that is fearful of downgrading to BBB may continue to avoid this path. Stable A-rated companies, however, will prefer moderate portfolio risk to the alternative of falling behind competitively.

Table 1.4 aids in quantifying the impact of an eventual renewal of interest in the high yield sector by insurance companies. Note that the industry-wide exposure of 4.9% of total assets includes private placements, as well as the public component with which we are mainly concerned. Observe as well that life companies dominate insurance industry participation in the high yield sector. Not only do they own 66% of the total holdings rated 3 through 6 by the National Association of Insurance Commissioners, but they are also considerably more

Table 1.4—Insurance Company Holdings of Noninvestment Grade Bonds As of December 31, 1990 ($ Thousands)

*NAIC Rating**	*Life*	*Property*	*Fraternal*	*Total*
3	$33,706,689	$4,965,477	$478,991	$39,151,157
4	34,603,642	2,791,405	472,678	37,867,725
5	13,299,063	796,531	76,121	14,171,715
6	3,503,348	345,633	56,150	3,905,704
Total	$85,112,751	$8,899,021	$1,083,932	$95,095,704
Classes 3–6 as Percentage of Total Bonds	11.4%	2.4%	5.4%	8.3%
Classes 3–6 as Percentage of Total Assets	6.7%	1.4%	3.7%	4.9%

* Generally speaking, the NAIC ratings parallel Moody's and Standard & Poor's ratings as follows:

3	Ba/BB
4	B/B
5	Caa/CCC
6	In or near default

Source: National Association of Insurance Commissioners.

concentrated in the noninvestment grade sector (at 6.7% of assets) than their property (1.4%) and fraternal (3.7%) counterparts. Added to the already-mentioned considerations is the absence of future purchases by First Executive and First Capital Holdings, which together accounted for 14.3% of the life insurance company holdings shown in Table 1.4. All things considered, we consider it reasonable to assume that public high yield bonds will eventually capture 4% of life insurance companies' asset growth. For the smaller category of property insurers, we simply assume a continuation of the present concentration of approximately 2%. As for the fraternal group, we note without any slight intended that our inherently rough estimates will be relatively insensitive to variations from their present 5.4% concentration, since their $1.1 billion high yield holdings represent just 1.1% of the industry's total. On a weighted average basis, then, we project that high yield bonds will capture about 3.3% of total insurance industry asset growth.

As shown in Table 1.5, life insurance assets grew at a hearty 11.5% average annual rate during the 1980s. A boom in annuity sales fueled this expansion in an environment of high consumer confidence in the

Table 1.5—U.S. Life Insurance Company Assets (\$ Millions)

	Amount	*Change from Preceding Year*
1980	$479,210	9.7%
1981	525,803	9.7
1982	588,163	11.9
1983	654,948	11.4
1984	722,979	10.4
1985	825,901	14.2
1986	937,551	13.5
1987	1,044,459	11.4
1988	1,166,870	11.7
1989	1,299,756	11.4
Average Annual Growth–1980s:		11.5%
1990	$1,408,208	8.3%

Source: American Council of Life Insurance.

life insurance industry. Today, by contrast, growth is hampered by public concerns about financial institutions generally and life insurance companies specifically. In 1990, asset growth slowed to 8.3%.

Specific forecasts of life insurance industry data are hard to come by. As a general statement, though, analysts are pessimistic about premium growth, one key determinant of asset growth. Similarly modest expectations prevail in the property area, given intense rate competition and the adverse effect of slow economic growth on such key variables as payroll growth (a determinant of demand for workmen's compensation coverage).

Projecting the above-mentioned 3.3% high yield market share onto average asset growth of 7% during the early 1990s produces annual net demand of around $5 billion. The insurance industry, in short, is likely to exceed the mutual fund sector in its appetite for high yield debt. Together, though, the market's two historically largest buyers will not be able to absorb anything approaching the 1986 peak-year $32 billion new-issue calendar on an ongoing basis. (Note that the amount to be absorbed is partly a function of the percentage of new issuance that simply represents refinancing of existing high yield debt.)

Pension Funds

Pension funds have long represented the noninvestment grade market's Great Possibility. If this $2.5 trillion[14] sector were to increase its 0.2% concentration[15] merely to 1%, the high yield sector would enjoy a $20 billion influx of capital.

No such shift appears imminent, however. Pension fund sponsors are generally conservative and most have long been wary of securities routinely vilified by the press as "junk bonds." During the hostile takeover frenzy of the 1980s, moreover, corporate sponsors commonly viewed the high yield market as a funding source for raiders, whose activities they did not wish to encourage. The steep market decline of 1989–1990 quashed the exploratory efforts of some sponsors who had just begun to perceive high yield bonds as a legitimate asset class. (A few sophisticated and aggressive pension funds, however, took advantage of the large sell-off by increasing their exposure at or close to the bottom.) The exceptionally high total return in high yield bonds in

---

[14] *EBRI Quarterly Investment Report* 5, no. 4 (Washington: Employee Benefit Research Institute, April 1991), pp. 44.

[15] *Source*: "Funds Sticking to Beaten Path," *Pensions & Investments* (January 21, 1991), p. 17.

1991 (34.58% on the Merrill Lynch High Yield Master Index) has provided some measure of reassurance. At the same time, though, the rally has underscored the high yield market's volatility, a characteristic that many pension fund sponsors abhor.

A survey reported in the September 1991 issue of *Institutional Investor*[16] demonstrates the magnitude of resistance to be overcome in converting pension sponsors to the high yield creed. Only 16.2% of the respondents acknowledged exposure to noninvestment grade bonds (public or private); 30.2% of those said they held such assets only as a result of buying higher-rated bonds that had suffered downgradings subsequent to purchase. More daunting still, only 1.5% of those surveyed stated intentions to initiate or increase high yield bond investment activities during the next two years. Even among the active high yield investors who perceived that the market was at or near its bottom, a mere 3.3% said they were increasing their exposure.

Over a longer period, proselytizing efforts by investment banks may yet produce significant allocations of assets to the high yield sector. Historical variance of returns is high in noninvestment grade corporates, but so is the diversification potential inherent in their low covariance with other major asset categories.[17] As a baseline forecast, however, a constant 0.2% share of expected growth is the most defensible hypothesis.

Unfortunately, the growth in pension fund assets will probably be modest over the next few years. Table 1.6 shows that after expanding at an average annual rate of 13.8% during the 1980s, assets contracted by 0.3% in 1990. The underlying trends shown in Table 1.7 are perhaps even more disturbing. For the private trusteed plans (which accounted for 46% of assets of all types of plans in 1990), net contributions turned negative in 1984 and have moved toward generally larger negative numbers in each subsequent year. In the last two years, dividend and interest income has not sufficed to offset these outflows. As a result, a period of zero or negative capital gains on investments, such as occurred during 1990, now produces net shrinkage in pension fund assets. This was not true as recently as 1984, a year of net capital losses for the private trusteed funds.

A primary cause of the negative contributions is the tightening, under the Federal Revenue Act of 1987, of the "full funding limita-

---

16 "Pensionforum: Still Wary of Junk Bonds," *Institutional Investor* (September 1991), p. 187.

17 *See* Martin S. Fridson, "The Mystery of the Missing Pension Funds," *Extra Credit* (October 1989), pp. 4–10.

Table 1.6—U.S. Pension Fund Assets
($ Billions)

	Amount	Change from Preceding Year
1980	$ 824.9	19.8%
1981	891.2	8.0
1982	1,049.6	17.8
1983	1,240.1	18.1
1984	1,356.9	9.4
1985	1,596.3	17.6
1986	1,791.6	12.2
1987	1,934.5	8.0
1988	2,163.5	11.8
1989	2,484.1	14.8
Average Annual Growth–1980s:		13.8%
1990	$2,476.8	(0.3)%

Source: Employee Benefit Research Institute.

Table 1.7—Net Flows of Private Trusteed Pension Funds
($ Billions)

	Earnings				
	Dividends & Interest	Capital Gains	Total Earnings	Net Contributions	Net Flows
1983	$50	$45	$95	$10	$105
1984	58	-3	55	-20	35
1985	59	128	187	-15	172
1986	60	98	159	-65	94
1987	64	24	87	-47	41
1988	69	82	151	-41	110
1989	77	179	256	-90	166
1990	77	-27	49	-89	-39

Source: Employee Benefit Research Institute.

tion," which determines the maximum deductible amounts that companies can contribute. An excise tax imposed by the Omnibus Budget Reconciliation Act of 1988, moreover, discourages nondeductible contributions. As a result of these laws, corporations have less of an opportunity than formerly to shelter excess cash from taxes by funneling it into their pension plans. The tightened funding limits apply to both private trusteed plans and private insured plans, which together hold 69% of total pension fund assets. (State and local governments' funds account for the balance.)

Taking into account as well the currently sluggish growth in the work force, as well as the competing funding need represented by health care benefits, asset growth promises to be low in U.S. pension funds during the timeframe of our forecast. A 1989 projection by the Employee Benefit Research Institute[18] predicted that asset growth would be in the 3.8% range during 1988–2000. In the early years of the EBRI projection, furthermore, the expected impact of the full funding limitation was expected to be particularly severe. We have accordingly assumed average asset growth of 3% a year on a 1990 base of around $2.5 trillion. Our 0.2% constant-share assumption produces estimated net demand for high yield bonds of just $160 million annually by U.S. pension funds. This figure equates to about one average-sized high yield offering.

Other

Besides the three classes of institutions already discussed, several other large pools of capital could theoretically generate sizable demand for high yield bonds. Practically speaking, though, participation by major depository institutions (commercial banks and federally chartered savings and loan associations) is impossible without regulatory or statutory changes that appear highly improbable in the present environment. Neither do we forecast sizable demand by individuals (other than through mutual funds) or corporations (other than through buybacks). Both groups have historically been comparatively small players, in any event.

Vulture capital funds are more likely to play a major role, but are inherently difficult to factor into a baseline forecast. Structured as limited partnerships and organized by firms with expertise in bankruptcy

---

[18] Jack VanDerhei, "What Do We Get from Today's Program? Savings and Capital Formation," Presented at a policy forum sponsored by the Employee Benefit Research Institute—Education and Research Fund, Washington, D.C., May 4, 1989.

and distressed investing, the vultures seek high returns[19] that are extremely dependent on market conditions. If distressed companies' bonds trade too close to par, the vulture capitalists' funds will probably remain uninvested. Furthermore, the vultures may elect in some cases to infuse equity and extinguish debt as the best means of repairing "sound companies with sick balance sheets." In that event, they will contribute to the contraction, rather than the expansion, of the high yield market. Given all the imponderables, we have decided to exclude vulture capital from our baseline projections, instead keeping them in mind as an "X factor."

The remaining potentially huge players are foreign institutions. Prominent among these in years past have been Japanese leasing companies, along with European and Middle Eastern banks.

Credit Lyonnais' $3.0 billion[20] bid to purchase Executive Life's high yield bond portfolio in October 1991 shows that individual offshore institutions can participate on a scale comparable, for example, to our total projected mutual fund demand. Bear in mind, though, that the Credit Lyonnais initiative was a play on the large upside potential of the seized insurer's distressed bonds and obscure private placements. Like the vulture capitalists, many of the potential foreign investors are opportunity-sensitive and inherently difficult to assess for purposes of a baseline forecast. Similarly, many potential overseas investors in nondistressed high yield paper will probably stay home if cross-border exchange rate and interest rate differentials are not favorable. As with the vulture capitalists, then, the imponderables force us to place foreign demand in the X category.

CONCLUSION

Two major conclusions emerge from an examination of summary baseline forecasts for the various components of high yield supply and demand (Figure 1.10).

First, the noninvestment grade market appears capable of absorbing a larger annual volume of net new supply than issuers have recently

[19] In a survey of distressed securities investors conducted in the fall of 1989, 92% of the respondents reported that they sought target returns of 25% or more. Twenty-six percent aimed for returns of 40% or higher; see Edward I. Altman, *Distressed Securities: Analyzing and Evaluating Market Potential and Investment Risk* (Chicago: Probus Publishing), p. 57.

[20] Credit Lyonnais' original bid, made in August 1991, was $2.7 billion.

Figure 1.10—Summary of Baseline Supply and Demand Forecasts Annual Levels: 1992–1996 ($ Billions)

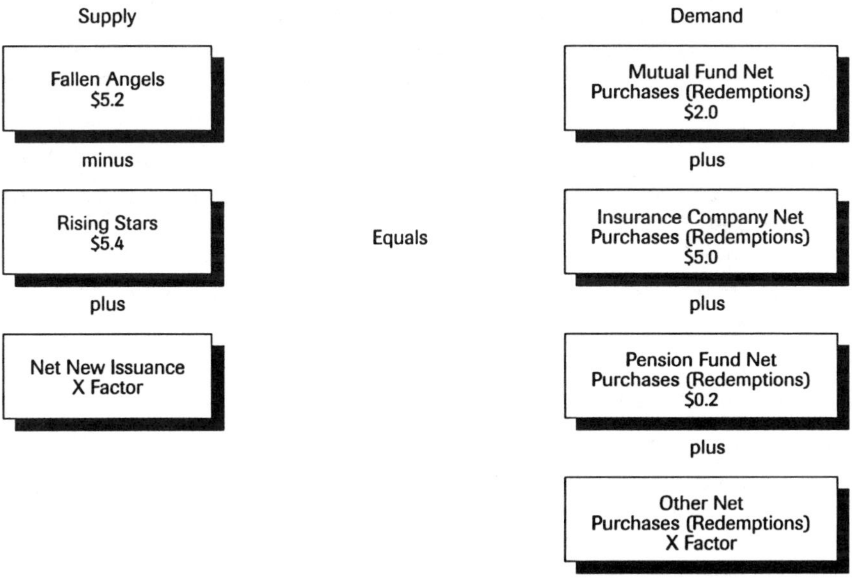

attempted to float. Even before considering "other" sources such as vulture capital funds and foreign investors, average annual demand should exceed $7 billion.

The second key point is that the "net new issuance" and "other net purchases" categories are frustratingly difficult to quantify. Without estimates for these two factors, there is vast uncertainty about the totals of the supply and demand sides of the equation.

Lack of closure does not negate the value of the exercise, however. From the available pieces of the puzzle we can see that high yield bonds continue to represent a viable business for money managers and investment banks. True, we do not foresee a sustained return to the $25 billion to $32 billion annual new issue volume of 1986–1989. The 1983–1985 range of $7.5 billion to $15 billion a year is not an unrealistic aspiration, though, particularly when we take into account refinancings.

The more modest level of expected financing activity probably bodes well for credit quality. As we have discussed elsewhere[21], the sharp decline in average ratings of new issues during 1987–1988 proceeded in part from a surge of capital into the high yield sector. Not surprisingly, default rates surged in the next two years. With the froth removed from the high yield primary market, credit quality of new issues (and, gradually, of the universe of outstanding bonds) should rise.

We believe, in short, that the high yield bond market is currently being rebuilt upon stronger foundations than its architects provided during the 1980s. If so, the prospect of extinction may never again seem as plausible as it did during the dark days of 1989 and 1990.

[21] See Martin S., Fridson, "Agency Costs: A Key to Spotting Tomorrow's Troubled Deals," *Extra Credit* (June 1991), p. 44.

Chapter Two

The High Yield Private Placement Market

by William B. Sacher
Associate Director
Bear Stearns & Co. Inc.

INTRODUCTION

The private placement market, once a quiet closed market dominated by insurance companies, has expanded dramatically in the last ten years in both size and sophistication. Where once the most exotic form of offering was a plain vanilla long-term debt financing, the market now is open to everything from highly structured asset backed financing to complex leveraged buy-outs and leveraged recapitalizations.

A look at the historical new issue volume statistics aptly reflects this transformation. In 1980 total new issuance in the private market was approximately $16.0 billion. By the close of the decade, when new issue volume was at its peak, total capital raised had grown to $165 billion. It is estimated that over 30% of all corporate debt outstanding, not including bank debt, was issued in the form of a private placement.

One important factor driving this growth has been the development of the high yield sector of the private placement marketplace. According to *Investment Dealers Digest,* 1988 acquisition-related high yield private placements alone totalled over $26 billion. This accounted for over 16% of the total new issue volume in that year. While it is difficult to get precise statistics for nonacquisition related high yield offerings because private placements were generally not rated during this period, by most estimates if included, total private high-yield issuance would have conservatively represented over 20% of the total new issue volume. Clearly, a highly developed market with a significant commitment of capital was available for below investment grade companies.

Aiding in the development of the high yield sector of the private placement market has been the emergence of many new classes of investors. While in the early 1980s the market was virtually the exclusive domain of insurance companies, today the investor base is much more diverse. In addition to insurance companies, the high yield sector has experienced increasing participation from commercial banks, credit/finance companies, both public and private pension funds, mutual funds, and special purpose funds established specifically to invest in high yield private placements. The market has also become more global with frequent participation from foreign investors fitting many of the above institutional categories.

To provide a basic overview of the current high yield private placement market, what follows is a description of the typical high yield issuer and why they would raise capital privately, profiles of the various high yield private placement investors, and the process involved in preparing and launching a new offering. This chapter will focus strictly on the issuance of debt oriented securities. Although many companies raise equity capital privately, this is generally considered a separate market.

THE HIGH YIELD PRIVATE PLACEMENT ISSUER

While high yield private borrowers fit many descriptions, in general, the typical issuer is a middle market company with annual sales ranging from $35 million to $250 million and whose debt, if rated, would be classified as non-investment grade. Despite the common perception that this is a limited collection of very small companies, these borrowers actually comprise a surprisingly large and important group. Of the approximately 22,000 American corporations with annual sales in excess of $35 million only about 800 have issued investment grade bonds publicly. Of the approximately 21,000 corporations remaining, it is estimated that 95% or more would be rated non-investment grade.[1]

---

1 "The Continental Bank Journal of Applied Corporate Finance," Vol. 4, Number 1 (Spring 1991), Pages 2-3.

The private placement market offers these companies many attractive benefits. Borrowers with conventional short-term floating rate bank debt often access the market to lock in an attractive fixed rate on a more long-term basis. Because issuers have the opportunity to negotiate directly with investors, the private market is also ideally suited for complex offerings requiring a high degree of explanation. Another attractive feature of the market is its private and confidential nature. Companies wishing to protect sensitive financial information from becoming available to competitors find this feature especially appealing.

The size of the financing is also a consideration in determining whether a company will choose to issue securities privately. Generally speaking, to provide sufficient liquidity for secondary trading the public market requires issue sizes of $75 million or more. Many middle market companies simply do not require this much capital. Because the private investor usually intends to hold its investment until maturity and is, therefore, not concerned with liquidity, the private placement market can easily accommodate financings of less than $100 million.

The time sensitivity of the financing can also make the private market a compelling alternative. Because a private placement is not filed with the Securities Exchange Commission the time required to secure commitments from lenders can be much more expeditious.

PRIVATE PLACEMENT INVESTORS

Insurance Companies

Insurance companies have historically been the largest investor in high yield private placements. Of the two major types of insurance companies (i.e., life companies and property/casualty companies) the life insurance company is the more active investor. One reason is the relatively predictable long-term nature of the life insurance company's liabilities (i.e., life insurance policies, annuities, and guaranteed investment contracts), negating the need for investment liquidity. Property and casualty insurance companies by comparison, because their insurance claims are less predictable, generally have a greater need for liquidity and, therefore, tend to favor public securities which are more easily sold.

An important characteristic of life insurance companies is that they are cash flow oriented lenders and do not look to the book value of the issuer's assets to determine lending limits. Consequently, insurance companies can, for issuers with strong cash flow characteristics, be extremely competitive with conventional asset based lenders. In terms of security, insurance companies will tend to lend on an unsecured basis. In a high yield credit, however, if there are other secured lenders most insurance companies will require that they be secured too.

Life insurance companies are also match funded spread lenders. By this we mean that the insurance company will match the cash flow generated by the private placement against the cash outflows associated with their liabilities and thus lock in a profit resulting from the spread. Because early redemptions will cause them to become unmatched, most insurance companies impose onerous prepayment penalties. The most common prepayment protection is the "make-whole" penalty. Essentially, the make-whole penalty requires the issuer to make a lump sum payment to the holder, that once reinvested, will be sufficient to produce the same cash flows the holder would have received had the loan not been prepaid. As the name implies, the holder is "made whole" because they are able to remain matched and preserve their profit spread.

The make-whole premium is calculated by taking the present value of the future payment stream remaining on the loan at the time of the prepayment. In most cases, the discount factor prescribed is the prevailing Treasury rate. In a low interest rate environment, which is when most issuers prepay their debt, the make-whole premium can be quite high, easily reaching 20% or more.

Because their liabilities are also largely fixed in nature, insurance companies are almost invariably fixed rate lenders. Pricing for most high yield issues is based on a spread over Treasury securities. The spread is determined by prevailing market conditions and the insurance company's assessment of the credit. Spreads for noninvestment grade issues are quite wide, generally ranging from 200 basis points to 450 basis points or more over the appropriate Treasury security. Unlike publicly issued securities which are priced off the Treasury with the same maturity as the loan, the private placement market prices off the Treasury with a maturity that most closely matches the average life of the loan. In an interest rate environment characterized by a steep positively sloped yield curve (short-term rates are lower than long-term rates) the private market can be very competitive with its public counterpart.

Depending on where the loan is determined to fall on the risk spectrum, an equity kicker may be required in addition to the coupon.

Generally, the equity kicker takes the form of warrants to purchase common equity in the issuing company. At times of limited demand for noninvestment grade securities, equity related inducements become more common.

For leveraged recapitalizations or leveraged acquisitions, pricing on the subordinated debt is rarely spread-based, rather, it is comprised of some fixed current return and a deferred return usually derived from an equity kicker. The fixed current return typically ranges from 12% to 15%. The all-in return including the equity kicker, calculated over a five-year time horizon, generally falls in the mid-twenties. Because of the subjective nature of calculating the equity value, the amount of kicker necessary to produce the required return can be the subject of intensive negotiation.

Another attractive distinguishing feature of the insurance company loan is the flexibility afforded the high yield issuer in designing an amortization schedule. Given the wide range of insurance company liabilities, almost any amortization need can be met. The one requirement most insurance companies have, however, is that the projected operating cash flow of the business be sufficient to repay the entire loan. Unlike more asset oriented lenders, insurance companies will not undertake the market-related risk of having to refinance the loan at maturity.

COMMERCIAL BANKS

The commercial banks, both foreign and domestic, are the most frequently considered alternative to a traditional insurance company private placement. In the high yield sector, the foreign banks, have become increasingly active lenders picking up market share from their domestic counterparts who have been scaling back their lending activity due to U.S. regulatory pressure.

Unlike insurance companies, the banks are very much asset oriented lenders. Although they look to cash flow to service the loan, they place a great deal of importance on asset values to cover their debt should cash flow fall short. As a consequence, capital availability for the borrower is frequently limited to the book value of the assets on its balance sheet. While banks do lend on an unsecured basis, for most noninvestment grade companies secured loans are more the norm. Security for a loan generally encompasses all the assets of the company including, in most instances, the stock of its operating subsidiaries, if any.

A major distinguishing feature between the banks and insurance companies is that the banks are not generally match funded. Their liabilities tend to be short term in nature, producing characteristics almost opposite of those found in an insurance company loan. For instance, bank loans are generally shorter in tenor. Loans to high yield companies are generally not longer than seven years with the majority falling into the three- to five-year range.

Because they are not match funded, banks are also able to commit to fund without the capital actually being drawn down. This enables the borrower to have the funds available for use when needed. This type of loan is commonly referred to as a revolving facility. Another result of not being match funded is that bank loans can generally be redeemed without onerous prepayment penalties.

A negative consequence of this preference for being prepaid, however, is that most bank loan agreements contain a feature referred to as an "excess cash sweep" which requires the company to apply any excess cash flow that remains after fixed charges to prepay the loan. Companies requiring the use of their excess cash flow for expansion or acquisitions can find this feature extremely constraining.

Another distinguishing feature of a bank loan is that they are almost invariably priced on a floating rate basis. For most non-investment grade companies, the loan rate will float at a spread over either the London Inter-Bank Offered Rate (LIBOR) or the U.S. Prime Rate. On a senior loan, spreads for noninvestment grade companies usually range from 150 to 300 basis points over LIBOR or from 100 to 200 basis points over prime. A typical loan agreement will also incorporate a mechanism that adjusts the spread up or down for either incremental improvements or deteriorations in the company's credit profile. Banks will also often require the borrower to fix the rate on a portion of the loan. This is accomplished by swapping a piece of the loan with another borrower who has a fixed-rate liability. Most banks are capable of arranging the swap as an additional service.

Banks are fee oriented and most loans carry a variety of ways for the bank to generate fee related income. Commitment fees are usually the largest and can range from 1% to 3% or more of the loan depending on the credit, the use of proceeds and the prevailing market conditions. Other aspects of the loan for which fees are charged include unused line fees, agent fees, and syndication fees.

Although some commercial banks have special funds available for subordinated debt, this is not a main line of businesses and their appetite, especially of late, has been extremely limited.

CREDIT/FINANCE COMPANIES

Credit/finance companies have become an increasingly important source of capital in the high yield private placement market. While the banks have recently been reducing their exposure to high yield credits, most of the credit/finance companies have stepped up their lending to fill the void. According to the Federal Reserve, from the beginning of 1990 to the end of July 1991, loans by finance companies to business increased by over $41 billion to total $300 billion. By comparison, during the same period, business loans by American banks fell by over $31 billion or approximately 6% to $480 billion.

The credit/finance company is a hybrid lender exhibiting characteristics common to both insurance companies and commercial banks. Like the banks, they are asset-based lenders and in most high-yield credits they like to have a secured position. But more like their insurance company counterparts, they also emphasize cash flow and will lend well beyond the limits imposed by asset coverage alone.

Like the banks, credit/finance companies are not match funded and are therefore able to provide revolving facilities and accommodate early loan redemptions. For the borrower this is an attractive characteristic because, like the banks, the credit/finance company loan generally does not contain expensive prepayment penalties.

But also like the banks, on the negative side, most credit/finance company loans contain an "excess cash sweep." Because they are funded with short-term liabilities, a typical credit/finance company loan will have a five- to seven-year maturity.

The credit/finance company loan is usually priced on a floating rate basis. Because the cost of capital for credit/finance companies is generally higher than that of their commercial bank counterparts, they usually concentrate on the higher yielding end of the noninvestment grade market. While a LIBOR based option can be negotiated, most of the credit/finance companies in the market today prefer prime based loans. Spreads usually charged range from 150 to 250 basis points over prime. Because they are not subject to the regulatory restrictions imposed on commercial banks, credit/finance companies have become increasingly active in acquisition related financings.

The degree of appetite for subordinated debt varies from company to company. Senior secured loans, however, are a credit/finance company's primary business.

Credit/finance companies, like the commercial banks, are also fee oriented. They charge for services on a similar basis to a bank, and because they concentrate on the higher yielding end of the market, their fees tend to run at the high end of the range.

THE FUNDS

Special purpose funds are a catch-all category which encompasses many different types of financial institutions. Collectively, this group has become an important source of capital for noninvestment grade companies. These institutions include public and private pension funds, private partnerships, and mutual funds.

The investment characteristics of each of these institutions varies not only from category to category but also from institution to institution. While it would be too voluminous to discuss each, the inclusion of these investors has generally broadened the market both in terms of capital availability and flexibility in accommodating unusual financings. While these investors all structure and price within the context of the market, because each institution has its own unique funding attributes and investment parameters, a financing can be structured with characteristics which heretofore had not been possible. This has elevated the importance of "knowing your market" and created the opportunity for agents who arrange financing on behalf of issuers to add significant value.

ISSUING A HIGH YIELD PRIVATE PLACEMENT

Because most high yield private placement offerings are highly structured and negotiation-intensive and most of the issuers are not widely recognized in the marketplace, a thoroughly prepared and planned offering is extremely important. While there will inevitably be some variation from transaction to transaction, the process of issuing a high yield private placement can be broadly broken down into the four steps outlined below. Although some companies will attempt to arrange their financing directly, most high yield issuers use an agent and as such this is assumed in the outline that follows. As can be seen from the chart below, the entire process from inception to closing should require from six to twelve weeks to complete.

Time Required	*Steps*
1 to 2 weeks	Due Diligence/Structuring
1 to 2 weeks	Preparing the Private Placement Memorandum
2 to 4 weeks	Marketing Transaction/Getting Commitments
2 to 4 weeks	Documentation/Closing
6 to 12 weeks	

DUE DILIGENCE/STRUCTURING

Depending on the condition of the company's records and financial reporting systems and the complexity of its business, the due diligence process will generally take from one to two weeks to complete.

The agent conducts due diligence for essentially three reasons. First, from a liability and franchise protection standpoint, the agent will want to ensure that the representations and information that will be disseminated to investors, who are also their clients, is accurate and correct. Secondly, the more the agent knows about the business the more effective they can be in advising the company as to structure and the type of financing that will best accomplish their goals and objectives. Lastly, since investors may not know the company, and at best have only a general understanding of the market in which they operate, the agent must have an in-depth appreciation for the business to effectively communicate the merits of the financing to the market.

An extremely important part of the structuring process which many issuers do not adequately address is the covenant package. The covenants which are the rules by which the issuer agrees to abide for the term of the loan, could significantly impair the company's operating flexibility if not carefully designed. This is an area where an experienced agent can add substantial value.

The covenant package will include affirmative and negative covenants. Affirmative covenants basically require the company "to do" something (i.e., to provide investors with timely financial statements or to comply with certain regulatory requirements). Negative covenants, require the company "not to do" something (i.e., not to allow net worth to drop below a certain level).

While affirmative covenants are important, it is the negative covenants that often require the most attention. Because a high yield loan by definition is a riskier proposition than an investment grade loan, private placement investors require a much more extensive and tighter set of covenants. In general, most high yield covenant packages will include: maintenance and incurrence tests for coverage of interest and leverage levels as well as restrictions on mergers, asset sales, investments, and the payment of dividends. Considerable attention should be paid to selecting the right type of covenants and setting the appropriate levels by which they will be measured to ensure adequate operating flexibility and a loan that the company will be able to live with until maturity.

PREPARING THE PRIVATE PLACEMENT MEMORANDUM

The private placement memorandum ("PPM") is the primary document used to offer the securities to the marketplace. It is also the last chance the issuer has to make a good first impression. The PPM must, therefore, be thorough, informative, and professionally produced. The PPM is not the document on which a final investment decision is based. Rather, its purpose is to provide prospective investors with sufficient information to form an initial impression of the company and the terms of the offering and to provide the basis for further discussion.

The PPM should begin with an executive summary introducing the company, outlining the financing and explaining the intended use of the proceeds. The areas following the executive summary which should be covered include:

- Proposed Terms of the Financing
- Investment Considerations
- Industry Overview
- In-depth Description of Business, its Customers & Competitors
- Management Profiles
- Historical Financial Statements
- Five Year Projected Financial Models

Other related information such as audited financial statements, independent research reports or relevant newspaper or trade articles should be included as exhibits.

MARKETING THE OFFERING

A marketing strategy should be developed once the PPM is complete. The importance of an effective marketing strategy should not be underestimated. Re-offering securities to the market after an initial failed marketing will be difficult at best and will seriously put the issuer at a disadvantage in negotiating acceptable terms. Considerations that should be made include:

- Is a pre-marketing required?
- Is there a need for a lead investor?
- Who should be the lead?
- Should a limited versus wide number of investors be approached?
- What types of investors should be targeted?
- When should the financing be launched?
- What should the ground rules be for committing to the offering?

With a marketing strategy in place the agent then begins contacting prospective investors to introduce and highlight the offering. If there is interest, the agent will then distribute the PPM to the investor.

After giving investors time to review the memorandum, the agent will begin arranging a schedule for investors to conduct their own due diligence. Preparation by the issuer for this time-consuming and exhaustive part of the process is vital. Being able to respond quickly and efficiently to investor requests for information is key to maintaining momentum behind the transaction.

Immediately after each investor completes its due diligence, negotiation on the basic terms of the financing should begin. If acceptable terms can be reached the agent will then be ready to "circle" the deal. The agent must be careful to strike a balance between attaining a level of specificity on the terms which makes the circle meaningful and not getting bogged down in detail that should be part of the documentation process. A successful closing could be jeopardized should this step in the process become too protracted.

Circling the financing is a commitment on the part of the investor to purchase a specific amount of securities at the agreed upon terms. Accepting a circle is a commitment on the part of the issuer to sell a specific amount of securities at the agreed upon terms and to withdraw the offering from the market.

It is extremely important to be familiar with the investing policy of the institution (s) providing the commitment to ensure completion of the offering. While most institutions consider their circle a binding commitment, some investors feel less bound by this market convention. Not being able to gauge the strength of the commitments can lead to very disappointing and costly conclusions.

It is generally advisable to maintain a dialogue with those institutions that expressed an interest in the financing but who for one reason or another were not circled. Keeping these investors in reserve can save a transaction should one or more of the investors drop out before closing.

DOCUMENTATION/CLOSING

Once the basic terms are set and the financing is fully circled, the lawyers begin drafting the final documentation. The documentation process takes the agreement to a much higher level of detail and thus opens a new round of negotiation. The more complex the financing the more intensive and protracted the negotiation. Whenever possible, representatives from both sides who have the authority to make decisions should be present. As terms and mechanics get drafted spontaneous decisions will invariably have to be made. It is also recommended that both sides agree up front on target deadlines for completion to impose some pressure on the parties to reach a consensus. While the documentation process will vary from financing to financing, most can be completed within a two to four week timeframe.

CONCLUSION

While the high yield private placement market has been a reliable source of capital for middle market companies for many years, the expanding ranks of institutions that participate in the market today has created a deep, vibrant, and dynamic new marketplace. Given the diverse and often unique financing needs of middle market companies, the private placement market should continue to attract both issuers and investors and extend its rapid growth and development.

Chapter Three

The Impact of Changes in the Highly Leveraged Transactions Debt Market on Business Values

by Mitchell F. Vernick
Senior Group President
Heller Financial, Inc.

In November 1987, an article by this writer entitled "Business Value Lending" was published in *Mergers and Acquisitions.* A similar but more detailed article was published in early 1990 in *Volume V of The Library of Investment Banking: Mortgage and Asset Securitization* and in the *Acquisition Yearbook 1991*. In both of these articles, the concept of discounting future cash flows was used in valuing a business. Further, these articles illustrated that high leveraged versus low leveraged capital structures had different weighted average after-tax costs of capital (WAATCC), which is the discount rate used in valuing a business.

HIGHLY LEVERAGED CAPITAL STRUCTURES IN 1987

What is particularly interesting three and one-half years later is the degree to which the examples of highly leveraged capital structures used in November 1987, which largely represented market conditions at that time, are radically different than is the case in May 1991. The table below replicates the example of a highly leveraged capital structure used in the 1987 article:

	% Capital	Pre-Tax Cost	[4]After-Tax Cost	Weighted Cost
Senior Debt (floating)	65%	[1] 9.75%	6.34%	4.12%
Subordinated Debt	30%	[2] 13.00%	8.45%	2.54%
Equity	5%	[3] 39.70%	39.70%	1.99%
WAATCC	100%			8.65%

[1] Prime rate of 8.25% plus 1.5% = 9.75%

[2] 30-year Treasury of 8.6% plus 4.4% = 13.00%

[3] 30-year Treasury of 8.6% plus 31.1% = 39.70%

[4] Tax rate of 35%

HIGHLY LEVERAGED CAPITAL STRUCTURES IN 1991

Assuming interest rates were unchanged from those in 1987 (May 1991 prime rate was 8.5% compared to 8.25% in 1987, with the 30-year Treasury rate basically unchanged), a typical highly leveraged capital structure in 1991 is as follows:

	% Capital	Pre-Tax Cost	[4]After-Tax Cost	Weighted Cost
Senior Debt (floating)	50%	[1] 9.75%	6.34%	3.17%
Subordinated Debt	30%	[2] 20.00%	[5]15.45%	4.64%
Equity	20%	[3] 30.00%	30.00%	6.00%
WAATCC	100%			13.81%

[1] Prime rate of 8.25% plus 1.5% = 9.75%

[2] 30-year Treasury of 8.6% plus 4.4% = 13.00%, plus warrants increasing expected return by 7.0% to 20.0%

[3] 30-year Treasury of 8.6% plus 21.4% = 30.0%

[4] Tax rate of 35%

[5] 13% debt rate less 35%, or 8.45%, plus 7.0% due to capital gain from warrant which is not tax deductible

FACTORS IMPACTING THE COST OF CAPITAL

Comparing the 1987 highly leveraged capital structure with that in 1991, one finds the weighted average after-tax cost of capital (WAATCC) is 60% higher in 1991 without any change in market interest rates. The increase in WAATTC in 1991 is due to three factors:

- Senior debt, which is the lowest cost source of capital, has been reduced from 65% to 50% of the capital structure, at the same 1.5% spread over the prime rate.
- The reduction in senior debt has been offset by an increase in equity from 5% to 20% of the capital structure, although at a lower cost of equity. The reduction in cost of equity from 39.7% to 30.0% reflects the lower risk premium required in a less levered capital structure (4:1 in 1991 versus 19:1 in 1989). Notwithstanding the lower cost of equity, 15% of the capital structure is now structured with equity returning 30% versus senior debt returning 6.34%.
- The cost of the subordinated debt has increased by 7% due to the inclusion of warrants. It may have been increased even more if only 5% equity remained below it in the capital structure. However, with 20% equity below the subordinated debt, a lower return is acceptable.

Since the WAATCC is the discount rate used to present value of a businesses' future expected stream of earnings, the higher cost in 1991 suggests that given the same view of future operating performance, one would pay 37% less for a business today as in 1987. To demonstrate, assume a business has $10 million in earnings before interest, taxes and depreciation, less capital expenditures (EBITD-CE), and for simplicity, earnings are assumed to be flat forever.[1] The value of this business would have declined from $75 million in 1987 to $47 million in 1991, as shown on the next page:

---

[1] Assuming no growth in after-tax cash flow results in multiples lower than were generally seen in 1987 and 1991, but the relative difference would not change even in a growth scenario.

	1987	*1991*
EBITD-CE	$10MM	$10MM
Less 35% Tax	(3.5MM)	(3.5MM)
	6.5MM	6.5MM
WAATCC	8.65%	13.81%
Business Value	$75MM	$47MM
Multiple of EBITD-CE	7.5 ×	4.7 ×

The table below summarizes the differences in highly leveraged capital structures between 1987 and 1991, leading to a different WAATCC in each year.

	1987 After-Tax Cost	*% Capital*	*WAATCC*	*1991 After-Tax Cost*	*% Capital*	*WAATCC*	*Change*
Senior Debt	6.34%	65%	4.12%	6.34%	50%	3.17%	
Subordinated Debt	8.45%	30%	2.54%	15.45%	30%	4.64%	
Equity	39.70%	5%	1.99%	30.00%	20%	6.00%	
WAATCC			8.65%			13.81%	5.16%

One way to analyze the 5.16% change in discount rates caused by changes in capital structure and pricing is to isolate the components of this change, as follows:

- *More Conservative Senior Lenders (.32%)*
  15% decrease in Senior Debt as a percentage of capital, replaced with subordinated debt at 1987's after-tax cost (15% × (8.45%–6.34%) = .32%)
- *More Conservative Subordinated Lenders (2.74%)*
  Equity has replaced subordinated debt in the eighty-first through ninety-fifth percentile of the capital structure. While the ninety-fifth through one hundredth percentile equity remains priced at 39.7% in both years, the eighty-first through ninety-fifth percentile equity is priced at 26.76% in 1991 to reflect the lower leverage in capital structure, computed as follows:

5/20	×	39.70%	=	9.93%
+ 15/20	×	X	=	20.07%
20/20				30.00%

where X = 26.76%

Comparing the after-tax cost of subordinated debt in 1987 with the cost of equity in the same position in the capital structure yields the following:

26.76% – 8.45% = 18.31% × 15% = 2.74%

- *Higher Return Demanded by Subordinated Lenders (2.10%)*
  Increase in the absolute cost of subordinated debt from 8.45% to 15.45%, representing 30% of the capital structure, yields 2.10%.

As the analysis above shows, only .32% of the change in WAATCC is due to senior lenders becoming more conservative as a percentage of the capital structure. The remaining 4.84% is due to the subordinated debt increasing in cost (by requiring a non-tax deductible warrant yielding 7%) and requiring a more conservative position in the capital structure through 15% more equity. This 60% increase in the WAATCC resulting from a radical shift in the risk/reward balance required by subordinated lenders (i.e., much less risk; much more reward) in highly leveraged capital structures has had profound effects on the valuation of large, publicly traded companies.

THE IMPACT OF COST OF CAPITAL ON LBOs

To understand effects on valuation of large, publicly traded companies, one must compare both 1987 and the 1991 WAATCC in highly leveraged capital structures with the WAATCC of low leveraged capital structures in both years. The November 1987 article illustrated the typical capital structure of a large, publicly traded company, as follows:

	% Capital	*Pre-Tax Cost*	*After-Tax Cost*	*Weighted Cost*
Senior Debt (fixed)	33%	[1] 9.75%	6.34%	2.09%
Equity	67%	[2] 14.40%	14.40%	9.65%
WAATCC				11.74%

[1] 30-year Treasury of 8.6% plus 1.15% = 9.75%

[2] 30-year Treasury of 8.6% plus 5.8% = 14.4%

Capital structures and costs for large, low leveraged public companies have not changed in 1991 compared to 1987. What has changed is that highly leveraged capital structures' WAATCC have increased from below low leverage levels to above between 1987 and 1991 (11.74% low leverage WAATCC compared to high leverage WAATCC of 8.65% in 1987 and 13.81% in 1991). Recalling the earlier example of the company with $10 million EBITD-CE, compare what has happened to business value between high and low leveraged capital structures between 1987 and 1991:

	High Leverage		*Low Leverage*
	1987	*1991*	*1987/1991*
EBITD-CE	$10MM	$10MM	$10MM
Less 35% Tax	(3.5MM)	(3.5MM)	(3.5MM)
	6.5	6.5	6.5
WAATCC	÷ 8.65%	÷ 13.81%	÷ 11.74%
Business Value	$75MM	$47MM	$55MM
Multiple of EBITD-CE	7.5 ×	4.7 ×	5.5 ×

As mentioned earlier, the absolute multiples and business values are lower than market due to assuming no growth in operating earnings, but the relative difference between the three capital structures is accurate. What is most noticeable is that the business value in the 1987 high leverage structure was 36% higher than the low leverage structure, whereas, the business value under the high leverage structure in 1991 is 15% *lower* than under the low leverage structure. This phenomenon helps to explain the substantial reduction in larger leveraged buyouts in 1991.

THE ROLE OF JUNK BONDS IN LBOs

Most large public companies have a low leveraged capital structure such as the one described above. With the development of the "junk bond" in the mid-1980s with the cost and capital structure characteristics described in the subordinated debt portion of the 1987 high leverage capital structure, the WAATCC of highly leveraged companies was significantly below low leveraged companies. Consequently, a buyer using such a highly leveraged capital structure could afford to pay more than the market capitalization of that same company using low leverage. By 1990, the situation reversed itself when the junk bond market collapsed, and the WAATCC of even less highly leveraged capital structures increased above that of low leveraged capital structures.

Now the market capitalization of low leveraged companies is more than high leveraged buyers can justify paying.

Will the situation reverse again? Some argue that the junk bonds in 1987 were fundamentally underpriced, given the risk. While it is still too early to know how well these bonds will perform after the final consummation of the transactions done in the 1980s, recent market values suggest these bonds were originally underpriced. Others will argue that the less optimistic forecast of general economic activity in 1991 compared with 1987 explains the radical change in risk/return characteristics of subordinated debt.

LBOs OF PRIVATE VERSUS PUBLIC COMPANIES

If one looks at the transactions that were completed in 1987 in the private market where private companies were purchased by private buyers, one finds that the subordinated debt provided by institutions such as insurance companies required *returns* similar to that required in 1991. However, these private subordinated lenders in 1987 required only 5%–10% equity and permitted 60%-65% senior debt, similar to the position in the capital structure of subordinated debt found in 1987's large transactions. One might surmise that junk bonds were partially underpriced, as evidenced by the higher return received in the private subordinated debt market in 1987, but not by the full degree to which they have declined in value since subordinated lenders in private transactions today have lowered the risk component of the equation by requiring more equity below them and less senior debt above them, suggesting that the current state of the economy partially reflects the lower value of junk bonds today.

Interestingly, the difference between the cost of private and public subordinated debt in 1987 was explained at that time as a function of the liquidity of the public debt. In other words, since an investment was liquid, it carried a lower return. Experience now shows that such liquidity is fleeting and primarily a function of how the investment is performing, unless one is prepared to accept a large discount to face value to increase the return to that required to balance risk and reward in the particular transaction.

In examining the question of whether leveraged buyouts (LBO) will return to their former popularity, the analysis above can be illuminating. First, it is important to differentiate between using an LBO to acquire a public company versus a private company. With respect to a public company, the sole purpose of an LBO is to arbitrage a perceived difference between the market price and the actual value of a company. While breaking up the components of a company and reselling them may result in this arbitrage opportunity, the opportunity occurs when conglomerates obfuscate the underlying value of their component companies for the average market investor. With the increasing sophistication of institutional market participants, these opportunities will be fewer and fewer in the future.

Another arbitrage opportunity is created through using a lower WAATCC to finance a business. As was shown earlier, highly leveraged capital structures created this arbitrage opportunity in 1987, compared with low leveraged structures, and reversed themselves by 1991 eliminating this arbitrage profit. Since the apparent imbalanced risk/reward ratio of junk bonds created this arbitrage opportunity, new opportunities of this type will not occur again until a new financing phenomenon underestimates risk in relation to reward. Given the unlikely arbitrage opportunities in the near term created by conglomerates or lower WAATCC in high leveraged companies, public companies taken private in LBOs are unlikely on a large scale for the foreseeable future.

Private companies primarily use LBOs to liquify owners' positions, not to arbitrage value opportunities. Since most private firms are not able to liquify their ownership in public markets, they are relegated to the sale of the company to an industrial buyer or to a financial investor. Sale to an investor can be more rewarding to the former owner if the investor leverages the equity investment through an LBO, since debt is less expensive than equity up to some level of leverage. Since private companies will continue to require liquidity and LBOs constitute one of the major sources of such liquidity, LBOs will continue to be used in this market segment.

While arbitrage opportunities theoretically exist for the private company market, they are much less pronounced since most are not conglomerates, and buyers and sellers tend to be reasonably sophisticated and close to the operations of these middle market businesses. Further, private providers of capital to this market are generally principals in that they directly underwrite and hold their own investments, and are therefore less susceptible to gross imbalances of risk and reward across many transactions. Consequently, LBOs will continue to be used with middle market companies, and values will move primarily as a function of these companies' operating performance rather than financial market conditions.

Chapter Four

Financing Mergers and Acquisitions in the 1990s

by Frank Torchen
Senior Vice President
General Electric Capital
and
Adjunct Professor
Pace University

Banks and other financiers are pickier about the m&a deals they will back and their loans are pricier than in the "easy money" days of the 1980s. And that's just for the relative handful that are still active in the acquisition finance game.

The mergers and acquisition boom of the 1980s was fueled by a seemingly limitless supply of funds from banks and other lenders.

It's no secret that times have changed. If the flow of borrowed money into the m&a market hasn't completely dried up, it has been slowed markedly to impose strong clamps on dealmaking.

Lenders who scrambled and scraped for deals in the 1980s, now are choosier on the transactions they will finance and the industries they will lend into, and are fiercely dedicated to minimizing risk. They are

---

Reprinted by permission of *Mergers & Acquisition* (July/August) 1991.

This chapter was written while the author was Senior Vice President and Deputy Division Manager at Heller Financial Inc.

committing smaller amounts per deal, charging more for the money they will put up, demanding greater margins of safety in terms of coverage ratios and other criteria, mandating greater equity contributions in leveraged transactions, and dictating tougher terms and schedules for repayments. The supply of funds has dwindled even further in real terms because many financing sources have simply dropped from the m&a market.

Included in the fallout of this tightfistedness are fewer transactions, reduced selling prices, and a dampening of competition for businesses being sold. The lending contraction has put the tightest squeeze on middle-sized transactions where huge numbers of deals are either leveraged buyouts or, whether executed by smaller companies, individuals, or investors, essentially debt-financed. However, even major strategic buyers haven't escaped the lenders' intensified selectivity. And while smaller deals are faring somewhat better because of the relatively modest amounts of money they require, they too must toe a tighter line.

I will concentrate initially on middle-sized leveraged transactions—in the $25 million to $300 million range—for several reasons. The lending guidelines in this category have undergone the most visible change and emerged, both quantitatively and qualitatively, in clearest terms. Moreover, the application of these guidelines has generated broader ripple effects across the entire m&a market by impeding financial buyers and curbing their abilities to compete.

During the boom in leveraged and debt-financed acquisitions of the mid- to late 1980s, buyers often appeared to be acquiring companies with other people's money—namely the lenders. Deal structures dominated by borrowings which were supplemented by minimal equity contributions from the buyers were common forms of acquisition financing.

With the expansion of the leveraged deal segment of the mergers and acquisitions market came a swing toward "business value" lending which based the financing on the market value of a target business. This was an oft-used alternative to the traditional "asset-based" lending in which financing was keyed to the liquidating values of hard assets. As acquisition pricing increased and the multiples (based on earnings before interest and taxes [EBIT], cash flow, or other bench marks) that drove prices expanded dramatically, business value lending techniques enabled lenders to justify higher levels of senior debt in leveraged transactions. But the combination of high leverage and inflated prices often put enormous strains on cash flows and forced lenders to either back end amortization schedules and/or rely on the proceeds of asset sales to get their money back.

WHO WILL FINANCE DEALS?

As the merger boom peaked and the economic slowdown began in late 1989 and continued into 1990, the excesses of the prior decade contributed to unprecedented levels of nonearning loans and write-offs for lenders. Further compounding their problems are the tougher standards that regulators have imposed on banks for making loans and maintaining adequate capital.

Not surprisingly, the tough conditions have taken a toll of lenders willing to finance leveraged acquisitions that once were considered extraordinarily lucrative. The early 1990s feature three types of leveraged lenders:

- The few that are still in the business;
- The bulk of lenders that are out of the business; and
- The far too many members of the group that purport to be in the business but really are not.

Obviously, the contraction in the ranks has reduced the supply of funds available for leveraged financing. But an even deeper cutback has resulted from the way the smallish band of survivors has changed the rules. Those still in the business have retreated to the credit disciplines and standards that last prevailed in the early 1980s, and are demanding more equity in deals and a far greater cushion in cash flow coverages of debt service. While the business value approach is still used, it now is based on more realistic earnings and cash flow projections at the target business, lower multiples and purchase prices, and stronger capital structures.

Some general criteria that have evolved from the shake-up in lending policies will be presented below. They are fairly typical standards for deals priced at $25 million to $300 million and financed through a leveraged structure of secured loans, subordinated debt, and equity.

DYNAMICS OF TARGETS AND BUYING GROUPS

To be considered viable candidates for financing, parties to the deal must show these characteristics:

- Defensible market share;
- Limited technology risk;

- Segmentation and diversification among customers, suppliers, products, geography, etc.;
- Strong historical performance and interim results;
- Realistic financial and operating projections;
- Capable and experienced management with an established hierarchy;
- Equity stake by management;
- Ability to recover from a recession and/or downside scenarios; and
- Experienced buyers or sponsor groups with strong track records.

PURCHASE PRICE

In the 1985–1990 period, the typical price multiple was seven to 10 times EBIT.

In the early 1990s, the multiple has declined to five to six times EBIT.

Sir Isaac Newton's law of gravity notes that what goes up, must come down. Multiples (regardless of which cash flow definition is used) have dropped significantly. In fact, certain buyout groups won't entertain prices for companies in excess of five to 5.5 times EBIT.

There are both theoretical and practical reasons for this retrenchment. In theory, all lenders—banks, finance companies, insurance companies, and other mezzanine lenders—are demanding higher rewards for contributing a smaller percentage of the capital structure. This has resulted in larger equity infusions that are partially accommodated by lower expected returns on equity, a higher cost of capital, and, therefore, lower prices. In practical terms, lenders are comfortable only when financing at lower multiples. Less credit is available, and recession has affected performance and dampened future expectations.

CAPITAL STRUCTURE OF THE DEAL

In the 1985–1990 period, the usual capital structure was:

- Senior debt—60% to 65%.
- Subordinated debt—25% to 30%.
- Equity—5% to 10%.

In the early 1990s, lenders are satisfied with a capital structure that reduces the debt portion and sharply raises the equity infusion. A more typical structure today is:

- Senior debt—50% to 60%.
- Subordinated debt—20% to 30%.
- Equity—20% to 30%.

HLTs, or highly leveraged transactions, are being supplanted by what I term LHLTs, or less than highly leveraged transactions. In fact, most lenders are looking for a minimum of 25% common equity in transactions.

Certain lenders are willing to have subordinated debt and equity together total 20% to 30% of the capital structure as long as the mezzanine piece has "payment-in-kind" or "pay-as-you-can" features. With a "payment-in-kind" feature, the interest expense is not paid out in cash but is added to the principal amount. Under a "pay-as-you-can" provision, the interest expense can be paid out in cash only if certain financial targets (such as if the company reaches a predetermined earnings level or fixed charge coverage goal) are met. If these targets are not met, the interest expense is added to the principal amount.

Seller notes, or obligations representing a portion of the purchase price and, at times, contingent on achievement of future earnings targets, are re-emerging.

THE PRICE OF FINANCING

In the 1985–1990 period, providers of capital typically charged these interest rates or required these rates of return:

- Senior debt—The prime rate plus 1.25 to 1.75 percentage points.
- Subordinated debt—The Treasury rate plus four to five percentage points (current coupon). Anticipated internal rate of return (IRR) was 20% to 25%.
- Equity—40% to 50% IRR.

In the early 1990s, interest rates and IRRs have trended upward for lenders and expected returns have declined for buyers in this pattern:

- Senior Debt—Prime plus 1.75 to 2.5 percentage points.

- Subordinated debt—The Treasury rate plus 5.5 to 6.5 percentage points (current coupon). Anticipated IRR of 25% to 28%.
- Equity—IRR of 35%.

In addition to the basic interest rate, senior lenders are looking for 2% to 3% in closing fees—up to 4% to 5% on occasions—and unused revolving line fees of 0.5%.

Loan pricing ranges are broader, and combinations of total pricing vary. Some senior lenders also want additional upside through a nominal warrant position or the ability to buy equity. Subordinated lenders are seeking total IRRs of at least 25%, and, in certain deals, upward of 28%. Fees also are in the 2% range. More realistic projections are being used by subordinated lenders to determine IRRs.

Most sub debt lenders continue to take warrants with a current coupon to reach IRR targets. However, a few of these lenders recently have foregone the upside potential of a warrant by locking in coupon rates in the 18% to 20% range, thus accepting that yield as their overall IRRs.

A number of buyers are willing to accept returns of 30% to 35% on their equity on certain deals. Buyers would like "base" case projections to generate IRRs in the 20% to 25% range.

COVERAGE RATIOS

Lenders are demanding a wider margin of safety in coverage of debt service by the cash or earnings generated by leveraged targets.

In the 1985–1990 period, the coverage ratios for run rates (performances in the trailing 12 months) were as follows:

- Senior debt interest—1.4 to 1.6 times the residue of earnings before interest, depreciation, amortization, and taxes (EBIDAT) minus capital expenditures/senior interest expense.
- Total interest—0.9 to 1.3 times the residue of EBIDAT minus capital expenditures/total interest expense.
- Fixed charges—0.8 to 1.1 times EBIDAT minus capital expenditures and taxes/total interest expense plus total principal payments.

In the early 1990s, the ratios, using the same base figures for each expense category, were as follows:

- Senior debt interest—1.8 to 2.0.
- Total interest—1.4 to 1.6.
- Fixed charges—1.2 to 1.4.

Lenders want stronger coverages. Changes in working capital may be included in the coverage ratio, when significant.

TERM LOAN REPAYMENT

Senior lenders still are making loans with five-year to seven-year maturities. Graduated payments are still available but are not as back-ended as in the past.

Lenders generally are looking to minimums of 50% to 60% term loan amortization in the first five years. Repayments are based on cash flow, not asset sales, as in the past. For subordinated lenders, 10-year loans with repayment at maturity, or repayment beginning or due after the senior lenders are repaid, are being continued.

COVENANTS/COLLATERAL

Collateral for senior lenders continues to be the assets and the stock of the operating company.

Senior lenders are looking for tighter financial covenants and more aggressive standstill periods and other intercreditor agreements.

ENVIRONMENTAL ISSUES

Environmental liability is of great concern to lenders, many of whom will not finance transactions with obvious or potential environmental problems. Due diligence by lenders has intensified. Phase I audits, involving tours of locations, reviews of filings with regulatory agencies and any citations or complaints, and evaluation of the history and background of particular sites, etc., are generally required. Phase II audits, involving ground, water, and air testing, and Phase III audits, involving intensified testing and due diligence, are required when needed.

VALUE CREATION

With their proportionally larger investment in transactions through greater equity contributions, financial buyers will be more closely monitoring the operating performance of their companies. Many have added industry specialists and veteran operating executives to their staffs.

To enhance value, financial buyers will be placing greater emphasis on improvement in operating efficiencies and synergistic add-ons, rather than straight repayment of debt, as in the past. They will be functioning more like strategic buyers in that mode.

LOAN SYNDICATION

With the decline in the number of lenders willing to take part in leveraged deals, commitment and placement activity by senior lenders, in which parts of an acquisition loan are dealt off to a number of other institutions, has declined. This also has had the effect of shortening credit supplies for acquisition financing. Club deals, in which a few lenders join to fund a specific deal, and proposals based on a "best efforts" basis are more common.

Generally speaking, lending in all layers of the capital structure is limited to a few players.

SENIOR LENDERS' EXIT STRATEGIES

In the 1985–1990 period, lenders relied on cash flow as the primary source for debt repayment. Corporate finance alternatives were regarded as supplemental sources. These steps included divesting subsidiaries, divisions, and other assets; streamlining operations; and reducing personnel.

In the early 1990s, cash flow and the restructuring alternatives still rank No. 1 and No. 2 as sources for debt reduction. However, the lenders have added a third measure in the form of the target's asset values. Thus, they are tightly analyzing key asset values, such as receivables, inventories, and fixed assets, to determine downside risk in case there is need to liquidate the business.

FINANCING LARGE TRANSACTIONS

The foregoing covers transactions that generally comprise the m&a middle market where acquisitions financed with borrowed funds account for large amounts of activity. What of the other two key m&a segments?

At the upper end are the large, financially strong strategic corporate buyers that, in general, are of investment grade quality. Loans to finance these kinds of transactions reflect the minimized risk. Lending criteria for this market have not materially changed from the 1980s. Pro forma total interest coverage after the deal is in excess of 2.5 to one and pro forma leverage is less than one to one. Lending charges for senior debt are at LIBOR (London Interbank Overnight Rate) plus up to 100 basis points and closing fees of 25 to 50 basis points. Loans usually are unsecured.

Lending criteria for this market have not materially changed from the 1980s.

FINANCING THE SMALL DEAL

At the lowest end of the market is the deal priced at $30 million and less. Financial buyers are major players in this segment and debt financing is important to getting the deal done, regardless of the acquirer's form. Purchase prices currently are pegged to multiples of three to 4.5 times EBIT. Financing is on an asset-based secured basis. Under that approach, lenders base their loans on the value of appropriate assets and advance the borrower portions of those values.

Currently prevailing advance formulas for key assets include:

- Receivables—70% to 80% of the value.
- Inventory—30% to 60% of the value.
- Machinery—60% to 75% against orderly liquidation values.
- Real Estate—65% to 75% against "fair" value.

Other characteristics of lending into smaller deals:

- The lending rate is prime plus 1.5% to 2.5% and 1% to 1.5% in closing fees.
- Equity infusions of 10% to 20% of the deal value are required.
- The term loan generally comprises less than 50% of the total credit facility.

Maturities for machinery and equipment loans are up to five years, generally without balloon payments. Maturities for loans against real estate are three to five years and are based at times on a 10-year to 15-year amortization.

Overall, the current criteria have changed from the 1980s in that advance rates are more conservative. Valuations of machinery and equipment and real estate have declined and pricing has slightly increased.

In a 1955 article, Dr. Geoffrey Moore, a well-known economist, described the evolution of a period of troubled credit in this manner:

"First and foremost is a rapid increase in the volume of credit or debt. Second, a rapid, speculative increase in the prices of the assets that are bought with the rapidly expanding credit. Third, vigorous competition among lenders for new business. Fourth, relaxation of credit terms or standards. Fifth, a reduction in the risk premiums sought or obtained by lenders."

Moore's scenario aptly and presciently sketched what occurred in the 1980s. These are the very policies that lenders are retreating from as they get back to basics in extending m&a credit.

Chapter Five

Rating Cash Flow Transactions Backed by Corporate Debt

by Douglas J. Lucas
Assistant Vice President
and
Raymond W. McDaniel, Esq.
Managing Director
Moody's Investors Service

INTRODUCTION

In a corporate-debt-backed cash flow transaction, the rating of the structured bond is based on the sufficiency of the cash flow generated by an underlying portfolio of corporate bonds or bank loans. Although collateralized bond obligations (CBOs) and collateralized loan obligations (CLOs) are typically backed by highly diversified pools of speculative-grade credits, they could be supported by investment-grade credits or credits in a single industry or even a single credit. Protection for the highly rated CBO or CLO is typically furnished by subordination or by a combination of subordination and third-party support.

A cash flow transaction reapportions the risk and the return of the collateral according to the preferences of the senior and subordinate investors. The senior bond has less credit risk and a lower expected yield than the underlying portfolio, while subordinated securities have more credit risk and higher expected yields than the portfolio. Arbitrage issuers expect that the structured securities they create can be sold for more than they paid for the underlying collateral. Moody's has rated over $5 billion of CBOs and CLOs since 1988.

These structures are markedly different from the market value structures that they have in large part replaced. The older structures have no subordination; instead they rely on the market value overcollateralization of the collateral pool relative to the par value of the rated structured bond. The portfolio is marked to market periodically and if its value falls below a specified multiple of the structured security's outstanding principal balance, the issuer is required to add to or replace assets in the portfolio. If the issuer is unable to raise the market value of the pool to the required amount or if the issuer becomes bankrupt, the portfolio is liquidated and proceeds are used to retire the structured securities.

Credit issues and the analysis involved in cash flow structures are different from those involved in market value structures. The concern in market value transactions is the possible decrease in collateral value between valuation dates, which could be caused by actual or anticipated defaults, an increase in interest rates, or a decline in market liquidity. Because the period between valuations is short, default risk on underlying assets is relatively less important to a market value transaction than it is to a cash flow transaction. In a cash flow transaction the issuer is not obligated to add more collateral to the structure in response to fluctuations in the collateral's market value. A cash flow transaction is sound as long as portfolio defaults do not threaten to diminish collateral cash flow below the level necessary to service and repay the rated structured debt. Changes in the market value of the collateral are of secondary importance.

A number of structural devices can be used to increase the safety of the structured cash flow security. Credit protection of a senior class can be accomplished through subordination of a junior class on a contemporaneous pay basis or, more commonly, through serial maturity tranches. Mechanisms within the transaction that divert cash flow from subordinate classes to a reserve fund or directly to the senior class in response to certain triggering events increase the credit protection furnished by subordination. Third-party support, such as letters of credit, surety bonds, and liquidity facilities, is an additional method of protection.

OVERVIEW OF CASH FLOW RATING PROCESS

Moody's rating methodology for cash flow corporate-debt-backed securities compares the credit risk inherent in the underlying portfolio with the credit protection offered by the structure. The portfolio's credit risk is based on the credit quality of each bond or bank loan in the portfolio, and on the number and diversity of firms represented in the portfolio, and is relative to the requested structured bond rating. The lower the credit quality and diversity of the collateral, and the higher the requested rating, the greater the portfolio's risk.

The structure's credit protection is quantified by the maximum collateral loss the structure is able to withstand without causing a loss to the structured rated securities. It varies according to the level of subordination and conditions under which cash flow is diverted from subordinated classes to the senior-rated classes. Cash flow models that accurately depict the features of the structure demonstrate the transaction's credit protection.

Based solely on a quantitative perspective, a CBO's or a CLO's rating is determined by whether the structure's credit protection is at least equal to the underlying portfolio's credit risk. The following sections outline the determination of portfolio credit risk and structural credit protection, and discuss legal as well as other structural issues.

PORTFOLIO CREDIT RISK

The aggregate credit risk of a corporate debt portfolio is composed of the default probability and potential loss severity of each asset in the pool. Such risk is explicitly addressed by the rating Moody's assigns to each asset in the portfolio. Academic research and Moody's own studies show that an increased incidence of default accompanies a decrease in rating quality. Table 5.1 presents average 10-year default rates for companies according to their senior unsecured rating, and includes defaults and distressed exchanges on more than 4,000 Moody's-rated companies from 1970 through 1990. (For a complete report on default rates, see "Corporate Bond Defaults and Default Rates 1970-1992," January 1993 Special Report.)

Table 5.1—Ten-Year Company Default Rates

Rating	*Default Rate*
Aaa	0.8%
Aa	1.0%
A	2.1%
Baa	5.0%
Ba	18.2%
B	34.7%

The averages cited, however, do not reflect the variation in default rates that could occur between different 10-year periods. For example, among companies rated Ba at the beginning of 1974, 6.1% defaulted over the next 10 years, compared with 21.2% over the 10-year period beginning in 1981. The magnitude of variations in these default rates suggests the presence of correlation, meaning that if one company defaults, there is a greater likelihood that others will default. Default correlation is only incidentally caused by one firm being the creditor of another; primarily it is the result of individual companies being linked to one another through the general economy. To a certain extent, all companies suffer or prosper together.

The increased variability in default rates caused by correlation increases the credit protection necessary for a portfolio to achieve an investment-grade rating. For example, suppose we know that on average a certain type of bond will default 10% of the time. If defaults were uncorrelated, or independent, the default rate on a large portfolio of similar bonds would not vary greatly from 10%. To protect the transaction against losses on such a portfolio, the structure would only need to be able to absorb losses from the approximate 10% of bonds expected to default.

Suppose, however, that default correlation was so extreme that whenever one bond defaults, all bonds default. To be consistent with the 10% default rate, it must follow that 90% of the time none of the bonds in the portfolio default and that 10% of the time all bonds in the portfolio default. To fully protect against portfolio losses, the structure would have to be capable of covering losses when 100% of the bonds default. The degree to which bonds are default-correlated determines whether credit protection should be closer to 10% or to 100%.

Default correlation caused by general conditions in the national or international economy cannot be diversified by adding companies or industries to the portfolio. To varying degrees, all businesses are adversely affected at the same time, regardless of their specific characteristics, because of their sensitivity to the general economy. Correlation from the general economy is the base level to which default correlation from other sources must be added.

Default correlation, beyond that induced by the general economy, exists between firms in the same industry because of industry-specific economic conditions. Despite a favorable overall economy, 22 companies in the oil or oil service industry defaulted between 1982 and 1986. Other concentrations in defaults have centered on railroad conglomerates, which experienced one default in each year from 1970 through 1977; airlines, with three defaults in 1970 and 1971 and four defaults from 1989 through the beginning of 1991; thrifts, with 11 defaults in 1989; and casino/hoteliers, with 10 defaults in 1990. Default correlation also exists between companies in different industries that rely on the same production inputs and among companies that rely on the same geographical market. The 1986 oil price crash, for example, had a negative effect on a variety of companies doing business in Texas.

ASSESSING PORTFOLIO CREDIT RISK

In assessing the credit risk of a portfolio, Moody's first calculates the average rating of the underlying collateral using the specific rating of each credit in the pool. If the portfolio contains unrated collateral, such as bank loans, Moody's uses a series of methods to establish the credit quality of each unrated asset in the portfolio. The simplest technique is to infer a rating on the unrated debt from the rating on another rated debt of the same issuer. If the issuer has no rated debt, a minimum allowance equivalent to a B3 rating may be given to a secured bank loan if the obligor meets certain financial tests and other requirements. More formally, a private assessment may be assigned to the asset following a review by a Moody's rating analyst. (See "Corporate-Debt-Backed Securities Update" in Moody's November 1990 *Structured Finance* for details.)

The next aspect of assessing the portfolio's risk involves the calculation of a Diversity Score, which measures how well the portfolio is diversified. Moody's looks at both the number of firms in the collateral pool and their distribution among industry groups. A 32-industry classification system is used to measure intra-industry correlation (see Appendix B). More subtle sources of correlation, such as that caused by production inputs, markets, and geographical concentration, are then evaluated. Both the portfolio's quality, as measured by the collateral's average rating, and the portfolio's diversity, as measured by its Diversity Score, determine the collateral's risk. The lower the credit quality and diversity of the collateral, and the higher the requested rating, the greater the portfolio's risk.

Portfolio credit risk is expressed in terms of the percentage loss of underlying collateral the structure should be able to withstand without causing a default on the rated structured bonds the collateral supports. For example, to achieve various investment-grade ratings, a structured security supported by 30 B2-rated obligations from companies in 30 different industries should be able to withstand the following percentage loss of the underlying collateral (after recoveries) without defaulting (Table 5.2).

Table 5.2

Desired Rating	*Portfolio Credit Risk (Net Loss After Recovery)*
Aaa	51%
Aa1	41%
Aa2	39%
Aa3	37%
A1	35%
A2	34%
A3	32%
Baa1	31%
Baa2	29%
Baa3	26%

As a rough test of the adequacy of the above portfolio credit risk numbers, it is instructive to compare them with historic default experience. The 39% loss necessary to achieve an Aa2 rating translates into a 55.7% default rate using a fairly conservative recovery estimate of 30%. Since the average 10-year default rate for B-rated companies is 31.6%, and its standard deviation is 5.2%, the Aa2 portfolio credit risk number represents the average historical default rate, plus 4.6 standard deviations. Furthermore, it should be noted that incremental losses exceeding the protection demanded by the portfolio credit risk would not have much of a negative impact on the structured bond's return, compared with the often catastrophic loss in value a traditional corporate bond experiences after default.

In sum, the portfolio's relative credit risk is the result of the portfolio's credit quality and default correlation and the desired rating of the structured obligation. Details of the approach are presented in Appendix A. Tables providing estimates of portfolio credit risk under a sampling of different collateral and diversity assumptions are shown in Appendix C.

STRUCTURAL CREDIT PROTECTION

The analytical complement to portfolio credit risk is structural credit protection. After determining the portfolio's credit risk, Moody's tests the proposed structure to determine whether its resiliency to collateral losses is at least as high. The structure's credit protections are quantified by the percentage of loss that can occur on the underlying collateral without interrupting promised payments to the rated securities. A cash flow model that accurately portrays structural protections and Moody's modeling assumptions is key to this analysis.

The structure's credit protection depends on several factors, including the amount of structured rated debt issued, the level of subordination or other credit support, the interest rate spread between the collateral and the structured bonds, and the conditions under which cash flows are diverted from subordinated classes and used to protect the senior-rated bonds. Diverted cash flows can be used to fund a reserve account or pay senior principal directly. Possible triggering mechanisms leading to the diversion of cash flow from subordinate classes include tests of interest coverage, asset coverage, portfolio defaults, and collateral credit ratings.

The structure's credit protection also varies by the assumption made regarding the timing of defaults. The longer the underlying obligations are outstanding before defaulting, the more interest income is generated by the defaulting debt and available to repay the structured bonds.

Moody's assumptions about the timing of losses are based on our default study of companies with speculative-grade ratings. About 66% of all the defaults that occur over 10 years happens in the first six years, with 35% of six-year cumulative defaults occurring in the first year. To ensure that our timing assumptions are more conservative than most actual historical loss patterns, Moody's added two standard deviations to these numbers. In that case, about 100% of 10-year defaults occur over the first six years; 50% in the first year. Accordingly, Moody's default scenario calls for 50% of all losses to occur in the first year, followed by 10% in each of years two through six. Furthermore, to protect against deterioration of credit protection at the end of the transaction, the structure is stressed by examining the losses it can sustain in its later years.

Additional modeling assumptions are made on a case-by-case basis to take into account risks unique to particular transactions, such as those associated with floating-rate collateral, noncallable structured debt, floating-rate structured debt, and certain interest rate mismatches.

OTHER STRUCTURAL ISSUES

In addition to the quantitative factors mentioned, Moody's considers the roles and relevant experience of parties to the transactions, including the collateral manager, placement agent, legal counsel, trustee, paying agent, accountant, and general partner. Of special concern is the insolvency risk of the issuer and the isolation of the transaction from the legal challenges of interested parties. In partnership structures, Moody's is concerned about the effects of partnership dissolution on the transaction, and in CLOs, Moody's conducts a further analysis on the credit quality of banks selling loan participations into the pool. As with all structured ratings, Moody's also completes an extensive review of transaction documents and legal opinions before assigning a rating.

APPENDIX A

The Mathematics of Calculating Portfolio Credit Risk

Moody's uses a probabilistic, expected loss approach to determine a portfolio's credit risk. Expected loss is the average of all possible principal losses weighted by their probability. A portfolio's credit risk is quantified as the amount of loss protection needed to lower a portfolio's expected loss to the expected loss benchmark of the desired rating of the structured bonds.

For illustrative purposes, suppose that a transaction is backed by a single speculative-grade bond with a 30% default probability, and the structured bond rating sought is associated with a 5% default probability benchmark. Assume for now that defaulted bonds always lose 70% of par.

The expected loss of the speculative-grade collateral with the 30% default probability and a 70% loss severity is 21%:

$$\text{Probability of Default} \times \text{Default Severity} = \text{Expected Loss}$$

$$30\% \times 70\% = 21\%$$

The expected loss of the investment-grade bond with the 5% default probability and a 70% loss severity is 3.5%:

$$\text{Probability of Default} \times \text{Default Severity} = \text{Expected Loss}$$

$$5\% \times 70\% = 3.5\%$$

We want to calculate the amount of credit protection necessary to lower the expected loss of the speculative-grade collateral to the expected loss of the investment-grade bond.

$$\text{Probability of Default} \times (\text{Default Severity} - \text{Credit Protection}) = \text{Expected Loss}$$

Solving the above equation, credit protection must equal 58.3%:

$$30\% \times (70\% - X) = 3.5\%$$

$$X = 70\% - 3.5\%/30\%$$

$$X = 58.3\%$$

Note that the credit protection is not the difference between the two security's expected losses (21% – 3.5% = 17.5%). An intuitive explanation of this is that the credit enhancement is only used if there is a default on the speculative-grade debt and is therefore weighted by the default probability of the speculative-grade bond.

$$\text{Probability of Default} \times \text{Credit Protection} = \text{Change in Expected Loss}$$

$$30\% \times 58.3\% = 17.5\%$$

With only one bond in the portfolio, there are only two possible outcomes: default or no default. As more bonds are added to the portfolio, the distribution of outcomes becomes more centered about the expected outcome. The more bonds added to the portfolio, the lower the necessary credit protection, as illustrated by adding one more speculative-grade bond in the example above:

Probability of 1 Default[1]

×

(Default Severity if 1 bond defaults – Credit Protection)

+

Probability of 2 Defaults[2]

×

(Default Severity if 2 bonds default – Credit Protection)

=

Expected Loss

or:

$$(2 \times 30\% \times 70\%) \times$$
$$(35\% - \text{Credit Protection})$$
$$+$$
$$(30\% \times 30\%) \times$$
$$(70\% - \text{Credit Protection})$$
$$=$$
$$3.5\%$$

Solving the equation, credit protection equals 34.3%, substantially reduced from the 58.3% credit protection necessary for one speculative-grade bond to achieve the same expected loss as the investment-

1 The probability of the first bond defaulting and the second bond not defaulting is the default probability of the first times one minus the default probability of the second. The probability of the first bond not defaulting and the second bond defaulting is one minus the default probability of the first times the default probability of the second. These two products are summed to obtain the probability of either one of the two bonds defaulting.

2 The probability of both bonds defaulting is the probability of the first bond defaulting times the probability of the second bond defaulting.

grade bond. That reduction in credit enhancement is a result of the decreased variance in the portfolio's expected loss.

Necessary credit protection also depends upon assumptions about the distribution of potential recovery rates on a defaulted bond. Suppose loss in the case of default can be 100%, 85%, 70%, 55%, and 40%, with equal probability.

$$
\begin{gathered}
\text{Probability of Default} \times \text{Probability of 100\% Loss} \times \\
(100\% - \text{Credit Protection}) + \\
\text{Probability of Default} \times \text{Probability of 85\% Loss} \times \\
(85\% - \text{Credit Protection}) + \\
\text{Probability of Default} \times \text{Probability of 70\% Loss} \times \\
(70\% - \text{Credit Protection}) + \\
\text{Probability of Default} \times \text{Probability of 55\% Loss} \times \\
(55\% - \text{Credit Protection}) + \\
\text{Probability of Default} \times \text{Probability of 40\% Loss} \times \\
(40\% - \text{Credit Protection}) \\
= \\
3.5\%
\end{gathered}
$$

In solving the equation, portfolio credit protection equals 65.6%. Note that the credit protection is higher than that in either the one- or the two-bond case, where loss was assumed to be constant at 70%. That is because when losses are 40% or 55%, credit protection is capped at 40% or 55%, respectively, because an investor never receives more than 100% of par. To offset the reduced probability of using the full credit protection, the amount of credit protection must be increased.

The above examples introduce the four important quantitative factors that must be considered when assessing the credit risks of a corporate debt portfolio:

- Moody's ratings of the collateral, quantified as a default probability.
- Default loss severity and distribution.
- Diversifiable and undiversifiable default correlation, quantified as higher default probability and as an adjustment to the number of bonds assumed in the portfolio.
- Desired rating of the structured security, quantified as the target expected credit loss.

Default Probability and Loss Severity

Moody's study of default rates found 10-year average cumulative default rates as low as 0.8% for companies with Aaa senior unsecured ratings and as high as 34.7% for companies with B senior unsecured ratings. These default rates refer to the company rating at the beginning of the 10-year period and include the defaults of companies subsequently downgraded. An interpolation of these results to show default rates by numerical rating modifiers yielded the results shown in the left-hand column of Table 5.3. Moody's stressed these interpolated default rates to allow for variations in future default rates caused by harsher economic conditions and undiversifiable default correlation. The resulting assumed default rates in any rating category are higher than those actually experienced over any 10-year period.

Table 5.3

Rating	*Historic 10-Year Default Rates*	*Assumed 10-Year Default Rates*
Aaa	0.8%	1.8%
Aa1	1.2%	1.9%
Aa2	1.4%	2.0%
Aa3	1.5%	2.2%
A1	1.7%	2.5%
A2	1.8%	3.0%
A3	2.3%	3.6%
Baa1	3.5%	4.4%
Baa2	4.4%	5.4%
Baa3	7.5%	7.9%
Ba1	11.9%	17.4%
Ba2	16.1%	21.5%
Ba3	20.6%	26.0%
B1	25.9%	32.1%
B2	31.6%	37.9%
B3	39.6%	45.8%

These default probabilities for single debt obligations are the basis for computing the probability of multiple defaults within a portfolio. A binomial distribution is assumed, where the probability of y defaults out of a portfolio of n debt obligations is as follows:

$$\binom{n}{y} \times$$

$$(\text{Probability of Default})^{y} \times$$

$$(1 - \text{Probability of Default})^{(n-y)}$$

Several historical studies of bond defaults have shown that the average price of a bond shortly after default, without regard to lien position, is approximately 40% of par. As illustrated above, Moody's uses a recovery distribution that varies from 0% to 60% and has a mean of 30%, which is lower than the historic average.

Moody's computes the portfolio's credit risk using the actual rating of the specific collateral in the portfolio (or, if trading is allowed, the limit to which trades may be made) and the 0% to 60% recovery assumption. That method is possible because Moody's assessment of portfolio credit risk is stated in terms of expected loss, which is the product of default probability and default severity, and because the rating system is designed so that obligations of the same rating have the same expected loss. A senior-secured bank loan, for example, would have a lower loss severity but an offsetting higher default probability than a subordinated bond of the same credit rating. Since the expected loss of all obligations of the same rating category is roughly the same, and since the approach to calculating portfolio credit risk focuses on expected loss, an accurate assessment of the portfolio can be made by adjusting default probability while maintaining the same recovery assumption. That simplification makes it easier to compute the portfolio's credit risk and to monitor the trading activity of transactions with nonstatic portfolios.

Diversifiable Default Correlation

Adding companies to a portfolio lessens the chance of extreme outcomes and reduces portfolio credit risk. These benefits are, however, diminished to the extent that companies are correlated in terms of default and tend to survive or fail together. The phenomenon of companies tracking each other's performance is particularly apparent for firms in the same industry.

Correlation caused by the general economy is taken into account by the higher than historic default rate and loss severity assumed for the collateral. Moody's takes industry-related correlation into account by means of a Diversity Score, which penalizes the structure for having issuers in the same industry. For example, Table 5.4 shows that the first firm in a particular industry earns the transaction a Diversity Score of 1. The second name in the same industry increases the Diversity Score in that particular industry to 1.5. The transaction's total Diversity Score is computed by summing the Diversity Scores of all industries represented in the portfolio. This methodology is adjusted to accommodate portfolios where the par amounts per issuer are unequal.

Table 5.4

Number of Firms in Same Industry	*Diversity Score*
1	1.00
2	1.50
3	2.00
4	2.33
5	2.67
6	3.00
7	3.25
8	3.50
9	3.75
10	4.00
>10	Evaluated on a case-by-case basis

It is industry practice to express concentration constraints by stating the maximum percentage of aggregate collateral to be held in any name or industry. To evaluate a diversity standard expressed this way, Moody's uses the lower of two diversity calculations. The first calculation assumes that the portfolio has the minimum number of names, the second calculation assumes the portfolio has the minimum number of industries. For example, if an issuer stated a diversity standard of 2% par per name and 5% par per industry, the fewest number of names would be 50. The 50 names would have to be spread over at least 25 industries, otherwise the industry ceiling would be violated. Two names in each of 25 industries would yield a Diversity Score of 1.5 per industry and a total score of 37. The second computation assumes the fewest number of industries. For example, if the portfolio only held 20 industries each with 5% of aggregate portfolio par, each industry would have to contain three names or else the name ceiling would be violated. Three names in each of 20 industries leads to a diversity index of 2 per industry, or 40 in total. Moody's would use the lower Diversity Score of 37.

Appendix B lists Moody's industrial classifications. Portfolios must also be examined for other correlation-causing attributes, such as geographic concentration or reliance upon the same production inputs or markets. Single-industry portfolios in particular are examined on a case-by-case basis.

Target Expected Returns

To determine expected losses commensurate with each investment-grade rating category, Moody's first computed historic default rates on investment-grade companies without counting defaults caused by special events. These defaults rates were then lowered to make investment-grade ratings harder to achieve, particularly for speculative-grade collateral. Finally, to arrive at expected loss, the reduced default rates were multiplied by a 60% loss severity assumption, which is a lower loss severity than that assumed for collateral (Table 5.5). These assumptions, which lower the target-expected loss that a structure must achieve, add another conservative bias to our approach to ensure that structured investors receive a structured security with the credit characteristics of the investment-grade rating.

Table 5.5

Rating	*Historic 10-Year Default Rates Without Special Events*	*Target Expected Loss*
Aaa	0.0%	0.002%
Aa1 to Aa3	0.9%	0.06% to 0.23%
A1 to A3	1.1%	0.37% to 0.86%
Baa1 to Baa3	3.4%	1.25% to 3.33%

APPENDIX B

Moody's Industry Classifications

1. Aerospace and Defense: Major Contractor, Subsystems, Research, Aircraft Manufacturing, Arms, Ammunition
2. Automobile: Automotive Equipment, Auto-Manufacturing, Auto Parts Manufacturing, Personal-Use Trailers, Motor Homes, Dealers
3. Banking: Bank Holding, Savings and Loans, Consumer Credit, Small Loan, Agency, Factoring, Receivables
4. Beverage, Food and Tobacco: Beer and Ale, Distillers, Wines and Liquors, Distributors, Soft Drink Syrup, Bottlers, Bakery, Mill Sugar, Canned Foods, Corn Refiners, Dairy Products, Meat Products, Poultry Products, Snacks, Packaged Foods, Distributors, Candy, Gum, Seafood, Frozen Food, Cigarettes, Cigars, Leaf/Snuff, Vegetable Oil
5. Buildings and Real Estate: Brick, Cement, Climate Controls, Contracting, Engineering, Construction, Hardware, Forest Products (building-related only), Plumbing, Roofing, Wallboard, Real Estate, Real Estate Development, REITs, Land Development
6. Chemicals, Plastics and Rubber: Chemicals (nonagriculture), Industrial Gases, Sulphur, Plastics, Plastic Products, Abrasives, Coatings, Paints, Varnish, Fabricating
7. Containers, Packaging and Glass: Glass, Fiberglass, Containers made of: Glass, Metal, Paper, Plastic, Wood, or Fiberglass
8. Personal and Nondurable Consumer Products (Manufacturing Only): Soaps, Perfumes, Cosmetics, Toiletries, Cleaning Supplies, School Supplies
9. Diversified/Conglomerate Manufacturing
10. Diversified/Conglomerate Service
11. Diversified Natural Resources, Precious Metals and Minerals: Fabricating, Distribution, Mining and Sales
12. Ecological: Pollution Control, Waste Removal, Waste Treatment, Waste Disposal
13. Electronics: Computer Hardware, Electric Equipment, Components, Controllers, Motors, Household Appliances, Information Service Communication Systems, Radios, TVs, Tape Machines, Speakers, Printers, Drivers, Technology
14. Finance: Investment Brokerage, Leasing, Syndication, Securities

15. Farming and Agriculture: Livestock, Grains, Produce; Agricultural Chemicals, Agricultural Equipment, Fertilizers
16. Grocery: Grocery Stores, Convenience Food Stores
17. Healthcare, Education and Childcare: Ethical Drugs, Proprietary Drugs, Research, Health Care Centers, Nursing Homes, HMOs, Hospitals, Hospital Supplies, Medical Equipment
18. Home and Office Furnishings, Housewares, and Durable Consumer Products: Carpets, Floor Coverings, Furniture, Cooking, Ranges
19. Hotels, Motels, Inns, and Gaming
20. Insurance: Life, Property and Casualty, Broker, Agent, Surety
21. Leisure, Amusement, Motion Pictures, Entertainment: Boating, Bowling, Billiards, Musical Instruments, Fishing, Photo Equipment, Records, Tapes, Sports, Outdoor Equipment (Camping), Tourism, Resorts, Games, Toy Manufacturing, Motion Picture Production Theaters, Motion Picture Distribution
22. Machinery (Nonagriculture, Nonconstruction, Nonelectronic): Industrial, Machine Tools, Steam Generators
23. Mining, Steel, Iron and Nonprecious Metals: Coal, Copper, Lead, Uranium, Zinc, Aluminum, Stainless Steel, Integrated Steel, Ore Production, Refractories, Steel Mill Machinery, Mini-Mills, Fabricating, Distribution and Sales
24. Oil and Gas: Crude Producer, Retailer, Well Supply, Service and Drilling
25. Personal, Food, and Miscellaneous Services
26. Printing, Publishing and Broadcasting: Graphic Arts, Paper, Paper Products, Business Forms, Magazines, Books, Periodicals, Newspapers, Textbooks, Radio, TV, Cable, Broadcasting Equipment
27. Cargo Transport: Rail, Shipping, Railroads, Railcar Builders, Ship Builders, Containers, Container Builders, Parts, Overnight Mail, Trucking, Truck Manufacturing, Trailer Manufacturing, Air Cargo, Transport
28. Retail Stores: Apparel, Toy, Variety, Drugs, Department, Mail Order Catalog, Showroom
29. Telecommunications: Local, Long Distance, Independent, Telephone, Telegraph, Satellite, Equipment, Research, Cellular
30. Textiles and Leather: Producer, Synthetic Fiber, Apparel Manufacturer, Leather Shoes
31. Personal Transportation: Air, Bus, Rail, Car Rental
32. Utilities: Electric, Water, Hydro Power, Gas, Diversified

APPENDIX C

Portfolio Credit Risk Tables

These tables show how collateral rating, portfolio diversity, and the desired rating on the structured security correspond to portfolio credit risk. The numbers in the matrices are the losses (defaults net of recovery) we look for a structure to withstand without causing a loss to the senior structured bonds. These numbers do not reflect certain qualitatively assessed factors that affect portfolio credit risk and are examined on a case-by-case basis. Portfolio risk numbers for transactions with low Diversity Scores are particularly open to qualitative adjustment based on the default correlation of the companies in the pool. Collateral Rating is the par-weighted average rating of assets in the portfolio. Diversity Score is a measure of portfolio diversity, as explained in Appendix A.

Structured Security Desired Rating: Aaa

Diversity Score	Collateral Rating														
	B3	*B2*	*B1*	*Ba3*	*Ba2*	*Ba1*	*Baa3*	*Baa2*	*Baa1*	*A3*	*A2*	*A1*	*Aa3*	*Aa2*	*Aa1*
1	← evaluated case-by-case →														
2	100%	100%	100%	100%	100%	100%	85%	71%	57%	52%	49%	47%	45%	42%	39%
3	99	98	97	95	95	92	75	59	43	38	36	35	33	32	30
4	95	92	91	87	84	80	64	50	36	33	31	29	27	25	24
5	90	87	85	83	76	73	58	44	30	27	25	23	22	21	20
7	81	77	73	69	66	60	49	38	27	24	22	20	19	18	17
10	75	69	65	59	58	51	41	33	25	22	20	19	18	17	16
15	66	60	56	51	46	43	36	30	24	21	19	18	17	16	15
20	62	56	51	46	42	38	33	28	23	20	18	17	16	15	14
25	58	53	48	43	38	35	30	26	22	19	17	16	15	14	13
30	56	51	46	40	35	32	28	24	20	17	16	15	14	13	12
35	54	48	44	38	35	30	26	22	19	16	15	14	13	12	11
40	52	47	42	37	33	29	24	20	17	15	14	13	12	11	10

Structured Security Desired Rating: Aa1

	Collateral Rating													
Diversity Score	*B3*	*B2*	*B1*	*Ba3*	*Ba2*	*Ba1*	*Baa3*	*Baa2*	*Baa1*	*A3*	*A2*	*A1*	*Aa3*	*Aa2*
1	← evaluated case-by-case →													
2	93%	92%	91%	88%	85%	82%	68%	56%	50%	47%	45%	43%	41%	37%
3	85	82	79	74	69	63	53	42	36	34	33	31	30	28
4	79	74	70	64	60	55	43	34	31	29	27	25	23	22
5	73	68	63	58	54	49	38	28	26	24	22	21	20	19
7	66	61	56	51	46	42	33	25	22	20	19	18	17	16
10	60	54	50	44	40	36	30	24	20	19	18	17	16	15
15	54	48	44	38	34	30	27	23	19	18	17	16	15	14
20	51	45	40	35	31	27	24	22	18	17	16	15	14	13
25	48	43	38	33	29	25	23	21	17	16	15	14	13	12
30	47	41	36	31	27	24	21	19	16	15	14	13	12	11
35	45	40	35	30	26	23	20	18	15	14	13	12	11	10
40	44	39	34	29	25	22	19	16	14	13	12	11	10	9

Structured Security Desired Rating: Aa2

	Collateral Rating												
Diversity Score	*B3*	*B2*	*B1*	*Ba3*	*Ba2*	*Ba1*	*Baa3*	*Baa2*	*Baa1*	*A3*	*A2*	*A1*	*Aa3*
1	←					evaluated case-by-case							→
2	91%	89%	86%	83%	80%	75%	55%	48%	46%	44%	42%	40%	36%
3	81	78	74	67	62	58	41	34	32	31	29	28	27
4	74	69	64	60	55	50	33	29	27	25	23	22	21
5	69	64	59	54	50	45	27	25	23	22	20	19	18
7	63	57	52	47	43	38	24	20	19	18	17	16	15
10	57	51	46	41	37	33	23	19	18	17	16	15	14
15	51	45	41	36	32	27	22	18	17	16	15	14	13
20	48	43	38	33	29	25	21	17	16	15	14	13	12
25	46	40	36	31	27	23	20	16	15	14	13	12	11
30	45	39	34	29	26	22	18	15	14	13	12	11	10
35	44	38	33	28	25	21	17	14	13	12	11	10	9
40	43	37	33	28	24	20	15	13	12	11	10	9	8

Structured Security Desired Rating: Aa3

Diversity Score	*Collateral Rating*											
	B3	*B2*	*B1*	*Ba3*	*Ba2*	*Ba1*	*Baa3*	*Baa2*	*Baa1*	*A3*	*A2*	*A1*
1	←					evaluated case-by-case						→
2	86%	84%	81%	77%	73%	68%	53%	47%	44%	42%	40%	36%
3	77	72	67	61	57	53	39	33	31	28	27	25
4	70	64	60	55	49	44	32	28	25	22	21	20
5	65	60	54	49	45	40	26	24	22	19	18	17
7	59	53	48	43	39	34	22	19	18	17	16	15
10	54	48	43	38	34	29	21	18	17	16	15	14
15	49	43	38	33	29	25	19	17	16	15	14	13
20	46	40	36	30	26	23	18	16	15	14	13	12
25	44	38	34	29	25	21	17	15	14	13	12	11
30	43	37	32	28	24	20	16	14	13	12	11	10
35	42	36	31	27	23	19	15	13	12	11	10	9
40	41	35	31	26	22	19	14	12	11	10	9	8

Structured Security Desired Rating: A1

Diversity Score	Collateral Rating										
	B3	*B2*	*B1*	*Ba3*	*Ba2*	*Ba1*	*Baa3*	*Baa2*	*Baa1*	*A3*	*A2*
1	← evaluated case-by-case →										
2	82%	79%	75%	70%	66%	59%	50%	45%	41%	39%	35%
3	72	66	61	56	52	48	36	32	28	26	24
4	65	60	55	49	45	40	30	26	21	20	18
5	61	55	50	45	40	36	24	22	18	18	16
7	55	49	45	39	35	31	21	18	17	15	14
10	50	45	40	34	30	26	20	17	16	14	13
15	46	40	36	30	26	23	18	16	15	13	12
20	44	38	33	28	24	21	17	15	14	12	11
25	42	36	32	27	23	20	16	14	13	11	10
30	41	35	31	26	22	19	15	13	12	10	9
35	40	34	30	25	21	18	14	12	11	9	8
40	39	33	29	24	21	17	13	11	10	8	7

Structured Security Desired Rating: A2

	Collateral Rating									
Diversity Score	*B3*	*B2*	*B1*	*Ba3*	*Ba2*	*Ba1*	*Baa3*	*Baa2*	*Baa1*	*A3*
1	← evaluated case-by-case →									
2	80%	77%	73%	68%	63%	55%	45%	41%	39%	35%
3	70	65	60	55	50	46	32	27	25	22
4	64	58	53	48	43	39	26	20	19	17
5	59	53	49	44	39	34	22	18	17	15
7	54	48	43	38	34	29	19	17	15	14
10	49	43	39	33	29	25	18	16	14	13
15	45	39	35	29	25	22	17	15	13	12
20	43	37	32	27	23	20	16	14	12	11
25	41	35	31	26	22	19	15	13	11	10
30	40	34	30	25	21	18	14	12	10	9
35	39	33	29	24	20	17	13	11	9	8
40	38	32	28	23	20	16	12	10	8	7

Structured Security Desired Rating: A3

Diversity Score	Collateral Rating								
	B3	*B2*	*B1*	*Ba3*	*Ba2*	*Ba1*	*Baa3*	*Baa2*	*Baa1*
1	← evaluated case-by-case →								
2	75%	71%	66%	60%	53%	48%	41%	38%	35%
3	64	59	54	49	45	39	30	25	22
4	59	53	48	43	38	34	24	19	17
5	55	49	44	39	34	30	20	17	15
7	50	44	39	34	30	26	18	16	14
10	46	40	35	30	26	22	17	15	13
15	42	37	32	27	23	19	15	13	12
20	40	35	30	25	21	18	14	12	11
25	39	33	29	24	20	17	13	11	10
30	38	32	28	23	19	16	12	10	9
35	37	32	27	22	19	16	11	9	8
40	37	31	27	22	18	15	10	8	7

Structured Security Desired Rating: Baa1

	Collateral Rating							
Diversity Score	*B3*	*B2*	*B1*	*Ba3*	*Ba2*	*Ba1*	*Baa3*	*Baa2*
1	← evaluated case-by-case →							
2	71%	66%	61%	53%	48%	43%	38%	34%
3	60	55	50	45	40	34	24	21
4	55	49	44	39	35	30	19	16
5	51	46	41	35	31	27	17	14
7	47	41	36	31	27	23	16	13
10	44	38	33	28	24	20	15	12
15	40	34	30	25	21	17	13	11
20	38	33	28	23	20	16	12	10
25	37	32	27	22	19	15	11	9
30	36	31	26	22	18	15	10	8
35	36	30	26	21	18	14	9	7
40	35	30	25	21	17	14	8	6

Structured Security Desired Rating: Baa2

	Collateral Rating						
Diversity Score	*B3*	*B2*	*B1*	*Ba3*	*Ba2*	*Ba1*	*Baa3*
1	← evaluated case-by-case →						
2	65%	59%	52%	46%	42%	38%	34%
3	56	50	45	39	33	29	21
4	51	44	40	34	30	25	16
5	47	41	37	31	27	23	14
7	44	37	33	28	23	20	13
10	40	34	30	25	21	17	12
15	38	32	27	22	19	15	11
20	36	30	26	21	17	14	10
25	35	29	25	20	17	13	9
30	34	29	24	20	16	13	8
35	34	28	24	19	16	12	7
40	33	28	23	19	15	12	6

Structured Security Desired Rating: Baa3

	Collateral Rating					
Diversity Score	*B3*	*B2*	*B1*	*Ba3*	*Ba2*	*Ba1*
1	← evaluated case-by-case →					
2	56%	49%	44%	39%	35%	31%
3	48	43	37	31	27	23
4	44	38	34	28	23	19
5	42	36	31	25	21	17
7	39	32	28	23	19	15
10	36	30	26	21	17	13
15	34	28	24	19	15	12
20	33	27	23	18	14	11
25	32	26	22	17	14	11
30	31	26	21	17	14	10
35	31	25	21	17	13	10
40	31	25	21	16	13	10

Analyzing Legal Risks in CBO and CLO Structures

Noel E.D. Kirnon
Associate Director
Moody's Investors Service

This article focuses on Moody's analysis of legal risks in collateralized bond obligations (CBOs) and collateralized loan obligations (CLOs). Such risks include issuer insolvency, effective asset transfer to the issuer, consolidation of the issuer with its parent, effective subordination of tranches ranking below the most senior of the notes, and enforceability of the agreements.

BANKRUPTCY REMOTENESS

In rating CBOs and CLOs, Moody's evaluates the bankruptcy-remote nature of the issuer. The concern is that issuer insolvency could cause a delay in payment to the noteholders, which would be inconsistent with the rating of the structured bonds. The article concentrates on the two predominant legal structures used by CBO and CLO issuers: corporations and limited partnerships. For additional information on the quantitative aspects of Moody's rating methodology, see "Rating Cash Flow Transactions Backed by Corporate Debt," *Structured Finance*, February 1991.

Corporations

When evaluating a corporate issuer, Moody's looks for several facts and mechanisms, such as those described below, to ensure that both the involuntary and voluntary filing of the issuer into bankruptcy is a remote possibility.

To protect against the involuntary filing of bankruptcy by interested third parties, the incorporation documents limit the corporation's purpose to (1) issuing the structured debt and (2) purchasing the collateral, which places severe restrictions on the issuer's ability to incur additional liabilities. Allowed liabilities include the fees for the ongoing services of the corporation's accountants, trustees, paying agents, and other associated parties. Moody's measures these projected liabilities and hence the risk of these parties commencing involuntary bankruptcy proceedings against the issuer when determining the credit enhancement. However, an agreement with outside creditors barring them from petitioning for bankruptcy until one year and one day following the final payment of the rated CBO or CLO bonds further limits the risk of an involuntary filing for bankruptcy against the issuer.

Prudent shareholders and boards of directors representing the shareholder would not usually voluntarily put an issuer into bankruptcy unless the issuer is unable to pay its bills when they are due. Instead of relying on the prudence of shareholders and the board of directors or examining the business reasons for a voluntary filing, Moody's seeks to reduce the risk of a voluntary filing. Mechanisms that reduce the risk of voluntary filing by an issuer's shareholders or board of directors include the requirement that shareholders unanimously approve the bankruptcy petition and that the board of directors must, at all times, have two independent directors, whose approval is required for filing a voluntary bankruptcy petition.

Limited Partnerships with Corporate Co-Issuers

CBOs are often co-issued by two entities: a limited partnership and a corporation wholly owned by the limited partnership. The limited partnership is managed by the general partner, who may have a nominal or substantial economic interest in the limited partnership, while the limited partners are passive investors. The corporation would be subject to the same analysis described above. Moody's assesses the effects of the insolvency of the general partner and of the limited partners on the partnership, and the bankruptcy-remote nature of the partnership.

Under the Uniform Limited Partnership Act, the insolvency of the general partner may require the dissolution of the partnership. Dissolution risk arises because the Act permits dissolution of the limited partnership if the general partner is bankrupt and if the limited partners fail to elect a replacement general partner within a certain time—usually 90 days. Partnership dissolution might force the partners to liquidate the collateral and cause the rated bondholders to incur a market-value loss, whereas maintaining the collateral intact would have furnished sufficient cash flow to retire the bonds without a loss.

Market-value risk is generally not assessed in the rating of a cash flow transaction, such as a CBO or a CLO, and must be either eliminated or reduced to a level commensurate with the rating.

Establishing a bankruptcy-remote general partner mitigates dissolution risk. So too does (1) an agreement between the partners, which appoints a replacement general partner *a priori* in the event of the general partner's bankruptcy, (2) the presence of several general partners, or (3) a highly rated general partner. The use of any of these mechanisms gives Moody's comfort that risks associated with the bankruptcy of a general partner have been minimized.

The insolvency of a limited partner is similar to the insolvency of a noncontrolling equity investor and would not have an adverse impact on the rated bonds. However, if a limited partner takes part in controlling the business, the limited partner could then be recharacterized as a general partner and the possible insolvency of the newly characterized general partner could become an issue. Opinions of counsel arguing that the partnership is duly organized under the Act as a limited partnership and an analysis of the partnership agreement can help support the conclusion that the probability of such a recharacterization is remote.

Aside from the effects of the general and the limited partner's insolvency, Moody's analysis of the partnership's bankruptcy-remote nature parallels that of an bankruptcy-remote corporation. The partnership is established for a specific purpose and has limited power to incur additional debt. The partnership agreement also establishes business offices and separate records and outlines the powers of the general and limited partners. These restrictions and requirements, and agreements with outside creditors, reduce the risk of involuntary bankruptcy filing.

Mechanisms that reduce the risk of voluntary bankruptcy must also be evident. The presence either of two independent directors on the board of directors of the general partner or or an independent general partner, whose approvals are necessary to enable the general partner to file a bankruptcy petition on behalf of the limited partnership, lessen the power of the general partner and the limited partners to file a voluntary bankruptcy petition on behalf of the partnership. In addition to a voluntary filing, a general partner may file an involuntary petition against the partnership; however, the restrictions against a voluntary filing make the likelihood of such an action remote.

Moody's looks also at the effects of the insolvency of interested third parties on the transaction and seeks to minimize those effects to a level consistent with the requested rating. In doing so, Moody's assesses the way in which the assets were transferred or sold to the issuer, as well as the relationship of the issuer with its parent.

ASSET TRANSFER

In the event of the bankruptcy of the seller/transferor of assets to the issuer, a creditor of the transferor may attempt to recharacterize the transfer as a secured financing instead of a true sale. If successful, the assets would be considered as assets of the transferor, and the automatic stay provisions of the bankruptcy code would apply.

For a true sale to occur, the transferor must convey the future economic risks and benefits of ownership of the assets to the issuer. In determining whether a true sale has occurred, Moody's assesses the extent of recourse to the transferor, the level of subordination, and the control the transferor has over the assets. The strength of a true sale opinion rendered by independent counsel would also be considered by Moody's.

In a CBO structure, issuers usually buy the collateral bonds at market price from an unaffiliated seller, and the seller retains no interest in the asset. For this reason, true sale issues are not as relevant in a CBO transaction as they are in a CLO transaction. CLO asset transfers, particularly participations, may raise true sale concerns to the extent that they contain recourse provisions. In a typical participation, the issuer buys a share of the originating bank/seller's benefits and obligations created under a loan agreement. The originating bank retains all rights to administer the loan and makes servicing decisions and provides the participants with information furnished by the borrower.

Participation language that either compels the seller to repurchase the loan in the event of a default or subordinates the seller's share of the loan vis a vis the participant's, and participations that either have a shorter term than that of the originating bank's obligation to the borrower or special payment arrangements that do not solely depend on payment from the borrower may lead the FDIC or a court of competent jurisdiction to recharacterize the participation as a loan from the participating bank to the originating bank rather than as a true sale. If such a determination is made, the issuer would become a creditor of the originating bank. Therefore, Moody's examines the participation certificates and legal opinions to confirm that the participations constitute a true sale.

To ensure that the noteholders benefit from the assets, the trustee, on behalf of the noteholders, maintains a perfected-security interest in all the assets of the issuer. That interest provides additional protection in the unlikely event the transfer from the seller/originator to the issuer were recharachterized as a secured financing or in the event the issuer were to become bankrupt. Such perfection is governed by the Uniform Commercial Code and usually requires (1) possession of assets if securities are certificated and (2) registration in the name of the issuer or trustee for the benefit of the noteholder by a financial intermediary if they are uncertificated. Moody's reviews a security interest opinion to make sure that all the necessary steps to convey and to perfect the security interest have been taken. In addition, security interest opinions are usually provided annually and must be received before removing collateral from the jurisdiction in which the security interest was initially granted.

The seller's creditors may also attempt to retrieve assets from the issuer's estate by establishing that a fraudulent transfer occurred. A fraudulent transfer occurs when a company transfers its assets for less than reasonable equivalent value at a time when the company is insolvent. If the creditors are successful, a court could void the transaction and leave the noteholders with no security interest in the collateral. To date, all CBO and CLO assets have been purchased in arms-length transactions at fair market value. In the event the issuer acquired the collateral from a single seller or from a limited number of sellers and the prices were determined in other than an arms-length manner, Moody's would study a fraudulent conveyance opinion among other factors to assess whether the seller received adequate consideration for the assets sold to the issuer.

CONSOLIDATION

Even though an issuer may be insolvency-proof, the bankruptcy of the issuer's parent could give rise to an action by the parent's creditors seeking to consolidate the issuer's assets and liabilities with those of the parent. Consolidation is an equitable remedy that is not imposed casually and is highly dependent on the facts of each transaction. Such an occurrence could interrupt the business of the issuer and delay payments to the bond holders.

In deciding against consolidation, the courts consider such factors as whether: (1) the issuer has established a separate business office; (2) at least one director has no affiliation with the parent company; (3) the issuer maintains separate corporate records and books of account, (4) the issuer's funds are commingled with those of the parent company, (5) the issuer's board of directors holds meetings to authorize corporate actions, (6) the issuer observes all corporate formalities, (7) the parent, in dealing with its creditors, acknowledges the separate existence of the issuer, (8) the transaction has a legitimate business purpose or is a sham, and (9) transactions between the parent and issuer are conducted on an arms-length basis. However, even though all these factors exist, nonconsolidation is not guaranteed.

Other facts such as, for example, loan guarantees between parent and issuer, may give rise to consolidation. In the CBO/CLO market, consolidation has not been a concern because in most cases the issuers and their parents have been bankruptcy-remote entities. In instances where the parents are charitable trusts, Moody's has gained comfort from the reasoning contained in independent counsel's nonconsolidation opinions.

SUBORDINATION AND ENFORCEABILITY

When rating transactions with multiple tranches, Moody's must be assured that the subordinated tranche events of default and available remedies do not interfere with the priority of the senior-most tranche. Most commonly, the lower tranches are structured as residual interests so that payments are due only to the extent that they are payable out of cash flows from the collateral. In such a case, the subordinated tranche securities have payment-in-kind features and, even if payments are not made on the securities, a subordinated tranche noteholder cannot take any action without the consent of the senior-most class of securities. In assessing whether the degree of subordination is consistent with the rating, Moody's may also examine an opinion indicating that the subordination provisions are legal, valid, and binding.

Moody's reviews enforceability opinions that indicate the transaction's agreements are legal, valid, and binding against the relevant parties. These opinions are typically furnished by the counsel of each entity upon whose performance the noteholders and/or the issuer rely.

SUMMARY

Legal analysis is an integral part of determining a credit rating in CBO and CLO structures. As the facts of each transaction vary, the legal conclusions and their rating impact will vary as well. Moody's analysis of any type of transaction evolves as new structures arise or as the legal context of structured transactions change.

Chapter Six

Financial Ratio Analysis and the Credit Cycle

by Martin S. Fridson, CFA
Merrill Lynch

"Experience is what teaches us to recognize a mistake when we make it again."

In the absence of more dependable methods of foretelling future market developments, investors have traditionally relied on studies of past cycles. This mode of analysis is subject to immediate challenge on the grounds that no cycle is ever perfectly replicated in terms of intervals between recognizable events. Every cycle, moreover, is characterized by anomalies in which certain data series fail to display their usual relationship to the overall cycle. Nevertheless, identifying general patterns may help investors to determine the point of a cycle at which they are and to make informed predictions concerning the sequence of future developments.

With specific reference to the high yield market, there is a potential benefit in tracking the cycle of credit quality. For one thing, a long-term performance edge might be gained by varying the allocation of funds to high yield according to how discriminating the market is at different times with respect to new-issue quality. That is, performance may be enhanced by being more selective during periods in the cycle in which lesser-quality deals can be sold at skimpy risk premiums. Active managers may likewise improve their performance by upgrading or downgrading in quality in anticipation of shifts between environments that reward risk-taking and environments that punish investors who step down in quality.

Figure 6.1 displays four data series that could be viewed as indicators of the high yield credit cycle. To a fair degree, the graphs capture the tendency of investors to accept lower average quality (indicated by declining new-issue ratings) as accelerating capital inflows (indicated by mutual fund net sales) create pressure to put funds to work. With some lag, default rates and the ratio of downgrades to upgrades within the high yield sector rise as a consequence of the preceding decline in average credit quality.

Because a number of other factors are at play, the data series do not combine to form a smooth, unambiguously cyclical pattern. Default rates, for example, respond not only to changes in the average quality of new issues but also to fluctuations in economic activity. Furthermore, most data series tend to move bumpily. Investors receiving news of an abrupt surge or drop cannot immediately determine whether the move marks a new direction or will appear, in retrospect, as a meaningless blip.

Given the complex interactions of variables influencing the credit cycle, as well as the inherent tendency of cycles not to unfold in precisely the same way each time around, it is unlikely that a perfectly reliable quantitative model can be constructed from the sorts of inputs depicted in Figure 6.1. Accordingly, investors should not feel reluctant to round out their analysis with "softer" information that can in many cases provide significant insights.

One qualitative approach we consider worthwhile is to be conscious of shifting fashions in financial ratios. Certain ratios, we have observed, were in style at the start of the last cycle, when investors were still recovering from the devastating back-to-back recessions of the early 1980s. As confidence waxed and risk aversion waned, a different set of ratios came into vogue. Still other ratios entered the limelight during the later phrase of the cycle, 1989-1990, when high yield bond prices plummeted, in part because of credit vulnerability that had previously been recognized but not emphasized. The next cycle, we are inclined to believe, will feature a similar—albeit not identical—rotation, with particular ratios gaining popularity for a time and then falling from favor.

Figure 6.1—Indicators of the High Yield Credit Cycle

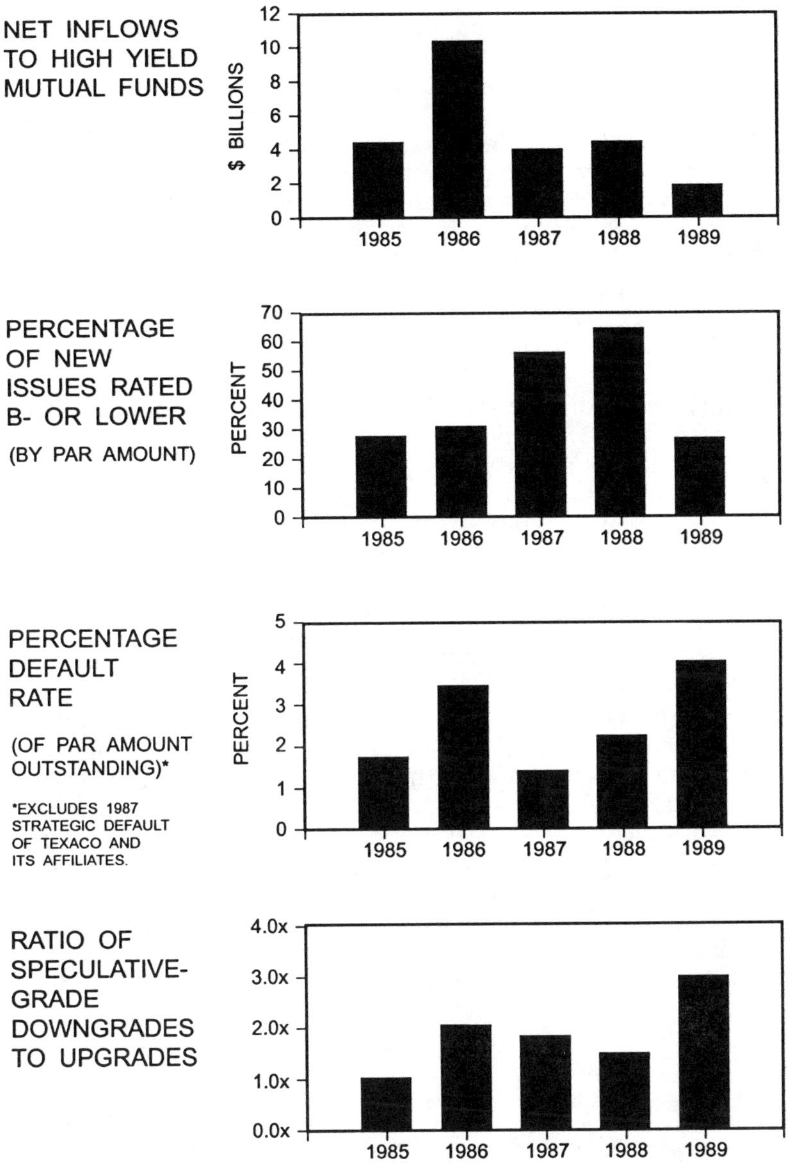

THE EARLY PHASE

At the latest cycle's inception, during the early 1980s, traditional measures of interest coverage **(Ratio 1)** and leverage **(Ratio 2)** were in common use. This was particularly the case among newcomers to the high yield sector.

With some justification, investors viewed these ratios as conservative credit tests. By looking solely to earnings (before deduction of interest and taxes) to cover interest charges, investors avoided giving credit for cash flow from depreciation in instances where depreciating assets were not being replaced through new capital expenditures. (Failure to replace plant and equipment amounts to gradual liquidation.) In a similarly conservative vein, recording debt at principal value when calculating the capitalization ratio recognized that in liquidation, borrowings would represent claims at full value even though the obligations might be trading at steep discounts. Book value of equity likewise represented a conservative standard, insulated as it was from the whims of the stock market.[1]

$$\frac{\text{Earnings Before Interest and Taxes*}}{\text{Interest Expense}} \qquad (1)$$

* **Abbreviated below as "EBIT."**

$$\frac{\text{Principal Amount of Total Debt}}{\text{Principal Amount of Total Debt + Book Value of Equity}} \qquad (2)$$

Strictly speaking, Ratios 1 and 2 did not invariably present the most conservative picture of a credit. For example, a given company might inflate its earnings (and therefore its EBIT coverage) by depreciating its assets over an unrealistically long period. Such overstatement, relative to the company's peer group, would be eliminated by measuring all of the competitors on the basis of EBITDA coverage **(Ratio 3)**. (Robbing the Peter of depreciation to pay the Paul of pretax earnings washes out when the numerator includes both numbers.) Likewise, book value of equity, as used in the conventional debt-to-capital ratio, can present too *favorable* a picture if a company has delayed taking an

---

1 During the early 1980s, if an investment banker argued for an upgrade on the grounds that the equity market "proved" that his client's leverage (on a book value basis) was overstated, the response from a rating analyst might be, "And do you want me to downgrade the company when stock prices decline?"

inevitable write-off. In that case, **Ratio 4**, a market-adjusted ratio of debt to capital, provides a more accurate reading:

$$\frac{\text{Earnings Before Interest, Taxes, Depreciation and Amortization **}}{\text{Interest Expense}} \quad (3)$$

** Abbreviated below as "EBITDA."

$$\frac{\text{Market Value of Total Debt}}{\text{Market Value of Total Debt + Market Value of Equity}} \quad (4)$$

Notwithstanding occasional anomalies of the "excessively liberal" variety, the rising popularity of Ratios 3 and 4 as the credit cycle advanced derived mostly from the traditional ratios' generally conservative bias. As multiples paid in leveraged buyouts rose, necessitating increased financial leverage in order to maintain expected equity returns, EBIT coverage ratios grew slimmer and equity at book value represented a narrower sliver of total capital.

Key psychological thresholds were reached when pro forma coverage, calculated in the traditional way, dropped to less than 1.0 times and when equity fell below 0%. (The latter situation generally results from the structuring of a highly leveraged transaction, or HLT, as a recapitalization rather than as a leveraged buyout. In the former case, no writeup of assets is permitted under Generally Accepted Accounting Principles.[2]) In hindsight, the increased debt loads represented by what some critics regarded as the piercing of the (financially) sound barrier did not prove incompatible with success in the aftermarket. This was especially true when the newly leveraged company possessed nonessential but marketable assets or else had potential for cutting fat out of its expenses. Among the high yield issues floated with prospectuses that showed either EBIT coverage of less than 1.0 times or negative equity were several that subsequently traded in the lowest quartile of yields (indicating highest perceived credit quality) among active speculative grade issues, including Borg-Warner Holdings, Colt Holdings, Duracell Holdings, FMC, Hospital Corporation of America, Loehmann's, Mueller Co., and Owens-Corning Fiberglas.

Despite such examples, underwriters preferred for semantic reasons to emphasize EBITDA coverage and market-adjusted capitalization,

---

2 For a fuller discussion of this subject, see Martin S. Fridson, "Who's Afraid of Negative Equity?" in *High Yield Bonds: Identifying Value and Assessing Risk of Speculative Grade Securities* (Chicago: Probus Publishing, 1989), pp. 121–126.

rather than to proclaim that "earnings failed to cover interest charges" or that "net worth was less than zero." Since depreciation and the aggregate value of all outstanding shares were invariably positive numbers, companies *sounded* better, financially speaking, when described by the newly fashionable (if not actually new) ratios. Company images were likewise enhanced by the marking down of debt to the market and, as it turned out, subsequent events (namely, distressed exchange offers at less than par) vindicated the practice in analytical terms.

Parenthetically, book value capitalization (Ratio 2) became problematic with the advent of negative-equity-through-recapitalization, entirely aside from any difficulties of investors' perceptions. As shown in Figure 6.2, a company with negative equity can actually experience a *rise* in its conventionally calculated debt-to-capital ratio if it pays down debt while simultaneously recognizing a gain on the sale of an asset. The possibility of such an absurd outcome helped to undermine the analytical usefulness of the old-style debt ratio.

Figure 6.2—How Negative Equity Subverts the Book Value Capitalization Ratio

XYZ Corporation
($Millions)

(a) Capital structure (with both debt and equity at book value) following recapitalization:

Total Debt	$350 =	130%
Equity	(80) =	(30)%
Total Capital	$270 =	100%

(b) Capital structure after company sells an asset for $50 million, booking a $5 million gain on the sale, and applies the proceeds to debt reduction:

Total Debt	$300 =	133%
Equity	(75) =	(33)%
Total Capital	$225 =	100%

Result:

Debt declines and equity increases, yet debt as a percentage of capital rises.

THE MIDDLE PHASE

As multiples paid in leveraged buyouts continued to rise, even EBITDA coverage figures started to look slim in many deals. To provide a bigger cash flow cushion, issuers began relying more heavily on zero/coupon and payment-in-kind (PIK) issues, which deferred cash payment of interest for specified periods. Coincident with these innovations, **Ratio 5**—EBITDA coverage of current cash interest only—became the latest fashion. This measure's time in the sun can be regarded as the peak of the most recent high yield credit cycle.

$$\frac{\text{EBITDA}}{\text{Cash Interest Expense}} \tag{5}$$

Meanwhile, in the area of leverage ratios, the switch to market value had alleviated many of the problems inherent in the book value capitalization ratio, but a complication arose when no market existed for the issuer's stock. This circumstance became more and more common as the high yield market was increasingly tapped by private companies.

Even in some instances in which high yield issuers had public equity outstanding (possibly in the form of "stub" stocks), analysts expressed dissatisfaction with market-adjusted capitalization ratios. They observed that certain classes of assets (notably cable television systems) consistently sold in private transactions at higher prices than the stock market appeared to reflect. That is, applying prevailing private market multiples of operating cash flow to the assets of a publicly traded cable operator usually produced a higher implied value than the product of the company's share price and its number of shares outstanding. This disparity was commonly attributed to private investors' greater willingness to incur depreciation-related losses in order to capture associated tax benefits. Public companies, in contrast, were thought to be more sensitive to reported earnings, which declined if they incurred heavier depreciation charges by paying higher prices. In view of the persistent private-public valuation gap, analysts argued that capitalization ratios derived from the stock market understated the true equity cushion enjoyed by cable companies.

Ratio 6, an asset coverage ratio incorporating equity calculated as cash flow times an appropriate multiple, came into vogue to address both of the just-described limitations of the market-adjusted Ratio 4. Note that in this format, equity is not included in the fraction but instead represents a residual. For example, if asset value (EBITDA ×

Multiple) is $500 million and total debt is $400 million, the implied equity cushion is $100 million.

$$\frac{\text{EBITDA} \times \text{Multiple}}{\text{Total Debt}} \tag{6}$$

Even when cash flow-based asset coverage was at its zenith of popularity, its analytical limitations were apparent. For one thing, most companies lacked widely-agreed-upon benchmarks for determining appropriate cash flow multiples. (Cable television systems, as relatively homogeneous assets for which comparable transaction prices frequently became available, were clearly the exception.) In some cases, inferences could be drawn from the stock prices—expressed as cash flow multiples—of publicly traded industry peers, but in other cases no such "comparables" existed. A second problem was that bondholders' protection could be overstated by an asset valuation based on cyclical peak cash flow during a period of speculatively elevated multiples. Liquidation of assets, if it ever became necessary, would be likely to occur during less ebullient times.

To keep themselves anchored in reality, especially as multiples and cash flow projections began to deflate with the maturing business cycle, high yield analysts tempered Ratio 6 with **Ratio 7**. Edging back toward the conservatism that had prevailed earlier in the credit cycle, fashion now dictated a recognition that neglecting capital expenditures for any extended period would eventually cause loss of competitiveness on costs, technology, and product features. Profitability (and hence cash flow) would inevitably suffer. High cash flow coverage of interest (Ratio 3) could therefore prove illusory.

$$\frac{\text{EBITDA} - \text{Capital Expenditures}}{\text{Interest Expense}} \tag{7}$$

For a company that was exactly offsetting its depreciation with capital expenditures, Ratio 6 was equivalent to Ratio 1, or simple EBIT coverage. In that sense, a full fashion cycle in financial ratios had already been completed.

The next move, however, was not the beginning of a swing back toward more liberal measures, but instead an intensified aversion to risk, consistent with the continuing slowdown in the economy. **Ratio 8** further refined the vogue in interest coverage, with analysts acknowledging that revenue growth (without which many deals were doomed to default) was impossible without the support of increased working capital. Another slice of EBITDA, in short, was as a practical matter unavailable to service debt.

$$\frac{\text{EBITDA} - \text{Capital Expenditures} - \text{Increase in Working Capital}}{\text{Interest Expense}} \quad (8)$$

THE LATE PHASE

After a period of inching toward more conservative measures, the high yield market lurched toward much stricter criteria amidst the unprecedented upheavals of 1989. The shock of a sudden, sharp contraction in liquidity focused analytical attention on a risk that had not previously received strong emphasis—a company's potential inability to refinance. With the new-issue door slamming shut on all but the best credits, companies could no longer take for granted the possibility of borrowing to compensate for shortfalls in cash flow projections or selling assets to investors who would raise the required funds in the high yield market.

Under the new conditions, the mere ability to cover current cash interest charges was no assurance of continued solvency. In part, a company's interest coverage might have been strong precisely because in its original LBO financing it had obtained the lowest possible rate from bank lenders by agreeing to a rapid and ultimately onerous principal repayment schedule. In the changed environment, the better credit risk was the company that, in contrast, had either agreed to pay its banks a bigger spread over LIBOR[3] (and therefore to post lower EBITDA coverage) for the comfort of an extended amortization holiday, or else depended more heavily on high-coupon subordinated debentures featuring long bullet maturities.

With their heightened awareness of refinancing risk, high yield investors shifted their attention to **Ratio 9**, adjusted EBITDA coverage of total current debt service (interest plus amortization and mandatory sinking fund payments).

$$\frac{\text{EBITDA} - \text{Capital Expenditures} - \text{Increase in Working Capital}}{\text{Interest Expense} + \text{Debt Maturities} + \text{Sinking Fund Payments}} \quad (9)$$

The change in circumstances also revived interest in an old measure of debt-servicing capacity, debt to cash flow **(Ratio 10)**. Expressed as shown here, the ratio theoretically indicates the number of years required to liquidate 100% of a company's debt through internal

3 The London Inter-Bank Offering Rate, a key money market cost-of-funds benchmark.

sources. Analysts can compare this figure with the issuer's maturity schedule to get a sense of whether the company enjoys financial flexibility or, alternatively, will be dependent on external sources to meet scheduled repayments. To illustrate, suppose a company has $500 million of debt and $80 million of EBITDA, implying an ability to liquidate all borrowings in 6.25 years. If essentially all debt matures in roughly equal installments over seven years, the company should in theory be able to amortize its debt even if all outside financing sources are shut off.

$$\frac{\text{Total Debt}}{\text{EBITDA}} \qquad (10)$$

In practice, Ratio 10 may give the lender false comfort under conditions of instability. First of all, the borrower's maturities may not in fact be evenly spaced, but may instead be concentrated in a one-year lump that greatly exceeds annual cash flow. Liquidity could be particularly jeopardized if the maturity bulge happened to coincide with a cyclical low in the borrower's EBITDA. Lenders might see their way clear to refinancing the large maturity if cash flow appeared to be in line with expectations, but a more serious problem with Ratio 10 is that it unrealistically assumes dedication of all cash flow to principal retirement. Like the simple measure of EBITDA coverage of interest expense (Ratio 3), Ratio 10 neglects the reality that to stay viable, a company must maintain its plant and equipment and, if its capital structure is premised on growth in sales, must devote a portion of cash flow to expanding its working capital.[4]

Given the impracticality of dedicating 100% of cash flow to debt retirement, **Ratio 11** may be preferable to Ratio 10 in a difficult refinancing environment. To be even more conservative, analysts may wish to consider cash flow available for debt service (the denominator of Ratio 11)[5] in light of the peak year in the issuer's maturity schedule. By the same token, individual companies' liquidity may be substantially understated by such measures, owing to fallback financing sources such as confirmed credit lines or deep-pocketed affiliates.

---

4 Cash paid out in taxes is obviously not available for debt retirement. The item is not deducted from EBITDA in Ratio 11, however, because it is ordinarily inconsequential for companies leveraged so highly that interest expense offsets 100% or more of pretax profits.

5 The denominator of Ratio 11 also goes by the name, "free cash flow." That term has no universally accepted definition, however, with interest expense and increase in working capital deducted or not, according to the custom of the research department or individual analyst.

$$\frac{\text{Total Debt}}{\text{EBITDA} - \text{Interest Expense} - \text{Capital Expenditures} - \text{Increase in Working Capital}} \quad (11)$$

The increased prominence of refinancing risk as a credit concern, beginning in 1989, created a twofold analytical need. Bondholders had not only to determine whether a high yield company was likely to remain solvent, but also to estimate the percentage of their investment they would lose if the worst came to pass.

For non-mark-to-market holders who had originally bought at par, Ratio 6—by now calculated with a multiple somewhat lower than at the credit cycle's peak—provided a rough idea of the cushion (or shortfall) in asset coverage of debt. Investors considering new purchases at prevailing, often severely depressed market levels could use the variant **Ratio 12**.

In either case, the investment decision had to reflect the time value of money, as well, on the grounds that the ultimate distribution of assets to bondholders would occur after a possibly lengthy reorganization or liquidation process. In addition, taking Ratio 6 or 12 at face value implicitly assumed that resolution of the bankruptcy would proceed according to the principle of absolute priority. That is, coverage of debt by asset value of precisely 100% ensures full principal recovery only if equity holders receive nothing. As a practical matter, unsecured creditors ordinarily must assume that on the strength of their ability to delay the approval of a plan of reorganization, classes junior to themselves will manage to extract some value, even if the company's assets appear insufficient to cover junior claims.

$$\frac{\text{EBITDA} \times \text{Multiple}}{\text{Market Value of Total Debt}} \quad (12)$$

This reality of the bankruptcy process, incidentally, explains at least in part the supposed anomaly of a positive value for the common stock of a company that—based on a steep market discount on its debt—appears to have no remaining equity value. From a financial ratio standpoint, moreover, the premise that discounted bonds imply zero equity poses a logical difficulty. Are we to infer that a Single-A company with debt trading at 70 cents on the dollar, simply because it carries a below-market-rate coupon, has no equity value? To be sure, speculative grade bonds with 14% and 15% coupons did not trade as low as 30 or 20 cents on the dollar during 1990 primarily because the general level of interest rates had risen. Neither was it true, however, that those same companies' equity claimants had no realistic hope of realizing value at the end of reorganization proceedings.

THE FINAL PHASE

Three last ratios deserve mention as symbolizing the final phase of the credit cycle, when financial distress is at, or at least approaching, its peak.

The first, **Ratio 13**, aids in both key tasks of end-of-cycle analysis, i.e., solvency determination and recovery estimation. If the senior bank lenders' exposure represents a low multiple of EBITDA, then their principal is probably safe. Analysts can consequently infer that the likelihood is small that banks will precipitate a financial crisis by calling their loans, on the basis of a technical default, in order to extract their money before their security is eroded.

$$\frac{\text{Bank Debt}}{\text{EBITDA}} \tag{13}$$

On the other hand, if a crisis is bound to come, the ratio of bank debt to EBITDA can furnish important clues concerning potential losses to subordinated holders. By way of illustration, there was a widely held view in 1990 that despite reduced prospects for cable television operators, banks would continue to finance the industry but cut their total HLT exposure by lending a smaller multiple of EBITDA than formerly. Against this backdrop, suppose a particular cable company had had senior bank debt equivalent to six times EBITDA and subordinated debt equivalent to two times. If interest payments on the combined borrowings had approached or exceeded EBITDA, a financial restructuring might have been inevitable. The difference between outstanding bank debt and the "loan limit" implied by the new multiple (say, five times) gave a feel for the size of the "haircut" that would be taken by subordinated and equity holders, barring covenants that gave the unsecured lenders a stronger-than-usual bargaining position vis-a-vis the banks.

Another way to get at recovery potential is to consider a bond's hypothetical value in a restructuring. This method relies heavily on assumptions yet can provide a worthwhile frame of reference.

We begin by determining the "supportable interest expense" required to calculate **Ratio 14**. For example, suppose EBITDA is $90 million and actual interest expense is currently $110 million, resulting in ordinary EBITDA coverage of 0.82 times. With no earnings turnaround in sight, a restructuring appears inevitable. Based on an assessment of the sustainability and variability of the company's cash flow, let us assume that lenders will not perceive the credit as viable going forward unless it has EBITDA coverage of at least 1.5 times. Solving for

90/x = 1.5, we find that supportable interest expense is $60 million. Senior secured bank lenders, who we presume would rather precipitate a bankruptcy than make concessions, are currently receiving $30 million in annual interest payments, leaving $30 million of supportable interest for subordinated holders.

$$\frac{\text{EBITDA}}{\text{Supportable Interest Expense}} \tag{14}$$

Assuming further that bondholders will demand a reasonable amount of current income, we translate the remaining $30 million annual interest outlay into a somewhat arbitrary 14% coupon, which implies $214 million of principal amount. To ensure a manageable maturity schedule, let us structure the hypothetical new bond as a 10-year bullet.

Based on prevailing yields on comparable-quality paper, with an added yield premium for the effect of a recent brush with default, we then conservatively price the 14%, 10-year bond at a 19% yield to maturity. The result, 78% of par, multiplied by $214 million principal amount of the hypothetical new bond, implies that subordinated holders will emerge with $167 million of market value following the restructuring. This figure, hypothetical though it is, may provide considerable comfort. If, as an example, the aggregate market value of all of the company's subordinated debt is currently $260 million, then bondholders have a sizable cushion against a successful effort by the supposedly wiped-out equity holders to retain value.

Inclusion of the last word in fashion, **Ratio 15**, addresses the fact that subordinated holders can be disadvantaged not only by predation from below (i.e., junior subordinated and equity classes) but also by intransigence above (i.e., senior secured lenders).

If senior lenders are confident that their security will enable them to recover their claims in full in event of liquidation, they can boldly veto any reorganization plan that deprives them of value in order to satisfy subordinated claims. Unsecured creditors, in contrast, play a dangerous game when they scuttle a reorganization plan by holding out. They run the risk that the apparent value supporting their unsecured claims will evaporate once the bankrupt company ceases to exist as a going concern.

$$\frac{\text{Principal Amount of Secured Debt}}{\text{Principal Amount of Total Debt}} \tag{15}$$

Given these dynamics, the value of unsecured holders' claims becomes highly leveraged, vis-a-vis small changes in total enterprise value as Ratio 15 rises.

To illustrate, suppose secured debt amounts to $275 million, or 80% of total debt of $344 million. Assume further that total enterprise value equals $310 million. Unsecured holders, with claims of $69 million (i.e., $344 million minus $275 million), can expect to recover just 51% ($310 million – $275 million/$69 million). (This calculation assumes no extraction of value by equity holders.)

If total enterprise value falls by 10% (or $31 million) to $279 million, secured holders can continue to expect full recovery of their $275 million of claims. On the other hand, unsecured holders—who bear the full brunt—see their expected proceeds plunge by $31 million to $38 million. A 45% decline in the bondholders' recovery, to summarize, results from a mere 10% decline in total enterprise value. By substituting different numbers, the reader can confirm that the sensitivity of subordinated holder's wealth to swings in total enterprise value is reduced when the percentage of secured debt to total debt declines.

CONCLUSION

The last-discussed ratios update through late 1990 our history of the most recent credit cycle. From the simple EBIT coverage and book value leverage ratios in common use at the start of the cycle, analysis shifted by degrees to hypothetical recapitalizations and liquidations. Along the way, certain subtleties that evaded the earlier ratios were elucidated, but perhaps less fortunately, the assessment of credit risk became more subjective.

It would reflect admirably on credit analysts, investors, and bankers alike if one could conclude that financial innovations during the period studied were driven to some meaningful extent by advances in the art of measuring credit risk. Instead, the impression that emerges from a review of the fashion trends is that intellectual justification followed changes in circumstances. Chief among these were an influx of capital into the high yield market, a consequently increased tolerance for leverage and an inevitable rise in the number of distressed companies. As the high yield market boomed, analysts channeled their energies into supplementing the numerator and shaving the denominator of the coverage ratio to accommodate the reality that portfolio managers could no longer invest huge sums while maintaining the standards that had previously applied. Similarly reactive was analysts' invention (or in some cases rediscovery) of ratios that measured the odds of staving off insolvency, as circumstances made that task more imperative.

While creativity in response to changing conditions is a virtue in an analyst, too readily bending with the whims of fashion is a fault. One of the chief benefits of ratio analysis, after all, is its identification of changes in financial strength over successive periods. That benefit is unachievable if the analyst uses a floating reference point.

In short, certain ratios are more useful at some points of the credit cycle than at others. Utilizing such ratios at the appropriate times lends a desirable suppleness to the analysis. Lest investors err by varying their standards to suit transitory fashions, however, they should calculate at least a few ratios on a constant basis throughout the cycle. Thus can two equally undesirable extremes, indifference and excessive risk aversion, both be avoided.

SOME CAVEATS REGARDING FINANCIAL RATIOS

Readers should not interpret the accompanying article's emphasis on financial ratios as a brief for the proposition that accurate credit assessments can be derived solely from the analysis of historical ratios. For one thing, a company's creditworthiness may be critically affected by factors not reflected in financial measures, such as contingent liabilities and abrupt changes in financial strategy. Furthermore, historical numbers must in many instances be adjusted in light of nonrecurring events or unconventional financial reporting practices. Aside from these considerations, raw historical ratios are ultimately less important than future ratios, which can be forecasted only with the expenditure of considerable mental energy.

Productive use of financial ratios, in short, precludes accepting ratios at face value, especially since some companies intentionally present their results in a manner calculated to humbug the unwary. Indeed, certain sects maintain that God elected to give people brains when He discovered that He could not create a tamper-proof accounting system.

As a final comment, the discussion omits certain refinements to the ratios described. In practice, credit analysts consider such matters as capitalized interest, rentals, intangible assets, and deferred taxes when calculating coverage and leverage ratios. The author has focused on more basic forms of the ratios in order to maximize clarity of exposition.

Chapter Seven

High Yield Indexes and Benchmark Portfolios

by Martin S. Fridson, CFA
Merrill Lynch

"You can't please everyone," as the saying goes, but high yield bond indexes seem to please no one. Whether viewed from the vantage point of an investment advisory firm's senior management, its clients or its portfolio managers, or else by a bond salesman, regulator, journalist, academician or consultant, the faults of indexes always appear fatal, yet at the same time easily remediable.

What explains the paradox of a costly problem that is universally recognized, yet perpetually resistant to seemingly simple and obvious solutions?

Perhaps the difficulty is that no high yield index can satisfy every category of user. The flaw perceived by a portfolio manager, whose performance is measured by the index, may be correctable with one stroke, but only at the cost of magnifying the shortcoming seen by a pension fund sponsor, who is the one doing the measuring. Tinkering with the index, meanwhile, accomplishes little for the chief investment officer, except to intensify his suspicion that somebody is trying to pull a fast one.

IRRECONCILABLE OBJECTIVES

If all interested parties were to list the attributes that would cause a high yield index to serve their parochial interests perfectly, the result might resemble Figure 7.1. Just a bit of reflection leads swiftly to the conclusion that reconciling all of the desired objectives is a puzzle with no solution. Some of the items listed are unachievable ideals, while certain others are mutually exclusive.

Universality is an example of an unattainable ideal, due to the dissimilar constraints under which various types of institutions operate. A market-weighted index does not truly represent the universe available to the manager of a collateralized bond obligation, who may be precluded from putting more than 3% of assets into a single name, even though RJR Nabisco paper represents 8% of the noninvestment grade market's par value. On the other hand, a manager who holds approximately a market weighting of RJR is not fairly measured by an index that fails to recognize the food and tobacco giant's disproportionate impact on overall sector performance.

As for the problem of mutually exclusive criteria, consider Objectivity and Transaction-Groundedness. The ultimate in objective selection for a high yield index is to include *all* securities that satisfy certain definitions, e.g., nonconvertible public debt obligations rated below Baa3 by Moody's or below BBB– by Standard & Poor's. Unfortunately, many of the 1,500 or so issues currently answering that description do not trade with any regularity. Nontransaction-based matrix prices[1] must therefore be used.

This remedy in turn produces a conflict with the Accuracy ideal, since matrixing is inherently prone to imprecision in a market where two issuers in the same rating "cell" can easily trade hundreds of basis points apart.

To avoid the problems of matrix pricing, the index constructor may decide to use only the most liquid issues for which bona fide market quotations are readily available. Objectivity can be preserved by using each issue's amount outstanding as a proxy for its liquidity, although the dollar amount cutoff that is chosen must inevitably be somewhat arbitrary. Many champions of Representativeness likewise

[1] Matrix pricing is a technique for providing quotations on issues for which no transaction price or trader's evaluation is available on a given date. A hypothetical price is assigned through an algorithm that adjusts the actual yield on a "key" issue of similar quality and structure for differences in such factors as name, maturity, and call protection.

Figure 7.1—Ideal Attributes of a High Yield Index

1. **Universality**–Acceptable for use by all high yield managers. Acknowledged by all market participants as a fair benchmark, even though another firm's proprietary index may produce slightly different yields and returns.
2. **Accuracy**–Shows true level and performance of the high yield universe. If comprised of a subset of all outstanding issues, closely tracks the full sample.
3. **Objectivity**–Issues included in index not selected by an arbitrary method that could bias results.
4. **Continuity**–Long performance record available, calculated on a consistent basis throughout.
5. **Integrity**–Produced by a good-faith effort to determine high yield market's level and performance.
6. **Comparability**–Directly comparable to standard indexes of other asset classes, thereby facilitating unbiased asset allocation decisions.
7. **Transaction-Groundedness**–Based on real prices rather than matrix-derived prices. (Latter effectively give extra weight to the "key issues," from which appraisals of issues that are not hand-priced are delivered.)
8. **Return-Indicativeness**–Correctly represents high yield market's periodic total return.
9. **Yield-Indicativeness**–Correctly represents high yield market's yield level.
10. **Price-Indicativeness**–Correctly represents high yield issues' average dollar prices.
11. **Representativeness**–Consists of bonds actually owned by portfolio managers; uncontaminated by issues that are not, for practical purposes, available for purchase.
12. **Adaptability**–Not so rigidly constructed as to become irrelevant to users as a result of profound changes in the marketplace.
13. **Accessibility**–Widely disseminated, making it easy for market participants to assess their performance as frequently as desired.
14. **Proprietary Uniqueness**–Provides a return to the entity that expends resources in developing and supporting the index, either through direct revenues or by generating other transactions.

favor an index composed solely of issues of $100 million or more outstanding (for example), since institutional portfolios typically have concentration requirements that preclude them from owning smaller deals.[2]

Unfortunately, cutting down on the total market capitalization represented by the constituent issues magnifies the impact of a large price change by a major issuer. In the short run, such a distortion can be sizable.

Suppose, by way of illustration, that a distressed but nondefaulted issuer with $750 million of public debt outstanding reports an unexpectedly sharp earnings drop, with the result that a critically important refinancing negotiation breaks down. With interest accrual partially offsetting the decline in average price from 50 to 30, the company's issues post a total return of –38% for the month. Assume further that during the same month, the total return on a $150 billion market-capitalization index is 1.0%. If the same –38% total return on the $750 million issuer is included in a "widely quoted issuers" index with a market capitalization of only $100 billion, the high yield sector's return for the period will be reported at 0.8%. In annualized terms, magnifying the outlier's effect in this manner reduces the market's reported total return from 12.68% to 10.31%.

Old hands at the high yield indexing game know how to eliminate such a distortion. In the name of Representativeness, the index constructor can discard the "unrepresentative" issue *retroactively*. This produces yet a third monthly return figure—1.1%, or 14.11% annualized.

Now the conflicts begin to multiply. The index's Accuracy is sure to be questioned by portfolio managers who earned total returns of 1.05% during the month, and who thought they had done well but now learn that they underperformed. They will facetiously wish that, like the index constructor, they too had in effect owned free puts on the bond that fell from 50 to 30. Objectivity is compromised, too, since a $750 million nondefaulted issue is now excluded from the index—solely because of its recent performance—while other nonde-

---

2 See Martin S. Fridson, "Establishing Investment Guidelines for a High Yield Portfolio" in *High Yield Bonds: Identifying Value and Assessing Risk of Speculative Grade Securities* (Chicago: Probus Publishing, 1989), pp. 3–20. A common mutual fund restriction limits holdings to 10% of the outstanding debt of a company and caps the investment in a single issuer at 5% of assets. To keep within these standards, a $1 billion fund investing in issuers with only $50 million outstanding would have to hold at least 200 different names, considerably more than many in-house research departments could monitor effectively. The arithmetic of the institutional market inexorably drives portfolio managers toward larger issues.

faulted issues of comparable size continue to be included. If the index constructor devises new rules on the fly to maintain some semblance of Objectivity, Continuity is in turn undermined. All of these developments, moreover, impair the high yield index's Comparability with indexes of other asset categories, which have been calculated consistently over many years. Lack of Comparability turns asset allocation decisions into an unreliable process of mixing apples and oranges. As a consequence, a conservative fiduciary may deem the data derived from this sort of improvisation to be an unsatisfactory rationale for entering the high yield sector.

Most problematic of all is the doubt cast upon the Integrity of a high yield index by constant revision. If a pension fund sponsor asks a high yield portfolio manager what he is measured against, the truthful answer under such circumstances must be, "An index that is tinkered with every month." In the fiduciary's mind, it is but a short step from tinkering to tampering, with a plausible suspicion that the goal is to portray managers' performance in the most favorable light possible. In reality, inaccurate performance measurement in high yield bonds probably results more from intractable problems of the available benchmarks than from conscious misrepresentation. Nevertheless, repeated alterations of methodology are bound to diminish an index's credibility.

Besides the particular thicket through which we have just led the reader, numerous other paths of contradictions can be traced from any item in Figure 7.1. Two examples will suffice.

1. Yield-Indicativeness (to facilitate new issue pricing, for instance) is perhaps best served by an index that excludes both exceptionally low-yielding bonds (e.g., Double-B issues of less than three years in maturity) and exceptionally high-yielding ones (e.g., distressed securities that continue to accrue interest at astronomical indicated yields but in reality trade on the basis of bondholders' expected recovery in bankruptcy). An index constructed on such principles, however, will not satisfy the Return-Indicativeness standard of a portfolio manager who invests across a broad spectrum of quality.
2. Adaptability is perpetually in conflict with Continuity. In late 1990, for example, some portfolio managers argued that it would be uneconomical to sell their defaulted bonds given the market's highly illiquid condition. If they held on, yet continued to be measured against an index that excluded defaulted issues (which have tended to be highly volatile), they faced an immense per-

formance handicap during bear markets. Accommodating managers on this point, though, might have necessitated adding defaulted issues to an index that had always excluded them[3] on the theory that noncurrent instruments did not belong in a benchmark designed for managers primarily concerned with current income. Whenever Adaptability is served in this way, however, Continuity suffers, with the specific consequence that pension fund sponsors may never see a track record calculated on a consistent basis over several years. Lack of such basic documentation makes fiduciaries wary of taking the high yield leap of faith.

A second manifestation of the Adaptability/Continuity conflict is the response of index constructors to product innovation. Conventionally structured new issues that meet the general requirements for inclusion should clearly be added to the index. Lower-rated convertible debentures and preferred stock, on the other hand, should undoubtedly be excluded from an index composed of high yield bonds (as usually defined), even though many high yield managers own these related securities. What about exchangeable debentures, usable bonds, commodity-indexed obligations and unrated commercial paper? At some point, too much innovation causes a financial instrument to fall outside the boundaries of the high yield market, as most investors conceive it. Introducing newly devised securities that plainly lie beyond the pale may undercut Continuity by making the index far more sensitive than it previously was to certain factors such as oil prices, money market rates or foreign exchange rates. Honest people can disagree about where to draw the line, but adapting an index too readily to innovations in financial structures can greatly reduce the value of its historical record as a predictor of its future performance.

Merrill Lynch's index specialists confronted this issue in connection with the introduction of zero-coupon (or deferred-interest) bonds and pay-in-kind securities during the mid-1980s. Their solution was to maintain the Master without DIBs and PIKs in the interest of Continuity, but to offer alongside it the Master II—augmented by the new, non-cash-pay securities—as an alternative for investors who elected to capitalize on these innovations in corporate finance. The Master has,

---

3 The typical practice has been to keep issues in the index until they default—so that the full impact of their credit deterioration will be reflected in total return—but to exclude them thereafter. Clearly, deleting a defaulted issue retroactively is inconsistent with the Integrity and Accuracy objectives.

in effect, become a specialized benchmark for investors who choose not to invest in DIBs and PIKs and therefore prefer not to be measured against an index that reflects their added volatility.

Invariably, then, solving one problem creates another problem. The perennial process of "fixing that @*?%#! high yield index" is an exercise in futility. In mathematical terms, the source of the problem is clear, namely: trying to create a perfect index—or even one that is satisfactory to all parties—is a vain attempt to solve an optimization problem by maximizing the value of every parameter. Unless the index constructor can identify one or more parameters for which the goal of total realization can be sacrificed, the juggling and balancing will continue indefinitely without tangible progress.

THE NORMAL SOLUTION

Few of the objectives in Figure 7.1, to be sure, leap out as candidates for the sacrificial block. Most market participants would be loath to scrimp on Integrity or Accuracy. Certain other criteria may not be important to all users of indexes, yet are vital to some. In our estimation, the solution that achieves the greatest good for the greatest number is to abandon the Universality objective. By this one simple expedient, the otherwise overwhelming conflicts are reduced to levels that allow everyone's highest priorities to be met. Far from introducing anarchy, as one might expect of a system that lets each manager adopt a customized index, the renunciation of Universality substitutes order for an inherently unstable arrangement.

The concept we advocate is not original, but has frequently appeared in the literature under the names "normal portfolio" and "benchmark portfolio" (see Bibliography). As one source defines the concept, "The *normal portfolio* for a particular manager is an index of securities designed to replicate the investment universe in which the manager routinely operates."[4] A recent article expands on this point as follows: "Rather than using the S&P 500 as a performance standard for all equity managers, for example, a benchmark approach would use a benchmark portfolio with value characteristics for a value manager, a benchmark portfolio with growth characteristics for a growth manager

[4] Walter R. Good and Douglas A. Love, *Managing Pension Assets* (New York: McGraw-Hill Publishing Company, 1990), p. 139.

and a benchmark portfolio with small-capitalization characteristics for a small-cap manager."[5]

In an equity context, the benchmark portfolio approach offers clear advantages to both clients and managers. Imagine, for example, the following scenario: The trustees of a pension fund decide that an allocation of $100 million to small-capitalization stocks is desirable in view of the fund's long-term return and diversification requirements. During the first year of the program, the Wilshire 4500 small-capitalization stock index returns 20%, well above the long-range objective. The market environment that year happens to favor large stocks, however, with the result that the Standard & Poor's 400 Industrials index returns 23%. At year end, the trustees review the performance of their small-capitalization manager, who has posted a 21% return. If they use the supposedly universal S&P 400 as a reference point, they will conclude that the manager has underperformed. They may even serve notice that a continuation of the unsatisfactory results will result in termination of the management agreement. By doing so, they will have done a disservice to the beneficiaries as well as an injustice to a portfolio manager who has actually outperformed the *relevant* index. If the manager possesses the skill to continue beating the Wilshire 4500 by 100 basis points a year, the trustees would be foolish to take their business elsewhere. Over the long run, small-capitalization stocks will do better than large-capitalization stocks in some years and worse in others. Assuming that the original decision to allocate a portion of the pension fund's assets to small-capitalization stocks was correct, firing a manager who can demonstrate superior ability in that sector must be wrong.

A similar logic holds in the high yield market. If a manager's orders are to limit risk by sticking to credits rated Single-B or better, he should not be penalized for underperforming an index that includes Triple-C and defaulted bonds during an economic rebound in which bottom-tier names record the biggest gains. By the same token, the client who chooses to follow the lower-risk "Single-B or better" strategy is the one who deserves the credit when his portfolio suffers less severe losses than an index spanning the full-quality spectrum from Double-B to D. The manager's evaluation in such circumstances should reflect only the extent—if any—to which he has outperformed the average of the Single-B-and-above universe. This desirable state of affairs is pre-

---

[5] Edward P. Rennie and Thomas J. Cowhey, "The Successful Use of Benchmark Portfolios: A Case Study," *Financial Analysts Journal* (September/October 1990), p. 18.

cluded by the widespread reliance on high yield indexes that are intended to be universal, an ideal they can never satisfy in a world where clients differ in their risk preferences, liquidity needs, and regulatory constraints.

HOW IMPORTANT IS PORTFOLIO MIX?

The use of custom-tailored high yield indexes may strike fixed-income generalists as a case of overengineering, since the high yield market itself is commonly regarded as a narrow specialty. Differences in investment parameters have enough impact on returns to make the benchmark portfolio well worthwhile, however. Table 7.1 strongly supports the case.

Table 7.1—Portfolio Composition Comparisons

	Index	*Selected Benchmark Portfolios*		
	Merrill Lynch Master	*Mutual Fund Proxy*	*No-Finance Paper*	*No-Finance Mutual Fund Proxy*
Cash	0%	5%	0%	5%
BB	37	10	|	|
B	52	70	100*	90*
CCC-C	11	10	|	|
Defaulted	0	5	0	5
Total	100%	100%	100%	100%
1990 Total Return	-4.35%	-6.14%	-3.18%	-3.36%
Monthly High	2.11%	2.14%	2.24%	2.16%
Monthly Low	-4.35%	-5.02%	-4.23%	-3.93%

* Represents aggregate of BB plus B plus CCC-C.

Notes: Portfolio composition figures are as of March 1991. Composition changes daily through rating changes, new issues, redemptions, etc. Ratings represent the higher of Moody's or Standard & Poor's rating for each constituent issue. Defaulted issues are represented by the Altman-Merrill Lynch Index.

The Merrill Lynch Master Index essentially holds up a mirror to the universe of public, nonconvertible bonds rated below investment grade by Moody's or Standard & Poor's or both. Except for a fairly low cutoff point ($50 million for amount outstanding), there is no trigger that excludes issues, making the Master just about the last word in Objectivity. Its composition, however, is quite different from the distribution of securities within the typical high yield mutual fund. For one thing, a sample of 41 funds tracked by Morningstar, a mutual fund research firm,[6] had a 9.1% concentration in cash as of January 11, 1991, versus 0% for the Master as of March 1991. In addition, Double-B paper represented 37% of the Master's market value, far above the 13% level reported for the Morningstar sample. The same 41 funds had 52% of their assets in Single-B debt, plus 10% in unrated paper, which is generally presumed to be *at best* Single-B in quality. These differences are critical, for both the cash position and the ratings mix have considerable bearing on performance.

On some observation dates, mutual funds' cash positions reflect market-timing decisions (i.e., defensiveness) for which their managers can properly be held accountable in performance measurement. At all times, though, funds must maintain minimum cash positions to accommodate redemptions. This requirement can create a considerable handicap vis-a-vis a cash-free index. During the 1989–1990 high yield bear market, holding cash actually helped performance, but over the longer term, cash's lower-risk/lower-return characteristics make it a drag on the total return of a high yield fund. Furthermore, the presence of cash reduces the volatility of returns, putting high yield funds at a disadvantage relative to most indexes during bull markets. Table 7.2 shows that between late 1988 and early 1991, cash had a monthly standard deviation of just 0.08%. Over the same period, the three rating categories of nondefaulted high yield bonds had a combined standard deviation of 3.11%.

Volatility of returns is also influenced by the mix of quality within the noncash portion of the fund. At 1.69%, the standard deviation of the Double-B sector, as shown in Table 7.1, is less than half as great as the Single-B sector's. The substantially higher weighting of Double-B paper in the Master relative to the typical high yield mutual fund should therefore cause the former to perform more steadily than the latter. (Cash positions in the funds will to some extent offset this effect.)

---

6 "Corporate Bond-High Yield Overview," *Mutual Fund Values* 13, no. 8 (Chicago: Morningstar, Inc., January 11, 1991), pp. 834–875.

Table 7.1's "Mutual Fund Proxy" benchmark portfolio is designed to show how the sensitivity of return and volatility to ratings distribution and the presence of cash affected the 1990 total return of a fund with the profile indicated. The hypothetical portfolio's 5% cash position, 70% Single-B exposure, and 5% defaulted bond component represent the long-range "normal" risk position specified by the board of directors, consistent with the fund's prospectus.[7] Any difference between the total return on this passively managed portfolio and the manager's actual results reflects the impact of specific investment decisions, including deviations from the normal ratings mix in response to changes in the investment climate. Credit decisions on individual names may likewise produce large positive or negative variances from the benchmark. The most appropriate benchmark for judging these micro-level decisions is an objectively selected group, rather than the index constructor's impression of "what managers actually own," i.e., 50 or 75 somewhat arbitrarily chosen issues. Accordingly, the 10% Double-B component in the Mutual Fund Proxy represents a smaller amount of the exact same mix of Double-B securities as the Master's 37% component.

The point of the comparison, in Table 7.1, between the Master and the Mutual Fund Proxy is not that the latter performed worse (–6.14% versus –4.35%) in 1990, but that the differential was so large (179 basis points). Compositional changes that might seem minor to generalists who perceive high yield bonds as an undifferentiated mass can, in fact, greatly alter returns. The sizable gap observed in 1990 dramatizes the potential benefits of a benchmark portfolio as an alternative to a universal index for performance measurement purposes.

Actually, the disparity between the Master and Mutual Fund Proxy is not surprising in view of the wide range of historical returns among the categories represented in Table 7.2.[8] By way of illustration, a shift of just 10% of assets from Single-B to Double-B would have raised a portfolio's average annual return by 49 basis points between September 1988 and February 1991. Monthly fluctuations in returns are likewise quite sensitive to differences in composition. Table 7.1 shows that the Mutual Fund Proxy not only underperformed the Master during 1990,

---

7 In an investment advisory context, the makeup of the benchmark portfolio can be regarded as the long-run investment strategy agreed upon by client and manager.

8 It happens that during the three-and-a-half-year period for which monthly returns are available for all of the indexes and subindexes, the relationship between risk and return is anomalous. The Single-B category shows a lower return than the less risky Double-B category, for example. The standard deviations increase monotonically and inversely with ratings, though, and over a longer period so should returns.

Table 7.2—Performance History—Selected Asset Categories September 1988 - February 1991

	Cash	*BB*	*B*	*CCC-C*	*Defaulted*
Average Annual Return	8.23%	8.81%	3.87%	-6.94%	-12.80%
Standard Deviation	0.08%	1.69%	3.85%	5.67%	5.14%

Note: Standard deviation is based on monthly returns. Defaulted issues are represented by the Altman-Merrill Lynch Index.

but also displayed a wider range of monthly returns (716 basis points versus 646 for the Master).

Clearly, tossing in even modest amounts of cash and defaulted issues, as well as altering the Double-B/Single-B distribution, can make a big difference in returns. A high yield manager can justly complain of an inappropriate bogey if he was criticized for underperforming the Master by 100 basis points in 1990. After all, at –5.35%, he did substantially better than the –6.14% produced by a passive portfolio of the universe of securities he was supposed to hold, in the proportions in which he was supposed to hold them.

On the criterion of Representativeness, the benchmark portfolio approach is unsurpassed, for the client and manager can define any universe they desire. Some investors, as a matter of policy, decline to hold finance paper, viewing investments of that nature as tantamount to paying fees to outsiders to manage financial assets. Discarding the Universality requirement enables such institutions to measure their managers against a better-suited benchmark such as the Master sans finance issues. Table 7.1 shows that in 1990, a benchmark constructed along those lines was a tougher bogey than the Master (–3.18% total return versus –4.35%), although the relationship might easily be reversed in another year. As a further refinement, the institution could create a hybrid such as the "No-Finance Mutual Fund Proxy," also depicted in Table 7.1, although the 1990 results suggest little incremental effect from adding cash and defaulted issues to the mix.

CONCLUSION

The high yield index designer who tries to satisfy everybody ends up satisfying nobody. Nevertheless, it is possible for high yield managers to compete against benchmarks that measure their results fairly, provided they do not all insist on using the same index.

Objections to the benchmark portfolio concept have been raised by managers who perceive it to be a device for shaving fees. There is no inherent reason, though, why improving the accuracy of performance measurement must reduce the value of managers' services. Fee income may indeed be jeopardized, however, if a manager has set out to "game the index," i.e., to produce the illusion of superior risk-adjusted returns by taking risks that escape detection under the imperfect measurement systems currently in place.

Ultimately, benchmark portfolios will supersede the index approach only if some forward-looking investment committees and pension fund sponsors are willing to be innovators. It is far easier to stick to established practice, even if, in the case of high yield performance measurement, that means applying an inappropriate standard. Given the importance of knowing whether one's managers are performing well or poorly, however, it behooves fiduciaries to explore the merits of a promising alternative.

BIBLIOGRAPHY

Brealey, Richard A. "Portfolio Theory versus Portfolio Practice." *The Journal of Portfolio Management*, Summer 1990, p. 6.

Brinson, Gary P., Jeffrey J. Diermeier and Gary G. Schlarbaum. "A Composite Portfolio Benchmark for Pension Plans." *Financial Analysts Journal* 42, no. 2 (March/April 1986), pp. 15–24.

Brinson, Gary P., L. Randolph Hood and Gilbert L. Beebower. "Determinants of Portfolio Performance." *Financial Analysts Journal* 42, no. 4 (July/August 1986), pp. 39–44.

"Corporate Bond-High Yield Overview." *Mutual Fund Values* 13, no. 8 (January 11, 1991), pp. 834–875. Chicago: Morningstar, Inc.

Dutton, Jacqueline. "GTE Edict to 24 Managers; Perform or Reduce Fees." *Pension & Investment Age*, January 25, 1988, p. 3.

Fen, Allan. "Creating a Benchmark for GIC Performance." *Pensions & Investment Age*, June 11, 1990, p. 38.

Fridson, Martin S. *High Yield Bonds: Identifying Value and Assessing Risk of Speculative Grade Securities*. Chicago: Probus Publishing, 1989.

Fridson, Martin S. "Performance Measurement." In *The New High-Yield Debt Market: A Handbook for Portfolio Managers and Analysts*, edited by Frank J. Fabozzi, pp. 249–269. New York: Harper-Business, 1990.

Good, Walter R. and Douglas A. Love. *Managing Pension Assets*, p. 139. New York: McGraw-Hill Publishing Company, 1990.

Gould, F.J. "Pigeonhole Mentality and Special Benchmarks." *Pensions & Investment Age*, April 30, 1990, p. 18.

Rennie, Edward P. and Thomas J. Cowhey. "The Successful Use of Benchmark Portfolios: A Case Study." *Financial Analysts Journal* 46, no. 5 (September/October 1990), pp. 18–26.

Richards, Thomas M. and Nancy E. McPike. "Benchmark Portfolios: Crafting a Valid Yardstick." *Cash Flow* 8, no. 2 (February 1987), pp. 47–48.

Ring, Trudy. "Abnormal Portfolios." *Pensions & Investments* 18, no. 7 (April 2, 1990), pp. 3, 50.

Tierney, David and Kenneth Winston. "Defining and Using Dynamic Completeness Funds to Enhance Total Fund Efficiency." *Financial Analysts Journal* 46, no. 4 (July/August 1990), pp. 49–54.

SECTION TWO:

EVALUATING CORPORATE BOND DOWNGRADES AND DEFAULTS

Chapter Eight

Changes in Corporate Credit Quality 1970–1992

by Douglas J. Lucas,
Assistant Vice President
and
John G. Lonski,
Senior Economist
Moody's Investors Service

SUMMARY

In 1993, Moody's revised its study of annual changes in the credit ratings of more than 4,000 rated U.S. and international debt issuers (industrial and utility companies, financial institutions, sovereign issuers, and structured finance issuers) from 1970 through 1992. The study analyzes trends in the direction and stability of the credit quality of rated issuers in the past 23 years.

Briefly, the study found:

- Corporate creditworthiness became progressively more volatile over the study period. On average, during the 1970s, 6% of rated issuers ended the calendar year in a different long-term, letter-rating category than they began. During the 1980s and so far in the 1990s, that percentage rose to 12%. For short-term commercial paper ratings, the percentage of companies experiencing a rating change over the course of a year also rose from

4%, on average, in the 1970s, to 6%, on average, in the 1980s and thus far in the 1990s.

- The increased volatility of credit ratings has been accompanied by a marked downward shift in corporate credit quality. The ratio of long-term downgrades to upgrades deteriorated from a 1.22:1 average in the 1970s to 2.21:1 in the 1980s and a record 4.93:1 in 1990. The ratio of downgrades to upgrades for short-term debt issuers also worsened substantially, from 1.32:1 in the 1970s to 2.86:1 in the 1980s to a record 9.60:1 in 1990.
- During the study period, the incidence of rating downgrades was spread fairly evenly across the rating spectrum. Downgrades tended to be more severe, however, in the lower rating categories. The incidence of upgrades generally increased in the lower rating categories.
- It was also found that 1% of Aaa-rated companies were downgraded into the speculative grades within five years. Over 10 years, the figure rises to 2%. For Baa-rated companies, 9% were downgraded into the speculative grades within two years, 15% within five years, and 17% within 10 years.
- Among speculative-grade issuers, 10% of all Ba-rated companies were upgraded into the investment grades within two years, 19% within five years and 29% within 10 years. For B-rated companies, 1% were upgraded into the investment grades within two years, 6% within five years, and 14% within 10 years.

METHODOLOGY

Moody's drew on a proprietary data base of public debt ratings of U.S.and non-U.S. industrial companies, utilities, financial institutions, sovereign issuers, and structured finance entities that issued commercial paper and long-term debt rated by Moody's. Municipal debt issuers were excluded. In total, our data base includes approximately 4,000 rated long-term issuers and 2,500 short-term debt issuers during the 23-year period studied. As of 1993, the data base contained ratings on 3,920 long-term issuers and 1,851 short-term issuers. These issuers account for almost the total dollar amount of corporate debt in the U.S. public market.

As with Moody's studies of default frequency among long-term issuers, rating change data presented here focus on the individual issuer in analyzing trends in the credit quality of corporate debt. Rating statistics are limited to one observation for each legal entity without regard to the number of securities issued or to the dollar amount of debt issued. However, the ratings of different issuers within an affiliated group of companies are tracked individually because affiliated companies are not always rated at the same level nor are their ratings always changed at the same time. For example, four legal entities affiliated with Texaco issue rated debt. Moody's tabulated the rating history of each one individually.

To track the long-term debt rating history of issuers with different types of debt (e.g., secured, senior unsecured, subordinate), all issuers were categorized by their actual or implied senior unsecured debt rating. Fifty-six percent of observations in the study were based directly on senior unsecured ratings and therefore required no modification. Twenty-six percent were implied from subordinated ratings by assuming a rating of one letter-grade above the subordinated rating or, following the introduction of numerical rating modifiers in 1982, one numerical notch above for investment grade and two numerical notches above for speculative grade. The final 18% of observations were implied from secured ratings by dropping one letter-grade below the secured rating or, following the introduction of numerical rating modifiers, one numerical rating notch below the secured rating.

TRENDS IN LONG-TERM RATING CHANGES

1970 through 1992 by Letter-Rating Category

To calculate long-term rating changes during a calendar year, each issuer's senior unsecured rating at the end of the particular year was compared with its rating at the beginning of the year. Multiple rating changes within a given year were ignored. Table 8.1 shows the number of upgrades and downgrades each year from 1970 through 1992, the percentage of total rated issuers affected in each case, and each year's ratio of downgrades to upgrades. For consistency, only changes in letter rating are included; changes in numeric modifiers are presented later in the study.

Aside from the 5% downgrade rate in 1974, associated with the 1974–1975 recession, annual upgrades and downgrades affected less than 5% of the universe of rated issuers in the 1970s. In the 1980s, the percentage of companies experiencing rating changes—in either direction—grew. In each year throughout the 1980s, at least 5% of all rated

Table 8.1—Long-Term Letter-Rating Upgrades and Downgrades, by Year 1970–1992

	Downgrades		Upgrades		Downgrades
	Number	*Percentage*	*Number*	*Percentage*	*Per Upgrade*
1970	21	2%	23	2%	0.91
1971	43	4%	19	2%	2.26
1972	22	2%	20	2%	1.10
1973	20	2%	20	2%	1.00
1974	55	5%	44	4%	1.25
1975	38	3%	48	4%	0.79
1976	27	2%	20	2%	1.35
1977	36	3%	31	3%	1.16
1978	29	2%	26	2%	1.12
1979	38	3%	31	3%	1.23
1980	68	5%	36	3%	1.89
1981	65	5%	43	3%	1.51
1982	126	9%	34	3%	3.71
1983	117	8%	60	4%	1.95
1984	100	7%	87	6%	1.15
1985	159	9%	67	4%	2.37
1986	213	11%	82	4%	2.60
1987	166	7%	78	4%	2.13
1988	220	9%	98	4%	2.24
1989	213	8%	83	3%	2.57
1990	301	10%	61	2%	4.93
1991	320	10%	89	3%	3.60
1992	309	9%	92	3%	3.36
Avg.	70–92	5.9%		3.1%	2.01
Avg.	70–79	2.8%		2.6%	1.22
Avg.	80–89	7.8%		3.8%	2.21

issuers were downgraded; upgrades were also higher than in the previous 10-year period. The 1990s showed a continuation of the trend set in the 1980s as a near-record (10%) of rated companies were downgraded in 1990 and 1991. Overall in the 1970s, 6% of companies ended the year with a different rating than at the beginning of the year, compared with 12% in the 1980s and 13% thus far in the 1990s.

While ratings became more volatile, they also listed decisively downward. The ratio of downgrades to upgrades increased from 1.22:1 in the 1970s to 2.21:1 in the 1980s to 3.96:1 thus far in the 1990s. The ratio of 4.93:1 for 1990 is the highest during the 23-year study period, reflecting the fact that the year saw the highest percentage of downgrades since 1986, and the lowest percentage of upgrades since 1978. The second highest ratio was in 1982, the year of probably the most severe of all post-WWII recessions. The high level of downgrades in 1986 reflects trouble in the energy sector and among banks lending to the energy sector. Roughly 35% of all industrial company downgrades and 60% of all financial company downgrades that year were traced to 1986's precipitous drop in oil prices. Downgrades in 1989 and 1990 reflect a variety of factors, including banks' problem loans in weakening real estate markets of the southwest and northeastern United States, as well as increasing difficulties for highly leveraged, speculative-grade companies, particularly in the wake of the speculative-grade market collapse.

Figure 8.1 illustrates the yearly percentage of upgrades and downgrades presented in Table 8.1.

Figure 8.1—Percentage of Long-Term Letter-Rating Upgrades and Downgrades, by Year 1970–1992

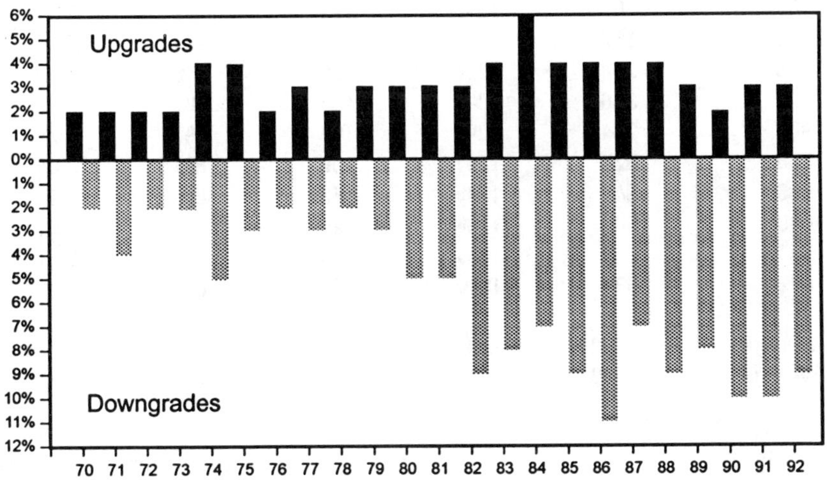

1983 through 1992 by Refined-Rating Category

In 1982, Moody's introduced numerical modifiers into its letter-rating system. Table 8.2 shows the number of company upgrades and downgrades per year from 1983 through 1992, including changes in numeric modifiers (using senior unsecured ratings), and each year's ratio of downgrades to upgrades. Multiple rating changes during the year were ignored.

Because upgrades and downgrades within as well as between letter categories are being counted now, the percentages of rating changes increase from those in Table 8.1. There was a general increase in the ratio of downgrades to upgrades over the nine-year period, with 1984 having the lowest ratio and 1990s the highest. Overall, the data show the same credit quality trends as for letter-rating changes during the 1983–1992 period, with the most significant deterioration during 1986 and 1989 through 1992.

Table 8.2—Long-Term Refined-Rating Upgrades and Downgrades, by Year 1983–1992

	Downgrades		*Upgrades*		*Downgrades*
	Number	*Percentage*	*Number*	*Percentage*	*Per Upgrade*
1983	182	13%	111	8%	1.64
1984	167	11%	189	12%	0.88
1985	214	12%	159	9%	1.35
1986	338	18%	156	8%	2.17
1987	264	12%	153	7%	1.73
1988	323	13%	158	6%	2.04
1989	342	13%	156	6%	2.19
1990	504	17%	129	4%	3.91
1991	571	18%	158	5%	3.61
1992	639	19%	187	6%	3.42
Average	83-92	14.6%		7.1%	2.17
Average	83-89	13.2%		8.1%	1.71

Figure 8.2 illustrates the yearly percentage of upgrades and downgrades presented in Table 8.2.

Figure 8.2—Percentage of Long-Term Refined-Rating Upgrades and Downgrades, by Year 1983–1992

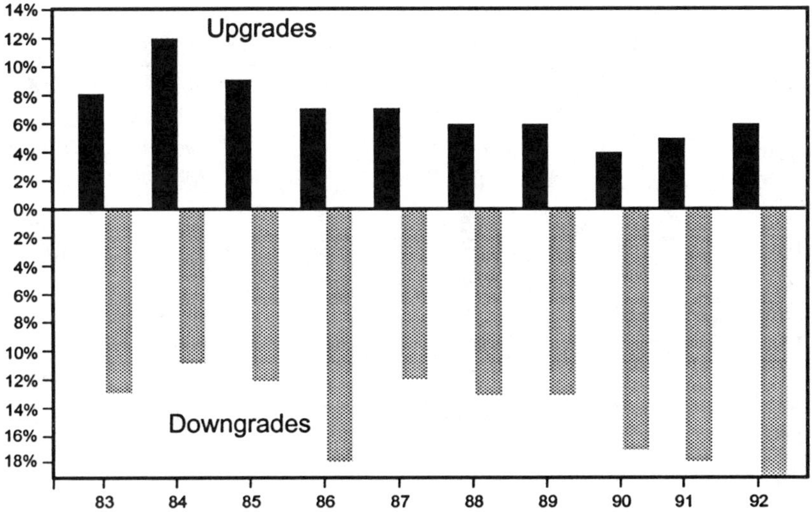

TRENDS IN SHORT-TERM RATING CHANGES

Moody's applied the same methodology in calculating short-term rating changes as that used for long-term rating changes. Each company's short-term rating at the end of the calendar year was compared with its rating at the beginning of the year, ignoring multiple rating changes within the year. Because short-term debt is typically a senior unsecured obligation of a firm, no adjustment to the rating is necessary.

Table 8.3 shows the number and percentage of upgrades and downgrades each year since 1973—the first full year in which Moody's included modifiers to its Prime category—as well as each year's ratio of downgrades to upgrades. As with long-term rating changes depicted in Table 8.1, the highest percentage of downgrades occurred in 1982, 1986, and 1990. However, because there are fewer short-term rating categories, short-term rating changes are less common than long-term rating changes.

Table 8.3—Short-Term Rating Upgrades and Downgrades, by Year 1973–1992

	Downgrades		*Upgrades*		*Downgrades*
	Number	*Percentage*	*Number*	*Percentage*	*Per Upgrade*
1973	7	1%	4	1%	1.75
1974	16	3%	8	2%	2.00
1975	19	4%	14	3%	1.36
1976	5	1%	15	3%	0.33
1977	9	2%	16	3%	0.56
1978	10	2%	8	1%	1.25
1979	10	2%	5	1%	2.00
1980	20	3%	8	1%	2.50
1981	19	3%	10	1%	1.90
1982	51	6%	8	1%	6.38
1983	22	3%	16	2%	1.38
1984	25	3%	25	3%	1.00
1985	53	5%	17	2%	3.12
1986	74	7%	14	1%	5.29
1987	30	2%	17	1%	1.76
1988	61	4%	29	2%	2.10
1989	80	5%	25	2%	3.20
1990	96	6%	10	1%	9.60
1991	66	4%	24	2%	2.75
1992	85	5%	27	2%	3.15
Avg.	73–92	3.6%		1.7%	2.67
Avg.	73–79	2.1%		2.0%	1.32
Avg.	80–89	4.1%		1.6%	2.86

Figure 8.3 illustrates the yearly percentage of upgrades and downgrades presented in Table 8.3.

Figure 8.3—Percentage of Short-Term Rating Upgrades and Downgrades, by Year 1973–1992

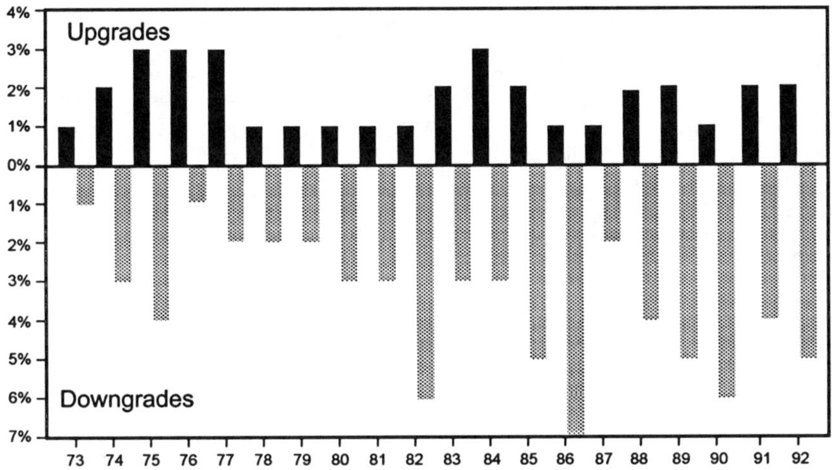

INCIDENCE OF LONG-TERM RATING CHANGES BY RATING CATEGORY

1970 through 1992 by Letter-Rating Category

Tables 8.4 through 8.6 present average long-term rating change activity, broken down by rating category at the beginning of a year. Throughout the 23-year period, rating downgrades were generally evenly distributed across rating categories, increasing slightly in the lower rating categories, but decreasing materially at the Ca and C rating levels, where issuers are already in default. This phenomena holds in both the 1970s (Table 8.5) and the 1980s (Table 8.6), except among Aaa-rated issuers, who were far less likely to be downgraded in the 1970s. By contrast, rating upgrades tended to occur with larger percentages of issuers in the lower rating categories, except among issuers already in default.

Table 8.4—Yearly Long-Term Rating Changes, by Letter-Rating Category 1970–1992

	Downgrades	*Upgrades*	*Total Changed*	*Downgrades Per Upgrade*
Aaa	8.9%	NA	8.9%	NA
Aa	7.5%	1.1%	8.6%	6.79
A	5.7%	2.2%	8.0%	2.56
Baa	5.8%	4.2%	10.0%	1.39
Ba	8.3%	5.3%	13.5%	1.57
B	8.8%	6.1%	15.0%	1.44
Caa	7.6%	7.3%	14.9%	1.05
Ca	1.8%	5.0%	6.8%	0.36
C	NA	2.5%	2.5%	NA

Table 8.5—Yearly Long-Term Rating Changes, by Letter-Rating Category 1970–1979

	Downgrades	*Upgrades*	*Total Changed*	*Downgrades Per Upgrade*
Aaa	1.3%	NA	1.3%	NA
Aa	3.6%	2.6%	6.2%	1.37
A	2.8%	1.5%	4.3%	1.88
Baa	3.1%	2.6%	5.7%	1.21
Ba	3.1%	4.7%	7.8%	0.65
B	4.3%	6.1%	10.4%	0.71
Caa	4.3%	1.7%	6.1%	2.50
Ca	1.6%	0.5%	2.1%	3.00
C	NA	0.0%	0.0%	NA

Table 8.6—Yearly Long-Term Rating Changes, by Letter-Rating Category 1980–1989

	Downgrades	*Upgrades*	*Total Changed*	*Downgrades Per Upgrade*
Aaa	7.7%	NA	7.7%	NA
Aa	8.3%	1.6%	9.9%	5.21
A	7.4%	3.0%	10.4%	2.46
Baa	8.6%	6.3%	15.0%	1.37
Ba	9.4%	5.6%	15.0%	1.70
B	6.6%	5.5%	12.1%	1.22
Caa	5.0%	9.9%	14.9%	0.50
Ca	0.0%	5.0%	5.0%	0.00
C	NA	1.6%	1.6%	NA

Ratings of issuers in the highest and lowest rating categories thus tended to be less volatile, mainly because they were less prone, respectively, to upgrades or downgrades. On average, during the 23-year period, 10% or fewer issuers in the investment-grade categories (Aaa, Aa, A, and Baa) finished each year in a different letter rating category. Fourteen-and-a-half percent of all companies in the next three rating categories (Ba, B, and Caa) experienced a rating change. These companies have the highest probability of defaulting and thus of being downgraded, but also the greatest chance of an upgrade should their financial circumstances improve. Defaulted issues in the Ca and C rating categories exhibited the greatest rating stability because of the impossibility of further downgrades. Comparing the ratio of downgrades to upgrades in the 1970s with that of the 1980s, the greatest portion of the secular decline in credit quality during the 1980s occurred at the upper and lower ends of the rating spectrum. From less than two downgrades per upgrade in the 1970s, downgrades outpaced upgrades by six to one for Aa-rated issuers and two-and-a-half to one for A-rated issuers in the 1980s. For Ba- and B-rated issuers, the ratio reversed itself from less than one in the 1970s to greater than one in the 1980s.

1983 through 1992 by Refined-Rating Category

Table 8.7 provides further detail of rating-specific trends in the 1980s and so far in the 1990s. As shown in Table 8.4 for letter-rating downgrades, numerical-rating downgrades were fairly evenly spread throughout the rating spectrum during the 1983–1992 period, but highest in the Aa2 and B3 categories. Upgrades were most frequent for issuers in the middle of the rating spectrum (A3 through Ba1), and the middle-rating categories thus tended to be more volatile. But while the middle of the rating spectrum was more volatile, the Aa1 through A2 range and the Ba2 to B2 range experienced the strongest overall decline in credit quality, as measured by the ratio of downgrades to upgrades.

Table 8.7—Yearly Long-Term Rating Changes, by Refined-Rating Category 1983–1992

	Downgrades	*Upgrades*	*Total Changed*	*Downgrades Per Upgrade*
Aaa	11.7%	NA	11.7%	NA
Aa1	12.1%	1.3%	13.3%	9.65
Aa2	22.3%	3.7%	26.0%	5.96
Aa3	17.6%	3.8%	21.4%	4.60
A1	13.9%	5.7%	19.6%	2.43
A2	14.8%	6.5%	21.3%	2.26
A3	15.3%	10.3%	25.6%	1.48
Baa1	16.6%	10.3%	26.9%	1.61
Baa2	14.3%	13.5%	27.8%	1.06
Baa3	17.2%	13.3%	30.4%	1.29
Ba1	16.5%	14.7%	31.2%	1.12
Ba2	16.6%	9.7%	26.3%	1.72
Ba3	16.5%	7.4%	24.0%	2.22
B1	15.5%	8.0%	23.5%	1.94
B2	17.7%	7.5%	25.2%	2.37
B3	20.4%	13.4%	33.8%	1.52
Caa	8.2%	8.7%	16.9%	0.95
Ca	1.4%	9.9%	11.3%	0.14
C	NA	5.8%	5.8%	NA

NA: Not Applicable

Magnitude of Rating Change by Letter-Rating Category, 1970–1992

Table 8.8 provides detail of how far ratings tended to move between categories during the 1970–1992 period. For each letter category listed on the vertical axis, the weighted average percentage of issuers in that category moving upward or downward over a year is listed by rating category on the horizontal axis. For example, on average, 91% of all Aaa-rated companies remained Aaa over the course of a year, 8% were downgraded to Aa, and 1% were downgraded to A.

It is clear that changes in ratings of more than one letter-grade are more frequent in the B through C rating categories than in the higher rating categories. While the probability of downgrade tended to be evenly distributed across all rating categories, the credit quality of companies in the B and Caa rating categories drop more precipitously when downgrades occur.

Table 8.8—Magnitude of Long-Term Rating Changes, by Letter-Rating Category Over One Year 1970–1992

	Rating at End of Year								
Rating at Beginning of Year	*Aaa*	*Aa*	*A*	*Baa*	*Ba*	*B*	*Caa*	*Ca*	*C*
Aaa	91%	8%	1%						
Aa	1%	91%	7%						
A		2%	92%	5%	1%				
Baa			4%	90%	5%	1%			
Ba				5%	86%	7%	1%		
B					5%	85%	7%	2%	
Caa					1%	5%	85%	6%	1%
Ca					1%	2%	1%	93%	2%
C					1%			2%	97%

Magnitude of Rating Change by Refined-Rating Category, 1983–1992

Table 8.9 gives additional detail on the intensity of rating changes from 1983 through 1992. As in the 1970–1992 period, downgrades

Table 8.9—Magnitude of Long-Term Rating Changes, by Refined-Rating Category Over One Year 1983–1992

Rating at Beginning of Year	Rating at End of Year																		
	Aaa	*Aa1*	*Aa2*	*Aa3*	*A1*	*A2*	*A3*	*Baa1*	*Baa2*	*Baa3*	*Ba1*	*Ba2*	*Ba3*	*B1*	*B2*	*B3*	*Caa*	*Ca*	*C*
Aaa	88%	6%	4%	1%	1%														
Aa1	1%	87%	4%	7%	1%														
Aa2	1%	3%	74%	12%	8%	1%	1%												
Aa3		2%	2%	79%	11%	4%	1%												
A1			1%	4%	80%	8%	3%	1%				1%							
A2				1%	5%	74%	8%	4%	1%										
A3					2%	8%	74%	7%	4%	2%				1%					
Baa1						3%	7%	73%	9%	4%	1%	1%	1%	1%					
Baa2						1%	3%	8%	72%	8%	3%	1%	1%	1%	1%				
Baa3							1%	3%	9%	70%	7%	4%	3%	1%	1%				
Ba1							1%	1%	4%	9%	69%	5%	5%	3%	2%		1%	1%	
Ba2									1%	3%	5%	74%	7%	6%	2%		1%		
Ba3										1%	2%	3%	76%	8%	6%		2%		
B1												3%	4%	76%	9%	1%	4%	1%	
B2												1%	2%	4%	75%	2%	13%	3%	
B3										1%	1%		2%	5%	3%	66%	12%	7%	1%
Caa													1%	2%	2%	2%	83%	7%	1%
Ca													2%	2%	1%	1%	1%	89%	1%
C											1%	1%						3%	94%

tended to be more severe for lower-quality issuers. In the Aaa through Aa3 categories, most downgrades involved adjustments of one refined rating category. For issuers rated Baa1 through B3, downgrades of more than two numerical notches were the norm.

INCIDENCE OF SHORT-TERM RATING CHANGES BY RATING CATEGORY

Table 8.10 shows the stability of issuer's short-term ratings by category. As with long-term ratings, short-term ratings are more volatile in the lower rating categories. Upgrades among Prime-3 and Not Prime issuers were not always caused by fundamental changes in the company's credit quality but by the issuer's purchase of letters of credit from highly rated financial institutions to increase the credit standing and the marketability of their commercial paper.

Table 8.10—Yearly Short-Term Rating Changes, by Rating Category 1973–1990

	Downgrades	*Upgrades*	*Total Changed*	*Downgrades Per Upgrade*
Prime-1	3.6%	NA	3.6%	NA
Prime-2	5.4%	6.3%	11.8%	0.85
Prime-3	11.6%	20.0%	31.6%	0.57
Not Prime	NA	12.8%	12.8%	NA

Table 8.11 demonstrates the magnitude of rating changes. The vertical axis shows ratings at the beginning of the year; the horizontal, at the end of the year. For example, an average of 96% of all Prime-1 commercial paper programs remained at Prime-1 in the course of a year; with 3% downgraded to Prime-2, 0.14% to Prime-3, and 0.20% to Not Prime. As with long-term ratings, lower-rated short-term issuers are more susceptible to rating changes of more than one category.

Table 8.11—Magnitude of Short-Term Rating Changes 1973–1990

	Prime-1	*Prime-2*	*Prime-3*	*Not Prime*
Prime-1	96%	3%	0.14%	0.20%
Prime-2	6%	88%	4%	1.08%
Prime-3	2%	18%	68%	12%
Not Prime	2%	3%	7%	87%

MAGNITUDE OF LONG-TERM RATING CHANGES BY LETTER-RATING CATEGORY OVER LONGER TIME PERIODS

To calculate long-term rating changes over intervals of more than one year, each issuer's senior unsecured rating at any given year was compared with its rating two or more years later. Table 8.12 shows, for example, the results when initial ratings every year from 1970 through 1988 were compared with ratings two years later from 1972 through 1990. The vertical axis shows the initial rating while the horizontal axis shows the rating dispersion after two years. In similar manner, Tables 8.13 and 8.14 show rating changes over five- and 10-year periods. Table 8.13 uses ratings at the beginning of five-year intervals from 1970 through 1985. Table 8.14 uses ratings at the beginning of 10-year intervals from 1970 through 1980.

As the length of time grows, the percentage of companies maintaining their original rating decreases, and the dispersion around the original rating increases. During the study period, 1% of Aaa-rated companies were downgraded into the speculative grades within five years. Over 10 years, the figure rises to 2%. For Baa-rated companies, 9% were downgraded into the speculative grades within two years, 15% within five years, and 17% within 10 years.

In contrast, 10% of Ba-rated companies were upgraded into the investment grades within two years, 19% within five years, and 29% within 10 years. For B-rated companies, the percentage upgraded into the investment grades was 1% in two years, 6% in five years, and 14% in 10 years. The percentage of companies losing their long-term rating altogether increases down the rating category, partly attributable to companies that lost their ratings following bankruptcy or other reorganization.

Table 8.12—Magnitude of Long-Term Rating Changes, by Letter-Rating Category Over Two Years 1970–1990

Rating at Beginning of Year	Rating at End of Two Years									
	Aaa	*Aa*	*A*	*Baa*	*Ba*	*B*	*Caa*	*Ca*	*C*	*NR*
Aaa	85%	9%	2%							4%
Aa	3%	80%	11%	1%	1%					5%
A		5%	81%	8%	1%					4%
Baa			9%	74%	7%	2%				7%
Ba			1%	9%	68%	10%	2%	1%		9%
B				1%	7%	70%	7%	3%		12%
Caa			1%	2%	2%	8%	63%	4%	2%	18%
Ca						3%	1%	77%	2%	17%
C								2%	92%	7%

Table 8.13—Magnitude of Long-Term Rating Changes, by Letter-Rating Category Over Five Years 1970–1990

Rating at Beginning of Year	Rating at End of Five Years									
	Aaa	*Aa*	*A*	*Baa*	*Ba*	*B*	*Caa*	*Ca*	*C*	*NR*
Aaa	65%	20%	5%	1%	1%					8%
Aa	7%	54%	22%	5%	2%	1%				9%
A	1%	10%	60%	14%	3%	1%				10%
Baa		2%	18%	51%	11%	3%	1%			14%
Ba			4%	15%	42%	15%	3%	1%		19%
B	1%		1%	4%	11%	42%	8%	5%	1%	28%
Caa		1%	1%	5%	4%	14%	35%	6%	1%	32%
Ca				1%		5%	1%	54%	4%	36%
C					1%	1%		4%	83%	11%

Table 8.14—Magnitude of Long-Term Rating Changes, by Letter-Rating Category Over Ten Years 1970–1990

	Rating at End of Ten Years									
Rating at Beginning of Year	*Aaa*	*Aa*	*A*	*Baa*	*Ba*	*B*	*Caa*	*Ca*	*C*	*NR*
Aaa	47%	30%	9%	3%	1%	1%				8%
Aa	10%	37%	30%	9%	3%	1%		1%		10%
A	1%	15%	43%	18%	6%	3%	1%			14%
Baa		4%	25%	31%	11%	4%	2%			22%
Ba		1%	11%	17%	22%	14%	3%	1%		30%
B	3%		5%	6%	11%	20%	3%	6%	1%	46%
Caa		3%	2%	9%	6%	11%	16%	9%	1%	44%
Ca				3%		4%	1%	31%	5%	56%
C								6%	82%	11%

Chapter Nine

A Study of Corporate Bond Defaults

by Gail I. Hessol
Managing Director
Standard & Poor's

Standard & Poor's new study of corporate bond defaults for the past decade confirms the high risk of speculative grade bonds, those rated BB+ and lower, commonly called junk bonds. The 10-year cumulative default rate for B-rated bonds was about 20%, compared to less than 8% for any of the investment grade categories. This was the first S&P study to calculate default rates for each of the rating categories. The findings support S&P's rating criteria by demonstrating the strong correlation between ratings and default risk. The findings also are similar to those reported in other published corporate bond default studies.

Default rates were calculated for all nonconvertible corporate bonds rated by S&P and outstanding during the 1981–1990 period. The data were broken into two groups: a static pool and the annual cohorts.

From Standard & Poor's *Credit Review*, September 16, 1991, by Gail I. Hessol. Reprinted with permission of Standard & Poor's Corporation.

STATIC POOL ANALYSIS

The static pool includes 1,271 issuers of rated bonds as of January 1, 1981. Their ratings were then tracked through December 31, 1990, measuring each year's defaults, annually and on a cumulative basis, as a percent of the rated issuers as of January 1, 1981. For example, there were 450 A-rated issuers at the beginning of 1981; Table 9.1 shows that none of them defaulted in the first year, two issuers or 0.44% in the second year, none in the third year, etc.; for the entire 10-year period the cumulative A default rate was 2.00% (see Figure 9.1).

Table 9.1—January 1, 1981 Static Pool Cumulative Default Rates (%)

	1981	*1982*	*1983*	*1984*	*1985*	*1986*	*1987*	*1988*	*1989*	*1990*
AAA	0.00	0.00	0.00	0.00	0.00	0.00	0.00	1.39	1.39	2.78
AA	0.00	0.00	0.00	0.00	0.00	0.00	0.54	1.62	1.62	1.62
A	0.00	0.44	0.44	0.44	0.44	1.11	1.33	1.56	1.56	2.00
BBB	0.00	1.18	1.18	1.57	1.96	2.35	2.75	3.92	3.92	5.10
BB	0.00	2.35	4.23	7.04	9.86	14.55	15.02	16.34	17.84	18.78
B	2.41	4.82	9.64	13.25	13.25	16.87	18.07	18.07	18.07	19.28
CCC	0.00	7.69	7.69	7.69	7.69	15.38	15.38	15.38	15.38	23.08

Default rates are attributed to the issuer's rating on January 1, 1981, even though that issuer's rating was typically lowered to speculative grade categories years before default. Default rates are based on the number of issuers, rather than the amount of debt, and the actual or implied senior debt rating is used for each issuer. This is the best way to measure the frequency, or probability, of default for each rating category. On January 1, 1981, the static pool contained a mix of relatively new bonds and those that had been seasoned. It resembles a bond portfolio that might have been purchased in 1981 and held for 10 years. Reflecting financing practices of that time, there were relatively few junk bonds (83 Bs and only 13 CCCs), and many of these were fallen angels, companies downgraded to speculative from investment grade. The key advantage of studying the static pool is that a full 10 years of data are available for each issuer. The 1985–1989 surge in junk bond financings, however, is not captured in the static pool.

Figure 9.1—Static Pool Cumulative Default Rates

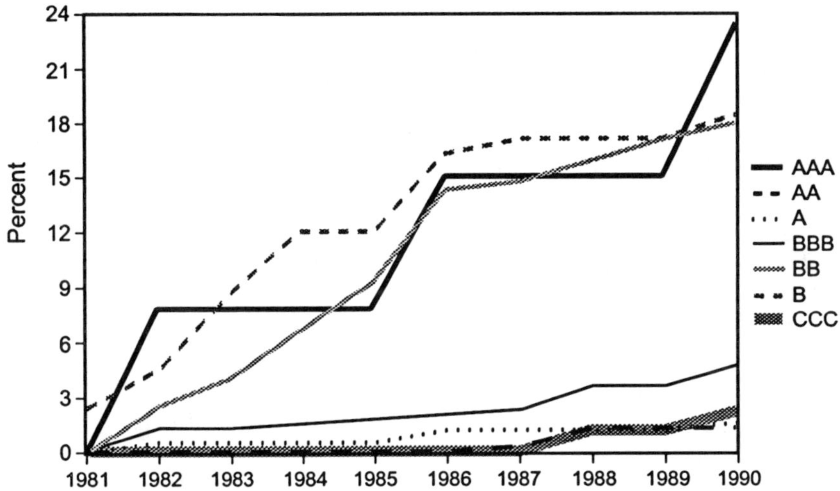

COHORT ANALYSIS

The annual cohorts were studied to gauge default rates for junk bonds sold in more recent years, even though default data are only available for shorter time periods. Each cohort consists of each year's first-time issuers for each rating category. For example, the first cohort consists of brand new issuers of AAA rated debt in 1981, and the last cohort represents new issuers of CCC debt in 1990. Table 9.2 shows the number of issuers in each cohort and in the static pool.

For each rating category, the defaulting members of the 10 yearly cohorts were summed and divided by all members of these cohorts to produce a first-year default rate; a second-year default rate was similarly calculated using the nine available cohorts; and so on. These data appear in Table 9.3. Then the annual rates were aggregated to produce cumulative rates as shown in Table 9.4. The five-year cumulative default rate for the B category cohorts was 14.70%, based on bonds issued 1981–1985. Simply put, a new bond rated B had a 14.70% chance of defaulting within five years and 18.01% within 10 years. (A more complete discussion of the methodology appears on page 158.)

Table 9.2—Number of Issuers per Cohort

	AAA	*AA*	*A*	*BBB*	*BB*	*B*	*CCC*
Cohort 81	2	6	18	14	12	20	1
Cohort 82	10	20	33	15	17	16	1
Cohort 83	8	30	53	45	30	39	3
Cohort 84	1	14	26	19	28	34	3
Cohort 85	12	33	65	35	49	72	2
Cohort 86	10	16	36	24	50	135	10
Cohort 87	4	21	26	31	59	119	11
Cohort 88	9	10	25	26	35	64	4
Cohort 89	3	18	20	12	37	69	5
Cohort 90	1	13	10	10	11	14	3
Total cohorts	60	181	312	231	328	582	43
Static pool	72	185	450	255	213	83	13

Table 9.3—1981–1990 Cohorts' Annual Default Rates (%)

	Years									
	1st	*2nd*	*3rd*	*4th*	*5th*	*6th*	*7th*	*8th*	*9th*	*10th*
AAA	0.00	0.00	0.00	0.00	0.00	0.00	0.00	0.00	0.00	0.00
AA	0.00	0.00	0.00	0.00	0.00	0.97	1.43	0.00	0.00	0.00
A	0.00	0.33	0.00	0.00	0.00	0.00	0.00	0.00	1.96	5.56
BBB	0.43	0.00	0.48	0.00	0.66	0.00	1.08	0.00	0.00	0.00
BB	0.61	1.26	2.50	4.08	4.30	2.94	1.15	0.00	0.00	0.00
B	1.03	2.82	4.01	3.68	3.16	3.31	0.00	0.00	0.00	0.00
CCC	9.30	7.50	8.57	6.45	0.00	0.00	0.00	0.00	0.00	N.M.

N.M. = Not meaningful

Table 9.4—1981–1990 Cohorts' Cumulative Default Rates

	Years									
	1	*2*	*3*	*4*	*5*	*6*	*7*	*8*	*9*	*10*
AAA	0.00	0.00	0.00	0.00	0.00	0.00	0.00	0.00	0.00	0.00
AA	0.00	0.00	0.00	0.00	0.00	0.97	2.40	2.40	2.40	2.40
A	0.00	0.33	0.33	0.33	0.33	0.33	0.33	0.33	2.29	7.85
BBB	0.43	0.43	0.91	0.91	1.57	1.57	2.64	2.64	2.64	2.64
BB	0.61	1.87	4.37	8.45	12.75	15.70	16.84	16.84	16.84	16.84
B	1.03	3.85	7.86	11.53	14.70	18.01	18.01	18.01	18.01	18.01
CCC	9.30	16.80	25.37	31.83	31.83	31.83	31.83	31.83	31.83	N.M.

N.M. = Not meaningful

The study does not measure defaults in each year as a percent of bonds outstanding in that year; thus, there is no default rate for 1990 or any other specific year. This method was not used because it tends to understate default rates in periods of heavy issuance, such as the 1985–1989 junk bond craze, and overstate default rates during periods of retrenchment (such as in 1990). Nevertheless, it is interesting to look at year-by-year defaults shown in Table 9.5 and Figure 9.2.

KEY FINDINGS

Lower-rated bonds have a higher risk of default. This is seen clearly in both the static pool and annual cohort studies. The distinction between investment grade and speculative grade is especially sharp. In the static pool, the 10-year cumulative default rate was 5.10% for BBB bonds and 18.78% for BB bonds (see Table 9.1).

Lower-rated bonds also default more quickly. Looking at the year-by-year defaults for the cohorts (see Table 9.3), none of the original AAA bonds defaulted in the study period, the first default on bonds originally rated AA was in year six, the first A default was in year two, and the next A default was in year nine. By comparison, the B and CCC categories began defaulting right away. The first-year default rate for the CCC cohorts was 9.30%, higher than the cumulative default rate for A bonds over 10 years.

Table 9.5—Rated Corporate Debt Defaulting

	Amount of Rated Debt (mil $)	*No. of Issuers*
1990	15,094	62
1989	5,965	33
1988	4,439	32
1987	9,056*	20
1986	3,263**	32
1985	1,176	17
1984	648	13
1983	417	11
1982	843+	14
1981	60	2
1980	220	4
1979	27	2
1978	76	4
1977	84	2

* Includes Texaco Inc.: $7,200 million
** Includes LTV Corp.: $1,650 million
+ Includes Manville Corp.: $175 million
Note: In this table, each issuer is counted separately, even if its debt is guaranteed by another issuer.

Figure 9.2—Amount of Rated Debt Defaulting

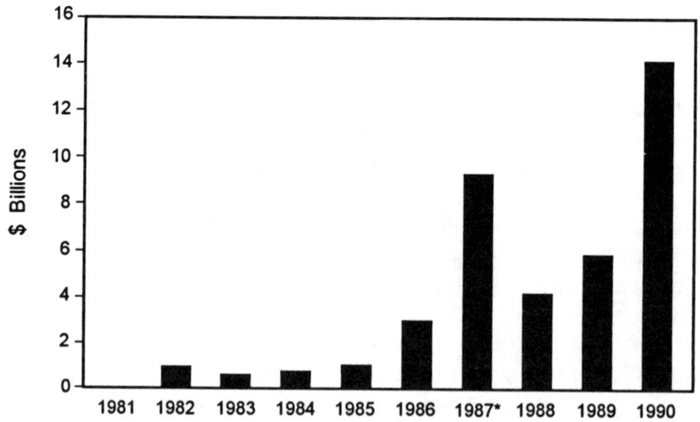

* Includes $7.2 billion for Texaco Inc.

The high default rates for junk bonds were correctly predicted by S&P. Nearly 1,000 newly rated companies in the 1981–1990 cohorts issued junk bonds. The low ratings initially assigned to these bonds typically reflected the companies' imprudent borrowing to finance acquisitions or stock buybacks. Sometimes business fundamentals were also weak. By the fifth year, 14.70% of those rated B had defaulted, confirming the low credit assessment.

A total of 218 companies defaulted. Table 9.6 shows their rating histories. Six months prior to default, 123 firms or 56.4% were rated B and 25.7% carried the lowest possible CCC (actual or implied) senior debt rating. A small number of issuers had relatively high ratings shortly before default. For example, Manville Corp. and its Johns-Manville Corp. subsidiary were rated A six months before their surprise bankruptcy filings. Their ratings were lowered to BBB about two months before the default. Only two defaulting companies, Federated Department Stores Inc. and IFRB Corp., had been rated as high as AAA (Texaco Inc. also had been rated AAA, but prior to 1981). Five and seven years, respectively, elapsed between the AAA rating and default.

Table 9.6—Ratings of Defaulting Companies

Years Prior to Default	*AAA*	*AA*	*A*	*BBB*	*BB*	*B*	*CCC*	*Total*
1/2	0	0	3	6	30	123	56	218
1	0	0	5	7	49	120	31	212
2	0	4	4	12	48	95	11	174
3	0	6	6	9	49	65	6	141
4	0	6	5	10	39	35	4	99
5	0	7	7	6	27	16	3	66
6	1	6	6	5	12	6	2	38
7	2	2	4	8	9	3	2	30
8	1	0	4	4	5	3	2	19
10	1	0	3	4	3	2	2	15

Note: Rating histories in the study do not go back prior to January 1981. Defaulting companies from the static pool may have had higher or lower ratings at an earlier date.

The study results were in line with S&P's expectations. The expectations of high junk bond default rates are embedded in S&P's criteria, developed in 1988, for rating collateralized bond obligations (CBOs). A

CBO is a security backed by a pool of high-yield bonds. The credit rating of the security is enhanced by excess collateral to cover losses due to bond defaults.

Speculative grade bonds defaulted at fairly high rates during the first five years, but then defaults tapered off. One might conclude that a risky speculative grade issuer surviving the first few years has either improved in credit quality or developed the skills to cope with high risk. (In some cases, the default has merely been postponed by payment-in-kind (PIK) or other deferred interest features.) The apparent seasoning pattern may be influenced by broad economic trends in the 1980s. By contrast, the risk of default for investment grade issuers grew in the later years. A company rated A, if it ultimately defaults, generally experiences several years of deterioration before defaulting. An upcoming S&P study will track these and other rating trends.

Default data for the CCC category should be regarded cautiously because of the small sample size. The static pool contained only 13 CCC issuers. In the cohort study only 10 CCC issuers had more than four years of history, which suggests that default rates for the fifth year and beyond may not be representative. A few issuers with CC or C senior ratings are counted in the CCC category for this study.

CAUSES OF DEFAULTS

A decade-long debt binge, often to finance acquisitions and massive stock buybacks, gave rise to skyrocketing bond defaults. New and more risky companies entered the public bond market in the 1980s, and existing borrowers assumed greater financial risk. Fears of being taken over compelled management to pile on the debt. Failed leveraged buyouts, some quite large, appear in recent years' default statistics.

Little-noticed 1979 changes in the U.S. Bankruptcy Code have lessened the sting of bankruptcy for borrowers. Criteria for seeking bankruptcy protection also were liberalized. A default on junior bonds and even senior bank loans has become a negotiating tactic to extract concessions from creditors. And a bankruptcy filing can also ease the burdens of onerous leases, product liability claims, and pensions. Seemingly solvent companies, such as Manville Corp., filed bankruptcy petitions to reduce these non-debt obligations.

The demise of the few highly rated companies that ultimately defaulted can be partly attributed to the 1980s takeover frenzy and costly legal problems. The static pool contains 707 issuers rated A or better, of which only 14 defaulted during the 10-year period. Five companies out of 553 rated A or better in the cohorts defaulted by the end of 1990.

Federated Department Stores and Allied Stores were acquired in 1988 and 1986, respectively, by Campeau Corp., a highly leveraged enterprise which soon filed for bankruptcy. Federated and Allied's ratings had been reduced sharply when they were acquired. Two other companies in the group, Interco Inc. and Southland Corp., thwarted takeovers by undertaking leveraged buyouts. The resulting debt burden was more than they could handle.

The unusual bankruptcies of Manville Corp., Texaco Inc., and their affiliates accounted for another four defaults in this group. Jim Walters Corp.'s default resulted from the unfortunate combination of a leveraged buyout and asbestos product liability.

Four firms (IFRB Corp., First RepublicBank Corp., M Corp. Inc., and Texas American Bancshares Inc.) were banks based in Texas which, subsequent to 1981, lent aggressively to real estate and energy projects resulting in the banks' collapse when energy prices plunged in the mid-1980s. Two oil field service companies (Smith International Inc. and Gearhart Industries Inc.) were enmeshed in the same energy boom and bust.

Only four of these 19 defaults were the result of "normal" business deterioration. While lawsuits and hostile takeovers are real risks in corporate America, anticipating these problems years before they surface is virtually impossible.

Chastened lenders under the more watchful eye of regulators have become more conservative in the past two years. High-yield bond investors are demanding less risky financial structures or, for those participating in the distressed debt sector, very high returns to compensate for the genuine risk. The economy appears to be turning around. Interest rates have fallen, and the spread between high-yield and high-grade bonds has narrowed. These developments would suggest fewer future defaults.

Although the overall slide in U.S. corporate credit quality may have halted—and there are signs that equity is back in fashion—defaults are expected to remain high through 1992. Many firms now rated B or lower are still limping under crushing debt burdens. As PIK bonds become cash-pay, struggling firms will be forced to restructure their obligations. Refinancing of maturing loans, blithely promised by many junk bond issuers in the 1980s, will only be available to companies that have bolstered their equity bases and exhibited cash flow growth. Others will "refinance" their debt via bankruptcy or an out-of-court debt rescheduling.

HOW THE STUDY WAS CONDUCTED

The study looked at the entire population of actual or implied public senior debt ratings for 3,008 companies issuing long-term debt in the United States. Foreign companies issuing debt in U.S. markets are included as are U.S guarantors of Eurobonds. Companies whose debts are guaranteed by another rated entity are excluded (the guarantor is included) as are structured financings, quasi-governmental corporations, and authorities. Issuers of exclusively convertible debt were excluded.

Defining a Default

Default is defined as failure to make an interest or principal payment on the due date or the filing of a company into bankruptcy. Distressed exchange offers were not treated as defaults in the primary study, although default rates using this broader definition of default are available on request. An issuer is deemed in default when it defaults on any rated issue, even if other issues are not in default.

Companies whose debt became not rated (N.R.) or was lowered to D and later rated AAA through C were treated as follows:

- Any N.R. companies whose rated debt matured, was called or tendered and which subsequently issued newly rated debt was treated as a new company in the year of the new debt issuance. This was done because the ratings prior to the N.R. only apply to debt which was completely extinguished. Companies whose ratings were withdrawn (N.R.) were tracked to determine whether there was a subsequent default.
- Companies which were rated D whose ratings were raised were treated in one of two ways. Where a company defaults on debt only to gain financial and/or covenant concessions from the bondholders, the company's rating incorporated this information, and the company's rating history was continued through the upgrade. All other defaulting companies were split into two, with a second rating history created after the default. Such a company was split because the pre-default ratings predicted the possibility of the original default and were not applicable to the situation post-default. The latter group typically includes companies that defaulted, sought bankruptcy protection, and issued new debt after emerging from bankruptcy.

Methodology

The study was completed using both static pool and cohort analyses. A static pool composed of all companies rated as of January 1, 1981 was constructed. This static pool is the equivalent of a seasoned bond portfolio purchased on January 1, 1981. This methodology is most useful for a buy-and-hold investor who uses point-in-time information and needs to determine if the pricing of an issue will cover the default risk.

Annual cohorts were composed of companies initially rated subsequent to January 1, 1981 and were constructed by rating category in the year in which the company was originally rated. In this methodology, each company is counted only once. The default experience of the static pool and the cohorts were measured through year-end 1990. Of the total population of 3,008 companies, the rating breakdown is as follows:

Companies by Rating Category

	All Companies	*Static 1981*	*Cohorts*
AAA	132	72	60
AA	366	185	181
A	762	450	312
BBB	486	255	231
BB	541	213	328
B	665	83	582
CCC or lower	56	13	43
	3,008	1,271	1,737

Thus, 1,746, or 58%, of the companies in the study were investment grade and 1,262, or 42%, were speculative grade. Within static 1981, 962 or 76% of the 1,271 companies in that pool were investment grade, and 309 or 24% were speculative grade. In the cohorts, 784, or 45%, of the 1,737 companies were investment grade, and 953 or 55% were speculative grade.

Method of Calculation

The default experience of the static pool and cohorts was measured by time elapsed as though each of the company's securities was rated on a single day. Default rates are computed by summing defaults across all companies in a rating category to compute annual default numbers and dividing by the total number of companies which originally had that rating and were outstanding for that length of time. Cumulative rates are computed by cumulating the annual rates.

Chapter Ten

Breakeven Default Rates

by Peter Niculescu
Vice President
Goldman Sachs

INTRODUCTION

Corporate bond yields incorporate a spread over Treasury yields to compensate investors for the risk of default. The breakeven default rate is the percentage of the value of outstanding corporate debt that must default to equalize the total return of a corporate bond portfolio and that of a Treasury portfolio. Because defaulting corporate debt typically pays substantially more than zero to the bondholder, the breakeven default rate will be higher than the breakeven loss rate.

Breakeven default rates provide a framework that helps investors with long time horizons translate their economic views into a decision about when to buy corporate debt. Because breakeven default rates are a fundamental, long-term measure of value, they are less relevant for investors with short-term horizons. In addition, while they provide a link between fundamentals and total returns for corporate debt, breakevens ignore the relative values of competing risky assets. This means they can tell you, in light of your economic forecast, whether you should buy corporates or Treasuries over the long term. But they cannot tell you whether to buy corporates as opposed to mortgages or asset-backed securities.

The market should be expecting defaults that actually are lower than breakeven default rates, because the bondholder usually gets an incremental return over the breakeven rate as extra compensation for bearing risk. Over the long term, the corporate bond buyer can usually expect to receive returns above Treasuries. The implication: Any investor whose economic scenario projects a default rate above the breakeven default rate would definitely not want to buy a corporate bond. If the investor expects a default rate below the breakeven default rate, he might or might not want to buy a corporate bond, depending on his time horizon and the price of alternative risky investments.

THE MECHANICS OF BREAKEVEN DEFAULT RATES

Let us simplify the problem by assuming the investor's time horizon is the maturity of the corporate bond. For example, consider an investor with a four-year horizon investing in a four-year maturity noncallable corporate note that yields 100 bp more than Treasuries. Suppose, for the moment, that the corporate note can default at maturity only. Finally, assume the Treasury is yielding 8.5%. If the corporate issue doesn't default, then its compounded four-year total return is 44.95%, while the Treasury would provide a 39.51% compounded total return. The difference between the two total returns (5.44%) is the incremental cumulative return of the corporate over the four-year horizon.

The incremental total return provides a performance cushion for the corporate issue. If the investor bought a diversified portfolio of corporates, all with spreads of 100 bp and maturities of four years, the portfolio could sustain a total loss on as much as 5.44% of the holdings at maturity and still offer a breakeven total return relative to Treasuries. If the loss happened before maturity, though (see below), the breakeven loss would be smaller. On the other hand, if the defaulting bonds paid more than zero, the breakeven default rate could be even higher. For example, if defaulting bonds paid 35% of par in bankruptcy (a conservative assumption, historically), 8.37% of the portfolio could default and the portfolio would still break even relative to Treasuries.

Early Default

What if the default happened earlier than Year 4? The earlier the default, the worse the total return experience for the bondholder. Investment grade debt typically needs several years before fundamentals deteriorate enough to cause a default. Let us be conservative, however, and assume the average default occurs shortly after issuance: If the default happens in Year 2 instead of Year 4, the breakeven default rate declines from 8.37% to 7%. Hence, over a four-year horizon, if you think that less than 7% of your holdings will default, you would do better owning corporates than Treasuries.[1] Table 10.1 gives a breakeven default matrix, assuming that the bondholder gets a 35% payoff in default and that the default happens within three years.

Table 10.1—Breakeven Default Probabilities (%)

Term (yrs.)	*Spreads Over Benchmark Treasuries (bp)* 50	75	100	125	150	200	300	500	650
1	0.8	1.2	1.5	1.9	2.3	3.1	4.6	7.6	9.8
2	1.6	2.4	3.2	4.0	4.8	6.4	9.6	15.9	20.5
3	2.5	3.8	5.0	6.3	7.5	10.0	14.9	24.8	32.2
4	3.5	5.2	7.0	8.7	10.4	13.9	20.8	34.5	44.7
5	4.5	6.8	9.1	11.3	13.6	18.1	27.1	45.0	58.4
6	5.7	8.5	11.3	14.2	17.0	22.6	33.9	56.4	73.2
7	6.6	9.9	13.2	16.4	19.7	26.2	39.0	64.3	82.9
8	7.5	11.3	15.0	18.7	22.3	29.6	44.0	71.8	92.1
9	8.5	12.6	16.8	20.9	25.0	33.0	48.8	79.1	NM
10	9.4	14.0	18.5	23.1	27.5	36.3	53.5	85.9	NM

Assumptions: Payoff in default = 35%.
Bonds default in three years or at one-half of term, whichever is sooner.
All Treasury yields are 8.50%.

Bankruptcy Value

Defaulting corporate bonds typically pay the bondholders more than zero. While bankruptcy value varies a lot across sector and structure, Altman's 1989 study of bankruptcies over the previous 20 years indicates that bondholders who own debt that was originally rated as investment grade got paid 40–80 cents on the par dollar of a bond. Hickman's 1958 study, which covered the period between 1912 and 1943, showed similar statistics. Debt originally issued as speculative grade paid an average of 35 cents on the dollar. The more leveraged

[1] For simplicity, I ignore the possibility that the absolute level of yields may influence corporate defaults. The evidence on this point is, in any case, quite mixed.

the company or the more junior the claim, the lower the payment. Table 10.2 shows the average price after default by original bond rating. In addition to these losses, bondholders typically lost one or more coupon payments.

Table 10.2—Payoff Percentages

	Altman: Original Issue Rating	*Hickman: Rating Five Years Before Default*
AAA	79	60
AA	79	52
A	46	42
BBB	45	34
BB	36	34
B	43	35
CCC	41	
C	10	
NR	31	48

It is possible that the situation today is more grave for many issuers than that shown in Table 10.2. For example, because of leverage and subordination, we expect that holders of bank debt, in the event of a bankruptcy, may receive only 15 to 20 cents on the dollar and that bondholders of some distressed corporations may in fact get close to zero. Southeast Banking Corp. debt, for example, is now trading at around 40 although the company is not in default. Many industrial corporations should do better, however, getting closer to 50 or 60 cents on the dollar. For comparison, Table 10.3 gives breakeven default probabilities if the payoff in default is only 15%.

HISTORICAL EVIDENCE

A 7% four-year default rate is a huge percentage in relation to historical default rates; the average four-year cumulative default rate over the last 20 years was 0.7% (Moody's, 1990). The average four-year cumulative default rate during the expansion of the 1920s was about 1%, not substantially different from recent historical experience. Over the four-year period from 1932 to 1935, about 6% of investment grade corpo-

Table 10.3—Breakeven Default Probabilities (%)

	Spreads Over Benchmark Treasuries (bp)								
Term (yrs.)	*50*	*75*	*100*	*125*	*150*	*200*	*300*	*500*	*650*
1	0.6	0.9	1.2	1.5	1.8	2.3	3.5	5.8	7.5
2	1.2	1.8	2.4	3.1	3.7	4.9	7.3	12.1	15.7
3	1.9	2.9	3.8	4.8	5.7	7.6	11.4	19.0	24.6
4	2.7	4.0	5.3	6.6	8.0	10.6	15.9	26.4	34.2
5	3.5	5.2	6.9	8.7	10.4	13.8	20.7	34.4	44.6
6	4.3	6.5	8.7	10.8	13.0	17.3	25.9	43.1	55.9
7	5.1	7.6	10.1	12.6	15.1	20.0	29.8	49.2	63.4
8	5.8	8.6	11.5	14.3	17.1	22.7	33.6	54.9	70.5
9	6.5	9.7	12.8	16.0	19.1	25.2	37.3	60.5	77.1
10	7.2	10.7	14.2	17.6	21.3	27.8	40.9	65.7	83.3

Assumptions: Payoff in default = 15%.
Bonds default in three years or at one-half of term, whichever is sooner.
All Treasury yields are 8.50%.

rate debt outstanding in 1932 defaulted. The rate then fell to 3% for the 1936–1939 period (Hickman, 1958).

While these rates are high, they are less than the breakeven default rates shown in Tables 10.2 and 10.3. And, although these numbers need more explanation, today's spreads suggest that a long-term investment in corporate bonds can survive a 1930s-style depression and still outperform Treasuries.

The most useful studies of historical defaults follow cohorts of bonds over long periods of time and find cumulative default rates for that cohort. This is because investment grade debt tends not to default quickly, but instead to be downgraded to speculative status some years prior to default. Hence, the proportion of debt rated investment grade that defaults *in any given year* is very small indeed, while the proportion of such debt that defaults *prior to maturity* may be much larger. The most useful studies also include both defaulting bonds and distressed exchanges.

The principal studies of defaults on investment grade debt are those of Moody's (1990), Altman (1989), Altman and Nammacher (1985), and Hickman (1958). In addition, the "Harvard Study" by

Asquith et al. (1989) deals exclusively with junk defaults. Because both the Moody's and Hickman studies use cohort data and include distressed exchanges, we will quote data from those studies.

The Moody's study, which covers 1970–1989, includes complete cohort data. Default rates shown in the Moody's study are relatively insensitive to the recessions of the 1970s and 1980s, perhaps because those experiences were relatively mild. Default rates for investment grade debt have increased gradually over the last 20 years. The increase may be associated with the general increase in measures of credit sensitivity, such as net interest expense as a percent of EBIT. Table 10.4 shows selected statistics on cumulative default rates.

In the 1920s, investment grade four-year cumulative default rates were generally a little under 1%, which is comparable with the experience of the 1970s and 1980s. Defaults had been higher at the outbreak of the First World War; the reason was a tremendous increase in demand for liquidity worldwide, which had led to extreme financial distress and had even resulted in the stock exchange closing for nearly five months.

As the economy passed from the expansion of the 1920s into the Great Depression of the 1930s, the four-year default rate on investment grade debt rose to 6% during 1932–1935 and ebbed to 3% for 1936–1939. Of the $17.7 billion of large-size investment grade debt outstanding in 1928, about 15% appears to have been downgraded to junk by 1932, while about 20% of the $17 billion outstanding in 1932 was downgraded to junk by 1936.

Speculative grade four-year default rates, which had been ticking along at about 20% in the expansion of the 1920s, rose to nearly 50% during the Depression years. That compares with an average four-year default rate of 11% in the last 20 years.

The Usefulness of Data From the 1920s and 1930s

Contrary to popular opinion, the similarities in the corporate bond market in the 1920s and in the 1990s are striking. The nonfinancial debt outstanding in the 1920s and 1930s was largely that of utilities, transportation companies (railroads), and industrial corporations. Corporate debt typically had long maturities and was callable at a premium. The market in the 1920s saw annual issuance (of nonfinancial debt) of up to $2 billion, which fell in the nadir of the Depression to less than $500 million. And the size of the investment grade nonfinancial corporate bond market peaked at about $17.7 billion in 1928. But GNP in 1928 was about $90 billion, in comparison to today's $5.7

Table 10.4—Four-Year Default Rates on Large Investment Grade Debt

Hickman (1912–1943)

	All	*AAA*	*AA*	*A*	*BBB*
1912–43:	3%				
1912–15:	5.9%	3.8%	2.7%	15.8%	13.1%
1916–19:	3.0	0	1.7	1.9	9.7
1920–23:	0.9	0	0	4	0
1924–27:	1.1	1.7	0	0	1.8
1928–31:	0.8	0	0.2	0.3	3.6
1932–35:	6.1	0.5	0.1	8.4	10.5
1936–39:	3.3	0	2.2	4.6	5.1
1940–43:	0.2	0	0	0	0.7
1920–27:		0.9	0	3.7	6.3
1928–39:		2.7	4.1	6.1	8.6
1932–39:		0.2	1.4	6.8	10.6
1920–39:		2.3	2.0	8.0	8.8

Moody's (1970–1989)

	All	*AAA*	*AA*	*A*	*BBB*
1970–89:	0.7				
1970–73:	0	0	0	1.2	
1974–77:		0	0	0	1.3
1978–81:		0	0	0	0
1982–85:		0	0	0.2	2.1
1986–89:		0	0.6	0.8	3.4
1970–79:		0	0	0.4	1.5
1980–89:		0.9	0.7	2.3	4.4

trillion. If the market were as large today, in proportion to GNP, as it was in 1928, its value would be $1,121 billion. In fact, the nonfinancial public investment grade corporate bond market today is only about $325 billion. Even if we exclude railroads (which had enormous capital requirements) from the 1928 numbers, the equivalent size today would be more than $500 billion.

Credit measures were very similar to today's. The times-interest-charges-earned ratio as reported by Hickman for the average investment grade nonfinancial corporation was better than 2 and it was better than 3 for the strongest corporations. In comparison, EBIT today is 2.3 times net interest expense for the average nonfinancial corporation (which is down from 3.7 times in 1980).

Four ratings agencies rated debt in the 1930s—Moody's, Fitch, Standard Statistics, and Poor's. The top four ratings of these agencies corresponded to investment grade debt. And market commentators then, as now, complained that the ratings agencies were too slow to lower ratings as the economic situation deteriorated.

The buyers then were similar to those today, although there appear to have been fewer pension funds in the market. The large, sophisticated, tax-exempt buyer dominated the corporate bond market; smaller investors bought tax-advantaged municipals or partially tax-exempt (PTE) Treasury issues. Investment grade corporate debt was bought largely by commercial banks, by savings banks (if it was on the legal or approved lists), and by insurance companies. Lower rated issues were deemed speculative and were not eligible for commercial bank or savings bank investment, nor could they be carried by insurance companies at amortized book value.

Spreads were not tremendously different in absolute magnitude either, although the absolute levels of yields were much lower. As a result, *percentage* spreads were huge by comparison with today's levels. Treasury bond yields, which were about 3.37% in 1928, fell to a low of 2.5% in 1936. Corporate AAA-to-BBB spreads fell to a low of 210 bp in 1928 and widened to 540 bp in 1932 before retreating to 230 bp in 1936.

PAYMENT FOR RISK: DEPRESSIONS AND DEVIATIONS

Table 10.5 shows the annualized total return increments over the past decade for investment grade corporates vs. governments (as measured by three major indexes)—both in basis points and as a percentage of the government returns. The data include the returns of bonds that were downgraded below investment grade during the month of the downgrade. Hence, the data reflect all price losses due to an increased default probability. Corporates outperformed governments by about 100 bp per year, on average, over much of the decade. Although corporates were beaten by governments in 1990 as recession fears intensified, their relatively strong performance during earlier years more than offsets the recent negative experience.

Table 10.5—Return Differences and Ratios: Corporates versus Governments*

Annualized differences in returns (bp)

	Years Ending September				
	1980–90	*1983–90*	*1985–90*	*1987–90*	*1990*
Merrill	108	110	93	83	-133
Salomon	120	128	106	113	-58
Shearson	134	115	97	94	-74
Average	121	118	99	97	-88

Annualized ratios of returns (%)

	Years Ending September				
	1980–90	*1983–90*	*1985–90*	*1987–90*	*1990*
Merrill	9%	10%	9%	8%	-19%
Salomon	10%	12%	11%	11%	-8%
Shearson	11%	10%	10%	9%	-11%
Average	10%	11%	10%	9%	-13%

* Treasuries and agencies.

Many would argue that corporate returns cannot remain above government returns for long without a violation of market efficiency. But corporate bonds do present more risk than government bonds, and some large portion of corporate default risk is systematic (nondiversifiable). Defaults by corporate bond issuers are strongly correlated with overall economic conditions, which implies they are examples of systematic risk. Accordingly, the investor should get paid wider spreads for bearing the risk and should benefit from better total return performance over the long run.

There is some evidence that long-term returns of the major risky asset classes in the bond market are related to their standard deviations of returns. This is consistent with the basic idea in financial theory that higher expected returns are required to compensate investors for bearing systematic risk. Figure 10.1 plots actual returns against standard deviations for returns over the last 10 years for governments, corporates, and mortgage securities.

Figure 10.1—10-Year Returns (percent)

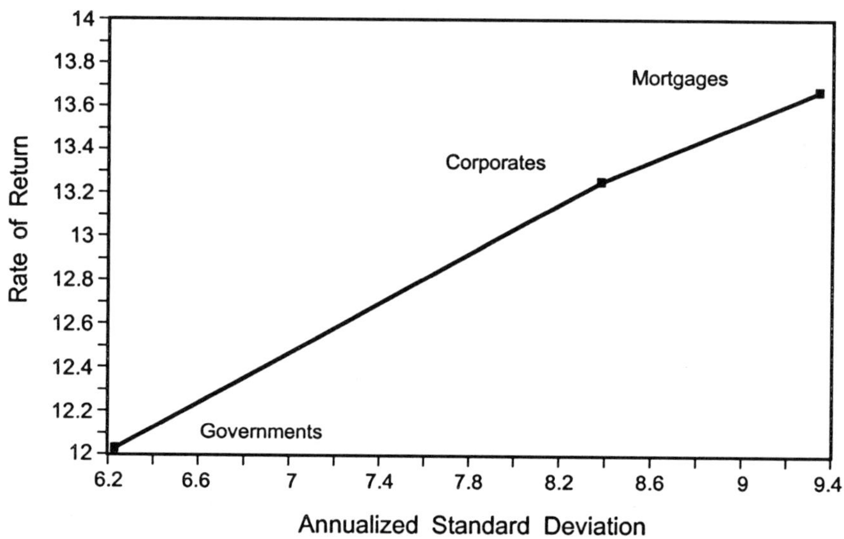

Source: Averages of major market indexes–Shearson Lehman, Salomon Brothers, and Merrill Lynch–as reported by Ryan Labs, Inc.

Perhaps, then, the good performance of corporates over the last 20 years is payment for recession risk and is an aberration precisely because we have avoided a major depression. Doomsayers can point to the worsening state of corporate debt statistics as evidence of increased sensitivity to an economic downturn (see Figure 10.2). The argument is that the investor is being paid for taking on the risk of a 1930s-style

Figure 10.2—Measures of Credit Quality

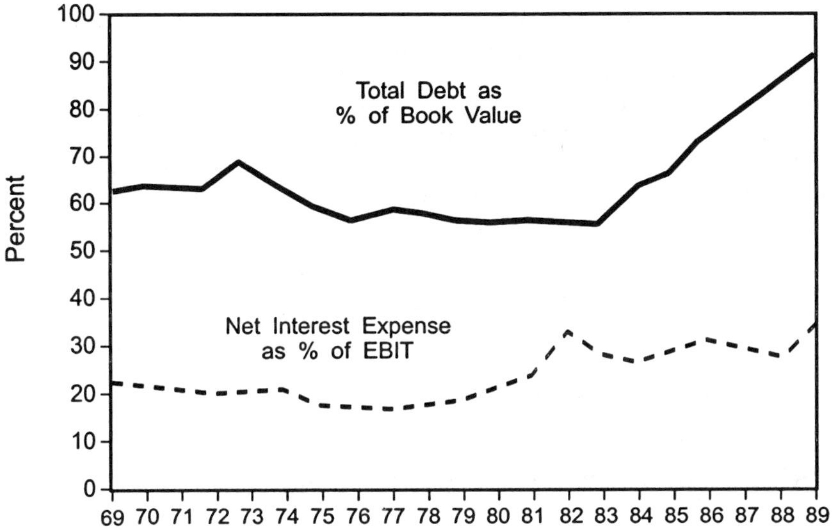

depression, which so far we have luckily avoided over the past half-century.

Nonetheless, it should at least be possible for corporates to underperform Treasuries in the long run. Surely we can conceive of a depression bad enough for corporates to underperform Treasuries. For if that were not the case, then the long-term investor would always buy corporates knowing that they would outperform Treasuries in good times and bad. But in fact, the worst corporate default experience from the 1930s shows corporate default rates to have been low enough that a long-term corporate investment would still have outperformed Treasuries. Perhaps the market is today discounting rational fears of some far worse default experience than any we have yet experienced. Or perhaps corporates really are likely to outperform Treasuries over the long run.

If corporates are likely to outperform Treasuries even in a "great" depression, do we have a violation of market efficiency? Efficient pricing is restored through actions by arbitragers, but in this case it may take far too long for any arbitrage to work out, and the arbitrage is in any case uncertain because of the possibility of short-term underperformance. To benefit from the expected long-run outperformance of corporates, the investor must buy and hold a portfolio of corporates for many years. But the situation is even worse than that: the long run may be extremely long. That is, the arbitrager may have to wait it out through several extended periods in case the one he experiences is an outlier—that once-in-a-lifetime depression scenario when his portfolio only matches (or even underperforms) Treasuries. In the meantime, before the long run finally runs its course, he may be faced with any number of shorter periods in which corporate spreads widen dramatically and his bonds underperform strongly. In human terms, he may expose himself to short-term career risk.

We can therefore conclude that it is conceivable, in principle, that corporates may outperform Treasuries in virtually any long-run scenario because their potential short-term underperformance prevents arbitragers from correcting the situation. The long-term investor who is willing to take short-term risk may, in fact, be very likely to outperform the Treasury investor significantly.

RECESSION RISK VERSUS EVENT RISK

So far, we have argued that corporate debt provides incremental returns over Treasuries as compensation for systematic risk. Corporates may indeed pay so generously for risk that a long-term investment in this market will outperform Treasuries in virtually any economic scenario. But corporate debt also faces unsystematic risk. A good example of that is event risk. And investors are in principle not paid incremental returns for bearing unsystematic risk.

When RJR/Nabisco debt sold off in the wake of the 1987 acquisition, many industrial companies' bonds also sold off in sympathy. The incremental yield spread on bonds that were considered possible event risk candidates compensated investors for the possible loss. Yield spreads for event risk names widened by about 30 bp, which was approximately equal to the average loss from an "event" (about 10 points of price) multiplied by the incidence of event risk over the previous year (about 3%).

The market compensated investors by paying an incremental return equal to the average loss multiplied by the probability of the loss. Because the risk was unsystematic, investors did not get additional compensation for bearing the risk. But investors who bear systematic risk will get an additional payment: their incremental returns will be higher than the probabilistic loss in compensation for bearing the risk.

BACK TO THE FUTURE: SPREADS, DEFAULTS, AND TOTAL RETURNS

Money Center Banks: An Example

If the investor can buy four-year bank at a 15% yield and a 650 bp spread to Treasuries, the debt would pay the bondholder a cumulative 78% return while four-year Treasury debt would pay a cumulative 40% return. If the bank debt defaults in two years and pays just 15 cents on the dollar, the breakeven default probability is 34%. Suppose four banks can be found whose debt trades at 15% in four years. A 34% default probability implies that there is an 81% chance that at least one of the four will default in two years. This can be seen from the mathematical formula: $1 - (1-0.34)^4 = 0.81$. In this example, 0.34 is the probability that any one bank will default, and 1–0.34 is therefore the probability that any one bank will not default. $(1-0.34)^4$ is the probability that all four banks will not default, and $1 - (1-0.34)^4 = 0.81$ is the probability that at least one of the four banks will default.

Industrial Corporate Debt: An Example

The trading of A-rated corporate debt at about 150 bp over Treasuries implies a cumulative 13.6% breakeven default rate in five years, assuming a 35% payoff. To put this in perspective, choose any industry at random and ask what that means for major changes in the structure of the industry. Paper companies issue frequently in the bond market because of high capital expenditures. Fourteen major investment grade domestic issuers exist, many of whom are rated single-A. Following the method outlined above, a 13.6% breakeven default rate implies there is an 87% chance that at least one of them will default within the next five years. Yet, no major paper company has defaulted within our memory.

IMPLICATIONS

An investor who believes that these breakeven default probabilities sound like an accurate description of his expectations will probably not want to buy corporate debt. He will be compensated for his probabilistic losses, but he will not be paid for taking risk. Such an investor would probably prefer to buy other risky assets that are expected to pay higher risk-adjusted returns.

But if the investor thinks the likelihood of experiencing these levels of defaults, which are worse than those seen in the 1930s, is extremely low, then he believes corporate debt is likely to outperform Treasuries over the long run. A long-term investor who thinks the breakeven default probabilities are high will want to consider corporate debt in place of Treasuries.

Chapter Eleven

An Approach to Forecasting Default Rates

by Jerome S. Fons
Moody's Investors Service

Using the results of Moody's historical default studies, changes in the rating composition of issuers, and a proxy for the state of the economy, this report presents a simple technique for forecasting default rates. Based on information available as of January 1, 1991, we forecast a 1991 full-year speculative grade default rate of 11.5%, up from 8.8% in 1990.

The sharp rise in the default rates of corporate bonds over the past two years has focused public attention on difficulties within this sector. Yet the focus on corporate bond defaults sharply illustrates the brevity of financial memory; interest in the subject of defaults predates nearly all modern financial theories. Compiled from the results of several different studies, Figure 11.1 below shows that the current wave of defaults is not the first such episode in history. It is safe to assume that it will not be the last.

The default rates presented in Figure 11.1 are for all corporate debt, not just speculative grade debt. Each study cited above used a different methodology. Default rates found in the Hickman and Atkinson studies were constructed as the par amount of rated corporate debt defaulting in each year divided by all rated corporate debt outstanding that year. On the other hand, Moody's historical default rates are defined as the number of defaulted *issuers* divided by the population of all rated

Figure 11.1—Historical Default Rates 1900–1990

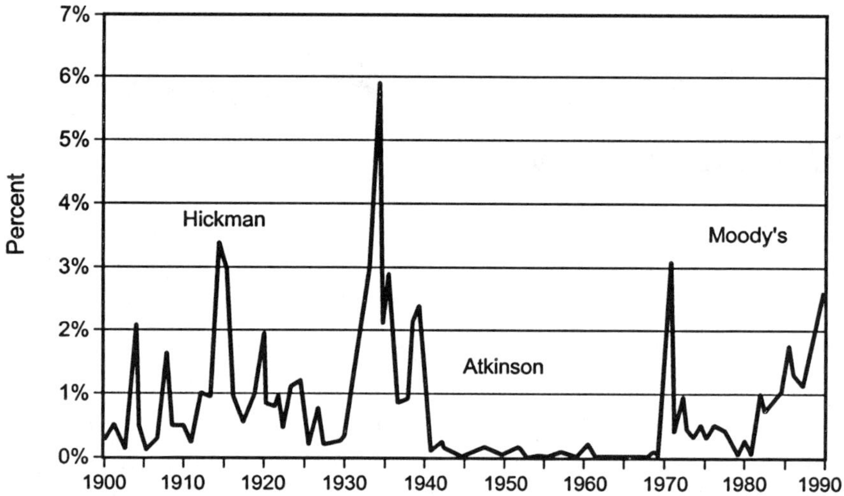

issuers. Nevertheless, we believe the studies to be roughly illustrative of the overall trend in default rates.

The spike in 1970 is due to the default of Penn Central Railroad and its 30 affiliates. The prior peak occurred in 1933 at the bottom of the Great Depression. The recent climb began in 1982, reflecting the 1981–1982 recession, and accelerated sharply in 1990. Moody's projects an even higher default rate for 1991.

Below we show that default rates are correlated with the business cycle and with changes in credit quality as measured by ratings. Thus, accurate forecasts of corporate default rates are possible and could help investment portfolio managers predict returns and plan reserve needs. We suggest in this report one possible means of forecasting default rates based on our historical research in this area.

Moody's default studies—which span default experience over several economic cycles—have shown that Moody's ratings are consistent proxies of default risk. Accordingly, as investor tolerance for credit risk grew in the mid- to late-1980s, Moody's ratings clearly reflected the market shift (see Figure 11.2). Prior to 1984, speculative grade debt (i.e., debt rated below the Baa category) constituted a small fraction of

Figure 11.2—New Issue Volume by Rating 1984–1990

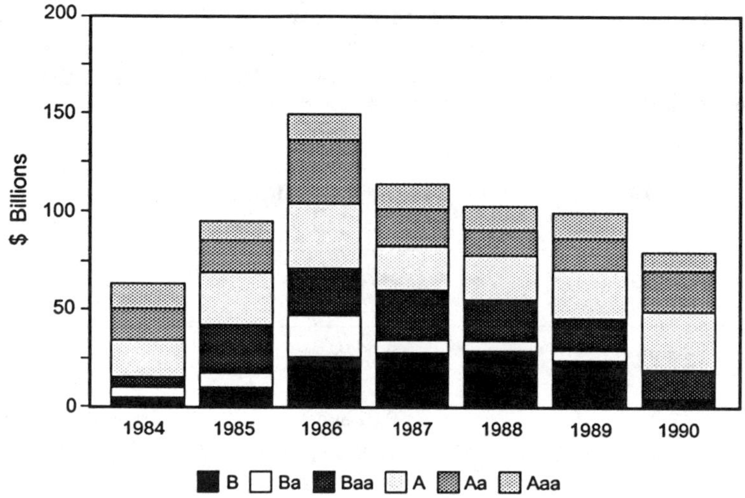

corporate new issue volume. In the 1986–1989 period, issuance of this debt class soared. But by 1991, there was very little new issuance of speculative grade debt. Over this entire period Moody's continued to focus on fundamental credit factors, despite pressures for an easing of standards.

Reflecting shifts in investor risk appetites, changes in the relative flow of new issuance of speculative grade debt can alter the overall rating composition of the corporate bond universe. This composition is also affected by changes in the ratings of companies with outstanding debt. For instance, in the first half of 1991, Moody's downgraded into or within the speculative grade population 156 issuers. Conversely, Moody's upgraded out of or within the speculative grade population only 39 companies.

Given a stable risk/rating relationship, changes in aggregate default experience could be explained in part by changes in the rating composition of the bond market. For instance, relatively high issuance of low-rated bonds or large-scale downgrading of issuers shifts the distribution of rated debt downwards. Relative increases in the number of issuers with low ratings, all else equal, raises the expected default rate for corporate bonds.

Using broad rating categories and historical default experience for each rating category, Moody's has computed expected one-year default rates.[1] Table 11.1 lists one year annual speculative grade and investment grade default rates by rating category for the period 1970 through 1990.[2] As expected, the likelihood of default rises as rating category declines. Furthermore, lower rating categories experience greater volatility in the expected default rate.

Table 11.1—One Year Default Rates by Rating

Moody's Rating	*Average Default Rate*	*Standard Deviation*
Aaa	0.00%	0.00%
Aa	0.01%	0.06%
A	0.01%	0.05%
Baa	0.18%	0.29%
Ba	1.61%	1.78%
B	6.56%	4.97%
Caa	22.91%	19.03%

To calculate an "expected" default rate for speculative grade issuers based on rating composition alone, we multiplied the number of issuers within a given rating category at the beginning of each year by the corresponding average default rate for that category. The products are then summed across all rating categories to give the expected number of rated defaults for that year. This figure is then divided by the num-

1 Broad rating categories, e.g., Aaa, Aa, A, etc., are used for the 1970–1990 study period because ratings with numerical modifiers have only been in use since 1982.

2 The default rates presented are simple averages of one-year default rates by rating category for each year between 1970 and 1990. Each one-year default rate is calculated as the percentage of issuers in each given rating category at the beginning of the year that defaulted by year end. We prefer this measure to one compiled by weighting each year according to the number of issuers outstanding, as the latter would be heavily influenced by recent default rates. Moody's also prefers the issuer as the unit of study as opposed to the par amount of debt affected as a better measure of the likelihood of any one issuer defaulting. In any event, our research has shown that issuer default rates are a good approximation to dollar default rates.

Figure 11.3—Actual Versus Expected Default Rates Based on Historical Experience

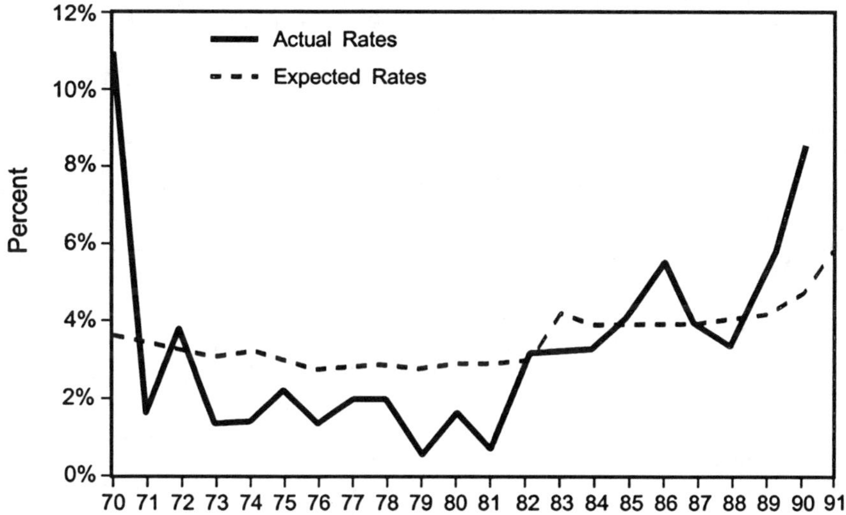

ber of issuers rated speculative grade at the beginning of the year to arrive at the year's expected default rate.[3]

Market practice is to state default rates as a fraction of the speculative grade universe. The rationale for excluding investment grade issuers is that the majority of defaulting issuers hold speculative grade ratings well before the default event. For instance, the year 1990 saw no defaults by issuers rated investment grade at the start of the year. Moreover, the "expected" number of defaults by all investment grade issuers during 1991, based on January ratings, is less than one.

The solid line in Figure 11.3 is a time series representation of speculative grade default rates for the period 1970 through 1990. The dashed line is the corresponding expected default rate as defined above. As expected, this series is much more stable than the actual

---

[3] For example, the rating distribution by issuers at the start of 1991 (Aaa: 289; Aa: 1165; A: 672; Baa: 402, Ba: 331; B: 397; Caa: 49) multiplied by the corresponding default rate gives the expected number of defaults as: $(289 \times 0) + (1165 \times 0.0001) + (672 \times 0.0001) + (402 \times 0.0018) + (331 \times 0.0161) + (397 \times 0.0656) + (49 \times 0.2291) = 43.5$. Dividing this by the 777 speculative grade issuers gives an expected default rate of 5.6%.

default rate, reflecting only slight shifts in the rating profile of corporate issuers. Nevertheless, it is clear that, vis-a-vis "expected" default rates, actual default rates were relatively low from 1971 through 1984 (excluding 1972 and 1982) and during 1988. A major shift in rating profiles, associated with a change in Moody's rating system to add numerical modifiers to the letter categories, occurred between 1982 and 1983, at which point the number of issuers rated single-B more than doubled relative to the prior year, reflecting Moody's new capability to make finer distinctions between senior and junior debt. This event led to an upward shift in "expected" default rates. A second shift, tied to more fundamental factors, appeared to begin in 1990 and continued through 1991. The expected default series forms the permanent, or trend, component of our default rate forecast.

It is well known that the state of the economy also plays a strong role in determining actual default rates. A healthy economy can often carry a financially weak firm that otherwise would face default. Consequently, fewer defaults are likely in a growing economy. This inverse effect can be seen when residual default rates—actual default rates minus "expected" default rates—are plotted with the percent change in real gross national product (GNP) (see Figure 11.4). This effect appears quite strong in recent years, though it held as far back as 1970. Sharp

Figure 11.4—Unexplained Default Rates and GNP Growth

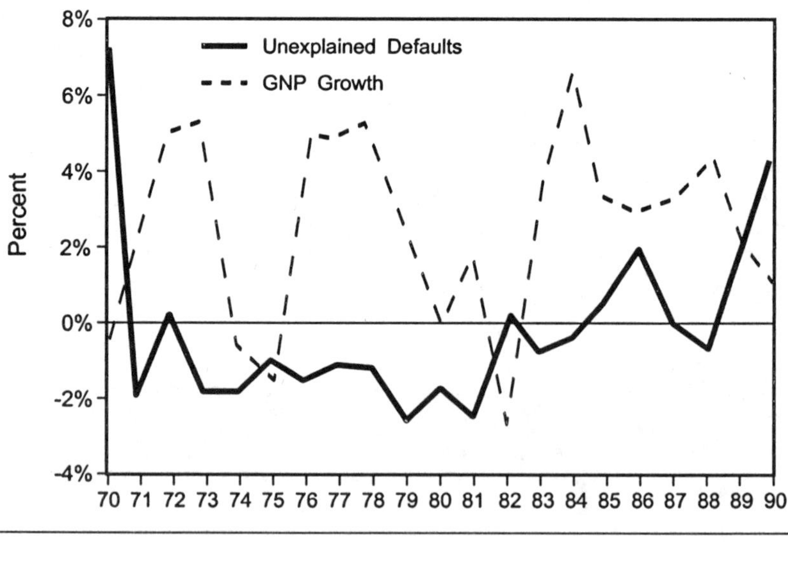

drops in the growth rate of GNP, generally associated with recessions, were often accompanied by high residual default rates.

Five of the 21 years shown in Figure 11.4 were affected by recession: 1970, 1974 and 1975, 1980, and 1982. Although the period 1982 to 1990 was characterized as an expansion by the National Bureau of Economic Research, broad sectors and regions of the economy suffered declines. These disturbances contributed to the minor dips in the growth rate of real GNP.

Our proposed forecasting model thus incorporates both changing rating profiles and the state of the overall economy. In the Appendix to this chapter we describe the model, noting that it derives from a posited simple statistical relationship between actual default rates, "expected" default rates, and real GNP growth. The model is estimated and it is used to predict default rates by incorporating GNP growth projections.

Based on data available as of January 1, 1991, the speculative grade default rate for Moody's-rated corporate issuers is expected to hit 11.5% for all of 1991 (see Figure 11.5). If realized, this would be the highest level of defaults experienced in over 50 years. How likely is this? Many developments over the past two years support such a fore-

Figure 11.5—Actual versus Predicted Default Rates (Based on Rating Profile and GNP Growth)

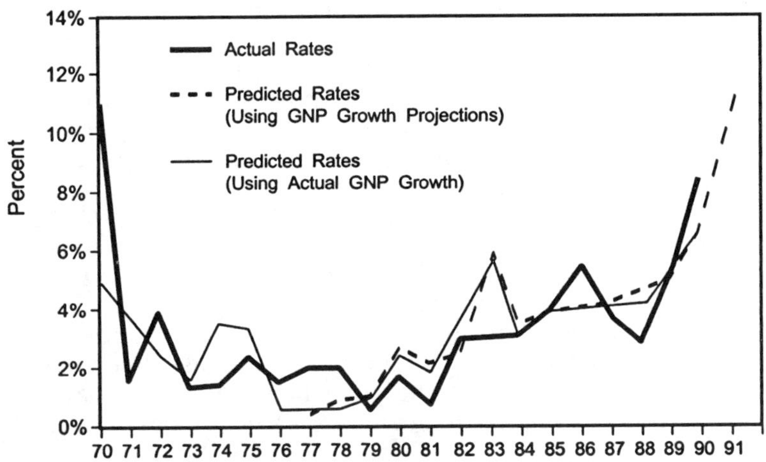

cast. First, a sizable number of firms still face enormous pressures to ease debt burdens accumulated in the late 1980s. Many firms still face difficulty finding sources for capital as existing high coupon debt comes due or proves insupportable by operating cash flows.

The collapse in late 1989 of the speculative grade bond market, in part precipitated by a tougher regulatory environment, continues to disrupt refinancing plans. Capital constrained banks and insurance companies have not led the charge to refinance highly leveraged deals nor have they provided financing to spark the asset sales required to support many struggling firms. The weak economy, though now showing signs of rebounding somewhat, has contributed to large operating losses at many firms. History has shown that default rates typically continue to rise for several months following a trough in the economic cycle. The rapid pace of rating downgrades witnessed in 1990 has begun to slow in 1991 but still remains high by historical standards. Thus the list of issuers with the lowest ratings continues to grow.

Finally, through the end of June 1991, 55 rated issuers have already defaulted in 1991, well ahead of last year's pace when 36 rated issuers defaulted by mid-year. During all of 1990, 78 rated issuers defaulted, giving a speculative grade default rate of 8.8%. To reach the 11.5% full year default rate figure for 1991, another 39 rated issuers would default in the second half of the year.

The 11.5% forecast for 1991 is based on the issuer rating profile and projections of GNP growth made at the start of the year. Median GNP growth forecasts as of January of each year from 1977 through 1991 were obtained from Blue Chip Economic Indicators of Sedona, Arizona, which polls a large group of forecasters. Figure 11.5 plots forecasted default rates derived both from actual reported GNP growth rates and from beginning-of-year GNP projections. Note that predicted default rates derived from GNP growth projections closely track predicted values using actual GNP growth.

The contribution of the GNP growth rate to our model is critical. Ratings alone are not meant to predict year to year fluctuations in default rates. The time horizon of a bond rating is long term. Its one-year default likelihood is an average of high default rates in economically troubled years and lower default rates in more settled times. It would be confusing and unproductive for a rating agency to undertake wholesale upgradings or downgradings of the corporate bond market to reflect the fluctuations in short-term default likelihood over the course of economic cycles. On the other hand, the bond market's assessment of the default risk inherent in a particular bond rating cate-

Figure 11.6 Model versus Market Forecast

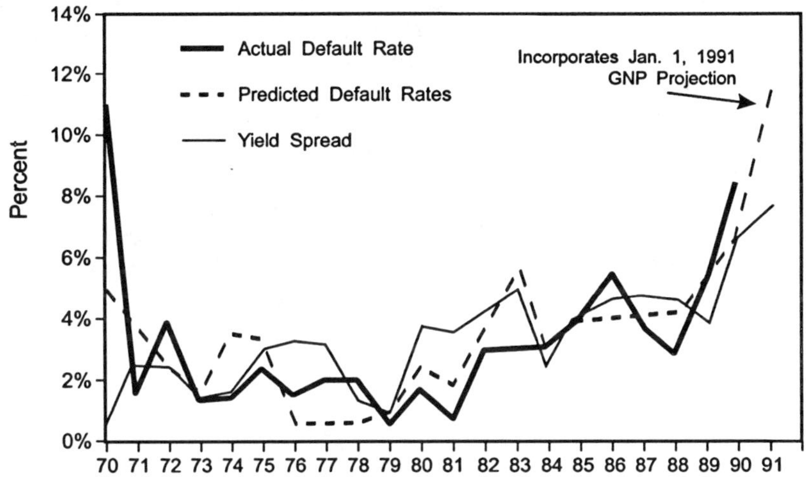

gory shifts with the phase of the business cycle. This is manifested in shifts in the yield spread of bonds within different rating categories.

Yield spreads are thus a natural source for default forecasts. Figure 11.6 compares actual default rates, the models' forecasts, and the beginning of the year spread between the yields of a low grade corporate bond index and treasury securities.[4] Because participants in the long-term corporate bond market must factor future default prospects into their decisions and yields are calculated from expected future cash flows, this spread incorporates a rough estimate of the bond market's forecast of default rates. Though not an exact market forecast of expected default rates, the yield spread does a surprisingly good job of predicting them.

Many of the "turning points" in actual default rates are captured by yield spreads, though the reaction to some appears to be lagging. In recent years, the yield spread may be reflecting factors other than default risk, such as liquidity problems or even supply factors. For in-

[4] From 1970 through 1979, we used the spread between the average yields on Moody's Baa industrial bonds and the 10-year constant maturity treasury yield. From 1980 through 1991, we used the spread between Salomon Brothers' long-term high yield bond index and the same treasury yield.

stance, despite our model's forecast of significantly higher default rates in 1991, yield spreads rose only slightly between the beginning of 1990 and the beginning of 1991.

In summary, we have introduced a forecasting method that explicitly incorporates two major factors explaining default rates for the past 21 years: changes in the risk distribution of corporate issuers as well as the impact of the economy. We developed a model based on these factors to forecast 1991 defaults, based on information available as of January 1, 1991. Had such a method been used historically, relatively accurate forecasts could have been achieved.

As is the case with all statistical tools, a forecast from this (or any other) model should be tempered with an understanding of other omitted factors that also contribute to the underlying process.

APPENDIX

The link between actual default rates, average "expected" default rates (as described above) and the percent change in GNP can be established using regression techniques. Although the sample is limited to just 21 cases (annual defaults from 1970 through 1990), a regression is still useful. The relationship between these variables is given by:

$$\text{Actual D.R.} = -0.079 + (3.462 \times \text{Expected D.R.}) - (0.274 \times \text{Percent Change in GNP})$$
$$\qquad\qquad\qquad\qquad (4.66) \qquad\qquad\qquad\qquad (-1.65)$$

The t-statistics are in parentheses, the Durbin Watson statistic is 1.71, and the adjusted $R^2 = 51.83\%$. That is, we can explain over 50% of the variation in actual default rates by our expected default rate measure and year-over-year GNP growth.

The above equation provides a simple and easy to use forecasting format. For forecasting purposes, the expected default rate figure is generally available at the beginning of the year in question. The final GNP growth estimate, however, is not usually known until well into the following year. On the other hand, median forecasts of GNP growth are widely disseminated by such services as Blue Chip Economic Indicators of Sedona, Arizona, who have tracked consensus forecasts since mid-1976.[5]

The "expected" default rate for 1991 (based on the rating profile) was 5.6%. Blue Chip Indicators reported at the start of 1991 a year-over-year GNP forecast of –0.1%. Thus, using the equation above, speculative grade default rates are forecast to reach 11.51% during 1991, up from 8.8% in 1990.

Changes in the input parameters due to, say, revised forecasts, can make a difference in the model's forecasts. For instance, at mid-year, the economists polled by Blue Chip Indicators had revised their GNP forecasts down from –0.1% to –0.2%. Incorporating this change slightly raises the 1991 default forecast to 11.54%.

---

[5] The 1970–1990 average default rates by rating category—used in the calculation of "expected" default rates—would, of course, not be available for much of the sample period. However, Moody's default studies show these rates to be fairly stable over time. Theoretically, a usable estimate could easily have been calculated early on and updated annually.

This paper evolved out of discussions with Irwin Vanderhoof and Martin S. Fridson.

SECTION THREE:

OPPORTUNITIES AND PITFALLS IN DISTRESSED SECURITIES

Chapter Twelve

Separating the Jewels from the Junk*

by Neil D. Dabney
and
Darryl L. Schall
Dabney/Resnick and Wagner, Inc.

> Speculative excess, referred to concisely as a mania, and revulsion from such excess in the form of a crisis, crash or panic can be shown to be, if not inevitable, at least historically common.
>
> —*Charles P. Kindelberger, Manias, Panics and Crashes*

Many leveraged buyouts, recapitalizations, mergers, and acquisitions executed in the late 1980s appear, with the help of hindsight, to have been speculative folly. In their time, these transactions appeared attractively priced and were based upon seemingly solid fundamentals: good management; steady earnings track records; recession-resistant busi-

*The authors are members of Dabney/Resnick and Wagner, Inc., a Los Angeles-based broker-dealer specializing in providing research and investment advice on debt securities of financially distressed companies. Mr. Dabney is a co-founder and senior portfolio manager. Mr. Schall is a senior member of the research department. The authors gratefully acknowledge their colleagues, David M. Millison, Joseph W. Phillips and Dana D. Messina, who contributed to this chapter.

nesses; commanding market shares; and significant barriers to entry. During this period, the U.S. economy was experiencing its longest run of growth and prosperity in the post-World War II era. Increased interest in the market for high-yield securities pushed underwritings to over $200 billion during the 1980s. To many market participants, it seemed as though the appetite for high-yield securities had no limits. However, by the end of the decade a "mania" had taken hold.

With increasing frequency, businesses which had displayed strong earnings momentum throughout the expansion incurred heavy debt loads at their cyclical peaks. Financial projections were based upon sustaining annual sales and earnings growth rates of 15% to 20%, which for many companies proved too aggressive to achieve. The success of many transactions relied on subsequent asset sales at record multiples. Accelerated debt amortization schedules left little room for error. Capital structures, which included pay-in-kind or discount/zero coupon bonds, were created to allow companies to defer current cash interest payments, so that they could "grow" into their debt burdens. Unfortunately for some companies, these securities turned out to be time bombs when envisioned growth did not materialize.

The high-yield market crashed in 1990, closing the doors to easy credit. In December 1989, the high-yield index traded at 625 basis points over treasuries. Within one year that spread had widened to over 1,325 basis points. What was thought of as a rational, functioning market for high-yield securities evaporated. Drexel Burnham Lambert Inc., the principal high-yield market maker, filed for Chapter 11 protection. Mounting negative economic pressures caused a cash flow squeeze among weaker, more leveraged borrowers. Bank and insurance companies tightened their lending standards. An ensuing credit crunch caused liquidity to dissipate. Motivated by political scapegoating, government regulators promulgated new rules that exacerbated the recessionary drift. The once buoyant high-yield market succumbed to gravity. Selling induced more selling. The market's deterioration was due as much to a supply/demand imbalance as it was to a decline in credit quality.

If one could step out of this quagmire and take an impartial view, what could be learned? Did value just vanish? Was the high-yield market based solely on hype and accounting puffery, or did the pendulum swing too far? Could solid keystones of earnings and asset quality be found, given sufficient examination and analysis?

In markets driven by panic, there are techniques and methods by which one can ascertain relative value and make calculated judgments that are conservative relative to apparent risk. What follows is a brief explanation of our methodology, introducing concepts of enterprise value, valuation of debt at "market" value versus face value, and calculation of asset and interest coverage ratios. We incorporate these analytic techniques into recent case study illustrations. After gaining a basic understanding of valuation techniques, we then discuss how the restructuring process impacts upon investing in distressed companies. We conclude by describing strategy considerations in purchasing and selling securities.

BASIC VALUATION METHODS

Many times an investment opportunity is brought to our attention in the following manner: "The bonds are trading at 10 cents on the dollar, how much lower can they get?" Our reflexive response is, "They can be worthless!" A severe discount might signal an investment opportunity, but without an understanding of intrinsic value, one merely would be gambling. The first step in our investment analysis is to measure the market value of debt against the underlying value of assets. The next procedure is to assess how the restructuring process may affect the estimated asset values.

In distressed situations, investment decisions based upon face value of debt can be likened to valuing assets based upon book value. Both may have had significance in the past, but today's market prices for assets and liabilities provide a better proxy for current and future value. By gauging the market value of debt against the market value of assets, one can measure downside risk. In other words, an investor can determine the extent to which the principal value of an investment is covered by company assets. In our first example, we analyze JPS Textile Group, Inc.

JPS Textile Group, Inc. ("JPS"), an industrial textile manufacturer, was an LBO organized in 1988 by Odyssey Partners, a New York investment firm. JPS acquired the assets of five operating divisions of J.P. Stevens & Co. at a cost of $563 million, a multiple of 8.0 times earnings before interest, taxes and depreciation ("EBITD"). The five divisions were organized into three segments by JPS: (1) Apparel Fabrics (31% of sales and 73% of operating profits)—a leading manufacturer of woven fabrics, yarn and elastic products; (2) Industrial Fabrics (46% of sales and 11% of operating profits)—a producer of automotive carpets and liner fabrics; and (3) Home Fashion Textiles (23% of sales and 16 of operating profits)—a manufacturer of home and commercial carpeting.

This transaction exhibited many of the symptoms of what has been described as speculative folly. The capital structure—composed of 88% debt, including $160 million of high-coupon 16.25% discount notes—was feasible only if the company could sustain then-current growth. Although the predecessor divisions indicated strong sales growth since 1986, gross margins had declined over 22.2% from 16.2% in 1986 to 12.6% in 1988. Many of the company's customers (automobile makers, construction companies and apparel manufacturers) were susceptible to a recession. JPS managed to make its cash interest payments and maintain certain capital expenditures. However, it faced an onerous increase in interest expense when the discount notes required cash coupon payments in 1992, as well as a tough bank debt amortization schedule. Anticipating a cash flow shortfall, the company tried in vain to execute an exchange offer for the various outstanding issues of debt. Eventually, JPS was able to negotiate a prepackaged bankruptcy restructuring with a bondholder steering committee. Table 12.1 shows the company's capital structure as of the restructuring's effective date, March 31, 1991.

As Table 12.1 denotes, the "market" value of JPS' total debt was significantly discounted from its face value ($273.5 million versus $524.3 million, or 52% of face value). Since one would invest based upon prevailing market prices, we calculated the company's ratio of asset value to the market value of debt (a "coverage ratio"). These calculations are shown in Table 12.2. Using readily available prices, one can simply calculate the market value of each class of debt. However, estimating asset value is a more involved and subjective process. Businesses such as these are not commodities. Additionally, there is not necessarily a liquid market for the assets, even if broken up and sold piecemeal.

As a start, to determine the company's value, we applied a valuation multiple to projected EBITD for the coming year. We estimated EBITD, incorporating the following variables:

- historic operating performance;
- comparable industrial performance;
- the company's current business plan;
- detailed analysis of financial statement accounts;
- conversations with company executives, industry experts, and market analysts;
- macroeconomic variables, such as employment data, interest rates, money supply, consumer savings and spending, etc.

Table 12.1—JPS Textiles, Inc.
Mark to Market Capitalization Table
($ millions)

	Face Value As of 3/31/91	*Market Price As of 3/31/91*	*Market Value As of 3/31/91*
Senior debt:			
Bank debt	$ 92.0	100.0%	$ 92.0
Senior notes	100.0	70.0	70.0
Total senior debt	$192.0		$162.0
Subordinated debt:			
16.25% Discount notes	133.7	28.0	37.4
15.25% Senior sub. notes	123.6	43.0	53.1
14.25% Sub. debentures	75.0	28.0	21.0
Total subordinated debt	322.2		111.5
Total debt	524.3		273.5
Senior preferred stock	37.7	10.0	3.8
Junior preferred stock	23.0	0.0	0.0
Common stock	5.0	0.0	0.0
Deficit	(150.8)		N/M
Total equity	$(122.8)		N/M
Total capitalization	$439.2		N/M

To arrive at a valuation multiple, our analysis included an examination of the following factors:

- estimating a range of comparable industry multiples;
- examining at what values companies with similar capital structures were trading in the public and, if available, private markets;
- valuing multiples of other timely restructuring transactions.

The resultant asset coverage ratio and valuation analysis is shown in Table 12.2.

**Table 12.2—JPS Textiles, Inc.
Coverage Ratios and Valuation Analysis
($ millions)**

Valuation as a whole:	*Low*	*Mid*	*High*
Projected 1991 EBITD	$75.0	$82.5	$87.0
Valuation multiple	4.0	4.5	5.0
Enterprise value ("EV")	$300.00	$371.3	$435.0
Asset coverage			
EV/Face value of debt	0.6x	0.7x	0.8x
EV/Market value of debt	1.1x	1.4x	1.6x
Strict priority[(1)]			
Bank Debt and Sr. variable notes	1.6x	1.9x	2.3x
Sr. subordinated notes[(2)]	1.1x	1.3x	1.5x
Sr. subordinated discount notes[(2)]	1.1x	1.3x	1.5x
Subordinated debentures	1.0x	1.2x	1.4x
Valuation segment by segment:			
Apparel Fabric			
Projected 1991 EBITD	$43.9	$48.3	$51.0
Valuation multiple	5.0	6.0	7.0
Segment EV	$219.5	$289.8	$357.0
Industrial Fabric			
Projected 1991 EBITD	29.3	32.2	33.9
Valuation multiple	3.0	3.5	4.0
Segment EV	$87.8	$112.6	$135.6
Home Fashion			
Projected 1991 EBITD	10.4	11.4	12.1
Valuation multiple	2.0	2.5	3.0
Segment EV	$20.8	$28.5	$36.3
Total segment EV	$328.1	$430.9	$528.9
Asset coverage			
Segment EV/Face value of debt	0.6x	0.8x	1.0x
Segment EV/Market value of debt	1.2x	1.6x	1.9x

(1) Recoveries for bank debt and senior variable notes are assumed at par; recoveries for all other securities based on market values.
(2) Senior subordinated notes and senior subordinated discount notes are pari passu.

In Table 12.2, we designated the "enterprise value" as the market value of company assets. We estimated the enterprise value on three levels—low, mid, and high—which incorporated three estimates of projected EBITD and three estimated valuation multiples. We performed this analysis on a global level (total company EBITD) and on a segment basis (applying different valuation multiples to the various business segments). We then measured the enterprise value against the debt claims to calculate an asset coverage ratio. Traditional financial analysis would suggest that we utilize the face value of debt as a proxy; however, in distressed situations, we believe that the market value of debt is a more relevant measure because: (1) investment decisions are based upon market value today, not par value; and (2) negotiations that resolve claims in distressed situations are based upon current recoveries, not historical values. The above analysis suggested that total enterprise value (range: $300 – $435 million) provided asset coverage of 1.1 times to 1.6 times, and using a segment valuation (range: $328 – $529 million) provided asset coverage of 1.2 times to 1.9 times. In other words, "market" debt claims appeared to be covered by asset values by 110% to 190%. Additionally, strict priority ratios (which allocate asset value to creditors in claim seniority) indicated that, even after assuming par recovery to bank debt and senior variable notes, each class of debt would be satisfied by company asset values. This analysis demonstrated that JPS' going concern value exceeded the market value of its debt claims. Barring a significant drop in operating cash flow, an investment in JPS debt appeared to have limited downside risk.

After determining asset coverage estimates, we proceed to layer on the following assumptions as applicable.

Capital Expenditures

What is the current quality of assets—do they need repairs, upgrades, replacements? If applicable, what then is a normalized level of capital expenditures to maintain the current asset base or to expand that base if management's business plan calls for such expansion? These estimates are made in context of historical experience and industry standards.

Working Capital Requirements

Does management's business plan require an increase or decrease of working capital accounts (inventory, accounts receivable, accounts payable, current maturities of debt, etc.)? This analysis is again performed in the context of industry standards, the current economic climate, and historical performance.

The impact of both our working capital and capital expenditure analyses will determine the level of cash flow available to amortize debt or to provide a cushion for future business needs. EBITD less capital expenditures and working capital requirements is defined as "free cash flow."

Demands of Parties in Interest

Different claimants to the company's assets have different agendas each with their own impact upon the restructuring process. Senior secured claimants (i.e., bank debt) might place certain demands upon the company that significantly impact its earnings capacity. For instance, they may insist that certain businesses be sold to pay down debt, or that cash generated from operations be applied exclusively to amortization, letters of credit, or capital improvements.

Economic Cycles

JPS' operations are cyclical. To understand recovery value, one must estimate whether the business is in its peak, mid, or trough phase. It is necessary to perform several variations of sensitivity analysis to test assumptions against varying degrees of risk.

Our preliminary analysis allowed us to conclude that based on a restructured balance sheet, JPS would have sufficient latitude to weather a protracted downturn and provide bondholders with significant risk-adjusted returns. Before an investment decision was made, we needed to assess the possibility of a successful restructuring and its impact on recovery values. Therefore, before completing the JPS case study, we incorporate a discussion of the financial restructuring process.

THE RESTRUCTURING PROCESS

We extend our analysis to focus on the *process* of restructuring the company's finances. Emphasis is added to the word process because a restructuring, in or out of court, is an extended negotiation with multiple parties, each with varied interests and motivations. Understanding the legal, accounting, and economic characteristics of a financial restructuring is critical to gauging recovery values and the timing of payoffs. A seemingly simple negotiation can deteriorate into a long, drawn-out battle, reducing value for all parties. One must learn as much as possible about the economic motivations and legal leverage that each party brings to the negotiating table.

Secured Lenders

Secured lenders (usually banks, credit corporations and insurance companies) focus much of their attention on maintaining their legal claim to collateral and on insuring that the value of this collateral does not diminish. Since they hold a collateral claim on the company's assets, they usually have a large degree of economic and legal leverage. In analyzing a credit with significant secured claims, it is important to determine that the secured lenders are comfortable with their collateral position and will work with the company to help satisfy parties with subordinate claims. We have seen many situations in which a rapid and significant reduction in asset value has caused secured lenders to exercise their foreclosure rights. This often results in chaos and, subsequently, reduces recovery values for other claimants. In the Eastern Airlines Chapter 11 proceedings, secured creditors eventually prevailed in bankruptcy court. The company was liquidated over the protestations of management and subordinated creditors as business operations consistently consumed cash and the market value of assets (principally jet aircraft, spare parts, and landing rights and gates at various airports) deteriorated. Eastern's unsecured creditors were virtually wiped out.

In order to consider investing in subordinated securities, our analysis allows for secured lenders' claims to be satisfied in full or bear the least degree of discount in either principal value or interest rate. We measure the relationship between the value of underlying collateral and the secured lender's claim using a strict priority analysis, where we allocate asset value to creditors in order of their seniority in the capital structure. This is important in determining recovery values as well as in measuring additional claims secured lenders can assert (specifically post-petition interest claims in Chapter 11 cases). We examine the extent to which security interests have been granted, and whether or not these interests have been properly perfected. If there is asset value in excess of secured claims, or if security agreements have not been properly maintained, then there may be additional value available to subordinated claimants. An exchange offer made by Journal Company, Inc. ("JCI") (formerly Ingersoll Newspapers) in mid-1991 allowed holders of senior subordinated and subordinated debt to exchange their securities for new senior secured debt guaranteed by and secured with pledges of the common stock of the operating subsidiaries of JCI. Investors choosing to participate in this offer essentially leap-frogged claims senior to them and, thus, improved their standing in JCI's capital structure. Had security interests been granted previously, this inventive exchange offer could not have been executed.

Additionally, there may be instances where secured lenders have overreached to protect their interests and, therefore, have helped to contribute to the company's financial distress. Issues of equitable subordination (a legal doctrine which allows for the subordination of claims of senior creditors because their adverse actions injured junior creditors) and fraudulent conveyance (a legal doctrine that requires the unwinding of a transaction found to have been constructively fraudulent) are being raised more frequently in examining unraveled LBOs. Interjecting these issues may improve the value of a subordinated claim. In the case of Interco, a manufacturer of furniture and footwear currently in Chapter 11 reorganization, the holders of Medium-Term Notes ("MTNs"), a senior unsecured claim, apparently have a good chance of full recovery by pressing fraudulent conveyance actions against the secured bank group. On face, the MTNs are pari passu with the bank claims and, thus, should be entitled to share equally with bank group recoveries. However, the MTN holders allege that the bank group helped structure the LBO transaction to their advantage and to the detriment of the MTNs. According to a court-appointed examiner, the MTN holders apparently have a strong argument. By using this legal leverage, these holders may gain a superior recovery vis-a-vis the secured bank group.

Subordinated Lenders

Most high-yield securities issued in the 1980s were unsecured and subordinated. Institutional holders, particularly insurance companies and mutual funds, are motivated by different accounting and economic conventions which shape their attitudes toward a restructuring. For instance, insurance companies historically do not mark their holdings to market and are resistant to reductions in their claims' principal value which would, in turn, penalize their capital position. Insurance companies often posture for outcomes that maintain relatively high face amounts, while accepting lower coupon rates.

In contrast, mutual funds, which do mark their holdings to market, are more flexible in accepting haircuts in par value. They tend to focus more on economic rather than accounting-driven outcomes. Additionally, tensions arise between original issue holders and holders who purchased at a discount. Discount purchasers achieve their return objectives at lower thresholds and, thus, tend to be more flexible in negotiations.

In the mid-1980s, there were hundreds of financial restructurings (e.g., exchange offers), in which bondholders would exchange one package of securities for another package. The exchange offer typically would contain a combination of the following: reduced coupon; reduced principal; enhanced or reduced security; changes in amortization schedules; company equity; and cutbacks in covenant protection. In many cases, interest rates were reduced and amortization schedules extended to assist the distressed investor, while principal values remained at or near par, thus obviating the dilemmas of marking to market. With the severe downturn in economic conditions and changes in state and federal regulations, original institutional holders have become more aggressive, and they tend not to accept exchange offers that are not heavily negotiated.

In today's financial markets, subordinated bondholders have become increasingly proactive because they are more knowledgeable, better organized and have better access to professional advice. Additionally, more professional investors have entered the market for distressed securities. Institutions, investment funds, and entrepreneurial investors purchase distressed securities at significant discounts and are willing to test managements' nerves by threatening foreclosure or involuntary bankruptcy. The mounting aggressiveness of original holders and the entry of professional investors are changing the expectations and recoveries of subordinated bondholders. Understanding the attitudes, skill, and resolve of these sophisticated participants is an essential step in the investment process.

Management and Sponsors

In most leveraged recapitalization and LBO transactions, the management and institutional investors that invested equity into these deals ("sponsors") are important constituencies in the process. Management, in almost all instances, has complete control over all business information and will use this information to their best advantage in maintaining their job status. Usually, only fraud or malfeasance can enable creditor groups to successfully effect a change in management. Therefore, for better or worse, the management team in place may be the team that leads the company forward, post-restructuring. Assessment of management capabilities is critical to determining enterprise value.

Sponsors, like Odyssey Partners, guide management through the leveraging process and, with capital and reputation, stand behind the transaction to insure its success. If a transaction is on the brink of collapse (as was JPS as we shall discuss further), the sponsor may be there to invest more equity to shore up finances and to lend expertise in restructuring negotiations. A financially strong sponsor may have as much to do with the ultimate outcome of a restructuring as would improving business or market conditions. A committed sponsor, in addition to investing new capital, may be the only party capable of quickly replacing a management team (sometimes a critical and always a difficult action).

Other Parties

As each situation of financial distress is different, there can be a multitude of other parties in interest that can impact upon the process. Tax agencies, pension guarantee agencies, governmental regulatory bodies, unions, organized equity holders, and trade creditors may all have their say in negotiations. Again, one must identify each constituent group and understand what degree of leverage it holds. Successful investing in distressed situations requires constant evaluation of each party's demands.

FORUMS OF NEGOTIATION

In today's market we have primarily focused on three distinct forums of negotiation: out-of-court restructurings; Chapter 11 reorganizations; and "pre-packaged" Chapter 11 reorganizations. There is a wide body of literature explaining the characteristics of each. We shall limit ourselves to the following brief outline of their advantages and disadvantages from an investor's perspective.

Out-Of-Court Restructurings

A negotiation conducted between the company and select creditor groups, an out-of-court restructuring may not impact upon all claimants and is conducted with the advice of professionals (attorneys, accountants, investment bankers) representing informally designated creditor groups. In many circumstances, out-of-court restructurings require a supermajority of claimants (sometimes over 90% of a creditor group) to approve the transaction. Often this allows a small minority of claimants to "hold out" for better treatment than the majority received.

Advantages:

1. Can be completed quickly and requires less attention from management. The business is less susceptible to managerial instability.
2. Less costly in terms of professional and court-related fees charged to the business.
3. Less uncertain in terms of business outcome. This process is more controlled by business interests. Economic recoveries have a greater chance of maximization.

Disadvantages:

1. Outcome may provide only a temporary solution. Negotiations may be continued to a later date based upon the future outcome of business plans.
2. May not comprehensively address all parties in interest.
3. Subject to "holdouts."
4. Management is less compelled to provide complete access to financial and business plans.

Chapter 11 Reorganizations

A company files for protection under Chapter 11 of the U.S. Bankruptcy Code to stay actions of creditors and allow for the comprehensive reorganization of claims under the supervision of the federal courts. In Chapter 11 cases, claimholders are organized into classes where they eventually vote for a plan of reorganization. This plan outlines the future business plan as well as contractually provides for the satisfaction of claims. For a plan to be accepted, 67% of the dollar value of each class as well as 50% of claimants in that class must approve the plan. Additionally, the plan must be approved by the bankruptcy court and must demonstrate that the probability of future reorganization is low.

Advantages:

1. Comprehensively addresses all categories of claims.
2. Compels a greater degree of disclosure of business and financial plans.
3. Eliminates holdouts and potential of preferred treatment of certain creditors.

4. Provides easier access for credit (e.g., debtor-in-possession financing).

Disadvantages:

1. Expensive in terms of court costs and professional fees.
2. May damage business relationships with trade credit and customers.
3. Consumes more management time.
4. Outcomes are not as easy to predict.

"Prepackaged" Chapter 11 Reorganizations

A prenegotiated, preapproved plan of reorganization structured under the U.S. Bankruptcy Code, the plan binds all parties as in traditional Chapter 11 cases; however, the plan is filed concurrently with the opening of the case. The plan and its disclosure statement document are subject to approval by the bankruptcy court.

Advantages:

1. Faster and cheaper than the traditional Chapter 11 process.
2. Binds holdouts.

Disadvantages:

1. Risk that a prepackaged plan is not approved by the court or claimholders and so becomes subject to normal Chapter 11 uncertainties.

APPLICATION OF RESTRUCTURING PROCESS

Taking into consideration an understanding of basic valuation methods and the restructuring process, we now apply our analysis to the JPS situation. After negotiating with an informal bondholder committee, JPS forwarded a restructuring plan to be executed through a prepackaged bankruptcy. As previously noted, in order for the plan to be approved, it had to have been supported by a majority of bondholders representing at least two-thirds of the face value of each class of debt. The JPS plan disclosed that the bondholder committee controlled 62% of the face amount of JPS debt; thus, the probability of significant opposition was reduced. Table 12.3 summarizes the salient terms of the prepackaged plan for bondholders.

Table 12.3—JPS Textiles, Inc.
Summary of Terms Under Prepackaged Bankruptcy Plan

	Old Senior Notes	*New Senior Notes*
Principal Amount:	$100 million	$100 million
Interest:	Variable/No less than 13.5%	11.75%
Mandatory Redemption:	$50 million on 6/1/95	$50 million on 6/1/94
Collateral:	General unsecured	Secured by second lien on subsidiaries' capital stock
Maturity:	6/1/96	6/1/95
Shares of Common Stock:	none	none
	Old Discount Notes	*New Discount Notes*
Principal Amount:	$160 million	To be determined on plan date
Interest:	16.25%	10.85%
Mandatory Redemption:	$40 million on 6/1/97 and 6/1/98	25% of issue on 6/1/97 and 6/1/98
Collateral:	General unsecured	General unsecured
Maturity:	6/1/99	6/1/99
Shares of Common Stock:	none	150,000 shares (15% of common equity)
	Old Subordinated Notes	*New Subordinated Notes*
Principal Amount:	$125 million	$125 million
Interest:	15.50%	9.25%
Mandatory Redemption:	$31.25 million on 6/1/97 and 6/1/98	$31.25 million on 6/1/97 and 6/1/98
Collateral:	General unsecured	General unsecured
Maturity:	6/1/99	6/1/99
Shares of Common Stock:	none	150,000 shares (15% of common equity)
	Old Debentures	*New Debentures*
Principal Amount:	$75 million	$75 million
Interest:	14.25%	7.00%
Mandatory Redemption:	$37.5 million on 5/15/99	$37.5 million on 5/15/99
Collateral:	General unsecured	General unsecured
Maturity:	5/15/00	5/15/00
Shares of Common Stock:	none	190,000 shares (19% of common equity)

The table denotes that while principal amounts remained the same, interest rates were reduced in exchange for shares of common stock or, in the case of the senior notes, liens on capital stock. Interest on all of the above issues was to accrue (or, in the case of the discount notes, accrete) at their original contracted rates until the earlier of the confirmation of the plan or 120 days after the bankruptcy filing. (Interest accruals at the old coupon rates produced current yields of 19% to 51%, depending upon the issue.) The common stock distributed to bondholders was not to be transferable (without prior approval of the board of directors) for two years after confirmation of the plan.

Concurrently with the confirmation of the plan, Odyssey Partners and the management group were to contribute $7.5 million to retain 51% of the common equity. Additionally, an amended credit agreement with the senior lenders would be executed. The interest rate on borrowings under the agreement would be at prime plus 200 basis points. The amended credit agreement would include a new $25 million subfacility for purchase of the company's bonds. In addition, new covenants in the restructured bonds contained a $50 million carve-out for debt repurchase. These two provisions would allow the company to repurchase high-cost debt at a significant discount, thus improving overall credit quality.

Improved Credit Quality

Given the plan provisions, as summarized in Table 12.3, the restructuring would enhance credit quality. In particular, the reduced interest expense would translate into better interest coverage ratios and additional funds for capital expenditures and debt amortization. In the plan disclosure statement, JPS indicated that it posted EBITD of $82.7 million in fiscal 1990. Based on its existing debt structure, with cash interest at $60 million and total interest at $80 million, cash interest coverage was 1.4x and total interest coverage was 1.0x. The restructuring plan would reduce cash interest expense to $41 million and total interest expense to $56 million, which would give the company pro forma coverages of 2.0x and 1.5x for cash interest expense and total interest expense, respectively. We estimated that pro forma coverages would remain at those levels during the 12 months following plan approval, since JPS projected that fiscal 1991 EBITD would be flat at $82.5 million. JPS planned to increase annual outlays on capital expenditures ("CapX") from less than $15 million to $20 million. Given pro forma results for a higher level of CapX and lower interest, free cash flow would cover cash interest 1.5x in 1991. Beyond 1991, we believed that coverages could improve when the apparel, auto and residential construction markets recovered and company cash flow increased. Company projections through 1995 are shown in Table 12.4.

Table 12.4—JPS Textiles, Inc.
Historical and Projected Cash Flow and Interest Coverages
($ millions)

FYE October:	*1990*[a]	*1991*[b]	*1992*	*1993*	*1994*	*1995*
Sales	$821.4	$792.7	$810.2	$825.5	$842.6	$860.0
EBITD	82.7	82.5	90.5	95.4	100.2	104.6
Total Interest	80.0	56.0	57.6	55.3	53.7	51.3
Cash Interest	60.0	41.0	46.1	52.1	50.2	47.4
CapX	Na	Na	20.0	20.0	20.0	20.0
Free Cash Flow	Na	Na	12.9	20.1	26.5	33.3
EBITD/Total Int.	1.0x	1.5x	1.6x	1.7x	1.9x	2.0x
EBITD/Cash Int.	1.4x	2.0x	2.0x	1.8x	2.0x	2.2x
EBITD-CapX/Cash Int.	Na	Na	1.5x	1.4x	1.6x	1.8x

[a] Interest expense for 1990 is estimated based on current debt structure.
[b] Interest expense for 1991 is pro forma for the proposed restructured debt load.

The table indicates that the proposed restructuring improved the credit quality by strengthening "interest coverages" (the ratio of EBITD to interest); however, projected free cash flow (while improved) remained minimal and certainly could not effectively amortize a large amount of debt. Since projected free cash flow was weak, this restructuring faced the possibility of a significant future adjustment in the form of a refinancing or asset sale.

Valuation of Securities

The combination of improved cash flow, ability to repurchase discounted debt, better amortization terms and reduced cash and total interest expense led us to conclude that JPS bonds would trade at prices substantially higher than were quoted at the time of the plan announcement. Table 12.5 shows the price levels at which the new bonds would trade given various returns (with and without the previously mentioned equity allocation), taking into account the new rates and assuming a March 31, 1991, effective date for the plan.

Table 12.5—JPS Textiles, Inc.
Expected Trading Ranges

Yield:	*15.0%*	*17.5%*	*20.0%*	*22.5%*	*25.0%*	*27.5%*	*30.0%*
Sr. Notes	90.1	83.4	77.3	71.8			
Disc. Notes		67.8	60.0	53.5	47.9	43.1	39.0
plus Equity		68.4	60.6	54.1	48.5	43.7	39.6
Sub. Notes		56.7	49.4	43.3	38.1	33.6	29.8
plus Equity		57.2	49.9	43.8	38.6	34.1	30.3
Sub. Debs.			46.4	40.9	36.4	32.5	29.3
plus Equity			47.6	42.1	37.6	33.7	30.5

From this analysis one could make judgments as to trading ranges of the prospective issues given an estimate of relative risk versus other restructured securities offered in the market at that time. Using Table 12.5, we made our own appraisal of bond value and calculated the expected returns given those estimates. Without taking into account the value of the equity to be received, the bonds offered 14%–29% capital appreciation potential from the then-quoted levels. To calculate the equity value, we used a five-year valuation model based on company projections of EBITD, the company's projected capital structure in 1995, an enterprise multiple of five times EBITD, and a 25% discount factor for determination of present value. Based upon these assumptions, we calculated that the equity was worth $4.9 million in total, or about half of a point of value per bond for the senior subordinated and discount notes, and 1.2 points for the subordinated debentures. If JPS used its $50 million carve-out to buy debt at a discount, these values could increase considerably. We assumed that if the company purchased $100 million of senior subordinated debt at approximately $50 per bond, equity value per bond would increase to 2.5 points for the senior subordinated notes, more than 3 points for the discount notes, and nearly 17 points for the subordinated debentures.

Table 12.6 summarizes the expected investment returns we estimated at the time of the restructuring offer.

Table 12.6—JPS Textiles, Inc.
Calculation of Expected Investment Returns

	Market Price	*Expected Price*	*Expected Cap. Gain*	*Interest Return*	*Expected Total Return*	*Annualized Return*
Senior Notes	70	80	14.3%	3.7%	18.0%	72.0%
Sr. Sub. Notes	43	51	18.6%	6.8%	25.4%	101.6%
Disc. Notes	28	36	28.6%	0	28.6%	114.4%
Sub. Debs.	28	35	25.0%	9.8%	31.8%	127.2%

Table 12.6 denotes that the combination of accrued interest and expected capital gains on price appreciation produced very attractive returns.

Asset Coverage and Downside Risk

In preparing our analysis to assess downside risk, we estimated expected and worst case asset coverages (Table 12.7). The expected case was based upon the company's estimated EBITD for 1991 of $82.5 million, while the worst case assumed a 9% decline to $75 million.

Table 12.7—JPS Textiles, Inc.
Evaluation of Expected Enterprise Values
($ millions)

	Expected Case	*Worst Case*
EBITD	$82.5	$75.0
EV Multiple	5	5
Enterprise Value	$412.5	$375.0

	Principal	*Expected Case Coverage*	*%*	*Worst Case Coverage*	*%*	*Market Price*
Bank Debt	$104	$104	100%	$104	100%	NA
Sr. Notes	100	100	100	100	100	70
Sr. Sub. Notes	125	88	75	72	57	43
Disc. Notes	134	94	75	77	57	28
Sub. Debs.	75	26	35	22	29	28
	$538	$412.5		$375		

Table 12.7 shows that on a worst case basis, the enterprise value covered the senior notes at 1.4 times the market price, senior subordinated notes at 1.7 times, discount notes at 2.7 times, and subordinated debentures at 0.78 times. Over the near term, on a worst case basis, it was only the subordinated debentures—the most junior security in the capital structure—that did not appear to be fully covered by our estimate of enterprise value.

MARKET STRATEGY CONSIDERATIONS

Understanding when to enter and exit the market for a particular security is just as important as assessing its underlying worth. With respect to JPS, the bonds were trading at significant discounts to our estimates of ultimate value at the time of the restructuring announcement. Given the uncertainty associated with executing the transaction, the limited level of quality research available and the generally weak market conditions, we were not surprised that the bonds were trading at these "fire sale" prices.

Buying smart is only one side of the equation. It is important to make an informed judgment as to when there is more market risk in holding a security than in realizing a gain or loss through a sale. For JPS, we questioned whether or not the restructuring addressed the longer-term considerations of debt amortization, since the face value of debt was not reduced. With pro forma total debt of $538 million and a current enterprise value of $412 million (using an EBITD multiple of 5), EBITD would have to grow by about $25 million (30%) for JPS to be considered solvent.

The company's financial position would have to show significant improvement before a subsequent refinancing could take place. Given this uncertainty, one should expect a premium yield on all outstanding JPS securities. Notwithstanding these concerns, JPS appeared to have sufficient liquidity to survive with its new capital structure through June 1994. Clearly, the opportunity to purchase the old securities at a steep discount to their apparent values was justified on a risk-adjusted basis. However, maintaining positions in the restructured JPS issues would require close monitoring on an ongoing basis.

Another example of profiting from proper investment timing was seen in Eastern Airlines. As previously mentioned, Eastern Airlines filed for Chapter 11 protection and was liquidated. Notwithstanding the outcome, in May 1990 we identified an investment opportunity in the second secured equipment notes (17.25%, due 3/1/93). These securities had a second priority lien on a pool of jet aircraft, spare engines and parts, and cash. Due to concerns over the creditworthiness of Eastern and its parent, Texas Air (which guaranteed two future semi-annual coupon payments on these notes), the bond prices dropped from 107 to the 93–95 range.

Our analysis focused on the value of the underlying collateral and the likely disruption of coupon payments. At 93–95, the notes yielded between 18% to 31% to maturity, depending on the timing and form of the ultimate resolution. Table 12.8 illustrates the collateral pool values.

Table 12.8—Eastern Airlines
Description of Collateralized Assets
($ millions)

Asset Description	*Appraised Value*[1]	*Discounted by 30%*	*Discounted by 50%*
Various Jet Aircraft	$187,305	$131,114	$93,653
Spare Engines	29,000	20,300	14,500
Total Equipment	$216,305	$151,414	$108,153
Cash in Escrow	387,000	387,000	387,000
Total Collateral	$603,305	$538,414	$495,153
LESS: First Lien	213,500	213,500	213,500
Available to Second Secured Equip. Notes	$389,805	$324,914	$281,653
Second Secured Equip. Notes	$200,000	$200,000	$200,000
Collateral Coverage	1.9x	1.6x	1.4x
Cash Coverage	86.7%	86.7%	86.7%

[1] Lowest value taken from appraisals performed by Avmark in January 1990.

As shown in Table 12.8, assuming that the first lien was paid out of the cash in escrow, there would be $173.5 million in cash remaining (or 86.7% of the $200 million face value) to satisfy the second priority notes. In addition, even after applying a 50% haircut to the appraised value of the remaining equipment, the notes were collateralized 1.4 times. The excess collateral value allowed us to conclude that future principal and interest payments would be covered.

On September 1, 1990, the company defaulted on interest payments after Texas Air refused to back its guarantee (Texas Air subsequently filed for Chapter 11 protection in December 1990). The company began to make principal prepayments as well as accrued interest payments at the 17.25% contract rate in April 1991. To date, approximately $777 in principal (plus accrued interest) has been prepaid. If one purchased the bonds in May 1990 at a price of 95, the annualized total return would have been approximately 20%.

As the Eastern Airlines case denotes, perceived risk often exceeds actual risk. This implies undervaluation and opportunity. If one were to rank the distressed securities universe according to real risk versus potential return, Journal Company, Inc. ("JCI"), deserves top-tier status. Rarely does one credit exhibit so many attractive qualities.

JCI's assets consist of a group of daily newspapers located in several states with a total circulation of 275,000, and a St. Louis free weekly with a circulation of 850,000. The company's bonds had steadily dropped in early 1990 due to concerns over a weak industry operating environment, and losses from an ill-conceived start-up operation that was subsequently abandoned. Cash flow margins declined by more than 55%, from 20.4% in 1988 to 9.2% in 1989. Notwithstanding then-current operating results, JCI possessed considerable intrinsic value principally based upon the following:

1. *Strong equity sponsorship*—Warburg Pincus & Co., an investment firm with $3 billion under management, controlled 100% of JCI's equity. Warburg had publicly stated that it would use its resources to improve and expand JCI's operations, implying that it would support the credit, if needed.
2. *Solid asset coverage*—JCI's estimated enterprise value greatly exceeded the market value of debt. Company assets were readily separable and reasonably liquid. JCI had recently sold assets for $120 million, representing multiples of 4.3 times revenues and 15.5 times cash flow. Proceeds were used to reduce senior debt. After the asset sale, face value of debt was $266 million, comprised of $28 million in senior debt and $238 million of subordinated debt. Market value of debt was approximately $120 million (45% of face value). We estimated that company assets were worth at least 2 times pro forma revenues of $178 million, or $356 million (11 times pro forma 1989 EBITD). Conservatively valued relative to recent asset sales, enterprise value covered market value of debt by at least 2.9 times.
3. *High current yield and yield to maturity*—On May 1, 1990, JCI debt traded as shown in Table 12.9.

Table 12.9—Journal Company, Inc.
Publicly Traded Debt Issues

Amount Outstanding	*Description*	*Coupon*	*Maturity*	*Price*	*Current Yield*	*Yield to Maturity*
$73 million	Sr. Sub. Debentures	14.625%	5/01/00	51	28.7%	30.5%
$65 million	Sr. Sub. Debentures	11.875	9/01/99	49	24.2	27.1
$50 million	Sub. Debentures	12.125	9/01/00	35	34.6	36.7
$50 million	Sub. Debentures	14.825	5/01/00	35	42.4	43.9

Even in the unlikely event of a Chapter 11 filing, these securities were still attractive based upon their discounted trading levels. Unlike JPS, Journal Company, Inc., had relatively very little senior debt and higher asset coverage ratios. Assuming a 24-month bankruptcy proceeding where bondholders would recover 100% face value, yields on these securities would have been: 36.67% for the 14.625s of 5/01/00; 39.05% for the 11.875s of 9/01/99; 60.02% for the 12.125s of 9/01/00; and 60.02% for the 14.825s of 5/01/00. Again, the recurring investment theme of committed sponsorship, strong asset coverage relative to market-adjusted debt values, and high current yields made JCI an outstanding investment candidate.

An emerging strategic trend has been to invest in subordinated debt where reorganization value is distributed to claimants entirely in the form of new equity. These instances have arisen when there is insufficient asset value or earnings capacity to support high degrees of leverage. In the previously mentioned Interco Chapter 11 case, there are several tranches of subordinated debt which are currently trading at cents on the dollar. Interco was a leveraged recapitalization that failed due to a dramatic drop in cash flow and asset values. While the core businesses appear viable, they could not support a heavily leveraged capital structure. Therefore, an investor in the senior subordinated debentures, subordinated discount notes, and junior subordinated pay-in-kind debentures should expect to receive value in the form of equity. To value this equity, traditional techniques based upon projected earnings multiples should be used to augment cash flow valuations. Allocation of value among various classes is another critical issue. In recent reorganizations where equity distributions have satisfied the bulk of subordinated claims (Southland Corporation, Memorex-Telex, Allied-Federated Stores), the allocation of value has more or less been dependent upon two factors: (1) the seniority and subordination provisions of bond indentures; and (2) the representation of each security class at the negotiating table. Although there appears to be an emerging pattern of equity distribution in these types of cases, we believe that each instance is unique and requires individual attention.

CONCLUDING REMARKS

Over the past two years, upheavals in the market for high-yield securities produced unprecedented opportunities for investors who could remove themselves from the panic of the moment. Successful investing in distressed securities requires application of fundamental financial analysis to quantify "real" risk versus "perceived" risk so that one can distinguish the jewels from the junk. In the distressed arena, it is preferable to invest in "good" companies with "bad" balance sheets: a restructuring is generally more profitable when underlying problems are related to capital structure, not continuing operations. Determining enterprise value using various case scenarios, marking debt to market and calculating asset coverages at each claim level, assessing sources of liquidity available to meet scheduled interest and principal payments, comparing yields relative to other similarly distressed situations, and anticipating the form of a financial restructuring and its implications for each class of debt are all part of this "bottom up" credit analysis. Moreover, understanding the legal, accounting, and economic characteristics of financial restructurings enhances this fundamental approach.

In the future there will be more financial restructurings as companies confront the excesses of the past. Since the inception of orderly financial markets, investors have experienced disappointment and pain caused by market crashes and panics. Often these situations cause an imbalance between perceived risk and real risk. Preparing to step into the fire to take advantage of these market opportunities requires the above-mentioned skill sets and the tenacity and resolve to act upon one's judgment.

Chapter Thirteen

Selling Troubled Loans: Another Way Out

by Michael C. Singer
R.D. Smith & Company, Inc.

As a direct result of the excesses of the leveraged buyout frenzy in the late 1980s and the recent economic slowdown, the nonperforming corporate debt held by banks has grown substantially in the last two years. The amount of such debt in default is hard to estimate, but $100 billion appears to be the order of magnitude. With many highly leveraged transactions still in their early stages, this figure can be expected to increase in the near to medium term, particularly with a weak economy.

Faced with a troubled loan, a bank has several alternatives (or ways out). This chapter discusses what is an increasingly common way out of a troubled loan: the sale of the loan itself, usually at a substantial discount from par. It will cover some of the apparent reasons underlying the growing trend and discuss why banks may want to sell and buyers may want to purchase troubled loans. Since each loan has unique characteristics, this chapter will review the implications of selling loans that differ in certain basic ways, such as level of collateral coverage, whether in or out of bankruptcy, and whether the company is public or private. It will summarize the principal factors that go into

Reprinted from Spring 1991 Edition of "Commercial Lending Review." Reprinted by permission, The John Colet Press, Inc.

the pricing decision and offer a practical guide to the selling process and the mechanics of transfer.

DIFFERENT WAYS OUT OF A TROUBLED LOAN

Given a nonperforming loan, a bank will wish to maximize its *net* return from this bad loan, that is, its present value of future cash to be received less the expenses of cost of capital, fees, management time, and so forth to be expended in working out the loan. Given this objective, there are several ways to attempt to achieve maximum value. The way chosen will depend on a number of factors—many discussed below—but there are a number of common alternatives.

Perhaps the most common method to maximize the value of a bad loan is to restructure the loan. Too often, this turns out to be only a temporary solution. Debt service payments are rescheduled to reflect a revised projected cash flow that is substantially different from that envisaged at the time of the original loan. This method is most appropriate when the business is expected to recover and lenders can reasonably expect to be made whole, albeit over a longer time.

To the extent the financial distress appears to result from bad management, lenders could decide to use their influence to bring in turnaround management. In conjunction with a restructuring, new management may give lenders renewed confidence that the obligation is now to an organization with much greater potential.

A bank also may assist a troubled company to seek out a third party willing to inject new capital into the enterprise, thereby creating a more financially viable company capable of repaying the loan. Alternatively, either to obtain a return of its principal or to improve the credit support for the loan, a lender may assist in an outright sale of the company to a financially stronger debtor.

Often as a last resort, or when an individual lender in a larger group has little say in the direction of debtor/creditor negotiations, a bank may choose to sell the loan.

RECENT DEVELOPMENTS IN THE DISTRESSED LOAN MARKET

As mentioned above, nonperforming loans have increased substantially in recent years. Nevertheless, only a very small fraction of these loans are even considered to be put up for sale, let alone actually sold. Since loan sales are private transactions, it is difficult to estimate the annual volume of trading of distressed loans. If one defines a "distressed corporate loan, extended by a bank," as one that trades below 80 cents on the dollar (for other than pure yield considerations), then a suggested order of magnitude for current trading volume might be $1 billion annually. This very approximate figure is likely to increase substantially as the market evolves.

The recent growth in the market for bank loans is due not only to the greater availability of merchandise but also to increasing pressure from both regulators and management to lower the ratio of nonperforming assets to capital, particularly at weaker banks. In addition, some banks have a growing tendency to consider selling a loan well before the full extent of problems affecting its value may be apparent—indicating a much more sophisticated attitude toward maintaining a healthier portfolio.

To meet this increased supply of distressed loans for sale and to take advantage of the perceived investment opportunities, the number of investors and amount of funds available for the purchase of these loans has proliferated in the last two years. While the size of this pool of funds is very small compared with the potential supply of troubled loans, it is a very meaningful amount at the margin: where supply meets demand at a realistic price. In other words, given a perceived investment opportunity that is appropriately priced, the market has become increasingly competitive and much more liquid.

An equally important factor in the growth of this market has been the development of vehicles and associated documentation that essentially "securitize" the bank loan, enabling it to be purchased in a size and form more acceptable to institutional investors. These vehicles not only facilitate the initial transfer between selling bank and investors but also enhance the liquidity of secondary transfers.

The returns achieved by some investors in distressed loans have encouraged the growth in this market. As in any market, though, examples of substantial gains by some investors are tempered by examples of substantial losses by others. The bank loan market, which usually involves the most senior debt of a company, tends to be the most conservative way to invest in distressed securities and offers a relatively low risk/reward relationship.

FRUSTRATION, PESSIMISM LEAD BANKS TO SELL

Banks that sell troubled loans do so for a number of reasons and are found across the spectrum of the industry.

Perhaps the simplest economic rationale inducing a bank to sell a troubled loan is that the expected sales price is above the price to which the bank has written it down. This generally does not occur until the borrower has been in default or in bankruptcy for a long time.

A related factor influencing a bank's decision to sell is what might be called lender fatigue. After many regular, seemingly interminable rounds of negotiations between debtor and creditors, a lender is far more willing to sell, particularly if the underlying business remains weak and no clear end to the process is in sight.

A bank also might sell if it believes that the value of its loan is likely to deteriorate further or even stagnate over time. Most trades occur when buyers and sellers have different outlooks for the prospects of a business or the reorganization process.

Banks sell for a number of technical reasons; in some instances, they are forced to sell troubled loans. A number of banks, particularly those under close regulatory scrutiny, are under extreme pressure to decrease their exposure to nonperforming assets. This pressure could even extend to regulators requiring the bank to generate cash from its workout portfolio by certain deadlines.

Banks that are members of a large syndicated bank group and have only a small exposure to a troubled credit may find it uneconomical to administer the loan. The management time and the direct expense of attending negotiating sessions and monitoring the situation may not be justified by the size of the loan.

Also, as the reorganization plan takes shape, banks may be destined to receive stock or illiquid debt or equity securities at the end of the process. Since banks will not or, in many instances, cannot hold these securities, they often sell the loans well before the reorganization process is completed.

INSTITUTIONAL BUYERS PREDOMINATE

Logic suggests that the most likely buyers of distressed bank debt would be other banks—particularly those involved in the same credit. With a few exceptions, however, banks do not buy distressed debt. The last thing most banks need is more nonperforming assets. Exceptions are the few banks that have established funds specifically to invest in troubled debt.

The principal purchasers of distressed loans are institutional funds that focus on and have expertise in distressed securities of one form or another. These buyers range from insurance companies to pension funds to mutual funds to money managers. In some cases, the funds invest only in bank debt; more commonly, they purchase public as well as private securities.

While most investing in troubled bank loans is on a passive basis for a desired financial return, sometimes investors seek a controlling position in the negotiations for a reorganization. Purchasers are able to bring a fresh point of view to the negotiating process. In a very contentious situation, for example, new investors may assist to break ground toward a new plan since they enter the process without the bad blood from prior negotiations. In addition, new investors have purchased their debt at substantial discounts, so they may be more willing to settle for a slightly lower value and thereby hasten the process for all.

PRICING THE DEBT

It is a common notion that once bank debt becomes distressed it should trade, on average, at a certain standard discount from par. Presumably, this notion assumes that the debt eventually will receive par and the discount exists because of intervening uncertainty. Nothing could be further from reality. Each distressed bank loan achieves a price level in the marketplace that depends on the many inherent characteristics of the loan, the prospects for the company and the reorganization process, and technical market variables. Four of these factors—whether or not the loan is secured, whether the borrower is a private or a public company, whether or not the borrower is in bankruptcy, and the fundamental valuation of the loan—are discussed below.

Is the debt secured or unsecured? A claim in bankruptcy that is overcollateralized generally will receive postpetition interest. Such interest may be paid on a current basis or may accrue. The market obviously prefers current pay; this will be reflected in the price paid for the loan. Assuming adequate collateral, the market also may differentiate between forms of collateral. For example, the market might prefer property, plant, and equipment over stock of subsidiaries, since the latter's value may be more subject to dispute. To the extent collateral for the claim is insufficient, the value of the unsecured portion of the debt will depend on factors such as the fundamental analysis of the overall value of the business, the ranking of the claim, the expected distribution of the estate value among claimants and interests, and the expected time it will take to receive such value.

Is the borrower a private or a public company? Given similar circumstances, the debt of private companies will sell at a greater discount than debt of public companies because of the more restricted market for private company debt. Fewer investors buy this debt, since the amount of analysis required to become familiar with the credit is at least as great as that for public company debt. With a public company, however, an investor usually is already familiar with the credit as a result of interest in the public securities. Or, the investor is more willing to do the analysis, since the effort could yield opportunities in a broad range of investments within the public company's capital structure. The illiquidity of private debt also affects the buyer's ability to resell the loan later, which detracts from the value of the loan. Nevertheless, there is still a market for private company bank debt, albeit a more limited one than that for public company debt.

Is the borrower in bankruptcy? The filing of a bankruptcy petition eliminates a degree of uncertainty about the reorganization process and may make bank debt more tradeable. Before the filing, with the financial viability of an enterprise still in question, it may be difficult to negotiate a compromise price at which seller and buyer are willing to trade. A potential buyer will assume the downside of a protracted bankruptcy process in determining a price at which it is willing to purchase the debt. A potential seller may believe that an out-of-court restructuring is possible; therefore, it may not be prepared to discount the price of the debt sufficiently to meet the buyer's objective. As the bankruptcy process progresses, more uncertainties often are eliminated, which facilitates trading further. These uncertainties include whether interest payments on the debt will be kept current, how contentious—and therefore how long—the process might be, and so on.

What is the fundamental value of the loan? Underpinning the price of the debt, whatever the influence of these technical factors, is the fundamental analysis of the value of the loan. This process involves traditional reorganization/bankruptcy analysis of estimating the enterprise value, allocating the value among the various claims and interests, and estimating the time to realize value. Additional factors that may apply specifically to the bank debt—such as the value of the collateral, ability to pay cash interest, and potential legal actions—also affect value.

To illustrate the rationale for arriving at an appropriate value, Figure 13.1 suggests some factors that buyers and sellers may have considered in agreeing to a price for bank debt of some distressed companies.

Figure 13.1—Pricing Bank Debt

Possible Reasons for Prices at the Time of Transactions

Ames Department Stores
Bank debt traded at 60 cents/dollar

Bank debt is overcollateralized but not current pay. Collateral is the stock of subsidiaries and intercompany receivables. Buyer saw ample asset protection, cash payment at the end of the bankruptcy, and a potential for postpetition interest. Seller feared a substantive consolidation, a long bankruptcy, or a gradual operational deterioration.

Integrated Resources
Bank debt traded at 24 cents/dollar

Bank debt is senior but unsecured. Trades at a small discount to publicly traded, pari passu (equal in ranking), senior debt. Buyer expected to receive value (cash, securities) of 45 to 50 cents/dollar at end of bankruptcy, estimated at a year to 18 months from time of purchase. Seller expected long, litigious bankruptcy; price had risen from a low of 15 cents/dollar four months before the trade.

Lomas Financial Corporation
Bank debt traded at 57 cents/dollar

Bank debt is senior but unsecured. Trades at a small discount to publicly traded, pari passu, senior debt. Buyer expected to receive value (cash, securities) of 80 to 90 cents/dollar at end of bankruptcy, estimated within a year from time of purchase. Seller expected longer, contentious bankruptcy and did not want to own postbankruptcy securities.

Pameco
Bank debt traded at 65 cents/dollar

Bank debt of this subsidiary of a public company (MLX Corporation) is secured and cash paying. Buyer expected to receive a restructured loan and securities valued well in excess of purchase price. Seller was wary of bankruptcy risk and fatigued by series of amendments and negotiations during restructuring process.

Southland
Bank debt traded at 80 cents/dollar

Bank debt is well overcollateralized and was paying interest and principal. Threat of bankruptcy encouraged seller to dispose of asset; buyer needed significant discount to take on risk of uncontrolled bankruptcy and possible interruption in payments. The debt was not expected to be tainted by any litigation.

The suggested rationales do not take into account unique internal (often undisclosed) considerations of the seller and buyer that may have influenced their decisions. Rather, Figure 13.1 describes the general issues affecting the price of each bank loan.

AN EXPERIENCED BUYER FACILITATES THE SALE

Having made the decision to sell a loan, a bank then has to make a judgment about the way to achieve the highest price available in the market. Which method of sale a bank chooses will depend on the characteristics of the loan and on the resources available internally at the bank, among other factors.

One cannot overestimate the benefit of working with a buyer familiar with documents required to effect the transfer. The mechanics of transfer for each bank loan are complex and different (discussed below). An experienced, flexible, and creative purchaser or agent often is key to a successful trade.

If the credit exposure is large, say, in excess of $10 million, it is likely that more than one buyer will be needed. The larger the loan, the more the bank needs an efficient broker that can, in effect, syndicate the loan to several buyers.

If the credit exposure contains an undrawn revolver commitment or letter of credit, it may be necessary to seek out another bank to buy this portion or, at the minimum, a creditworthy purchaser who can fund possible future commitments.

When attempting to sell a loan involving a complex credit, a less-known name, or a private company, it is even more important that the purchaser or agent have capable and in-depth research to understand and analyze the credit. Only with this resource will a purchaser be able to establish quickly a price at which it would be prepared to buy.

In sum, to obtain the best price as efficiently as possible, it is crucial to work with an entity that has a thorough knowledge of all potential purchasers of the distressed loan, a professional and expert documentation staff, and a sound and respected ability to analyze financially troubled investments.

MECHANICS OF TRANSFER

The transfer of a bank loan is usually accomplished with the negotiation of an assignment agreement between seller and buyer. In general, the assignment agreement confirms the rights and liens associated with the loan. It provides representations and warranties that acknowledge, to one degree or another, that the seller is responsible for its actions with respect to the loan before closing of the transfer and the buyer is responsible for its actions after closing.

Before negotiating the conditions of transfer, it is customary to arrive at a price at which buyer and seller are willing to trade—subject, of course, to agreeable documentation—due to the time and expense of documenting these transactions. The record shows that nearly all transfers are successfully completed in this way and at the original price agreed to by buyer and seller. However, in a few cases, the sale of loans has not been completed because of representation, warranty, and indemnification issues. To facilitate a transfer in the event of unforeseen representations and warranties, it may be appropriate to renegotiate the price as a quid pro quo.

The toughest negotiations often relate to representations or warranties that the loan purchaser may require of the seller. The buyer may want assurances that the loan was not party to a fraudulent transfer, that no preference payments were received in connection with the loan, and that any of the seller's actions will not lead to a subordination of the claim. The purchaser also may seek certain remedies if any of these risks come to fruition. To the extent any of these risks are known when the price is negotiated, it is appropriate to specify the expected treatment then to minimize the likelihood of major differences when the documentation is prepared.

Another item to deal with at the time or pricing is the treatment of any undrawn funds in the commitment that is being purchased. There are several ways to address this, depending on the size of the undrawn commitment, the nature of the purchaser, and the objectives of the seller. These methods usually involve a future commitment to fund on a pro rata basis at the same price agreed to at the time of the transfer.

Other common technicalities that affect documentation include whether the loan is a direct assignment or a participation, the need for consents from the agent bank or the debtor, the transfer of voting rights, and so forth. Often, the purchaser will not want to be considered an insider. Therefore, it will waive any rights to receive nonpublic information and will not be a member of the bank creditors committee.

For certain transfers, particularly those involving larger loans, the loan may be securitized to facilitate its purchase by several investors. Securitization can be accomplished by structuring the transfer as a series of smaller direct participations or as a trust where purchasers buy interests in the trust. Many institutional investors prefer the latter structure because it provides an investment vehicle they are familiar with and a more efficient means for subsequent transfers by trust participants.

Whatever form of transfer is used, a bank that has chosen to sell a loan as its way out of a distressed situation should expect it to take approximately two to four weeks to close a transaction once price has been agreed to.

CONCLUSION

Selling a troubled loan is likely to become an increasingly common way out for banks as they look to reduce their level of nonperforming assets. The market can be expected to become more efficient as the number of investors in these loans increases and as documentation to facilitate transfers is improved. Banks looking to enter this market should be comfortable not only with the ultimate valuation of their asset as they negotiate its sale but also with the selling process in order to achieve the optimal value as quickly as possible.

Chapter Fourteen

Managing Default: Some Evidence on How Firms Choose Between Workouts and Chapter 11

by Stuart C. Gilson
Harvard Business School*

As more and more U.S. companies default on their debt and file for bankruptcy, financial economists have become increasingly interested in understanding how companies deal with financial distress. In particular, academic concern has focused on whether the costs of resolving default are excessive, and whether the process by which firms recontract with their creditors can be made more efficient.

Companies have good reason to be concerned with these issues as well. In 1990, almost $25 billion worth of junk bonds went into de-

*I am grateful for the helpful comments of Max Holmes, the valuable research assistance of Joe Basset, and the research support provided by the Division of Research of the Harvard Business School.

Reprinted by permission of *The Journal of Applied Corporate Finance.*

fault, and 749,956 U.S. firms filed for bankruptcy.[1] The costs of restructuring the balance sheets of troubled companies can be daunting. LTV Corporation, for example, has spent over $150 million on legal and other professional fees since it filed for Chapter 11 in 1986. And this figure ignores other, potentially greater, costs of financial distress such as any loss of business occasioned by the bankruptcy.

There are two basic methods for reorganizing troubled companies: private workouts and formal bankruptcy. In either case, new financial claims are exchanged for the firm's outstanding debt contracts on terms the firm finds more affordable. The net effect of the exchange is either to reduce the level of interest and principal payments, to extend the payment dates, or to substitute equity for debt. The main difference between the two approaches is that, in bankruptcy, this exchange is supervised by the court.

Viewed in this light, the workout-bankruptcy choice has an obvious parallel with the decision faced by plaintiffs and defendants over whether to settle out of court or go to trial. If settling privately is appreciably less expensive, then both sides have an incentive to avoid going to court. But if the affected parties are unable to agree on how to split the cost savings, then a trial may still be necessary even though the combined wealth of both parties is ultimately lower.

Recently, Professor Michael Jensen has suggested that today's highly-leveraged companies that get into trouble have far stronger incentives to reorganize privately than their low-leveraged counterparts of the early 1980s. When a highly leveraged company misses an interest payment, management is forced to take corrective action much sooner than otherwise, thus leaving more of the company's operating value intact. In the absence of such an "early warning system," operating performance could be allowed to deteriorate much longer—in the extreme, making liquidation the only sensible alternative. To the extent private workouts are less costly than the formal Chapter 11 process, the "privatization of bankruptcy" envisioned by Jensen should ensure that more of the firm's value survives the recontracting process, thus benefiting creditors as well as shareholders.[2]

Workouts in the 1980s. In a recently published study, Kose John, Larry Lang, and I examined a sample of 160 New York and American

---

1 Source: *Turnarounds and Workouts*. Washington, D.C.

2 See Michael Jensen, "Active Investors, LBOs, and the Privatization of Bankruptcy," *Journal of Applied Corporate Finance* (Spring, 1989).

Stock Exchange-listed companies that defaulted on their debt during the 1980s.[3] Eighty, or almost half, of these companies successfully restructured their debt in workouts while the rest filed for Chapter 11. And for 62 of the 89 companies (or almost 70%) that ended up in bankruptcy, we found reports in the *Wall Street Journal* of attempts to restructure privately. (Because a good number of other attempts at restructuring almost certainly were unreported, this 70% figure should be construed as a "lower bound.")

Thus, during the 1980s, private restructuring was generally the preferred method for dealing with default. The fact that attempts at private restructuring have been so frequent would seem to confirm that workouts are indeed less costly on average than Chapter 11.

To the alarm of many, however, a recent bankruptcy court ruling ("the LTV decision") and changes in the tax law have made such private restructuring much more difficult. To understand the import of these developments, it is necessary to know more about the relative costs of workouts versus Chapter 11. In the pages that follow, I begin by reviewing recent academic research on the costs of financial restructuring. I then go on to present the findings of my own work that attempts to determine what factors distressed companies consider in choosing between private workouts and bankruptcy.

COSTS OF WORKOUTS versus CHAPTER 11

Legal and Professional Fees

For several reasons, payments for legal and other professional services are likely to be higher if a company restructures its debt in bankruptcy court. Lawyer and investment banker fees effectively accrue on an hourly basis, and therefore increase with the length of time spent in creditor negotiations. In the Gilson-John-Lang study cited earlier, the average length of time spent by 89 companies in Chapter 11 was over

3 Stuart Gilson, Kose John, and Larry Lang, "Troubled Debt Restructurings: An Empirical Study of Private Reorganization of Firms in Default," *Journal of Financial Economics 26 (1990)*. We constructed our sample by first ranking all New York and American Stock Exchange-listed companies by their common stock returns (measured over three consecutive years), and then identifying all firms in the bottom five percent of the returns that were either in default on their debt, bankrupt, or restructuring their debt to avoid bankruptcy, based on coverage of these firms in the *Wall Street Journal*. This selection process was repeated for various years, resulting in a sample of firms that first experienced financial difficulty throughout the period 1978-1987.

20 months; the average length of the 80 workouts was about 15 months.

This difference was significantly greater in the 30 cases in our sample that involved the private restructuring of publicly-traded debt. Such debt was always restructured through exchange offers in which bondholders were free to tender, or not tender, their bonds in exchange for a package of new securities. (In 87% of these exchanges, moreover, this package included new common stock or securities that could be converted into common stock.) The average length of exchange offers in our sample was just under seven months.

Workouts may be less time-consuming in part because firms need deal only with creditors whose claims are in default. Of the workouts we examined, 30% of the firms with publicly-traded debt, as well as 10% of the firms with debt owed to banks and insurance companies, avoided having to restructure such debt. By contrast, cross-default provisions included in most debt contracts virtually guarantee that, when a company files for Chapter 11, it will have to negotiate with all its creditors.

In addition, total legal fees in Chapter 11 are based on the number of billable hours.[4] Because legal and other professional fees have priority over all the firm's other claims in Chapter 11, the professional advisers involved in the case have no obvious financial incentive to minimize the amount of time the firm spends in Chapter 11. Although bankruptcy judges will often scale back requested fees or partially withhold payment of fees until the end of the case ("withholding rates" of 25% are common), lawyers can easily anticipate the adjustments and charge accordingly.

A potential solution to this problem would be to pay lawyers and investment bankers using the same securities distributed to shareholders and creditors as currency, thus giving them an interest in preserving the value of the *surviving* firm and an incentive to get out of Chapter 11 quickly.[5] An interesting alternative approach was recently taken by Ames Department Stores, which filed for Chapter 11 in April 1990. Ames established a special bonus plan for its CEO, Stephen Pistner, which would have paid him $3.5 million if Ames was successfully

---

4 A darkly humorous account of how the Bankruptcy Code sometimes creates perverse incentives for lawyers to prolong the firm's stay in Chapter 11 (for example, by filing excessive motions with the court) can be found in Sol Stern, *A Feast for Lawyers* (M. Evans and Company, Inc., 1989).

5 See proposals by Michael Price and Wilbur Ross in Roundtable Discussion in the *Journal of Applied Corporate Finance* (Summer 1991).

Table 14.1—Direct Costs of Exchange Offers for Troubled Junk Bonds*

	Mean	*Median*	*Range*
Exchange offer costs ($1,000s)	799	424	200–2,500
Offer costs as a percentage of the book value of assets	0.65	0.32	0.01–3.40
Offer costs as a percentage of the face value of bonds restructured under offer	2.16	2.29	0.27–6.84

* Sample consists of 18 exchange offers undertaken during 1981–1988 for which data were available. Costs consist of cash compensation paid to the exchange and information agent, legal, accounting, brokerage, and investment banking fees, and the value of any common stock warrants issued to the firm's investment bank advisor (as estimated in the exchange offer prospectus).

reorganized within 18 months of its Chapter 11 filing, and successively smaller amounts if the reorganization took longer; no bonus would be paid if Ames was still in Chapter 11 after 39 months. Such innovative compensation schemes, however, are all too rare.[6]

A direct comparison of legal and professional fees for Chapter 11 and private restructuring is difficult because firms are not required to report these costs outside of Chapter 11. Nevertheless, firms that privately restructure their bonds through exchange offers are required to disclose an estimate of all offer-related costs in the exchange offer circular distributed to bondholders. As a result, I was able to obtain reliable cost data for a sample of 18 exchange offers undertaken by New York and American Stock Exchange-listed companies.[7]

---

[6] For evidence on how distressed firms pay their senior managers, see Stuart Gilson and Michael Vetsuypens, "CEO Compensation in Financially Distressed Firms," unpublished Harvard University and Southern Methodist University working paper (1993).

[7] This table is taken from Gilson, John, and Lang, cited in note 3. Exchange offer costs include cash compensation paid to the exchange and information agent, legal, accounting, brokerage, and investment banking fees, and the value of any common stock warrants issused to the firm's investment bank (as estimated in the offer circular).

As summarized in Table 14.1, these costs amounted on average to only 0.65% of the book value of assets (measured just prior to the exchange offer); the corresponding median percentage was only 0.32%. By contrast, academic studies have found that average legal and professional fees reported by Chapter 11 companies range from 2.8% to 7.5% of total assets (generally measured within one year of the filing).[8] Although comparisons across studies are made difficult by differences in the samples and the definitions of costs, these results clearly suggest that private restructuring through exchange offers is much less costly than formal reorganization in Chapter 11, perhaps by as much as a factor of ten.

Management by Bankruptcy Judges

Greater waste of corporate assets is also possible in Chapter 11 because the Bankruptcy Code effectively requires judges to set corporate operating polices. Of course, judges can also add value by arbitrating disputes among the firm's claimholders, thus reducing the length of time required to restructure the debt.

In their traditional role, judges are supposed to interpret and administer the law. In Chapter 11, however, because they must approve all major business decisions, bankruptcy judges have broad powers to influence how the firm's assets are managed. A company's future profitability may depend critically on how the bankruptcy judge rules on proposed corporate actions such as major asset divestitures and capital expenditures.

Moreover, the Bankruptcy Code does not require judges to base their decisions on whether corporate assets will be put to uses that produce the highest rate of return to all investors. For a company's plan of reorganization to be "confirmed" in bankruptcy court (the last legal hurdle to be crossed before exiting from Chapter 11), the judge is required by law to ensure only that two conditions are met: (1) each claimholder must receive at least what he or she would have been paid

---

8 See Jerold Warner, "Bankruptcy Costs: Some Evidence," *Journal of Finance* 32 (1977); James Ang, Jess Chua, and John McConnell, "The Administrative Costs of Corporate Bankruptcy; A Note," *Journal of Finance* 37 (1982); and Lawrence A. Weiss, "Bankruptcy Resolution: Direct Costs and Violation of Priority of Claims," *Journal of Financial Economics* 26 (1990). These studies calculate average costs using different definitions of the firm's assets, including the assets' market value (Warner, Weiss), liquidation value (Ang et al), and book value (Weiss).

if the firm were liquidated;[9] and (2) the company must not appear to be in danger of going bankrupt again in the near future. However honorable their intentions, judges have no financial interest in the outcome of reorganizations, and generally lack relevant management experience. It is thus hardly surprising that corporate assets end up being worth less when judges set corporate policies.

Lost Investment Opportunities

To the extent dealing with creditors (and, in bankruptcy, the judge) diverts management's attention from operating the business, then the firm may forgo profitable investment opportunities. Value lost by not capitalizing on such opportunities is no less real a cost of financial distress than lawyers' fees, and should also be considered in the context of the workout-bankruptcy decision. Although these costs cannot be directly measured, it is reasonable to assume that the extent of any damage will be greater the longer it takes to renegotiate the firm's debts. Hence the "opportunity costs" of financial trouble are likely to be greater in Chapter 11 than in private workouts.

Chapter 11 creates additional delays and distractions due to various procedural demands placed on managers. Before making any decision not in the ordinary course of the firm's business (such as hiring an investment bank to provide advice on asset sales), management must file an application with the court. They may file such an application, moreover, only after first notifying creditors in writing and allowing them sufficient time to file objections. Because the firm can act only after the judge approves the application, otherwise routine decisions can take months to complete. After Public Service Company of New Hampshire filed for bankruptcy in 1988, D.P.G. Cameron, the firm's vice president and general counsel, commented that "the proceedings . . . left us breathless."[10]

One proxy, admittedly crude, for the extent of a company's investment opportunities is the difference between its value as an ongoing

---

9 This is referred to as the "best interests of creditors" test in Section 1129(a)(7) of the Bankruptcy Code. Strictly speaking, this standard only applies if all impaired classes of claimholders assent to the proposed plan (which generally happens). If one or more classes votes against the plan, then the relevant standard is the "fair and equitable" test {Section 1129(b)(2)}, which basically requires that each impaired class receives the present value of its allowed claims under the plan (or whatever is available after all senior classes have been paid in full, provided more junior classes receive nothing). If a plan is fair and equitable, then dissenting classes can be forced to accept its terms under a court-imposed "cramdown."

10 See Stein, cited in note 4.

concern and its liquidation value—what I refer to as "excess going concern value."[11] To the extent investment opportunities are more likely to be lost in Chapter 11 than in private workouts, troubled companies have incentives to avoid bankruptcy and restructure their debt privately. In the extreme, if Chapter 11 leads to liquidation, creditors and shareholders effectively forfeit all of the firm's excess going concern value by not settling privately.[12]

The importance of preserving going concern value in these situations is well demonstrated by the case of Tiger International, a cargo shipper and lessor of transportation equipment. In early 1983, the company initiated what turned out to be a successful workout. As reported at the time in *The Wall Street Journal* (February 16, 1983),

> Wayne M. Hoffman, Tiger chairman, said the company was getting "excellent cooperation" in the early meetings with lenders. He said that he expects sessions to continue "for some weeks," but that he was confident a rescheduling of debt would be the result. "It's in the lender's interest to do this. All of them agree that the going concern is the important thing."

Consistent with the outcome of this case, the Gilson-John-Lang study found that troubled companies are more likely to reorganize privately when they have greater excess going concern value. For companies that successfully restructured their debt out of court, the average ratio of excess going concern value to liquidation value prior to restructuring was 0.83; for firms that filed for Chapter 11 that average ratio was only 0.61.

HOW DO SHAREHOLDERS FARE?

To the extent private workouts are less costly than Chapter 11, both shareholders and creditors should be made better off when attempts to

[11] Of course, excess going concern value will also reflect other sources of value such as monopoly power and goodwill.

[12] Of the Chapter 11 companies I examined (all of them New York and American Stock Exchange companies), only 5% were completely liquidated through a conversion to Chapter 7. For smaller, private companies, the rate is generally higher.

restructure debt privately succeed.[13] My own research suggests shareholders have generally done better in workouts than in Chapter 11.[14] The Gilson-John-Lang study found that shareholders of companies that successfully restructured their debt out of court realized an average 41% increase in the value of their common stockholdings over the period of restructuring (beginning with announcement of the default and net of general market movements). By contrast, for companies that tried to restructure privately but failed, average cumulative returns to shareholders were *negative* 40% over the period of restructuring that ended with a Chapter 11 filing. At least part of the 80% difference in these returns can be viewed as the market's estimate of the shareholder portion of the total cost savings from avoiding Chapter 11 and restructuring privately. (Some part of this 80%, of course, may also reflect the possibility that firms ultimately filing Chapter 11 were systematically less profitable *after* negotiations with creditors began—or that operating problems were far worse than investors initially suspected at the time of default—than firms that did not end up filing.)

Shareholders are also typically allowed to retain a significantly higher percentage of the equity in workouts than in bankruptcy. As I found in a recent study, creditors on average receive 20% of the common stock in workouts, as compared to 67% of the outstanding stock in Chapter 11.[15] Shareholders will be harmed by dilution of their equity to the extent creditors effectively purchase the new shares at a below-market price, or if the value of control conferred by large blocks is dissipated by the issuance of new shares. In some Chapter 11s, of course, shareholders are completely wiped out, as happened recently in the bankruptcy of Sharon Steel (which emerged from Chapter 11 late

---

13 If only a subset of the firm's debt is restructured, a private restructuring plan could in principle harm nonparticipating creditors (for example, participating creditors' claims could be given more security or made more senior). However, such harms will be limited by the right of nonparticipating creditors to sue the firm (and other creditors), by covenants that restrict the issuance of more senior debt, and by cross-default covenants that restrict the firm's ability to exclude certain creditors from participating in the restructuring.

14 Assessing the relative returns to creditors is more difficult because their claims trade much less frequently and market price data are either unreliable or nonexistent. There is nonetheless some evidence that creditors take bigger writedowns of their claims in Chapter 11 than in workouts. See Julian Franks and Walter Torous, "How Firms Fare in Workouts and Chapter 11 Reorganizations," London Business School and University of California at Los Angeles working paper (1991).

15 See Stuart Gilson, "Bankruptcy, Boards, Banks, and Blockholders," *Journal of Financial Economics* 26 (1990). Such percentages assume that none of the warrants or convertible debt and preferred stock received by creditors are eventually converted. Assuming such securities are fully converted, the average creditor holdings increase to approximately 40% and 80%, respectively.

in 1990). In workouts, obviously, shareholders never voluntarily consent to such a plan.

ADVANTAGES OF CHAPTER 11

Although evidence from the 1980s suggests that Chapter 11 is more costly than private restructuring *in the average case,* bankruptcy also provides certain benefits that offset at least part of this cost difference and cause some companies to file for Chapter 11 directly. There are four principal advantages to filing.

First, the Bankruptcy Code allows firms to issue new debt that ranks senior to all debt incurred prior to filing ("prepetition debt"). Such "debtor-in-possession (DIP)" financing is valuable because the firm can borrow on cheaper terms and thus conserve on scarce cash.[16] Over the last few years, increasing sophistication of DIP lenders and growth of the market for tradable bank debt have resulted in more firms entering Chapter 11 with a DIP facility already in place (two recent examples are Ames Department Stores and Pan Am).

Second, interest on prepetition unsecured debt stops accruing while the firm is in bankruptcy, again freeing up cash.[17]

Third, the Bankruptcy Code's automatic stay provision protects the firm from creditor harassment while it reorganizes, thus allowing the business to function with fewer disruptions.

Fourth, it is easier to get a reorganization plan accepted in Chapter 11 because the voting rules are less restrictive. Acceptance of the plan requires an affirmative vote by only a majority (one-half in number, but representing two-thirds in value) of the claimholders in each class whose claims are impaired. By contrast, a workout cannot pass without the consent of all who participate, thus increasing the incidence of creditor holdouts.

THE HOLDOUT PROBLEM

Whether the cost savings from private restructuring are realized will depend on whether creditors unanimously agree to the terms of the

---

[16] For an excellent description of current DIP lending practices see Mark Rohman and Michael Policiano, "Financing Chapter 11 Companies in the 1990s," *Journal of Applied Corporate Finance* (Summer, 1990).

[17] Interest on secured debt continues to accrue up to the excess, if any, of the security's assessed value over the debt's face value.

restructuring. Any factors that increase the likelihood of creditor holdouts thus make attempts at private workouts less likely to succeed. Of course, many of these factors are either difficult or impossible to quantify, such as creditors' relative bargaining strength or the amount of antipathy that creditors feel towards shareholders and management. Nonetheless, some academic work has succeeded in identifying factors that can be used to predict the likelihood of holdouts.

The extent of the holdout problem depends partly on what type of debt is restructured. As noted previously, publicly traded bonds have traditionally been restructured through voluntary exchange offers. The holdout problem in these offers can be quite severe. Provided enough bonds are tendered that the firm stays out of bankruptcy, the bondholders who do not tender (and thus, typically, do not agree to a reduction in the value of their claims) benefit at the expense of those who do. The alternative to an exchange offer—namely, modifying the interest rate, principal amount, or maturity of the outstanding bonds by a vote of bondholders—is made virtually impossible by the Trust Indenture Act of 1939, which requires *every* bondholder to agree to such changes. (Modification of all other, "noncore" covenants of the bond indenture usually requires only a simple or two-thirds majority.)

To address this problem, exchange offers are structured to penalize holdouts. New bonds offered in these exchanges, in addition to having a lower coupon rate or principal amount, are also typically more senior, and of shorter maturity, than the outstanding bonds they will replace.[18] Holders are also sometimes asked jointly to tender their bonds and vote for the elimination of noncore protective covenants in the old bonds (called an "exit consent solicitation"). By so doing, bondholders who tendered will be in a better position than those who don't if the firm later files for bankruptcy.

This situation changed dramatically, however, in January 1990 when Judge Burton Lifland ruled in LTV's bankruptcy that bondholders who tendered in a previous exchange offer were entitled to a claim in bankruptcy equal only to the *market* value of the bonds accepted under the offer; bondholders who held onto their original bonds were allowed a claim equal to the bonds' full face value. Since bonds of distressed companies usually sell at big discounts, the effect of this ruling was to reward LTV's holdouts. Although the LTV decision was re-

[18] As pointed out to me by an investment banker acquaintance, the effect of the exchange is similar to offering passengers on the Titanic the chance to move up from steerage to first class.

versed on appear in early 1992, the immediate effect of the ruling was a dramatic fall-off in the number of attempted exchange offers.[19]

With regard to private debt, my research suggests that holdouts are less common, and private restructurings thus more likely to succeed, when more of the firm's debt is owed to commercial banks—and, to a lesser extent, to insurance companies. The Gilson-John-Lang study found that, on average, bank debt amounted to 40% of total liabilities in firms that successfully restructured, but only 25% in firms that filed for Chapter 11 (median debt ratios were 36% and 20%, respectively).

As one would expect, bank lenders tend to be more sophisticated and fewer in number than other kinds of creditors, and are more likely to recognize the potential benefits of private restructuring. Trade creditors, by contrast, are generally less predisposed to settle. Bankruptcy professionals frequently characterize trade creditors as "unsophisticated" and "acrimonious." Consistent with this characterization, so-called vulture investors often buy out a firm's trade debt at the very start of their involvement with the company.

Our results also indicate that private restructuring succeeds more often when there are fewer distinct classes of long-term debt outstanding.[20] The simplest way to interpret this evidence is that having more creditors increases the likelihood that any one creditor will hold out, and thus make disputes among creditors more likely. The number of debt classes also serves as a measure of the complexity of a firm's capital structure. Complex capital structures will be more difficult to restructure privately, especially if the claims are more difficult to value and there is greater disagreement among creditors over whether they are being treated "fairly" relative to other creditors or shareholders.

---

[19] David Schulte calls 1990 a "very bad year for exchange offers" (see Roundtable Discussion, cited in note 5). And according to investment bankers with whom I have spoken privately, an additional consequence of the ruling was that companies gave up more easily (and filed for Chapter 11) when an exchange offer generated a low initial tender rate. During the 1980s, by contrast, it was not uncommon for companies to revise the terms of exchange offers up to half a dozen times until some desired tender rate was attained.

[20] As identified in the notes to the firm's balance sheet in its annual 10-K report. More precisely, we deflate this variable by the book value of long term debt, to provide a measure of the number of creditors *per dollar of debt owed*. The rationale for this adjustment is that smaller creditors have less of their wealth at risk if a private restructuring attempt fails, and therefore are more likely to hold out, everything else unchanged.

Figure 14.1—Percentage of Original Senior Managers (CEO, Chairman, and President) Who Remain with Their Firms Throughout Period of Financial Distress

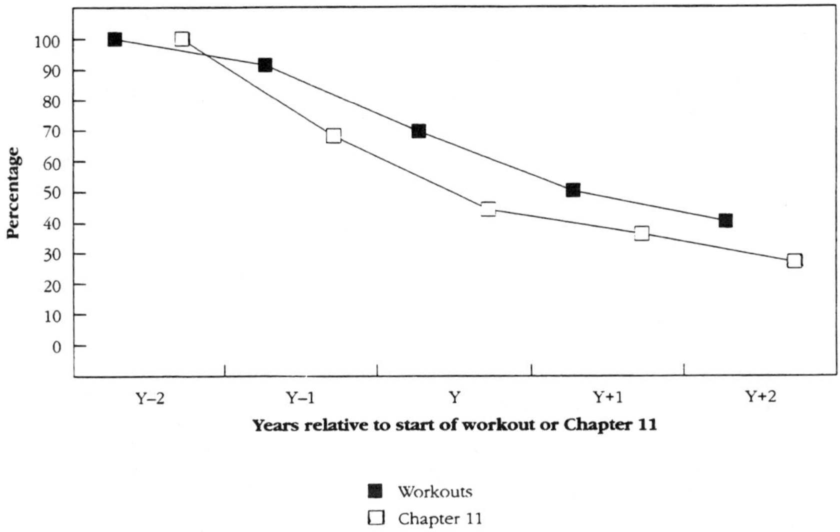

Note: Sample consists of 196 managers initially employed by 126 New York and American Stock Exchange listed companies (sixty-nine firms in Chapter 11 and fifty-seven private workouts) that first defaulted on their debt during 1979–1984.

INCENTIVES OF MANAGERS AND DIRECTORS

Although the workout-bankruptcy decision has a significant impact on a company's stock price, surprisingly few workout proposals are formally put to a shareholder vote. In only one out of every five workouts that I studied did firms first solicit shareholders' approval, either to increase the number of authorized shares or to sell off assets. This raises the interesting question whether managers can personally gain by settling with credits on overly generous terms, and thus at shareholders' expense. One obvious reason why managers might strike a deal with creditors is to protect their jobs.

To investigate this possibility, I analyzed turnover among the senior managers (the CEO, chairman, and president) of 126 New York and American Stock Exchange-listed firms that defaulted on their debt during the early 1980s.[21] As shown in Figure 14.1, management turnover

[21] See Stuart Gilson, "Management Turnover and Financial Distress," *Journal of Financial Economics* 25 (1980).

was substantial regardless of which restructuring method was chosen. At the end of a four-year period starting two years prior to the start of a workout of Chapter 11 filing, only 40% of the original senior managers remained in firms that privately restructured, and only 30% were left in firms that filed for Chapter 11. Turnover among directors of these firms was also high; approximately half the board was replaced during a typical workout or bankruptcy.[22]

Executives' professional reputations also appear to suffer when they are replaced. Although the average age of departing managers in my study was only 52 years, not one of these managers later found work with another exchange-listed firm for at least three years after leaving. Similarly, departing directors subsequently sat on a third fewer boards of other companies three years after leaving, suggesting that their services as directors were valued less highly by other firms. (Of course, these individuals may also have been generally less inclined to serve with large public corporations as managers or directors after their experience with financial distress.)

In short, my own research suggests that managers and other corporate insiders do not gain from systematically choosing a particular restructuring method. Moreover, it lends no support to the popular view, so often aired in the financial press, that Chapter 11 offers a "safe harbor" for the firm's managers.[23] To be sure, Chapter 11 does give the filing firm the exclusive right to file the first reorganization plan for at least 120 days; and it's also true that bankruptcy judges usually grant extensions—sometimes for several years. But such extensions, however potentially costly for investors, represent at most a temporary reprieve for senior managers.

Indeed, in the ten largest bankruptcies in 1990, seven firms replaced their CEOs, generally within one month of filing. In the bankruptcy of Circle K, for example, Karl Eller resigned as chairman and CEO approximately one week before his firm filed (despite his ownership of over 7% of Circle K's common stock). Peter Hollis resigned as president and CEO of Ames Department Stores two days after it filed for Chapter 11.

In addition to my finding that managers are routinely displaced when their firms file, I also found that one of every five top-level management changes was initiated at the behest of creditors—in particular,

---

22 See Gilson, cited in note 15.

23 For example, see Roger Lowenstein and George Anders, "Firms that default find their troubles have just begun," *The Wall Street Journal* (April 17, 1991), p.A1.

bank lenders. Creditors are thus far from powerless in these situations. In short, Chapter 11's automatic stay protects the *firm* from creditor harassment, but not its managers.

POLICY IMPLICATIONS

Distressed firms can preserve more of their value by restructuring their debt privately, when possible, and thus avoiding Chapter 11. My own research suggests that the professional fees incurred in exchange offers are about one-tenth those incurred in a typical Chapter 11 case.

Unfortunately, recent developments threaten to turn more troubled companies towards bankruptcy courts. First, as discussed above, the LTV decision undermined bondholders' incentives to tender in exchange offers for publicly traded junk debt. Second, there has been a steady shift in the tax law toward less favorable treatment of firms that restructure their debt outside of Chapter 11.

Following the Tax Reform Act of 1986, distressed firms have found it more difficult to preserve their net operating loss carryforwards, and to avoid paying taxes on forgiveness-of-debt income, when they operate outside of bankruptcy. Since late last year, firms have been subject to a new tax on private exchange offers. Under the Revenue Reconciliation Act of 1990, whenever new bonds issued in an exchange offer sell at a discount below their stated face value (as is most often the case), the firm must book the difference as taxable income. Prior to the Act, such original issue discounts were tax exempt.[24]

However, the 1990 Act reduced the effectiveness of the stock-for-debt exception by also imposing tougher standards with respect to the type and amount of stock that must be issued for an exchange to receive favorable tax treatment.

Although it is still too early to assess the full impact of these developments on corporate reorganizations, some preliminary evidence suggests that troubled firms are more often choosing to deal with default in Chapter 11. I examined press reports for all firms that were identi-

---

[24] The tax on OIDs could be avoided in two ways. First, an OID was nontaxable if the new bonds had the same face value as the old bonds retired under the exchange offer, and both old and new bonds were considered "securities" for tax purposes (among other things, this effectively required both issues to have a term to maturity of at least five years). Second, firms could qualify for the "stock-for-debt" exception, under which the OID would be nontaxable if stock was also issued under the exchange (in sufficient amount to satisfy the IRS that the firm's principal motive for issuing stock was not simply to avoid paying taxes).

fied in *The Wall Street Journal* as having filed for Chapter 11 between January 1990 and February 1991.[25] Almost 70% of these companies apparently made no attempt to restructure their debt privately before filing. During the 1980s, by contrast, only 30% of financially distressed firms sought Chapter 11 protection as a first resort. Also, for those companies that did attempt to restructure privately in 1990, only three months elapsed, on average, before a Chapter 11 filing. In the 80s, companies spent an average of eight months attempting to find a private solution before filing Chapter 11.

Society loses when firms are forced to use the more expensive method for dealing with financial distress. Until finally being overturned, the LTV decision made it less likely that bondholders would consent to private exchanges, even though the other cost benefits of private workouts relative to Chapter 11 were unaltered. Although entering Chapter 11 to preserve tax benefits helps the firm's security holders, these gains are essentially financed by other taxpayers; as such, they represent wealth transferred rather than wealth created.

Public policy should be directed toward breaking down these and other barriers to private contracting (or recontracting). For example, a strong case can be made for repealing the Trust Indenture Act to facilitate private restructuring of publicly held debt.[26]

Corporate default could also be made less costly by relaxing current regulatory constraints on commercial banks' ability to hold equity in distressed firms; banks are currently required to divest any stock received under a bankruptcy or restructuring in approximately two years. Allowing creditors to hold equity and debt jointly, which is the norm in Japan and Germany, would also streamline the reorganization process by reducing costly, time-consuming conflicts between creditors and shareholders.

One recent development that offers hope is the increasing use of "prepackaged" Chapter 11, in which a firm jointly files its bankruptcy petition and reorganization plan (after having first secured creditors' informal consent to the plan). Prepackaged bankruptcy is a hybrid of private restructuring and Chapter 11—one that potentially incorporates the best features of both methods. Provided the firm has adequately disclosed details of its financial condition to creditors before

---

[25] I excluded firms that were already attempting to privately restructure their debt at the beginning of 1990.

[26] See Mark Roe, "The Voting Prohibition on Bond Workouts," *The Yale Law Review 97* (1987), and Robert Gertner and David Scharfstein, "A Theory of Workouts and the Effects of Reorganization Law," *The Journal of Finance* (forthcoming).

filing, it is possible for the plan to be confirmed almost immediately. Republic Health recently completed a prepackaged bankruptcy in only four months. Such innovations in financial contracting deserve the full support of lawmakers and economists alike.

Chapter Fifteen

Penn Central: A Case Study in Distressed Securities

by Martin S. Fridson, CFA
and
Michael A. Cherry
Analyst
Merrill Lynch

In the investment business, the study of history is not an exercise in intellectual gratification, but rather has a thoroughly practical purpose. At the most basic fact-gathering level, investors search historical price changes for exploitable patterns or evidence that particular securities have deviated from their normal valuation ranges. A more sophisticated sort of historical analysis aims at identifying generalizable cause-and-effect relationships between events and price movements.

Clearly, a strategy of applying lessons of the past to a current investment decision can misfire for any of several reasons. First, the historical record may not have been studied with sufficient rigor to justify the inferences that have been drawn. Second, the investor may derive the wrong lesson from the right facts. The latter risk increases if another party emphasizes selected facts with the intention of inducing a particular decision. Finally, there is always a danger that history will not repeat itself, making even a well-documented and logically argued strategy a prescription for failure.

Perhaps the pitfall that is most important to avoid, however, is acting upon second- or third-hand impressions of past events, rather than knowledge obtained by more direct means. Sticklers for accuracy know that general history is rife with familiar events that never happened, e.g., Marie-Antoinette's exhortation to the masses to eat cake, Abner Doubleday's invention of baseball in Cooperstown, Abraham Lincoln's composing of his celebrated address on the back of an envelope while en route to Gettysburg, Charles Darwin's deathbed recantation, David Sarnoff's discovery via radio signal of the sinking of the Titanic, etc. In light of such discrepancies between what people know and what actually occurred, it would seem even more important in the case of financial history to mistrust popular recollections, given that real money is at stake.

The current revival of interest in distressed and defaulted securities provides many opportunities to learn—and to mislearn—from history. In particular, the recounting of past "killings" made in bonds of bankrupt companies fosters hopes that similarly spectacular opportunities lie among the ruins of yesteryear's leveraged buyouts. Whether those hopes neglect the aforementioned pitfalls—insufficient facts, incorrect facts, nonrepeating history—remains to be demonstrated.

DID BONDHOLDERS EARN EXCESS RETURNS?

One of the most dramatic chapters in the popular history of bankruptcy investing involves the 1970 collapse of the Penn Central Transportation Company (PCTC).[1] For many who were not intimately involved but know the story only as it has been passed down over the years, the following points probably summarize an understanding of the facts and resulting implications:

1. Unsophisticated holders panicked when Penn Central Transportation filed for bankruptcy and dumped their bonds at fire sale levels.
2. Shrewd, steel-nerved investors capitalized on the sellers' irrational fears by buying at prices that did not reflect the hidden value of PCTC's vast real estate holdings.

1 Although usage in some of the sources quoted in this article is inconsistent, we shall generally use "Penn Central Transportation" or "PCTC" to designate the transportation company that went bankrupt in 1970; "the Penn Central" to signify its railroad operations; "Penn Central Co." to indicate its prebankruptcy parent; and "Penn Central Corp." to refer to the nonrailroad company that continued to operate after the bankruptcy ended.

Figure 15.1

Courtesy of R.M. Smythe & Co.

3. As the market began to recognize the true worth underlying the misunderstood securities, patient holders realized spectacular gains.
4. The sure road to success in distressed securities investing, as plainly shown by the foregoing, is to acquire assets on the cheap from holders who are too traumatized to see the situation clearly.[2]

Observe that if clear-sightedness is all that a successful investor in distressed bonds requires, then Wall Street is making a colossally expensive error by employing specialized distressed-security analysts versed in the intricacies of bankruptcy law. Popular chroniclers of the markets lend ample editorial space to victorious speculators to explain

[2] Mark Hulbert, writing in *Forbes* (February 18, 1991), cites Penn Central Transportation and Interstate Stores (which was transformed into the hugely successful Toys "R" Us chain) as past stimulators of interest in the distressed securities sector. Over the course of a recurring cycle, Hulbert argues, the bargains disappear from what was previously an ignored group of securities.

how they triumphed by simply "seeing the big picture" and "hanging tough." Others, who went broke with equally brilliant insights, rarely get the chance to tell their stories. Upon closer examination, Penn Central Transportation's history is perhaps less a tale of courage rewarded than of violent lurches in intrinsic value. At both high and low points, the facts could have justified selling out as strongly as they argued for holding on to the supposedly unloved bonds.

To be sure, the record superficially supports the contention that post-bankruptcy-filing buyers of Penn Central Transportation bonds enjoyed good returns. As readers will discover below, however, the *spectacular* returns that are imprinted in the public consciousness accrued only to investors who got in at later stages. As an example of the appreciation that occurred in Penn Central Transportation issues, subsidiary New York Central's 4 1/2s due 2013 were quoted "flat" (i.e., without accrued interest) at 19 (or $190 per bond) on June 22, 1970 (Table 15.1).[3] A cool-headed investor who bought on that day and held on for the duration would have received a distribution of cash and securities with total value of $320.72 on June 22, 1979, following confirmation of Penn Central Transportation's plan of reorganization. In addition, the investor would have received securities for which the value was in large measure dependent on litigation involving assets taken over by Conrail, a government-sponsored rail operator. By waiting another 20 months for the outcome of the Valuation Case, the investor would have been able to sell these additional securities for a total of $809.80, before transaction costs. Taking into account the proceeds received in 1981 as well as those received in 1979, the internal rate of return (IRR) realized by the fearless purchase of New York Central 4 1/2s was 19.35%. (Selling out entirely in 1979 reaped a lower, but still quite respectable 14.44% return.) Other of the actively quoted Penn Central Transportation bonds produced returns (calculated on the basis of the two-stage distribution assumption) mostly in the range of 15.86% to 19.85%, with one outlier returning a much more modest 12.55%.

At first blush, the nervous nellies who dumped on news of the bankruptcy appear to have left sizable gains on the table. The dumpers, however, can truly be said to have acted unwisely—and the post-filing buyers to have realized extraordinary profits—only if the returns on the PCTC bonds were out of line with their observed risk. On this

[3] Penn Central Transportation filed for bankruptcy on Sunday, June 21, 1970. Our base date for calculating returns on its issues is the first subsequent trading day, June 22, 1970.

Table 15.1—Post-Bankruptcy Cash Flows[1] on Selected Penn Central Transportation Issues

Security	*Post-Default Price June 22, 1970*	*Cash Distribution (Date as Indicated)*	*Redemption of Valuation Case Bonds (February 18, 1981)*	*Liquidation of Reorganizati on Equity (February 23, 1981)*	*Internal rate of Return*
NY Central 6s 1990	$290.00	$155.00[2]	$440.00	$816.18	15.86%
NY Central 4s 1998	$177.50	$145.00[2]	$395.00	$733.40	19.85%
NY Central 4 1/2s 2013	$190.00	$152.00[4]	$405.00	$751.36	19.35%
NY Central 5s 2013	$202.50	$156.00[4]	$416.00	$772.84	18.97%
NY Central & Hudson River 3 1/2s 1997	$300.00	$135.00[2]	$384.00	$535.10	12.55%
Pennsylvania RR 4 1/2s 1981	$230.00	$141.00[2]	$398.00	$740.42	17.27%

[1] Per $1,000 face amount
[2] On October 24, 1978
[3] On March 27, 1979
[4] On June 22, 1979

Source: Capital Changes Reporter, *Wall Street Journal*

basis, the "high" IRR forgone by the early sellers of New York Central 4 1/2s may not have represented any great sacrifice.

The 19.35% IRR on New York Central 4 1/2s between filing date and final distribution was 2.4 times as high as the 8.07% compounded annual return on the Standard & Poor's 500 index of common stocks over the period June 30, 1970 to June 30, 1979.[4] As Figure 15.2 shows, however, the volatility of annual returns was far greater for the New York Central bonds. In the stock market's worst year of the decade (1974), total return plunged to –26.52%. That level of pain was surpassed twice during the seven full calendar years encompassed by PCTC's bankruptcy, as returns plunged to –30.10% in 1972 and –74.19% in 1974. Excluded from these figures, moreover, is the effect

[4] We use equity returns as the basis of comparison in this discussion of bankrupt railroad securities, rather than "riskless" government fixed income obligations. Statements by buyers of distressed bonds make it clear that they seek returns comfortably in the range of "risky asset" returns. In a survey of distressed security investors, Edward I. Altman reported that the most frequent response was a target return of 30% and a minimum return of 20%–25%.

Figure 15.2 Comparison of Annual Returns

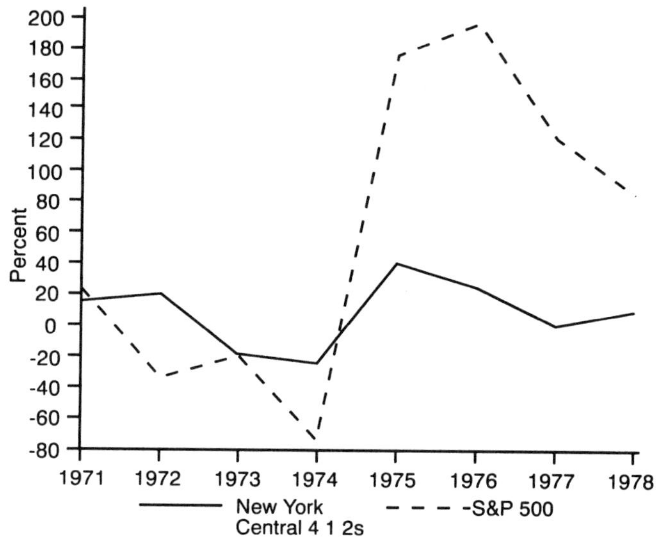

of the drop in New York Central 4 1/2s from their immediate post-bankruptcy price of 19 to 10 1/2 at the end of 1970, a 45% loss of value in just over six months.

This manner of comparing the returns and standard deviations of a defaulted bond with those of the stock market is highly sensitive to period-specific distortions. Furthermore, it would be surprising not to find lower variances of return in a widely diversified portfolio like the S&P 500 than in a single, high-risk security. Still, the figures show that the premium returns earned on defaulted Penn Central Transportation bonds came at a considerable cost in interim fluctuations.

To this last point, it might be answered that a rational, "basic value" buyer ought not to have been perturbed by interim price swings. Having determined in June 1970 that Penn Central Transportation's asset base would produce handsome returns for creditors—the only question being how long it would take—the smart investor ought to have laughed at the weak-willed types who caused quotations to fluctuate wildly in response to trivial news reports.

Realistically, however, sweeping judgments of this sort are easier to make in retrospect than when one's position is underwater by 89% (i.e., New York Central 4 1/2s at 2 at year-end 1975 versus 19 on June 22, 1970). Quite conceivably, the interim swings in Penn Central bond prices were insignificant blips en route to the inevitable, large payouts in 1979 and 1981. It is also possible, however, that the fluctuations were fundamentally grounded, that material new facts altered the present value of expected cash flows along the way and that investors who "chickened out" at 2 were no less rational than those who bought at 19 and never wavered.

Given the myriad of factors affecting a security's value on any given day, as well as the impossibility of quantifying a great many of them, it is impractical to render absolute judgments about the appropriateness of a given quotation many years after the fact. A brief (and therefore unavoidably selective) recapitulation of developments during Penn Central Transportation's bankruptcy can, however, provide some basis for judging whether the original purchase decision was indeed correct all along and that the market's tardiness in recognizing the company's value was all a misunderstanding.

THE 1970 AFTERSHOCK

Let us begin by considering whether it was truly a case of obtuseness (as the "stick-to-your-guns" argument implies) for investors to stand on the sidelines for the first six months while the New York Central 4 1/2s fell by 45% from their initial post-filing price.

As contemporary press reports listed in the Bibliography demonstrate, two key themes of the positive story emerged within a short while after Penn Central Transportation's June 1970 bankruptcy.[5] First, PCTC bulls argued that the company could raise cash by selling its vast real estate holdings. These included Manhattan's Waldorf-Astoria, Biltmore and Commodore hotels, as well as properties in California, Texas, Georgia, and Hawaii. Second, the railroad had the potential of greatly improving its profitability by exiting the passenger service business, which had lost more than $100 million in 1969. The "hidden value story," in short, was well disseminated from the outset, rather than a widely ignored valuation factor.

Bears pointed out, however, that selling real estate quickly would be difficult—since much of it was already pledged as collateral for loans or subject to liens—as well as economically questionable on the grounds that fire sales would not maximize value. Exiting the business

---

[5] Nine days after the bankruptcy filing, for example, a front-page story in the *Wall Street Journal* carried the subtitle, "The Issue of Tapping Assets" and pointed out that the railroad had "sizeable assets in real estate," which it enumerated.

of providing passenger service also promised to be a lengthy undertaking, given the regulatory approvals that would be required. In addition, the bankruptcy process was thought likely to be protracted; some analysts believed reorganization proceedings would take up to 20 years.[6] (On that basis, a recovery of 113% of face value—the actual experience of holders of the New York Centrals 4 1/2s—would have provided an IRR of just 9% to those who bought at 19 in June 1970.) While the clock ticked, moreover, Penn Central Transportation was without a clearly available source of financing for essential repairs and replacements of its long-neglected equipment.

In light of the substantial risks that came to light in the months immediately following the default, it may be judging investors too harshly to say that they were blind to PCTC's underlying values. Perhaps the truth is that analysts applied discount rates that were appropriate in view of the uncertainties that existed at the time, even though it might seem from the vantage point of 1991 that the company's difficulties were bound to be overcome.

BACK ON TRACK: 1971

Certainly, the 22.62% gain in New York Central 4 1/2s during 1971 lends credence to the view that the preceding period's decline represented an excess of pessimism, which patient holders could have exploited with high confidence of success. Some contemporary accounts, however, characterized the price rise as a sucker's rally. "The more sophisticated you are, the less value you can see in Penn Central," said one equity analyst, supporting the view that small, uninformed investors were fueling the rebound. Perhaps the little people simply believed that a stock priced not much earlier at $85 a share was bound to rise from $7, just as the St. Louis Southwestern Railway's stock—regarded as worthless following the carrier's 1944 bankruptcy—rebounded to $320 seven years later. One "insider" who thought otherwise was a porter in Philadelphia, who ventured, "It'll take a heap of baking powder before the Penn Central rises again."

---

6 Opinions varied widely on this point. John W. Barriger, a veteran of reorganizations dating back to the Great Depression, opined, "The situation is desperate, but it is not serious." Under capable management, he told *Forbes*, the Penn Central railroad could be rehabilitated in two to three years.

A TIME OF TROUBLES: 1972–1974

Those words proved prophetic, for the heroic recovery of the New York Central 4 1/2s to fully 12 7/8% of face value at the start of 1972 was akin to Richard Nixon's landslide reelection in the same year. Both the President and the bonds promptly suffered spectacular reversals of fortune, with the former resigning under threat of ouster and the latter plunging to 2 at the end of 1974. Not until 1976 would the New York Central 4 1/2s finish a year at a level as high as their 1970 close. A waggish remark that was current during Nixon's truncated second term was especially apt for describing the predicament of Penn Central Transportation's long-suffering lenders: "We have seen the light at the end of the tunnel, but is has turned out to be the headlamp of an oncoming locomotive."

Like the 1971 deterioration from levels that might have been thought already unjustifiably low, the 1972–1974 price relapse cannot easily be dismissed as a short-lived outbreak of hysteria. Even though earlier purchases at higher prices produced handsome returns in the long run, there is a plausible case that value was fairly reflected at 7 3/4 in 1973 and even at 2 in 1974.

For starters, the selloff in Penn Central Transportation bonds occurred amidst horrendous economic conditions. Between January and August of 1973, interest rates (as represented by three-month Treasury bills) soared from 5.41% to 8.67%. Gross National Product, which grew at a robust 9.72% seasonally adjusted annual rate during 1973's first quarter, slowed to 1.03% in the second quarter and turned negative (–0.39%) in the third. The economy posted three more negative quarters before the end of 1975, bottoming at –7.59% in the first quarter of that year. In New York City, where much of the railroad's vaunted real estate lay, office vacancy rates soared from 1.0% in 1969 to 14.8% in 1972 and did not recede to less than 10% until 1977.[7]

Based on these figures, it was rational for investors to assign not only a higher risk-free rate, but also a higher risk premium (in view of the increased danger of corporate failure), to expected cash flows generally. With an economic downturn further trimming cash flow forecasts, it is not surprising that the Standard & Poor's 500 common stock index fell by 22% during 1973–1975. The New York Central 4 1/2%, which unlike the S&P 500 lacked the stabilizing factor of dividend support, was in effect an equity with above-average price volatility during

---

[7] Source: Real Estate Board of New York.

the period, falling 78%. (Looking only at the 1973–1974 period, during which time the S&P bottomed out some 43% below its initial level, the New York Central 4 1/2s showed *less* price volatility, falling by just 14%.)

On top of the higher discount rates that reduced the values of all corporate assets, Penn Central Transportation securities warranted a sizable company-specific risk premium during the period. As 1973 opened, the railroad faced the threat of a strike by the United Transportation Union. In addition, the company's cash position had fallen during the preceding year from $45 million to $24 million, a level just $4 million above the bare minimum some analysts thought was needed to keep the railroad running. Potential relief existed in the form of $48 million in a court-controlled escrow account, but there was a danger that the funds would never reach creditors, but instead be diverted to maintenance of an essential public service, i.e., to meeting the railroad's day-to-day cash needs. Creditors spoke of their property rights, but acknowledged that they would have to fight in court to block the diversion of sale proceeds.

From the vantage point of the Nineties, following Ronald Reagan's revival of laissez-faire policies and the repudiation of centrally planned economies in Eastern Europe, readers may have difficulty appreciating the seriousness with which threats of effective confiscation were regarded by investors assessing Penn Central Transportation in the 1970s. Federal bailouts of Lockheed (1971) and Chrysler (1979), as well as the imposition of federal wage and price controls (1971), demonstrated the willingness of administrations both Republican and Democratic to allow perceived public interest to override the invigorating force of unfettered competition (to paraphrase the increasingly self-confident free marketers of the 1980s in their manner of explaining how the world worked). Therefore, the analysts who evaluated New York Central 4 1/2s at 2 as of the end of 1975, were not inclined to shrug off the possibility of an appropriation that would have dwarfed the diversion of $48 million of escrowed funds. They viewed as only too real the threat of a federal takeover of the Penn Central, with compensation to its owners that would have represented but a small fraction of true value.

In light of the railroad's grim operating prospects, political support began to mount for the formation of a federally financed corporation that would own and operate a streamlined rail network in the Northeastern United States, built around Penn Central Transportation's assets. The idea, not surprisingly, was anathema to railroad executives, who knew that broader nationalization was not unprecedented in the

United States, having occurred during the First World War. Shippers likewise preferred to keep Uncle Sam out of the picture, with one auto executive saying of the Penn Central, "God help us if the government ever takes it over."

Officially, President Nixon's directive was "to have a private, free enterprise solution," according to a Treasury spokesman, and there was general agreement that a veto of highly expensive legislation would not be overridden by Congress. On the other hand, the trustees' proposal to begin liquidating the railroad by October 31, 1973 was politically unpalatable to many. Closing down the Penn Central, by one estimate, would have cut total output in the U.S. economy by 3%. Bethlehem Steel chairman Stewart S. Cort warned that if rail service ceased, his company's operation would "be closed up as tight as a clam within 10 days, putting 70,000 workers out on the bricks." There was also a fear that winter fuel shortages would be exacerbated by a shutdown of the Penn Central, one of the railroad industry's largest haulers of coal. Even the less extreme proposal of abandoning unprofitable trackage to shore up finances, the subject of hearings during 1973, encountered stiff resistance. Pennsylvania governor Milton J. Shapp, for example, objected that track abandonment would greatly inhibit efforts to attract new industry to the state.

After much posturing by the Administration and Congress, neither of which wanted to appear responsible for a costly federal takeover, the 1973 Regional Rail Reorganization Act became law. The act reorganized several distressed Northeastern railroads into the Consolidated Rail Corporation (Conrail).

A Philadelphia district court soon struck down parts of the legislation, based on creditors' complaints that their asset value would be eroded while Conrail was being formed, during which time the Penn Central would be barred from abandoning track or liquidating. (Creditors contended that such erosion was occurring at a $200 million annual rate.) The U.S. Supreme Court upheld the 1973 legislation, however, concluding that creditors had available adequate means of recovering losses through the Tucker Act, a law enabling citizens to bring suit against the United States for unfair taking of property. Dissenting from the majority, Justice William O. Douglas groused that an action like Congress's acquisition of the Penn Central's assets, "if done by private parties in control of a bankrupt estate, would be a fraudulent conveyance."

Fraudulent or not, the appropriation of property that had secured Penn Central Transportation's creditors, with no assurance of adequate compensation, had now received the Supreme Court's seal of approval.

Under the circumstances, the price slippage in New York Central's 4 1/2s during 1973–1974 could not be ascribed exclusively to a generalized hysteria among investors. It surely had some rational justification, even if one can perhaps argue that the bears overshot the target.

THE VALUATION STRUGGLE: 1975–1978

Once the Supreme Court upheld the Regional Rail Reorganization Act, uncertainty regarding the value of Penn Central Transportation securities revolved around the compensation that would ultimately be paid for the assets taken by Conrail. In the end, a favorable resolution produced the eye-popping returns that have since been incorporated into the myth of Penn Central Transportation as a demonstration of the rich rewards inherent in the misunderstood securities of bankrupt companies. As in the earlier period, however, spectacular changes in the value of New York Central 4 1/2s—from 2 at the start of 1975 to 57 1/2 at the beginning of 1979—reflected risks that made the favorable outcome seem less assured at the time than in hindsight.

The wide range of potential values for Penn Central Transportation obligations was closely related to the disparity between what the federal government wanted to pay for the Conrail assets and what creditors wished to receive. Even allowing for aggressive assumptions on both sides to support extreme initial negotiating positions, the disparity in valuations was gargantuan. The United States Railway Association (USRA), which had been set up in 1973 as a branch of the U.S. Department of Transportation, valued the acquired assets at $471.2 million. The railroad's trustees, in contrast, put the figure in a range of $3.5 billion to $13.6 billion, with a most reasonable value of $7.4 billion.

As is typical in bankruptcy cases, the divergent asset valuations were supported by dissimilar calculation methods. The USRA assumed sale of the Penn Central's assets for scrap, which under normal conditions, would have produced a $3.6 billion estimate. The USRA further assumed, however, that placing assets as massive as Penn Central's on the auction block would have depressed prices, so that only $471 million would have been realized. Vehemently contesting this "fire sale" methodology, the railroad's trustees cited one example in which a line out of Charleston, West Virginia that earned $10 million a year was presumed to be worth just $3.5 million in the USRA's analysis. Penn Central Transportation's $7.4 billion most-reasonable estimate proceeded from the premise that the sale-for-scrap approach was irrelevant in light of the vital importance to the Northeastern economy of the railroad's continued operation. The trustees' valuation at a level far above the USRA's estimate reflected the railroad's worth on an ongoing basis.

From the investor's viewpoint, the extremes of $471 million and $13.6 billion may have represented outcomes that, if possible at all, had low probabilities. Indeed, Penn Central Co. chairman Archibald Johnson publicly characterized the USRA valuation theory as "unfair, unreasonable, and transparently confiscatory" and intimated that its actual purpose might be "to coerce the owners and creditors . . . to settle out of court for less than the minimum constitutional compensation." The mere fact of a large gap between the negotiating parties posed a serious risk to creditors, however, since their estate was now reportedly eroding by more than $1 million a day while the parties haggled.

To make matters worse, the value of Penn Central Transportation obligations circa 1976 depended heavily on the duration of the haggling. On June 3 of that year, the *Wall Street Journal* speculated that "at least 10, and perhaps 20 years of court wrangling" were likely before litigation over compensation to creditors could be resolved. In round numbers, Penn Central Transportation had $1.7 billion of secured bonds outstanding, an additional $1.7 billion of acknowledged liabilities and potential claims of another $1.6 billion from individuals, small businesses, tax-collecting municipalities, etc. According to a reorganization plan presented by a group of creditors, cash on hand, real estate, and rail assets not taken by Conrail were in aggregate sufficient to distribute about 10% of the $1,300-per-bond claim (including postpetition interest) in cash, plus $390 face amount of new 7% first mortgage bonds, amortizing in installments over seven years. On a strict priority basis, secured holders were entitled to an additional $480 per bond (i.e., $1,000 less $130, less $390).[8] Realization of the trustees' most likely estimate of the value of the assets acquired by Conrail, $7.4 billion, would have made secured creditors whole, but a 10-year delay would have reduced the $480 of additional proceeds to $78 at an assumed 20% discount rate for high-risk investments. By extension, the market-based present value in 1976 of a secured bond (such as the New York Central 4 1/2s) would have been $501, assuming immediate re-

[8] The economic value of the proposed distribution to secured holders was reduced by the difference between face and market value of the proposed 7% mortgage bonds. One contemporary analyst appraised the issue at 75% of face value, or about $293 per $1,000 face amount.

ceipt of the initial proceeds under the above-described reorganization plan. A lengthier litigation to evaluate the Conrail assets, running 20 years, would have reduced the present value of the deferred portion of the distribution to $12 and of the entire bond to $435.

Furthermore, investors had no particular reason to feel confident, as the foregoing calculations assume they did, that receipt of the non-Conrail-related proceeds was as imminent as some onlookers suggested. In the June 3, 1976 *Wall Street Journal* article previously referred to, Chief Trustee Robert W. Blanchette said that an agreement among creditors would take one year "under the best of circumstances" and suggested that the process could drag on for considerably longer than that. Even a two-year delay would have reduced the present value of the proposed cash-plus-mortgage-bond distribution from $423 (i.e., $130 cash plus $293 of market value of new mortgage bonds) to $294. If, as the aforementioned pessimistic case supposed, secured holders were paid the balance of their claims in full but only after 20 years, the present value of the full package would have been just $306.

That estimate might have been reduced even further by investors viewing the situation in 1976, given several additional uncertainties. First, compensation for the Conrail assets might have failed, in the end, to cover secured holders' claims. The USRA's $47 million valuation was less than the $900 million or so of secured claims not extinguishable through the immediate distribution contemplated in the major creditors' plan. Second, unsecured creditors had a large incentive to "hold out," i.e., to use the leverage represented by the requirement that their consent be obtained for any plan of reorganization. Compensation at the level of the USRA valuation would have left nothing for them, so junior creditors had nothing to lose by stalling the process in hopes of receiving concessions. Consequently, secured holders were viewed as likely to cede a non-negligible portion of their asset value (at least of the deferred portion) to unsecured holders in order to avoid further losses in time value of money. More uncertainty was added by two key players whose willingness to go along with the major creditors' plan was unknown.

These were Penn Central Transportation's common shareholder, Penn Central Co., and the federal government. (Among other things, Uncle Sam had guaranteed $100 million of private loans to the Penn Central back in 1971 and advanced $350 million to Conrail to pay disputed liabilities that it had acquired along with PCTC rail assets.) Finally, the sheer complexity of the proposed reorganization validated investors' fears of a prolonged struggle to achieve agreement on the major creditors' plan. Claims against more than 200 subsidiaries and leased lines had to be resolved, along with the issue of back taxes owed to some 2,200 state and local governments. Further complicating matters was the unclear status of the New York, New Haven & Hartford Railroad, which had been acquired by Penn Central in 1968 but never paid for.

Certainly, analysts who now know the outcome may find it difficult to reconcile the 1976 opening price of 5 3/8 for the New York Central 4 1/2s with the size of the initial distribution proposed in the reorganization plan. A contemporary investor, however, need not have been a pathological pessimist to fear that the vast array of creditors would not reach agreement by the end of 1977. Some "key insiders" had their doubts on this point, according to *Forbes*, and the plan still faced bitter opposition from certain quarters. John G. Brown, a large holder of Pittsburgh, Cincinnati, Chicago & St. Louis Railway bonds, complained to the *Wall Street Journal*, "They're taking the assets belonging to the leased lines, which are often large amounts of money held in escrow for the benefit of the leased-line bondholders. And they're distributing those among the holders of third-lien obligations of the New York Central, which are nothing but two streaks of rust running through a swamp!"

THE LONG WRAP-UP: 1979–1981

As it turned out, creditors did not receive the cash and reorganization securities by the end of 1977, but instead had to wait until June 22, 1979. Fears of even lengthier delays proved not to have been unfounded, particularly when one considers that only after hard bargaining did the federal government help to clear the way for an agreement by accepting senior bonds in lieu of cash for most of its claims. With the parties drawing closer together during the negotiations, though, the New York Central 4 1/2s climbed steeply toward their confirmation-date value, reaching 33 1/2 by the outset of 1979.

Holders who elected to forgo the further suspense of awaiting the outcome of the Conrail Valuation case could have sold the package of cash and securities for $662.50 in mid-1979. That alternative represented a 14.44% internal rate of return from purchase, nine years earlier, at $190 per bond. More sensational gains—the stuff of which legends were made over the next two years—remained for those who continue to play.

The endgame for Penn Central Transportation bondholders consisted primarily of speculation regrading the outcome of the Valuation

Case. Along the way, to be sure, the reorganized Penn Central Corp. sold some assets, including a former railroad yard in Manhattan and the Pittsburgh & Lake Erie and Detroit, Toledo & Ironton lines. Business prospects and acquisitions of Penn Central Corp., a diversified energy, recreation, and real estate company, also made some difference. The real action, however, derived from the size and timing of the compensation that Conrail would be obliged to pay for the rail assets it had taken from PCTC.

A key figure in investors' calculations was $2 billion. By the terms of the reorganization plan, the full proceeds up to that amount had to be applied to par redemptions of the bonds and preference shares given to creditors. The bonds naturally had priority, so that they could have been redeemed in full in the event of an award of as little as $1.3 billion. Proceeds above $2 billion, on the other hand, would go to common stock, 96% of which had been distributed to the creditors.

Like the earlier negotiations concerning the reorganization plan, the Valuation Case was an acrimonious affair that threatened to become extremely long-lived. The USRA had moderated its original stance somewhat, now saying it would approve a payment (still based on scrap value) of approximately $550 million plus accrued interest from 1976. That amount, however, was far below the $1.3 billion needed just to redeem the reorganization bonds, never mind the preference stock. For its part, Penn Central Corp. argued that its New York-New Jersey tunnel alone would cost over half a billion dollars to replace and, moreover, would last for a thousand years. With the parties extremely far apart, a special court that was hearing the case urged settlement as a means of avoiding protracted, costly litigation. Several months after settlement talks began, however, Penn Central Corp. characterized them as "still in a preliminary stage" and subject to discontinuation at any time.

In short, the ex-holder of New York Central 4 1/2s, having been partly cashed out in 1979, experienced fluctuations in the value of the remaining package of securities of approximately $457.10 to $1,161.27. Given the vagaries of the litigation process,[9] valuations well below the top figure were rationally justifiable. The circumstance that Series A bonds were available at 93 on October 31, 1980 does not establish that

---

[9] For a discussion of the limitations of financial analysis in valuing securities that are strongly affected by unresolved lawsuits, see Martin S. Fridson, "Does Legal Risk Belong in a High Yield Portfolio?" in *High Yield Bonds: Identifying Risk and Assessing Value of Speculative Grade Securities* (Chicago: Probus Publishing, 1989), pp. 161–176.

they were undervalued, even though they were redeemed at par less than five months later, producing a 25.71% annualized return.

On Monday, November 17, 1980, the federal government agreed to settle creditors' claims for $2.11 billion, a figure slightly above the $2 billion required to redeem the reorganization securities in full. USRA chairman Stephen Berger estimated that had a settlement not been reached, resolving the case in court might have taken three more years. On that assumption, and based on a 20% discount rate, the par securities issued in PCTC's reorganization would then have been worth just 56. Investors who lacked omniscience, in other words, could have reasonably valued the bonds on November 14 well below the prices they attained after the succeeding weekend.

For holders of the New York Central 4 1/2s and the 5s of 2013, the story was still not completely over. They had successfully sued for additional distributions of reorganization securities and received further mortgage bonds which were ultimately worth $276 per original debenture in the case of the 4 1/2s. By selling both Valuation Case distributions upon receipt, holders of the 4 1/2s realized the 19.35% IRR previously discussed (see "Did Bondholders Earn Excess Returns?" above).

EPILOGUE

Looking back at the bitter, 10 1/2-year struggle to settle the bankruptcy of Penn Central Transportation, the message that emerges is surely not that easy profits can be had at the expense of the cowards who flee in panic when they hear the phrase, "bankruptcy." Turning tail was initially the more successful, if not the more glorious course, as the New York Central 4 1/2s plummeted by 53%.

Staunch defenders of distressed securities sometimes urge that the trick is merely to wait until the first, convulsive disgorging of bonds is over before stepping up. In PCTC's case, however, stepping up during the first five years consistently resulted in losses, so the standard advice was not especially helpful.

Those who bought somewhere near the low tick can proudly point to their astuteness, but with all due respect, their post hoc explanations of "how they did it" do not conclusively demonstrate that they profited from anything other than luck. Viewed in isolation, the Penn Central Transportation bonds circa 1975 appear to represent a case of dramatic undervaluation. On the other hand, in the context of a number of securities that similar logic labeled "cheap" in 1970, PCTC paper may simply be the tail of a bell-shaped distribution of subsequent returns, some of which were lackluster or decidedly negative.

To illustrate this point with some more contemporary examples, we offer for consideration the common shares of L.E. Myers Group and Amdura. Both stocks traded at merely seven times earnings at the end of 1989, when the Standard & Poor's 500 index was priced at a multiple of 15 1/2. Myers's boosters foresaw expanded business opportunities in an expected resurgence of capital spending by electric utilities. There was likewise considerable upside in the Amdura turnaround/takeover scenario. In the event, however, Myers prospered, closing 1990 up 124% at 15 1/8, while Amdura sank 98% to 3/32 in the wake of a bankruptcy filing.

Knowing both sides of the story, a rational investor would not regard the history of L.E. Myers as proof that a below-average earnings multiple invariably reflects the madness of crowds and foreshadows a return to a "normal" valuation. Neither does the fact that a portfolio manager selected L.E. Myers at the end of 1989 constitute proof, in and of itself, of superior analytical skills. Indeed, there must be a presumption of luck unless the manager can document a statistically significant record of excess returns through security selections, premised on some consistent analytical approach.

Indiscriminately buying a selection of defaulted bonds, solely on the basis of isolated case histories like Penn Central Transportion, would be just as irrational as scooping up every low-multiple stock available. Even if the evidence confirmed the popular impression that PCTC bondholders received extraordinary returns relative to the risk they incurred, it would still be a prodigious leap to the conclusion that defaulted securities are, as a group, systematically undervalued because of an unwarranted stigma attached to bankruptcy. In fact, if one accepts the premise that markets are inefficient enough to permit a wholesale undervaluation, must one not also allow for the possibility that at a point in time defaulted securities may be collectively *over*valued as a consequence of too many dollars chasing a fad? Alternatively, if defaulted securities are, as a class, valued fairly at most times, they may be regarded as eminently attractive vehicles for investors of a particular risk preference. Selected issues, moreover, may at times represent genuine bargains even if defaulted bonds are collectively neither rich nor cheap.

Unlike the anecdotal evidence that is energetically recycled by some practitioners, the financial literature is far from a ringing endorsement of the belief that investors, by shunning defaulted securities, cause them in aggregate to be consistently undervalued. In a 1969 study, the strongest statement Edward I. Altman could make regarding value was, "We have shown that investments in bankrupt corporate equity securities appear to be at least as attractive as average returns on listed securities, as long as the securities are purchased after bankruptcy. The results, however, must be tempered by a possible upward bias in our . . . calculations."[10] In 1977 Jerold Warner studied a sample of railroad bankruptcies over the period 1930–1955 and found that no abnormal returns were earned by bondholders, once the effects of unusual results for 1940–1942 were removed. Warner thought that the brief episode of general undervaluation was perhaps related to certain Supreme Court decisions, which may or may not have been efficiently reflected in security price adjustments.[11] Dale Morse and Wayne Shaw picked up the thread following the Bankruptcy Reform Act of 1978. According to them, "After the 1978 Act, bankrupt firms had residual returns very close to zero." Morse and Shaw also found that in the 36 months following default, "half the securities had price increases and half the securities had prices decreases." They added that publicly available accounting data seemed to provide no help in predicting which issues would do well.[12] Finally, Allan Eberhart has recently observed 248 firms that filed for Chapter 11 after the October 1, 1979 effective date of the 1978 Bankruptcy Act and found that bond prices on the bankruptcy date represented unbiased forecasts of the amounts received upon confirmation of reorganization plans. That is, buying a market basket of bankrupt companies' bonds would have produced nothing other than a normal, risk-adjusted rate of return.[13]

An implication of Morse and Shaw's finding on the use of accounting data is that detailed analysis of the particulars of a bankrupt firm's financial *prospects* (as opposed to reported results) and of its reorganization proceedings is required to identify the firm in advance as a superior performer. Bankrupt securities, considered as a whole, do not represent an area in which courageous investors benefit from any inherent bias toward superior risk-adjusted performance. Indeed, from its base period of December 1986 through December 1990, the Altman-

---

10 Edward I. Altman, "Bankrupt Firms' Equity Securities as an Investment Alternative," *Financial Analysts Journal* (July/August 1979), pp. 129–133.

11 Jerold B. Warner, "Bankruptcy, Absolute Priority, and the Pricing of Risky Debt Claims," *Journal of Financial Economics* 4 (1977), pp. 239–276.

12 Dale Morse and Wayne Shaw, "Investing in Bankrupt Firms," *The Journal of Finance* 43, No. 5 (December 1988), pp. 1193–1206.

13 Allan C. Eberhart, William T. Moore, and Rodney L. Roenfeldt, "Security Pricing and Deviations from the Absolute Priority Rule in Bankruptcy Proceedings." *The Journal of Finance* 45, No. 5 (December 1990), pp. 1457–1469.

Merrill Lynch Index of Defaulted Debt Securities rose by a scant 11.6%, representing a compounded annual return of just 2.8%. In some interim periods, to be sure, the index's returns were higher, but inasmuch as one-year Treasury bills produced a compounded annual return of 7.55% over the same period, one cannot easily posit a perennial bargain in defaulted bonds as a class, even if occasional standouts like Penn Central Transportation have legitimately whetted speculators' appetites.

Also worth reflecting upon in connection with Penn Central Transportation bonds is the question of whether their undervaluation, if one indeed existed, displayed exploitable parallels with other situations. "Buying claims on hidden assets" may truly have been the principle underlying the success of PCTC bondholders (although the Biltmore Hotel and other real properties were remarkably ill-kept secrets, judging by their frequent mention in contemporary press accounts), yet the formula may prove useless in other instances. The specific analytical points that identified value at PCTC may simply not be generalizable to any other distressed company.

In summary, successful investing in bankrupt securities probably depends more on exhaustive scrutiny of financial statements and legal documents than on remarkable insights. The notion that con-conventional money managers shun defaulted bonds provides, in all likelihood, no useful guidance to investors. When hearing the distilled recollection of some hugely successful past speculation, investors should presume that many essential details have been discarded in the course of countless retellings. Hard work, rather than easy money, is the key to investing in distressed debt.

BIBLIOGRAPHY

Altman, Edward I. "Bankrupt Firms' Equity Securities as an Alternative Investment." *Financial Analysts Journal*, July/August 1969, pp. 129–133.

Altman, Edward I. "Investing in Distressed Securities." Los Angeles: The Foothill Group, April 1990.

Anderson, Harry B. "Bid Filed to End Penn Central's Bankruptcy Case." *Wall Street Journal*, December 20, 1976, p. 2.

Anderson, Harry B. "Long, Long Trail: Penn Central Settlement Will Take Years Even If Accord Is Reached Fairly Quickly." *Wall Street Journal*, June 3, 1976, p. 34.

Anderson, Harry B. "Managerial Miracle: How Penn Central, Minus Railroad, Got a Recoganization Plan." *Wall Street Journal*, March 10, 1978, p. 1.

"Another Cash Crisis at Penn Central." *Business Week*, January 13, 1973, pp. 44ff.

Bilby, Kenneth. *The General: David Sarnoff and the Rise of the Communications Industry*. New York: Harper & Row, Publishers, 1986, pp. 30-35.

Blustein, Paul. "The Reincarnation of Penn Central." *Forbes*, May 1, 1977, p. 50.

"Can Penn Central Come Back?" *Forbes*, As I See It, August 15, 1970, pp. 38ff.

Capital Changes Reporter. Chicago: Commerce Clearing House, 1990.

Doughen, Joseph R. and Peter Binzen. *The Wreck of the Penn Central*. Boston: Little, Brown & Co., 1971.

Eberhart, Allan C., William T. Moore and Rodney Roenfeldt. "Security Pricing and Deviations from the Absolute Priority Rule in Bankruptcy Proceedings." The Journal of Finance 45, No. 5 (December 1990), pp. 1457–1479.

Faulkner, Ben and Roderick Craib. "The Bitter Battle over the Penn Central's Value." *Business Week*, October 27, 1975, p. 114.

"A Ghost in the Closet?" *Forbes*, May 1, 1973, pp. 24–25.

"Hearings Set for Claims Against Penn Central." *Railway Age*, January 10, 1977, pp. 6–8.

"Holders of Penn Central Bonds and Stocks Keep Asking: What Will Be the Final Result of Bankruptcy Step?" *Insurance*, July 15, 1970, pp. 37–38.

Hulbert, Mark. "Up from the Ashes." *Forbes*, February 18, 1981, p. 135.

Karr, Albert and Bill Paul. "Road to Ruin: Penn Central Railroad Nears End of the Line; Rescue Effort Falters." *Wall Street Journal*, September 28, 1973, p. 1.

Kurland, M., et al. "L. E. Myers—Company Report." Mabon, Nugent & Company, April 2, 1990.

Madrick, Jeffrey. "Uncovering the Wealth at Penn Central." *Inside Wall Street*, September 7, 1976, p. 60.

Maples, R. C. "Amdura—Company Report." Piper, Jaffray & Hopwood Incorporated, March 6, 1989.

Marcial, Gene C. "Foreign Buying of U.S. Concerns Jumped 20% in First Half as Merger Pace Continues Strong." *Wall Street Journal*, Heard on the Street, August 31, 1978, p. 35.

Moody's Transportation Manual. New York: Moody's Investors Service, 1979, pp. 322ff.

Morris, Jack H. "No One is Sure Why, but Investors Flock to a Not-So-Hot Issue." *Wall Street Journal*, March 17, 1971, p.1.

Morse, Dale and Wayne Shaw. "Investing in Bankrupt Firms." *The Journal of Finance* 43, No. 5 (December 1988), pp. 1193–1206.

"Northeast Roads' Creditors Can Only Get Liquidation Value of Assets, Court Rules." *Wall Street Journal*, October 13, 1977, p. 48.

Paul, Bill. "Supreme Court's Upholding of Rail Act Far from Solves Penn Central's Woes." *Wall Street Journal*, December 24, 1974, p. 5.

"The Penn Central: A Year Later." *Business Week*, June 19, 1971, pp. 92ff.

"Penn Central Agrees to Sell 2 Inactive Yards." *Wall Street Journal*, March 11, 1975, p. 2.

"Penn Central and U.S. Hold Talks Seeking to Settle Firm's Suit." *Wall Street Journal*, March 1, 1979, p. 46.

"Penn Central Bankruptcy Case Near End; Plan Ruled Equitable, Subject to Changes." *Wall Street Journal*, March 10, 1978, p. 37.

"Penn Central Confirms Talks." *Wall Street Journal*, November 30, 1976, p. 25.

"Penn Central Creditors End Legal Bid to Upset Plan of Reorganization." *Wall Street Journal*, October 3, 1979, p. 23.

"Penn Central Holders, Lenders and Claimants Clear Reorganization." *Wall Street Journal*, May 26, 1978, p. 35.

"Penn Central: It's Time for Investors to Switch Trains." *Financial World*, August 1, 1978, pp. 26–27.

"Penn Central Rail Unit Could Close in Early '73 Due to Cash Shortage." *Wall Street Journal*, December 13, 1972, p. 16.

"Penn Central Scores U.S. Take-Over Plan for Ailing Roads, Especially Valuation." *Wall Street Journal*, September 16, 1975, p. 4.

"Penn Central to Sell Manhattan Rail Yard for Total $28 Million." *Wall Street Journal*, May 7, 1979, p. 23.

"Penn Central Unit's Trustees to Sue U.S. for Line's Alleged Value Loss Since 1970." *Wall Street Journal*, September 17, 1975, p. 13.

"Penn Central's Creditors to Get $2.11 Billion." *Wall Street Journal*, November 18, 1980, p. 2.

"Penn Central's Deficits Soar." *Railway Age*, January 26, 1976, p. 16.

"Penn Central's Former Creditors Are Rebuffed." *Wall Street Journal*, April 22, 1977, p. 8.

Pinkerton, Jr., W. Stewart. "Long Haul Ahead: Penn Central Faces Lengthy Legal Snarls Under Bankruptcy Laws." *Wall Street Journal*, June 30, 1970, p. 1.

Putnam III, George. *The Ten Largest Bankruptcies—And Their Lessons for Investors*. Boston: New Generation Investments, Inc. 1987, pp. 11–15.

Santry, David G. "Investors Can Ride Penn Central Again." *Business Week*, July 3, 1978, p. 85.

Shakin, Bernard. "Alive and Kicking: Penn Central Has Gone from Bankruptcy to Prosperity." *Barron's*, March 19, 1979, p. 9.

"A Shattered Railroad Becomes a Land Company." *Business Week*, January 24, 1977, p. 46.

Standard & Poor's Bond Guide. New York: Standard & Poor's Corporation, 1970-1981 monthly editions.

"Sunken Treasure." *Financial World*, September 1, 1976, p. 26.

"Top Court Backs Plan to Revamp Northeast Rails." *Wall Street Journal*, December 17, 1974, p. 4.

"A Trustee Who Worries about Creditors." *Business Week*, January 27, 1975, p. 105.

Warner, Jerold B., "Bankruptcy, Absolute Priority, and the Pricing of Risky Debt Claims." *Journal of Financial Economics* 4 (1977), pp. 239–276.

Williams, John D. "On the Block: How Penn Central Seeks Financial Success by Offering—or Is It?—to Sell Real Estate." *Wall Street Journal*, September 10, 1971, p. 1.

Williams, John D. "Victor Palmieri Finds a Nugget of Gold in the Ashes of the Penn Central Railroad." *Wall Street Journal*, January 27, 1978, p. 17.

PART TWO:

ALTERNATIVE HIGH YIELD MARKETS

SECTION ONE:

OPPORTUNITIES IN SOVEREIGN BONDS

Chapter Sixteen

Developing Country Sovereign Bonds: 1991

by John F.H. Purcell
Joyce Chang
Dirk W. Damrau
Sovereign Assessment Group
Vincent J. Palermo
Bond Portfolio Analysis
Mark R. Franklin
Corporate Bond Trading
Salomon Brothers

A GROWING AND INCREASINGLY DIVERSE MARKET

The developing country sovereign bond market has grown from more than \$56 billion in April 1990 to more than \$89 billion as of mid-1991. This rapid expansion reflects three factors: (1) New Brady Plan bond exchange agreements have been signed. (2) The credit of some countries, such as Mexico, is sufficiently well perceived to allow them to issue new bonds. (3) Some countries, especially in Eastern Europe, that previously had not been considered part of this market now are included. Tables 16.1 and 16.2 summarize the size and variety of the market.

Table 16.1—Total Outstanding Developing Country Sovereign Bonds Maturing Aug 91 and Beyond (Currencies in Millions)

		Denominated in			
Country	*Total*[a]	*US$*	*DM*	*¥*	*Other Currencies*[a]
Algeria	$1,818.81	$809.50	DM950.00	¥60,700.00	$39.09
Argentina	4,621.26	4,549.20	-	10,000.00	-
Brazil	2,456.61	2,340.70	-	15,000.00	7.82
Bulgaria	335.56	-	200.00	31,000.00	-
Chile	272.06	200.00	-	10,000.00	-
Colombia	477.64	434.40	-	6,000.00	-
Costa Rica	639.00	639.00	-	-	-
Egypt	50.00	50.00	-	-	-
Guatemala	151.10	151.10	-	-	-
Hungary	4,678.97	1,005.00	2,800.00	240,000.00	374.10
India	2,196.05	931.00	950.00	65,000.00	263.84
Mexico	44,595.23	38,967.40	3,828.00	52,686.00	3,101.22
Panama	177.69	72.50	-	13,000.00	11.51
Philippines	1,028.51	919.00	-	13,000.00	15.83
Poland	210.00	210.00	-	-	-
Soviet Union	1,587.83	-	2,250.00	-	325.91
Uruguay	2,769.52	2,742.50	-	3,750.00	-
Venezuela	21,330.56	19,626.00	1,589.00	13,600.00	715.36
Yugoslavia	152.06	80.00	-	10,000.00	-
Total	*$89,548.46*	*$73,727.30*	*DM12,567.00*	*¥543,740.00*	*$4,854.68*

[a] U.S. dollar equivalent, calculated at spot exchange rates of June 24, 1991

As shown in Table 16.2, more than $28 billion of new bonds has been issued in only the past 15 months. While more than two thirds of these are due to the Brady Plan agreement that Venezuela signed with its commercial bank creditors, a very diverse set of countries issued new bonds in 1990 and in the first half of 1991.

Table 16.2—New Issuances of Developing Country Sovereign Bonds, 1 Apr 90–31 Jul 91 (Currencies in Millions)

		Denominated in			
Country	*Total*[a]	*US$*	*DM*	*¥*	*Other Currencies*[a]
Algeria	-	-	-	-	-
Argentina	$41.00	$41.00	-	-	-
Brazil	250.00	250.00	-	-	-
Bulgaria	-	-	-	-	-
Chile	200.00	200.00	-	-	-
Colombia	200.00	200.00	-	-	-
Costa Rica	597.00	597.00	-	-	-
Egypt	-	-	-	-	-
Guatemala	-	-	-	-	-
Hungary	940.60	300.00	DM750.00	¥25,000.00	$39.81
India	356.40	-	250.00	30,000.00	-
Mexico	4,898.40	4,382.00	650.00	-	151.85
Panama	-	-	-	-	-
Philippines	835.00	835.00	-	-	-
Poland	-	-	-	-	-
Soviet Union	-	-	-	-	-
Uruguay	1,067.50	1,067.50	-	-	-
Venezuela	19,497.38	18,003.00	1,389.00	-	715.35
Yugoslavia	-	-	-	-	-
Total	*$28,883.28*	*$25,875.50*	*DM3,039.00*	*¥V55,000.00*	*$907.01*

[a] U.S. dollar equivalent, calculated at spot exchange rates of June 24, 1991

Both Venezuela and Uruguay completed Brady agreements in 1990, and Costa Rica and the Philippines also reached Brady-style agreements to buy back some of their debt. The variety of bonds issued under these Brady Plans has increased, as well. While Mexico was limited to par and discount options, Venezuela issued four exchange bond series and two new money bonds, while Uruguay issued two exchange bonds and a new money bond. The Philippines also issued new money bonds in 1990. In the case of both Venezuela and Uruguay, the Brady Plan agreements were viewed as successful, enhancing market perceptions of the sovereigns. As a result, market prices of both countries rose following the announcement of their plans.

In some ways, the most surprising and impressive trend since early 1990 is the ability of the developing countries, whose bank debt trades at a significant discount to par, nevertheless to issue bonds on international markets. Mexico by far overshadowed other direct issuers in this market, with more than $3 billion in new issues during the period.

Another related trend is the appearance, for the first time in virtually a decade, of several corporate issuers in countries such as Mexico, Venezuela, Brazil, and Argentina. While such corporate bonds still represent a small portion of outstandings, private corporations clearly will play an increasingly important role in the developing country bond market—at least in countries whose sovereign credit trends are improving.

Finally, several new sovereign debtors have entered the secondary market. Political events in Eastern Europe and the Middle East, combined with the liquidity squeeze confronting many major international banks, has caused the debt of a number of sovereign debtors to be traded on the secondary market for the first time. Banks searching for liquidity are more willing to sell certain sovereign assets at a discount regardless of whether the country is servicing its bank debt.

Accordingly, we have added the bonds of Bulgaria, Hungary, India, and the Soviet Union—a total of $8.9 billion of outstanding bonds—to our universe. The basis for inclusion in our study is that countries must either be rated noninvestment grade or not rated by the two major U.S. rating agencies and that their bank debt must trade at a significant discount on the secondary market. Several countries that continue to service their debt fully meet these criteria: Hungary, India, and the Soviet Union, for example, have fully serviced both their bond debt and direct sovereign bank debt. For example, although Moody's downgraded Hungary to noninvestment grade in July 1990, we maintain that it is still a low investment-grade borrower.

The aforementioned trends have increased the diversity of the developing country sovereign debt market. As shown in Table 16.3, non-Latin American debt comprised nearly 38% of total commercial bank debt outstanding at year-end 1990, up dramatically from only 16% just a year earlier. The non-Latin American debt portion of total bonds outstanding also increased notably over the same period—from 4.2% to 13.5%.

Table 16.3—Developing Country Sovereign Debt Outstanding—Latin America versus Other Regions (U.S. Dollars in Millions)

	Commercial Bank Medium/Long-Term Debt		*Bonds Outstanding*	
	End-1989	*End-1990*	*1 April 90*	*31 July 91*
Total	*$241,243*	*$300,376*	*$56,227.89*	*$89,548.46*
Latin America	$201,530	$185,511	$53,849.65	$77,490,67
• Percent of Total	83.54%	61.76%	95.77%	86.53%
Other Regions	$39,713	$114,865	$2,378.24	$12,057.79
• Percent of Total	16.46%	38.24%	4.23%	13.47%

MARKET PERFORMANCE

For those countries participating in—or perceived as likely candidates for—Brady Plan restructurings, the plan has had a strong positive effect on the prices for developing country debt. Table 16.4 reports the impressive total returns turned in by the most liquid Brady bonds from their date of issue to the present. Total return is a measure of investment performance that encompasses both price appreciation and coupon income.

Table 16.4—Brady Bonds—Total Return Performance, 31 July 91

Brady Bond	*Issue Date*	*Total Return*
Mexico Par Bond	Mar 90	65.61%
Mexico Discount Bond	Mar 90	47.25
Venezuela Par Bond	Dec 90	42.67
Venezuela Discount Bond	Dec 90	14.73

Despite these superior gains, Mexican and Venezuelan Brady bonds still traded at stripped yields of 14%–17% as recently as June 17. As these countries continue their progress toward an investment-grade rating, further gains are likely. Recent new issues by these countries of shorter maturities (around five years) have been trading at yields of 10%. Countries currently in discussion with official and commercial bank creditors to receive Brady Plans also have experienced large price gains. Poland, Morocco, and Nigeria have been in negotiations with their commercial bank creditors possibly to arrange Brady Plans, and Argentina and Brazil hope to conclude Brady agreements next year. As Table 16.5 shows, the price of Poland's debt increased from 13.63 to 27.50 between November 1990 and July 1991, while Brazil's commercial bank restructured debt appreciated from 23.13 to 34.50 over the same period—a gain of 49.16%—following the recent agreement on interest arrears. The price of Nigerian debt advanced by 34.24% from 32.13 in November 1990 to 43.13 at the end of July 1991, but has

Table 16.5—Price Appreciation of Brady Bonds and "Pre-Brady" Debt, April 90–July 91

Brady Bonds	*16 Apr. 90*	*1 Nov. 90*	*% Change 16 Apr. 90– 1 Nov. 90*	*31 July 91*	*% Change 1 Nov. 90– 31 July 91*
Costa Rica Series A	21.50	34.00	58.14%	50.13	47.44%
Mexican Par Bonds	41.62	42.62	2.40	56.75	33.15
Mexican Discount Bonds	63.13	64.37	1.97	75.81	17.77
Venezuela Par Bonds	NYI	49.50[a]	-	62.63	26.53
Venezuela Discount Bonds	NYI	69.00[a]	-	76.00	10.14
"Pre-Brady" Debt					
Brazil MYDFA[b]	26.13	23.13	-11.48%	34.50	49.16%
Morocco Restructured	40.50	38.63	-4.62	53.75	39.14
Nigeria Restructured	26.13	32.13	22.96	43.13	34.24
Poland DDRA[c]	15.50	13.63	-12.06	27.50	101.76

[a] Price quotations on when-issued basis trading; bonds were issued on December 18, 1990.
[b] MYFDA Multiyear deposit facility Agreement.
[c] DDRA Debt deferral and restructure agreement.
NYI Not yet issued.

Figure 16.1—Mexican and Venezuelan Brady Bonds—Spreads Over U.S. Treasuries, 16 Apr 90–31 July 91

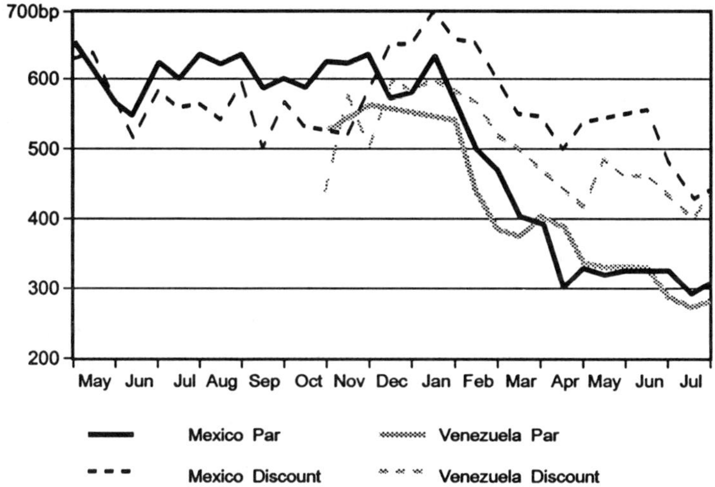

weakened with the dispute between creditors and the Nigerian government on the type of collateral used for the proposed Brady bonds.

Thus, the developing country bond and debt markets have been rallying strongly since the summer of 1990, and this uptrend is continuing. The causes for this rally are probably fourfold. First, interest rates in the United States have declined, making Brady bond collateral (such as zero-coupon U.S. Treasury bonds and U.S. Government agency bonds) more valuable. However, as Figure 16.1 demonstrates, spreads over benchmark U.S. Treasury bonds for the two largest Latin American issues—the Mexican and Venezuelan Brady bonds—have tightened significantly. Second, the extension of the Brady Plan to new countries and sovereign credit improvement both have added to market optimism. Third, technical supply and demand factors—such as debt-equity deals, buybacks, and the lack of massive selling programs by banks—have strengthened the markets. And finally, the Persian Gulf war produced a windfall price increase for oil producers that did not last long enough to severely damage nonoil producers.[1]

---

1 The abortive coup in the Soviet Union may have had a (possibly temporary) "safe haven" effect which further increased Latin American debt prices in late August 1991.

Certain of these factors—such as the extension of the Brady Plan to new countries and other official measures like Paris Club debt relief to alleviate sovereign debt burdens—are likely to continue. In addition, several important countries' creditworthiness probably will improve further. And technical factors, including privatization using some debt component and sovereign buybacks of their own debt, are still in progress.

Spreads have tightened not only in the secondary market but even more significantly in the primary issue market. Thus, Mexican sovereign-supported entities have been able to issue an impressive variety of Eurobonds during 1990 and 1991 at narrow issue spreads over U.S. Treasuries (see Table 16.6).

Table 16.6—Mexican Eurobonds—Spreads Over U.S. Treasuries, 1989–1991 (Currencies in Millions)

Issuer	*Coupon*	*Size*	*Issue Date*	*Maturity*	*Spreads Over Treasuries*[b]
BNCE	10 1/4%	US$100	Jun 89	Jun 94	909bp
Nafinsa	11	DM150	Jun 90	Jun 95	308
BNCE	11	DM100	Jul 90	Jul 95	328
Nafinsa	11 1/4	US$100	Aug 90	Aug 95	435
Pemex	11 5/8	US$150	Oct 90	Oct 93	363
Pemex	10	US$125	Mar 91	Mar 93	320
United Mexican States	10 1/2	DM300	Mar 91	Mar 96	234
Nafinsa[a]	10	US$125	Apr 91	Apr 96	285
BNCE	9 5/8	US$100	Jun 91	Jun 96	250
Pemex	11 1/2	ECU100	Jul 91	Aug 94	235
Banobras	10 1/4	US$100	Jul 91	Jul 96	240

a The issue is a private placement putable in three years, and the spread is over three-year U.S. Treasuries.

b Non US$ denominated bond spreads were calculated over equivalent U.S. Treasuries by using Swap curve.

Banobras Banco Nacional de Obras y Servicios Publicos. BNCE Banco Nacional de Comercio Exterior. SNC Pemex Petroleos Mexicano Nafinsa Nacional Financiera. bp basis points.

LIQUIDITY

With the securitization of the developing country debt market, liquidity has improved, as a number of observers had predicted. For example, Mexican and Venezuelan Brady bond transactions now are processed through the Eurobond clearing institutions. Euroclear and CEDEL, and future Brady bonds are likely to do so, as well. In fact, Mexican par bonds were the largest single issue traded through Euroclear and CEDEL during June and July 1990 and March 1991 (see Figure 16.2).

Figure 16.2—Brady Bonds Traded through Euroclear and CEDEL, April 90–March 91 (Dollars in Billions)

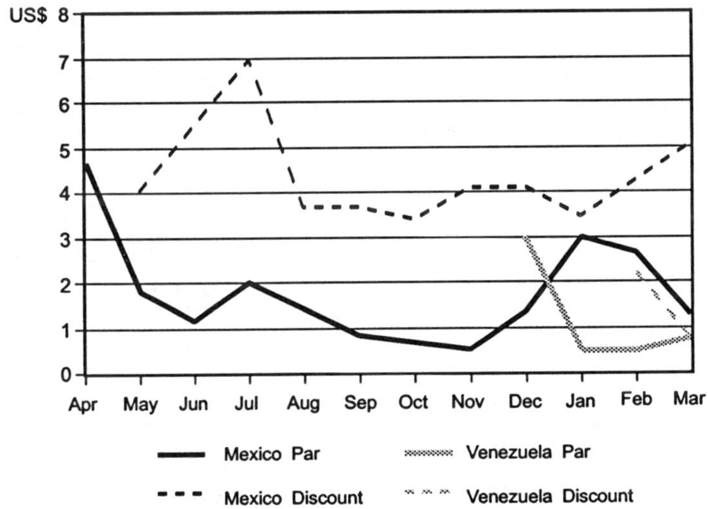

We estimate that the more than $50 billion of bonds traded during the past year represented nearly 50% of trading in the developing country secondary market.

AN IMPROVING POLICY AND SOVEREIGN CREDIT ENVIRONMENT

Market participants clearly have grown more optimistic about long-term improvements in the credit fundamentals of a number of countries in Latin America and elsewhere, lending strength to the developing country sovereign bond market.

In the first place, Brady initiatives continue, and new market-oriented bond instruments are being created to meet special situations. Venezuela and Uruguay completed Brady Plans, and Chile reached a voluntary refinancing agreement with its commercial bank creditors. Algeria is negotiating a refinancing package with its commercial bank creditors. Furthermore, the "menu of options" for creditors participating in Brady Plans has expanded beyond par and discount bonds to include debt buybacks, a variety of bearer and registered bonds with different maturities, "step-up" coupons, more tradeable attached warrants (Venezuela), and bonds for interest arrears (Brazil and others). Appendix A1 details the new bonds issued since our last report on this market.

Second, official debt-reduction initiatives have gained increased support. Several African countries have benefited from the Toronto Plan, which calls for increased financial flows to the continent in conjunction with concessional rescheduling from official Paris Club creditors. President Bush's "Enterprise for the Americas" initiative began last year; the initiative, which includes debt, trade, and investment components, will assist selected Latin American and Caribbean countries in reducing their official debt to the United States. In July, the United Kingdom held a summit to gain support for the Trinidad Terms, intended to help countries in sub-Saharan Africa qualify for concessional financing. And finally, the negotiation of free trade agreements throughout Latin America provides a much improved environment for developing countries to initiate political and economic reforms.

Third, developing counties have demonstrated their resilience by withstanding external shocks during the Gulf crisis. Countries that are heavily dependent on oil imports, such as the Philippines, Morocco, and Costa Rica, continued to make interest payments on a timely basis, even though their oil import costs increased by $1–$2.5 billion last year. Hungary smoothly absorbed the dual shock of higher oil prices and payment for energy imports from the Soviet Union in hard currency. And oil-exporting countries such as Venezuela and Algeria played down the benefits of higher world oil prices and continued to push ahead with economic reforms. These countries used the windfall from higher oil prices to make strategic longer-term gains. Venezuela, for example, is implementing a $25-billion expansion program for its state-owned oil company, Petroleos de Venezuela SA, over the next five years. And Algeria has become the key supplier of hydrocarbons and natural gas to Europe, recently beginning joint venture operations with the United States.

Finally, certain countries have made substantial advances in their fundamental level of credit quality. In our opinion, Chile and Mexico have demonstrated the most dramatic improvement. Indeed, we believe that Chile already warrants an investment-grade credit rating while Mexico is close behind; Venezuela also deserves mention in this category.[2] In Eastern Europe, Hungary's debt servicing prospects have improved markedly over the past year, sharply reducing the likelihood of any commercial bank debt rescheduling. Smaller countries that have made major advances include Uruguay and Costa Rica. Colombia remains a sound credit from an economic perspective.

Several countries that have relatively heavy debt and debt service burdens continue to honor their obligations and have begun or continued efforts to reform both their political systems and their economies. Algeria and Hungary are prime examples. Other countries, such as Morocco, have had to reschedule their bank debt, but they have made important progress in stabilizing their economies.

The demonstration effect of these improving sovereign credits continues to serve as a model for a larger category of countries that, while making serious efforts at reform, have yet to achieve a clear improving trend. In virtually all the countries that comprise the developing country bond market, government and business leaders now accept the principals of open markets, serious economic restructuring, and acroeconomic (particularly fiscal) discipline—a marked change from the environment that prevailed in the 1970s and early 1980s.

BROADENING OF THE INVESTOR BASE

During the latter part of 1990 and early 1991, nonbank institutional investors entered the market in a serious way. Early nonbank participants included retail investors, many of them citizens of Latin American countries, and speculative institutional accounts specializing in uniquely risky situations. However, the institutional investor base had broadened considerably since our first publication on this market.

Table 16.6 outlines our observations on the types of institutional investors that have entered this market, as well as their investment

---

2 See *Mexico: A World Class Economy in the 1990s*, Salomon Brothers Inc, August 1990; *Venezuela: Development Prospects Brighten*, Salomon Brothers Inc, March 1991; and *Chile: An Investment-Grade Credit*, Salomon Brothers Inc, May 1991.

goals and the kinds of instruments they buy. The table below illustrates the great diversity of investors that recently have been attracted to the developing country sovereign debt market.

Table 16.6—New Investors in the Developing Country Debt Market

Characterization and Goals	*Type of Institution*	*Product Purchased*
Mainstream Buy and Hold • Minimize Risk (Likes Collateral) • Familiar With Euros (Likes Senior Status and Shorter Euros)	Insurance Companies Money Managers Pension funds Mutual Funds	Brady Bonds Eurobonds
First-Time "Toe in the Water" Buyers • Short Term • Comfortable With Corporates • Low Risk • Could Graduate to Other Categories	Money Managers Insurance Companies Finance Companies	Mexican "Cetes" Mexican Bank CDs Private Sector Eurobonds
Aggressive, Informed Money Managers • Want Yield • Will Take Controlled Risk • Want Liquidity (Will Trade)	Mutual Funds Some High-Yield Investors	Brady "Arbitrage" New Money Bonds Some Special Situations (Such as Brazil IOs)
Equity Players in "Penny Stocks" • Story Account • Want Quick Upside	Equity Accounts Risk Arbitrage	Cheap Nonperforming Loans (Such as Ivory Coast, Peru, Panama, North Korea, and Bulgaria)
• Comfortable With Risk		

CDs Certificates of deposit. IOs Interest Only Bonds

RATINGS

Several important events have occurred on the rating agency front since our previous publication. In December 1990, Moody's Investors Service assigned Mexico a sovereign ceiling rating of Ba2 and rated the Brady bonds Ba3. Since then, the agency has rated several Mexican Eurobonds Ba2. In addition, Moody's upgraded Venezuela's sovereign ceiling rating to Ba1 from Ba3 on August 7, 1991, and assigned new ratings to Venezuelan Brady bonds. The new money bonds, debt-conversion bonds and front-loaded interest reduction bonds were assigned a Ba1 rating, the same level as the sovereign ceiling rating, and par and discount bonds were given a Ba2 rating. Standard & Poor's also upgraded Venezuelan Eurobonds to BB from B+ on July 25, 1991, and has maintained the country's "positive" rating outlook. We expect that Standard & Poor's soon will rate Mexico in the BB category. On the negative side, Moody's downgraded the sovereign debt of Hungary from Baa2 to Ba1 in July 1990. And in May 1991, Standard & Poor's moved India into the noninvestment-grade category, downgrading it from BBB– to BB+. Moody's followed suit on June 24, 1991, reducing its rating in two steps from Baa3 to Ba2; as late as the third quarter of 1990, India had been rated A2 by Moody's.

Several other sovereign states that entered the developing country market in 1990, such as Bulgaria and the Soviet Union, remain unrated. Over the next two years, however, we expect ratings for several new countries, including Chile and the Soviet Union.

CONCLUSION

The growth and performance of the developing country sovereign bond market has exceeded the expectations of even optimistic observers in early 1990. In our view, many of the factors working to enlarge and institutionalize this market remain in force. In addition, the fundamental credit quality of many sovereigns in the market is improving. Nevertheless, enough uncertainties remain and enough debt is still in "Pre-Brady" loan form to offer high yields and considerable relative value potential for knowledgeable investors.

APPENDIX A1

New Issues of Countries Listed in *Developing Country Sovereign Bonds: Opportunity in a New Asset Class* (Currencies in Millions)

Direct Issue Bonds

Issuer	Coupon	Size	Issue Date	Maturity	Listing	Lead Manager
Argentina						
Molinos Rio de la Plata	9 %	US$15	Jul 91	Dec 92	Luxembourg	Chase Investment Bank
Molinos Rio de la Plata Series A	LIBOR + 4.6	US$5	Dec 90	Dec 95	Luxembourg	Merrill Lynch
Molinos Rio de la Plata Series B	11	US$21	Dec 90	Dec 95	Luxembourg	Merrill Lynch
Brazil						
Petrobras	10 %	US$250	Jul 91	Aug 93	Luxembourg	Chase Investment Bank
Mexico						
BNCE	11 %	DM100	Jul 90	Jul 95	Frankfurt	Swiss Bank
BNCE	9 7/8	US$100	Jun 91	Jun 96	Luxembourg	Goldman Sachs
Banobras	10 3/4	US$100	Jul 91	Jul 96	Luxembourg	CSFB
Barton Corporation	12	US$92	Sep 90	Sep 93	Luxembourg	Bankers Trust
Nacional Financiera SNC (Nafinsa)	11	DM150	Jun 90	Jun 95	Frankfurt	Dresdner Bank
Nacional Financiera SNC (Nafinsa)	11 3/4	US$100	Aug 90	Aug 95	Luxembourg	CSFB
Euronovum	12	US$60	Sep 90	Sep 93	Luxembourg	First Interstate
Petroleos Mexicanos (Pemex)	10	US$125	Mar 91	Mar 93	Luxembourg	Swiss Bank
Petroleos Mexicanos (Pemex)	11 5/8	US$150	Oct 90	Oct 93	Luxembourg	Swiss Bank
Petroleos Mexicanos (Pemex)	11 1/2	ECU100	Jul 91	Aug 94	Luxembourg	Paribas Capital Markets
Petroleos Mexicanos (Pemex)	11 1/4	DM100	Apr 90	Apr 95	Dusseldorf	WLB
Petroleos Mexicanos (Pemex)	11	A$500	Jul 90	Jul 96	Vienna	Creditanstalt Bankverein
Ponder, LDC	11	US$22	May 90	May 92	NL	Lazard Freres
Sidek International Finance	12	US$50	Dec 90	Dec 95	Luxembourg	Kidder Peabody
Tamsa (Tamtrade)	12	US$33	Apr 90	Apr 92	Luxembourg	Bankers Trust
Tamsa	7 1/2	US$50	Jun 91	Jun 97	Luxembourg	Bankers Trust
United Mexican States	10 1/2	DM300	Feb 91	Mar 96	Frankfurt	Deutsche Bank
Philippines						
Republic of Philippines	LIBOR	US$120	Aug 90	Aug 91	NL	Lazard Freres
Venezuela						
BA Proven (Gtd. PDVSA)	11 1/8%	DM200	Oct 90	Oct 95	Frankfurt	Bankers Trust
Corimon International Finance	10 1/4	US$35	Oct 90	Oct 95	Luxembourg	Merrill Lynch

New Money Bonds

Issuer	Form	Coupon	Size	Issue Date	Maturity	Listing	Lead Bank
Chile New Money Bonds[a]	Bearer	LIBOR + 1 1/2%	US$200	Mar 91	Mar 96	Luxembourg	MHT
Colombian Bearer Instruments	Bearer	LIBOR + 1 1/2	US$200	Aug 91	Aug 96	Luxembourg	Chemical
Philippine New Money Bonds	Registered	LIBOR + 13/16	US$715	May 90	May 05	Luxembourg	MHT
Uruguay New Money Bonds	Registered	LIBOR + 1	US$89.5	Feb 91	Feb 06	Luxembourg	Citibank
Venezuela New Money Series A Bonds	Bearer	LIBOR + 1	US$478	Dec 90	Dec 05	Luxembourg	Chase Investment Bank
Venezuela New Money Series BP Bonds	Bearer	LIBOR + 7/8	US$356	Dec 90	Dec 05	Luxembourg	Chase Investment Bank
Venezuela New Money Series BNP Bonds	Bearer	LIBOR + 7/8	US$356	Dec 90	Dec 05	Luxembourg	Chase Investment Bank

Exchange Bonds

Issuer	Form	Coupon	Size	Issue Date	Maturity
Costa Rica					
Costa Rica Exchange Bonds	Bearer	6.25%	US$228	May 90	May 15
Costa Rica Collateralized Exchange Bonds	Bearer	6.25	US$235	May 90	May 10
Costa Rica Interest Claims	Bearer	LIBOR + 13/16	US$67	May 90	May 05
Costa Rica Collateralized Interest Claims	Bearer	LIBOR + 13/16	US$67	May 90	May 05
Mexico					
Floating Rate Privatization Notes	Bearer/Regis.	LIBOR + 13/16%	US$1.150	Jul 91	Jul 01

[a] Intention of issuing another US$120 million in March 1992. [b] Interest rate will be 5% for the first and second years, 6% for the third and fourth years and 7% for the fifth year; from the sixth year until maturity, interest rates will be fixed at LIBOR + 7/8%. [c] 11% interest for the first three years, 13.54% for the next nine years. BNCE Banco Nacional de Comercio Exterior, SNC. CSFB Credit Suisse First Boston. LIBOR London interbank offered rate. MHT Manufacturers Hanover Trust. NL Not listed.

New Issues of Countries Listed in *Developing Country Sovereign Bonds: Opportunity in a New Asset Class* (Currencies in Millions) (Continued)

Exchange Bonds (Continued)

Issuer	Form	Coupon	Size	Issue Date	Maturity
Venezuela					
Interest-Reduction Bonds					
• US$ Par Series A	Registered	6 3/4%	US$5.032	Dec 90	Mar 20
• US$ Par Series B	Registered	6 3/4	US$1,638	Dec 90	Mar 20
• Lir Par Series	Registered	6 3/4	Lir318,881	Dec 90	Mar 20
• FFr Par Series	Registered	6 3/4	Ffr321	Dec 90	Mar 20
• SFr Par Series	Registered	6 3/4	Sfr100	Dec 90	Mar 20
• DM Par Series	Registered	6 3/4	DM508	Dec 90	Mar 20
Principal-Reduction Bonds					
• US$ Discount Series A	Registered	LIBOR + 13/16	US$958	Dec 90	Mar 20
• US$ Discount Series B	Registered	LIBOR + 13/16	US$211	Dec 90	Mar 20
• DM Discount Series	Registered	LIBOR + 13/16	DM131	Dec 90	Mar 20
Temporary Interest-Reduction Bonds[b]					
• US$ Series A	Bearer	LIBOR + 7/8	US$2,259	Dec 90	Apr 07
• US$ Series B	Bearer	LIBOR + 7/8	US$989	Dec 90	Apr 07
• DM Series	Bearer	LIBOR + 7/8	DM341	Dec 90	Apr 07
• £ Series	Bearer	LIBOR + 7/8	£37	Dec 90	Apr 07
• SFr Series	Bearer	LIBOR + 7/8	Sfr153	Dec 90	Apr 07
Debt-Conversion Bonds					
• US$ Series DL	Bearer	LIBOR + 7/8	US$5,327	Dec 90	Apr 07
• US$ Series IL	Bearer	LIBOR + 7/8	US$304	Dec 90	Apr 08
• DM Series	Bearer	LIBOR + 7/8	DM209	Dec 90	Apr 07
• £ Series	Bearer	LIBOR + 7/8	£119	Dec 90	Apr 07
Uruguay					
Banco Central del Uruguay	Registered	6 3/4%	US$530	Feb 91	Feb 21
Uruguay Debt-Conversion Bonds	Registered	LIBOR + 7/8	US$448	Feb 91	Feb 08

United States Private Placements

Issuer	Type	Coupon	Size	Placement Date	Maturity	Arranger
Mexico						
Banamex	Secured Notes	11 %	US$130	May 90	1993	Citibank
Banca Serfin SNC	Bonds	10 1/2	US$70	Jan 91	1996	Yamaichi
Bancomer	Securitized Credit Card Receivables	LIBOR + 5/8	US$230	Jul 90	1995	Citibank
Cemex	Notes	9.41	US$425	May 91	1996	JP Morgan
Cemex[c]	Convertible Eurobonds	11	US$100	Jun 90	2002	Citibank
Grupo San Luis	Secured Notes	12	US$75	Aug 90	1993	Bankers Trust
Nacional Financiera SNC (Nafinsa)	Notes	10	US$125	May 91	1996	JP Morgan
Petroleos Mexicanos (Pemex)	Unsecured Notes	11.43	US$100	Aug 90	1995	Paine Webber
Telmex	Notes	11	US$335	Apr 90	1995	Citibank
Telmex	Unsecured Notes	12 1/4	US$150	Jul 90	1992	JP Morgan
Telmex	Notes	8.9	US$570	Dec 90	1995	Citibank
United Mexican States	Bonds	9 1/2	US$40	Jan 91	2000	Merrill Lynch
Venezuela						
Tytan Securities/SIDETUR Steel	Bonds	LIBOR + 1 3/8%	US$60	Dec 90	1996	Citibank

APPENDIX A2

Bond Issues of Newly Added Countries (Currencies in Millions)

Direct Issue Bonds

Issuer	Coupon	Size	Issue Date	Maturity	Listing	Lead Manager
Bulgaria						
Bulgarian Foreign Trade Bank	8 1/2%	DM200	Jul 89	Jul 96	Frankfurt	Bayerische Vereinsbank
Hungary						
Continental Bermuda Lts.	LIBOR + 1/4%	US$250	Apr 86	Feb 06	Luxembourg	Giro u Bk der Oesterr Spakssn
Hungary State Development Institute	10 1/2	US$200	Aug 90	Aug 00	London	Daiwa
National Bank of Hungary	7 3/4	DM100	Feb 85	Feb 93	Frankfurt	Commerzbank
National Bank of Hungary	7	DM150	Sep 85	Oct 93	Frankfurt	Deutsche Bank
National Bank of Hungary	6 3/4	DM200	Mar 87	Mar 94	Frankfurt	Dresdner Bank
National Bank of Hungary	6 1/4	DM200	Jul 88	Jul 94	Frankfurt	Deutsche Bank
National Bank of Hungary	5 1/2	Sfr75	Dec 88	Dec 94	Zurich	Warburg
National Bank of Hungary	10	DM200	Oct 90	Oct 95	Frankfurt	Deutsche Bank
National Bank of Hungary	9	¥10,000	Nov 90	Nov 95	Tokyo	Daiwa
National Bank of Hungary	9	¥15,000	Nov 90	Nov 95	Tokyo	Daiwa
National Bank of Hungary	6 5/8	DM200	Feb 89	Feb 96	Frankfurt	Bayerische Vereinsbank
National Bank of Hungary	7 1/4	DM150	Feb 86	Feb 96	Frankfurt	Dresdner Bank
National Bank of Hungary	10 1/2	DM200	Mar 91	Mar 96	Frankfurt	Commerzbank
National Bank of Hungary	10 1/2	DM150	Apr 91	Mar 96	Frankfurt	Commerzbank
National Bank of Hungary	9 3/4	DM200	May 90	May 96	Frankfurt	DG
National Bank of Hungary	10 1/2	US$100	Jun 91	Jul 96	Luxembourg	Bankers Trust
National Bank of Hungary	8 1/4	AS1,500	Sep 89	Sep 96	Vienna	OeLB
National Bank of Hungary	6 7/8	DM150	Sep 86	Sep 96	Dusseldorf	WLB
National Bank of Hungary	10	ECU75	Sep 89	Sep 96	Luxembourg	Kredietbank
National Bank of Hungary	8	DM200	Nov 89	Nov 96	Dusseldorf	WLB
National Bank of Hungary	5.7	¥20,000	Feb 87	Feb 97	Tokyo	Daiwa
National Bank of Hungary	9 1/2	AS1,000	Feb 90	Feb 97	Vienna	Creditanstalt Bankverein
National Bank of Hungary	10	DM300	Mar 90	Mar 97	Frankfurt	Commerzbank
National Bank of Hungary	8	DM200	Jun 89	Jun 97	Frankfurt	DG
National Bank of Hungary	10 5/8	AS500	Oct 90	Oct 97	Vienna	OeLB
National Bank of Hungary	6.3	¥40,000	Oct 87	Oct 97	Tokyo	Daiwa
National Bank of Hungary	5.7	¥25,000	Mar 88	Mar 98	Tokyo	Daiwa
National Bank of Hungary	5.7	¥35,000	Mar 89	Mar 99	Tokyo	Daiwa
National Bank of Hungary	6	¥25,000	Sep 89	Sep 99	Tokyo	Daiwa
National Bank of Hungary	LIBOR + 5/8	US$100	Jan 85	Jan 00	Luxembourg	Nomura
National Bank of Hungary	LIBOR + 1/4	US$200	Aug 85	Sep 00	Luxembourg	Nomura
National Bank of Hungary	LIBOR + 1/4	US$100	Jan 86	Jan 01	Singapore	Daiwa
India						
Indian Oil Corporation	LIBOR + 3/16%	US$200	Nov 89	Nov 94	Luxembourg	CSFB
Industrial Credit & Investment Corp. of India	LIBOR + 1/4	US$6	Nov 81	Dec 91	London	Credit Lyonnais
Industrial Credit & Investment Corp. of India	5 1/4	Sfr80	Aug 88	Oct 95	Basle	Swiss Bank
Industrial Credit & Investment Corp. of India	5 3/4	Sfr75	Nov 86	Nov 96	Zurich	UBS
Industrial Development Bank of India	7	DM100	Feb 86	Feb 93	Frankfurt	Dresdner Bank
Industrial Development Bank of India	6 3/8	DM200	Dec 87	Dec 94	Frankfurt	Commerzbank
Industrial Development Bank of India	6 5/8	DM250	Sep 88	Sep 95	Frankfurt	Dresdner Bank
Industrial Development Bank of India	10	US$100	Jun 86	Jun 96	Luxembourg	CSFB
Industrial Development Bank of India	5 5/8	Sfr100	Mar 87	Mar 97	Basle	UBS
Oil and Natural Gas Commission	9 3/4	US$125	Dec 88	Nov 93	Luxembourg	CSFB
Oil and Natural Gas Commission	6 3/8	DM150	Feb 87	Feb 94	Frankfurt	Commerzbank
Oil and Natural Gas Commission	LIBOR + 3/16	US$125	Mar 86	Mar 96	London	CSFB
Oil and Natural Gas Commission	LIBOR + 1/8	US$150	Feb 85	Feb 97	London	Merrill Lynch
Oil and Natural Gas Commission	10	US$125	Mar 90	Mar 97	Luxembourg	Nomura
Oil and Natural Gas Commission	9 1/2	DM250	Jul 90	Jul 97	Frankfurt	Commerzbank
Oil and Natural Gas Commission	5 3/8	Sfr150	Apr 88	Apr 98	Zurich	CSFB
State Bank of India	5 1/4	¥15,000	Jun 88	Jun 93	London	IBJ Intl. Ltd.
State Bank of India	LIBOR + 0.1	US$100	Dec 85	Dec 97	London	Lloyds Merchant Bank
Soviet Union						
Vneshekonombank[a]	12 1/4%	Lir75,000	Mar 89	Mar 94	Luxembourg	Banco di Roma
Vneshekonombank	8 7/8	DM500	Feb 90	Feb 95	Dusseldorf	WLB
Vneshekonombank	6 3/8	DM500	Aug 88	Aug 95	Frankfurt	Dresdner Bank
Vneshekonombank	7 1/2	DM500	Sep 89	Sep 95	Frankfurt	Commerzbank
Vneshekonombank	8	AS1,000	Sep 89	Sep 95	Vienna	Creditanstat Bankverein
Vneshekonombank	7	DM750	Mar 89	Mar 96	Frankfurt	Deutsche Bank
Vneshekonombank	8	Fl250	Jul 89	Jul 96	Amsterdam	ABN
Vneshekonombank	5	Sfr100	Feb 88	Feb 98	Zurich	BKA

[a] Bank for Foreign Economic Affairs of the USSR, formerly Vneshtorobank. ABN Algemene Bank Ned. BKA Bank fur Kredit und Aussenhandel AG. CSFB Credit Suisse First Boston. DG Deutsche Genossenschaftbank. IBJ Industrial Bank of Japan., Ltd. LIBOR London interbank offered rate. OeLB Osterreichische Landesbank. UBS A consortium of Swiss Bank. WLB Westdeutsche Landesbank.

Bond Issues of Newly Added Countries (Currencies in Millions) (Continued)

Issuer	Type	Coupon	Size	Placement Date	Maturity	Arranger
United States Private Placements						
Hungary						
National Bank of Hungary	Bonds	8 7/8%	US$55	Nov 86	1993	Dai-Ichi Kangyo
Japan Private Placements						
Bulgaria						
Bulgarian Foreign Trade Bank	Shibosai	5.7%	¥10.000	Nov 88	1998	Bank of Tokyo
Bulgarian Foreign Trade Bank	Shibosai	5.9	¥6.000	Oct 89	1999	IBJ
Bulgarian Foreign Trade Bank	Private MT Bonds	5.8	¥10.000	Mar 89	1999	Nikko Securities
Mineral Bank of Bulgaria	Private Bonds	5.8	¥5.000	Jun 89	1996	IBJ
Hungary						
National Bank of Hungary	Shibosai	7.9%	¥10.000	1984	1991	LTCB
National Bank of Hungary	Shibosai	7.6	¥10.000	Mar 85	1992	LTCB
National Bank of Hungary	Shibosai	5.7	¥20.000	Feb 87	1997	Daiwa
National Bank of Hungary	Shibosai	5.9	¥30.000	Oct 88	1998	Daiwa
India						
Industrial Devel. Bank of India	Bonds	5.7%	¥20.000	Oct 89	1999	Daiwa
Oil and Natural Gas Commission	Bonds	8 1/2	¥30.000	Dec 90	2000	Nikko Securities

* * *

APPENDIX B

Developing Country Bonds Outstanding Maturing August 1991 and Beyond (Currencies in Millions)

Direct Issue Bonds

Issuer	Coupon	Size	Issue Date	Maturity	Listing	Lead Manager
Algeria						
Banque Algerienne de Developement	LIBOR + $\frac{1}{2}$%	Sfr60	Nov 86	Nov 96	Zurich	Swiss Bank
Banque Exterieure d'Algerie	$6\frac{3}{4}$	DM200	Jul 86	Jul 92	Frankfurt	DG /BAII
Banque Exterieure d'Algerie	7	DM150	Sep 88	Sep 93	Frankfurt	DG /BAII
Banque Exterieure d'Algerie	$7\frac{3}{4}$	DM150	May 89	May 94	Frankfurt	DG /BAII
Banque Exterieure d'Algerie	LIBOR + $\frac{1}{4}$	US$500	May 85	May 00	Luxembourg	BAII/Chemical
Banque Nationale d'Algerie	$6\frac{1}{2}$	¥8,000	Mar 88	Mar 93	NL	Nomura
Banque Nationale d'Algerie	$6\frac{1}{4}$	DM150	Mar 88	Mar 94	Frankfurt	Dresdner Bank
Banque Nationale d'Algerie	$8\frac{1}{2}$	DM150	Aug 89	Aug 94	Frankfurt	BHF Bank
Sonatrach	LIBOR + $\frac{3}{4}$	US$50	Nov 78	Dec 92	Luxembourg	CCF
Sonatrach	LIBOR + 1	US$100	Mar 90	Mar 97	Luxembourg	Chase Investment Bank
Sonatrach/Beneficial Interest[a]	LIBOR + $\frac{7}{8}$	US$85.6	May 85	May 92	NL	BAII
Sonatrach/Beneficial Interest[a]	LIBOR + $\frac{7}{8}$	US$21.4	May 85	May 92	NL	BAII
Sonelgaz	$9\frac{1}{2}$	DM150	Feb 90	Feb 95	Frankfurt	BHF Bank
Argentina						
Banco de la Nacion Argentina	LIBOR + $\frac{3}{4}$%	US$195	Nov 87	Oct 97	Luxembourg	IBJ/Sumitomo
Molinos Rio de la Plata	**9**	**US$15**	**Jul 91**	**Dec 92**	**Luxembourg**	**Chase Investment Bank**
Molinos Rio de la Plata - Series A	**LIBOR + 4.6**	**US$5**	**Dec 90**	**Dec 95**	**Luxembourg**	**Merrill Lynch**
Molinos Rio de la Plata - Series B	**11**	**US$21**	**Dec 90**	**Dec 95**	**Luxembourg**	**Merrill Lynch**
Brazil						
Banco Itau SA	LIBOR	US$85	Feb 90	Feb 05	NL	First Chicago
Light-Servicos de Electricidad	LIBOR + 2%	Sfr12	Jul 81	Aug 91	Zurich	BGKB
Petrobras	**10**	**US$250**	**Jul 91**	**Aug 93**	**Luxembourg**	**Chase Investment Bank**
Bulgaria						
Bulgarian Foreign Trade Bank	$8\frac{1}{2}$%	DM200	Jul 89	Jul 96	Frankfurt	Bayerische Vereinsbank
Colombia						
Republic of Colombia	LIBOR + $1\frac{1}{8}$%	US$50	Apr 87	Apr 94	Luxembourg	Citibank
Costa Rica						
Banco Central de Costa Rica	LIBOR + $1\frac{1}{4}$%	US$42	Apr 85	Oct 92	Luxembourg	Bankers Trust
Hungary						
Continental Bermuda Lts.	LIBOR + $\frac{1}{4}$%	US$250	Apr 86	Feb 06	Luxembourg	Giro u Bk der Oesterr Sparkssn
Hungary State Development Institute	**$10\frac{1}{2}$**	**US$200**	**Aug 90**	**Aug 00**	**London**	**Daiwa**
National Bank of Hungary	$7\frac{3}{4}$	DM100	Feb 85	Feb 93	Frankfurt	Commerzbank
National Bank of Hungary	7	DM150	Sep 85	Oct 93	Frankfurt	Deutsche Bank
National Bank of Hungary	$6\frac{3}{4}$	DM200	Mar 87	Mar 94	Frankfurt	Dresdner Bank
National Bank of Hungary	$6\frac{1}{4}$	DM200	Jul 88	Jul 94	Frankfurt	Deutsche Bank
National Bank of Hungary	$5\frac{1}{2}$	Sfr75	Dec 88	Dec 94	Zurich	Warburg
National Bank of Hungary	$6\frac{1}{4}$	DM200	Mar 88	Mar 95	Frankfurt	DG
National Bank of Hungary	**10**	**DM200**	**Oct 90**	**Oct 95**	**Frankfurt**	**Deutsche Bank**
National Bank of Hungary	**9**	**¥10,000**	**Nov 90**	**Nov 95**	**Tokyo**	**Daiwa**
National Bank of Hungary	**9**	**¥15,000**	**Nov 90**	**Nov 95**	**Tokyo**	**Daiwa**
National Bank of Hungary	$6\frac{5}{8}$	DM200	Feb 89	Feb 96	Frankfurt	Bayerische Vereinsbank
National Bank of Hungary	$7\frac{1}{4}$	DM150	Feb 86	Feb 96	Frankfurt	Dresdner Bank
National Bank of Hungary	**$10\frac{1}{2}$**	**DM200**	**Mar 91**	**Mar 96**	**Frankfurt**	**Commerzbank**
National Bank of Hungary	**$10\frac{1}{2}$**	**DM150**	**Apr 91**	**Mar 96**	**Frankfurt**	**Commerzbank**
National Bank of Hungary	**$9\frac{3}{4}$**	**DM200**	**May 90**	**May 96**	**Frankfurt**	**DG**
National Bank of Hungary	**$10\frac{1}{2}$**	**US$100**	**Jun 91**	**Jul 96**	**Luxembourg**	**Bankers Trust**

[a] Minimum 10.25%. [b] Bank for Foreign Economic Affairs of the USSR, formerly Vneshtorobank. [c] Intention of issuing another US$120 million in March 1992. [d] Interest rate will be 5% for the first and second years, 6% for the third and fourth years and 7% for the fifth year; from the sixth year until maturity, interest rates will be fixed at LIBOR + 7/8%. [e] 11% interest for the first three years, 13.54% for the next nine years. ABN Algemene Bank Ned. BKA Bank fur Kredit und Aussenhandel AG. BGKB Banque Gutzwiller Kurz Bungenev. BNCE Banco Nacional de Comercio Exterior, SNC. CDs Certificates of deposit. CSFB Credit Suisse First Boston. DG Deutsche Genossenschaftbank. IBJ Industrial Bank of Japan, Ltd. LIBOR London interbank offered rate. LTCB LongTerm Credit Bank. MHT Manufacturers Hanover Trust. NA Not available. NL Not listed. OeLB Osterreichische Landesbank. PDVSA Petroleos de Venezuela, SA. UBS A consortium of Swiss Bank. WLB Westdeutsche Landesbank.

Note: Bold issues are bonds that have been issued since April 1990.

Developing Country Bonds Outstanding Maturing August 1991 and Beyond (Currencies in Millions) (Continued)

Direct Issue Bonds (Continued)

Issuer	Coupon	Size	Issue Date	Maturity	Listing	Lead Manager
Hungary (Continued)						
National Bank of Hungary	8 1/4%	AS1.500	Sep 89	Sep 96	Vienna	OeLB
National Bank of Hungary	6 7/8	DM150	Sep 86	Sep 96	Dusseldorf	WLB
National Bank of Hungary	10	ECU75	Sep 89	Sep 96	Luxembourg	Kredietbank
National Bank of Hungary	8	DM200	Nov 89	Nov 96	Dusseldorf	WLB
National Bank of Hungary	5.7	¥20.000	Feb 87	Feb 97	Tokyo	Daiwa
National Bank of Hungary	9 1/2	AS1,000	Feb 90	Feb 97	Vienna	Creditanstalt Bankverein
National Bank of Hungary	10	DM300	Mar 90	Mar 97	Frankfurt	Commerzbank
National Bank of Hungary	8	DM200	Jun 89	Jun 97	Frankfurt	DG
National Bank of Hungary	6.3	¥40.000	Oct 87	Oct 97	Tokyo	Daiwa
National Bank of Hungary	**10 5/8**	**AS500**	**Oct 90**	**Oct 97**	**Vienna**	**OeLB**
National Bank of Hungary	5.7	¥25.000	Mar 88	Mar 98	Tokyo	Daiwa
National Bank of Hungary	5.7	¥35,000	Mar 89	Mar 99	Tokyo	Daiwa
National Bank of Hungary	6	¥25.000	Sep 89	Sep 99	Tokyo	Daiwa
National Bank of Hungary	LIBOR + 5/8	US$100	Jan 85	Jan 00	Luxembourg	Nomura
National Bank of Hungary	LIBOR + 1/4	US$200	Aug 85	Sep 00	Luxembourg	Nomura
National Bank of Hungary	LIBOR + 1/4	US$100	Jan 86	Jan 01	Singapore	Daiwa
India						
Indian Oil Corporation	LIBOR + 3/16%	US$200	Nov 89	Nov 94	Luxembourg	CSFB
Industrial Credit & Investment Corp. of India	LIBOR + 1/4	US$6	Nov 81	Dec 91	London	Credit Lyonnais
Industrial Credit & Investment Corp. of India	5 1/4	Sfr80	Aug 88	Oct 95	Basle	Swiss Bank
Industrial Credit & Investment Corp. of India	5 3/4	Sfr75	Nov 86	Nov 96	Zurich	UBS
Industrial Development Bank of India	7	DM100	Feb 86	Feb 93	Frankfurt	Dresdner Bank
Industrial Development Bank of India	6 3/8	DM200	Dec 87	Dec 94	Frankfurt	Commerzbank
Industrial Development Bank of India	6 5/8	DM250	Sep 88	Sep 95	Frankfurt	Dresdner Bank
Industrial Development Bank of India	10	US$100	Jun 86	Jun 96	Luxembourg	CSFB
Industrial Development Bank of India	5 5/8	Sfr100	Mar 87	Mar 97	Basle	UBS
Oil and Natural Gas Commission	9 3/4	US$125	Dec 88	Nov 93	Luxembourg	CSFB
Oil and Natural Gas Commission	6 3/8	DM150	Feb 87	Feb 94	Frankfurt	Commerzbank
Oil and Natural Gas Commission	LIBOR + 3/16	US$125	Mar 86	Mar 96	London	CSFB
Oil and Natural Gas Commission	LIBOR + 1/8	US$150	Feb 85	Feb 97	London	Merrill Lynch
Oil and Natural Gas Commission	10	US$125	Mar 90	Mar 97	Luxembourg	Nomura
Oil and Natural Gas Commission	**9 1/2**	**DM250**	**Jul 90**	**Jul 97**	**Frankfurt**	**Commerzbank**
Oil and Natural Gas Commission	5 3/8	Sfr150	Apr 88	Apr 98	Zurich	CSFB
State Bank of India	5 1/4	¥15,000	Jun 88	Jun 93	London	IBJ Intl. Ltd.
State Bank of India	LIBOR + 0.1	US$100	Dec 85	Dec 97	London	Lloyds Merchant
Mexico						
BNCE	10 1/4%	US$75	Jun 89	Jun 94	Amsterdam	Merrill Lynch
BNCE	**11**	**DM100**	**Jul 90**	**Jul 95**	**Frankfurt**	**Swiss Bank**
BNCE	**9 7/8**	**US$100**	**Jun 91**	**Jun 96**	**Luxembourg**	**Goldman Sachs**
Banamex	LIBOR + 1/4	US$54	Jan 82	Feb 92	London	CSFB
Banobras	**10 3/4**	**US$100**	**Jul 91**	**Jul 96**	**Luxembourg**	**CSFB**
Banobras	17 1/4	US$150	Mar 82	Apr 92	London	Warburg
Barton Corporation	**12**	**US$92**	**Sep 90**	**Sep 93**	**Luxembourg**	**Bankers Trust**
Commission Federal de Electricidad	8 1/4	Sfr41	Mar 82	Apr 92	Zurich	Handelsbank
Cydsa SA	LIBOR + 3/4	US$50	Oct 81	Nov 91	London	Continental Capital
Nacional Financiera SNC (Nafinsa)	8 1/4	Sfr60	Jun 82	Jun 92	Zurich	UBS
Nacional Financiera SNC (Nafinsa)	LIBOR + 1	US$100	Dec 77	Jan 93	Luxembourg	CCF
Nacional Financiera SNC (Nafinsa)	**11**	**DM150**	**Jun 90**	**Jun 95**	**Frankfurt**	**Dresdner Bank**
Nacional Financiera SNC (Nafinsa)	**11 3/4**	**US$100**	**Aug 90**	**Aug 95**	**Luxembourg**	**CSFB**
Euronovum	**12**	**US$60**	**Sep 90**	**Sep 93**	**Luxembourg**	**First Interstate**
Petroleos Mexicanos (Pemex)	**10**	**US$125**	**Mar 91**	**Mar 93**	**Luxembourg**	**Swiss Bank**
Petroleos Mexicanos (Pemex)	**11 5/8**	**US$150**	**Oct 90**	**Oct 93**	**Luxembourg**	**Swiss Bank**
Petroleos Mexicanos (Pemex)	17 3/4	US$150	May 82	Jun 94	Luxembourg	Citibank
Petroleos Mexicanos (Pemex)	**11 1/2**	**ECU100**	**Jul 91**	**Aug 94**	**Luxembourg**	**Paribas Capital Mkts.**
Petroleos Mexicanos (Pemex)	**11 1/4**	**DM100**	**Apr 90**	**Apr 95**	**Dusseldorf**	**WLB**
Petroleos Mexicanos (Pemex)	**11**	**AS500**	**Jul 90**	**Jul 96**	**Vienna**	**Creditanstalt Bankverein**
Petroleos Mexicanos (Pemex)	14 1/2	£50	Apr 81	Mar 06	London	Lloyds Banks
Ponder, LDC	**11**	**US$22**	**May 90**	**May 92**	**NL**	**Lazard Freres**
Sidek International Finance	**12**	**US$50**	**Dec 90**	**Dec 95**	**Luxembourg**	**Kidder Peabody**
Tamsa (Tamtrade)	**12**	**US$33**	**Apr 90**	**Apr 92**	**Luxembourg**	**Bankers Trust**

Developing Country Bonds Outstanding Maturing August 1991 and Beyond (Currencies in Millions) (Continued)

Direct Issue Bonds (Continued)

Issuer	Coupon	Size	Issue Date	Maturity	Listing	Lead Manager
Mexico (Continued)						
Tamsa	**$7\frac{1}{2}$**	**US$50**	**Jun 91**	**Jun 97**	**Luxembourg**	**Bankers Trust**
Transportacion Maritima Mexicana SA	LIBOR + $1\frac{1}{2}$	US$30	Dec 87	Dec 94	Luxembourg	Citibank
United Mexican States	$8\frac{3}{4}$	US$10	Nov 73	Dec 91	London	Rothschild
United Mexican States	16.45	US$29	Apr 82	Apr 92	Luxembourg	Bankers Trust
United Mexican States	**$10\frac{1}{2}$**	**DM300**	**Feb 91**	**Mar 96**	**Frankfurt**	**Deutsche Bank**
United Mexican States	$8\frac{1}{8}$	US$13.4	Dec 72	Dec 97	New York	Merrill Lynch
United Mexican States	$16\frac{1}{2}$	£50	Sep 81	Sep 08	London	County Bank
Panama						
Republic of Panama	LIBOR + $1\frac{3}{4}$	US$30	Mar 87	Mar 92	NA	IBJ
Republic of Panama	LIBOR + 1	US$20	Jun 85	Jun 92	London	Citibank
Republic of Panama	LIBOR + $\frac{5}{8}$	US$12.5	Sep 80	Sep 92	Singapore	Yamaichi
Republic of Panama	$8\frac{1}{4}$	ECU10	Sep 78	Oct 93	Luxembourg	Kredietbank
Philippines						
Republic of Philippines	**LIBOR**	**US$120**	**Aug 90**	**Aug 91**	**NL**	**Lazard Freres**
Republic of Philippines	8.9%	¥3,000	Dec 81	Dec 91	Tokyo	Nikko Securities
Republic of Philippines	17.65	Pesos419	May 89	Jun 93	NL	Lazard Freres
Soviet Union						
Vneshekonombank[b]	$12\frac{1}{4}$%	Lir75,000	Mar 89	Mar 94	Luxembourg	Banco di Roma
Vneshekonombank	$8\frac{7}{8}$	DM500	Feb 90	Feb 95	Dusseldorf	WLB
Vneshekonombank	$6\frac{3}{8}$	DM500	Aug 88	Aug 95	Frankfurt	Dresdner Bank
Vneshekonombank	$7\frac{1}{2}$	DM500	Sep 89	Sep 95	Frankfurt	Commerzbank
Vneshekonombank	8	AS1,000	Sep 89	Sep 95	Vienna	Creditanstalt Bankverein
Vneshekonombank	7	DM750	Mar 89	Mar 96	Frankfurt	Deutsche Bank
Vneshekonombank	8	Fl 250	Jul 89	Jul 96	Amsterdam	ABN
Vneshekonombank	5	Sfr100	Feb 88	Feb 98	Zurich	BKA
Venezuela						
BA Proven (Gtd. PDVSA)	**$11\frac{1}{8}$%**	**DM200**	**Oct 90**	**Oct 95**	**Frankfurt**	**Bankers Trust**
Corimon International Finance	**$10\frac{1}{4}$**	**US$35**	**Oct 90**	**Oct 95**	**Luxembourg**	**Merrill Lynch**
Republic of Venezuela	$11\frac{1}{2}$	DM100	Nov 81	Dec 91	Dusseldorf	WLB
Republic of Venezuela	$11\frac{1}{8}$	US$100	Feb 88	Feb 93	Luxembourg	JP Morgan
Republic of Venezuela	8.6	¥13,600	Mar 81	Mar 93	Tokyo	Daiwa
Republic of Venezuela	Libor + $1\frac{7}{8}$	US$100	Aug 88	Aug 93	Luxembourg	Samuel Montagu
Republic of Venezuela	$8\frac{1}{4}$	DM100	Nov 88	Nov 93	Dusseldorf	WLB

New Money Bonds

Issuer	Form	Coupon	Size	Issue Date	Maturity	Listing	Lead Bank
Argentina New Money Bonds	Bearer	LIBOR + $\frac{7}{8}$%	US$88.2	Aug 87	Oct 99	NL	Citibank
Brazil New Money Bonds	Bearer	LIBOR + $\frac{13}{16}$	US$674.7	Nov 88	Oct 99	Luxembourg	Morgan
Chile New Money Bonds[c]	**Bearer**	**LIBOR + $1\frac{1}{2}$**	**US$200**	**Mar 91**	**Mar 96**	**Luxembourg**	**MHT**
Colombian Registered Instruments/ Keystone Facility	Registered	LIBOR + $1\frac{1}{2}$	US$184.4	Jun 89	Jun 97	NL	Chemical Bank
Colombian Bearer Instruments	**Bearer**	**LIBOR + $1\frac{1}{2}$**	**US$200**	**Aug 91**	**Aug 96**	**Luxembourg**	**Chemical Bank**
Mexico New Money Bonds	Registered	LIBOR + $\frac{13}{16}$	US$183.5	Mar 90	Mar 05	Luxembourg	Citibank
Philippine New Money Bonds	**Registered**	**LIBOR + $\frac{13}{16}$**	**US$715**	**May 90**	**May 05**	**Luxembourg**	**MHT**
Uruguay New Money Bonds	**Registered**	**LIBOR + 1**	**US$89.5**	**Feb 91**	**Feb 06**	**Luxembourg**	**Citibank**
Venezuela New Money Series A Bonds	**Bearer**	**LIBOR + 1**	**US$478**	**Dec 90**	**Dec 05**	**Luxembourg**	**Chase Invest. Bank**
Venezuela New Money Series BP Bonds	**Bearer**	**LIBOR + $\frac{7}{8}$**	**US$356**	**Dec 90**	**Dec 05**	**Luxembourg**	**Chase Invest. Bank**
Venezuela New Money Series BNP Bonds	**Bearer**	**LIBOR + $\frac{7}{8}$**	**US$356**	**Dec 90**	**Dec 05**	**Luxembourg**	**Chase Invest. Bank**

Exchange Bonds

Issuer	Form	Coupon	Size	Issue Date	Maturity
Brazil					
Brazil Investment Bonds	Bearer	6%	US$1,056	Aug 89	Sep 14

Developing Country Bonds Outstanding Maturing August 1991 and Beyond (Currencies in Millions) (Continued)

Exchange Bonds (Continued)

Issuer	Form	Coupon	Size	Issue Date	Maturity
Costa Rica					
Costa Rica Exchange Bonds	Bearer	6.25%	US$228	May 90	May 15
Costa Rica Collateralized Exchange Bonds	Bearer	6.25	US$235	May 90	May 10
Costa Rica Interest Claims	Bearer	LIBOR + $\frac{13}{16}$	US$67	May 90	May 05
Costa Rica Collateralized Interest Claims	Bearer	LIBOR + $\frac{13}{16}$	US$67	May 90	May 05
Mexico					
Mexican Collateralized Exchange Bonds	Registered	LIBOR + $1\frac{5}{8}$%	US$2,560	Mar 88	Mar 08
Williams Bond	Registered	LIBOR + $\frac{3}{4}$	US$200	Nov 88	Nov 08
United Mexican States					
• C$ Discount Series	Registered	LIBOR + $\frac{13}{16}$	C$250	Mar 90	Dec 19
• DFl Discount Series	Registered	LIBOR + $\frac{13}{16}$	Fl46	Mar 90	Dec 19
• DFl Par Series	Registered	5.31	Fl401	Mar 90	Dec 19
• DM Discount Series	Registered	LIBOR + $\frac{13}{16}$	DM661	Feb 90	Dec 19
• DM Par Series	Registered	5.01	DM2,517	Mar 90	Dec 19
• FFr Discount Series	Registered	LIBOR + $\frac{13}{16}$	Ffr97	Mar 90	Dec 19
• FFr Par Series	Registered	6.63	Ffr6,971	Mar 90	Dec 19
• Lir Par Series	Registered	$10\frac{3}{4}$	Lir1,128,204	Mar 90	Dec 19
• SFr Par Series	Registered	$3\frac{3}{4}$	Sfr397	Mar 90	Dec 19
• ¥ Discount Series	Registered	LIBOR + $\frac{13}{16}$	¥5,540	Mar 90	Dec 19
• ¥ Par Series	Registered	3.85	¥32,146	Mar 90	Dec 19
Floating Rate Bonds					
• US$ Discount Series A	Registered	LIBOR + $\frac{13}{16}$	US$2,478	Mar 90	Dec 19
• US$ Discount Series B	Registered	LIBOR + $\frac{13}{16}$	US$2,476	Mar 90	Dec 19
• US$ Discount Series C	Registered	LIBOR + $\frac{13}{16}$	US$2,476	Mar 90	Dec 19
• US$ Discount Series D	Registered	LIBOR + $\frac{13}{16}$	US$4,068	Mar 90	Dec 19
Fixed Rate Bonds					
• US$ Par Series A	Registered	$6\frac{1}{4}$	US$6,211	Mar 90	Dec 19
• US$ Par Series B	Registered	$6\frac{1}{4}$	US$11,663	Mar 90	Dec 19
Floating Rate Privatization Notes	**Bearer/Regis.**	**LIBOR + $\frac{13}{16}$**	**US$1,150**	**Jul 91**	**Jul 01**
Venezuela					
Republic of Venezuela	Bearer	LIBOR + $1\frac{1}{8}$%	US$166	Dec 88	Dec 94
Republic of Venezuela	Bearer	LIBOR + $1\frac{1}{4}$	US$263	Jan 89	Dec 95
Republic of Venezuela	Bearer	LIBOR + $1\frac{1}{8}$	US$167	Dec 88	Dec 98
Republic of Venezuela	Bearer	LIBOR + $1\frac{1}{8}$	US$167	Dec 88	Dec 03
Interest-Reduction Bonds					
• US$ Par Series A	**Registered**	**$6\frac{3}{4}$**	**US$5,032**	**Dec 90**	**Mar 20**
• US$ Par Series B	**Registered**	**$6\frac{3}{4}$**	**US$1,638**	**Dec 90**	**Mar 20**
• Lir Par Series	**Registered**	**$6\frac{3}{4}$**	**Lir318,881**	**Dec 90**	**Mar 20**
• FFr Par Series	**Registered**	**$6\frac{3}{4}$**	**Ffr321**	**Dec 90**	**Mar 20**
• SFr Par Series	**Registered**	**$6\frac{3}{4}$**	**Sfr100**	**Dec 90**	**Mar 20**
• DM Par Series	**Registered**	**$6\frac{3}{4}$**	**DM508**	**Dec 90**	**Mar 20**
Principal-Reduction Bonds					
• US$ Discount Series A	**Registered**	**LIBOR + $\frac{13}{16}$**	**US$958**	**Dec 90**	**Mar 20**
• US$ Discount Series B	**Registered**	**LIBOR + $\frac{13}{16}$**	**US$211**	**Dec 90**	**Mar 20**
• DM Discount Series	**Registered**	**LIBOR + $\frac{13}{16}$**	**DM131**	**Dec 90**	**Mar 20**
Temporary Interest-Reduction Bonds[d]					
• US$ Series A	**Bearer**	**LIBOR + $\frac{7}{8}$**	**US$2,259**	**Dec 90**	**Apr 07**
• US$ Series B	**Bearer**	**LIBOR + $\frac{7}{8}$**	**US$989**	**Dec 90**	**Apr 07**
• DM Series	**Bearer**	**LIBOR + $\frac{7}{8}$**	**DM341**	**Dec 90**	**Apr 07**
• £ Series	**Bearer**	**LIBOR + $\frac{7}{8}$**	**£37**	**Dec 90**	**Apr 07**
• SFr Series	**Bearer**	**LIBOR + $\frac{7}{8}$**	**Sfr153**	**Dec 90**	**Apr 07**
Debt-Conversion Bonds					
• US$ Series DL	**Bearer**	**LIBOR + $\frac{7}{8}$**	**US$5,327**	**Dec 90**	**Apr 07**
• US$ Series IL	**Bearer**	**LIBOR + $\frac{7}{8}$**	**US$304**	**Dec 90**	**Apr 07**
• DM Series	**Bearer**	**LIBOR + $\frac{7}{8}$**	**DM209**	**Dec 90**	**Apr 07**
• £ Series	**Bearer**	**LIBOR + $\frac{7}{8}$**	**£119**	**Dec 90**	**Apr 07**

Developing Country Bonds Outstanding Maturing August 1991 and Beyond (Currencies in Millions) (Continued)

Exchange Bonds (Continued)

Issuer	Form	Coupon	Size	Issue Date	Maturity
Uruguay					
Banco Central del Uruguay	**Registered**	**6¾%**	**US$530**	**Feb 91**	**Feb 21**
Uruguay Debt-Conversion Bonds	**Registered**	**LIBOR + ⅞**	**US$448**	**Feb 91**	**Feb 08**
Yugoslavia					
National Bank of Yugoslavia	Registered	5¾%	US$80	Oct 88	Oct 08
Domestic U.S. Dollar Instruments					
Argentina					
Bonos Externos '82 (BONEX)	Bearer	LIBOR	US$375	Feb 82	Feb 92
Bonos Externos '84 (BONEX)	Bearer	LIBOR	US$500	Dec 84	Dec 94
Bonos Externos '87 (BONEX)	Bearer	LIBOR	US$350	Sep 87	Sep 97
Bonos Externos '89 (BONEX)	Bearer	LIBOR	US$3,000	Dec 89	Dec 99
Egypt					
Dollar Treasuries	Bearer	LIBOR + ½%	US$50	Nov 89	1999
Guatemala					
Stabilization Bonds	Bearer	10%	US$151.1	1988	1998
Uruguay					
Dollar Treasury Bills (19 Issues)	Bearer	Fixed: 8.5%-11%	US$710	1980-90	1991-99
Dollar Treasury Bonds (5 Issues)	Bearer	Fixed: 7.5-11	US$97	1983-87	1991-95
Dollar Treasury Bonds (20 Issues)	Bearer	LIBOR-LIBOR + 2	US$868	1983-91	1991-99
Venezuela					
Banco Central de Venezuela Promissory Notes	Registered	LIBOR + ⅞%	US$60	Sep 89	Up to 1992
Ministerio de Hacienda Promissory Notes	Registered	LIBOR	US$600	1982-90	Up to 1997

United States Private Placements

Issuer	Type	Coupon	Size	Placement Date	Maturity	Arranger
Algeria						
Sonatrach	Bonds	10¼%	US$42	Jun 78	1992	Credit Lyonnais
Sonatrach	Bonds	Zero	US$10.50	Jun 78	1992	Credit Lyonnais
Brazil						
Varig	Lease Financing	NA	US$125	Dec 88	2000	GAGX/CL Air
Hungary						
National Bank of Hungary	Bonds	8⅞%	US$55	Nov 86	1993	Dai-Ichi Kangyo
Mexico						
Aeronaves de Mexico SA	Secured Notes	17½%	US$8	Dec 81	1993	LKL/MLWW
Aeronaves de Mexico SA	Secured Notes	19¾	US$19	Jun 84	1994	SLAE
Aeronaves de Mexico SA	Equipment Trust Cert.	15¾	US$33	Jun 81	1996	LKL/MLWW
Aeronaves de Mexico SA	Secured Notes	18.20	US$13.5	Dec 81	1996	LKL/MLWW
Aeronaves de Mexico SA	Secured Notes	17½	US$14	Dec 81	1996	LKL/MLWW
Aeronaves de Mexico SA	Equipment Trust Cert.	19¾	US$34	Dec 81	1996	MLWW
Aeronaves de Mexico SA	Secured Notes	17½	US$23	Jun 82	1997	LKL/MLWW

Developing Country Bonds Outstanding Maturing August 1991 and Beyond (Currencies in Millions) (Continued)

United States Private Placements (Continued)

Issuer	Type	Coupon	Size	Placement Date	Maturity	Arranger
Mexico (Continued)						
Banamex	**Secured Notes**	**11%**	**US$130**	**May 90**	**1993**	**Citibank**
Banca Serfin SNC	**Bonds**	**10 1/2**	**US$70**	**Jan 91**	**1996**	**Yamaichi**
Bancomer	**Securitized Credit Card Receivables**	**LIBOR + 5/8**	**US$230**	**Jul 90**	**1995**	**Citibank**
Banco International SNC	Bonds	LIBOR + 3/4	US$188	Sep 86	1991	First Interstate
Banco International SNC	Bonds	LIBOR + 3/4	US$53	Feb 90	2000	First Interstate
Banco Mexicano Somex SNC	Bonds	LIBOR + 3/4	US$75	Sep 86	1991	First Interstate
Cemex	**Notes**	**9.41**	**US$425**	**May 91**	**1996**	**JP Morgan**
Cemex[e]	**Convertible Eurobonds**	**11**	**US$100**	**Jun 90**	**2002**	**Citibank**
Commission Federal de Electricidad	Notes	11 1/2	US$235	Mar 90	1995	Salomon Brothers
Companhia Mexicana de Aviacion	Floating Rate CDs	LIBOR + 3/4	US$135	Sep 86	1991	First Interstate
Companhia Mexicana de Aviacion	Secured Notes	16 1/4	US$24	Oct 82	1992	Citibank
Companhia Mexicana de Aviacion	Secured Loan Cert.	15 1/2	US$100	Jun 81	1993	LKL/MLWW
Companhia Mexicana de Aviacion	Secured Notes	16 1/4	US$28	Dec 81	1996	LKL/MLWW
ELM.International	Notes	13 1/2	US$65	Jan 90	1992	Bear Stearns
Empresas Tolteca de Mexico SA	Secured Notes	17 3/4	US$15	Jun 82	1992	Bank of America
Grupo San Luis	**Secured Notes**	**12**	**US$75**	**Aug 90**	**1993**	**Bankers Trust**
Mexican Airlines	Secured Loan Cert.	15 1/2	US$100	Jun 81	1993	LKL/MLWW
Multibanco Comermex SNC	Floating Rate CDs	LIBOR + 3/4	US$135	Sep 86	1991	First Interstate
Nacional Financiera SNC (Nafinsa)	**Notes**	**10**	**US$125**	**May 91**	**1996**	**JP Morgan**
Petroleos Mexicanos (Pemex)	Notes	9 7/8	US$90	Oct 77	1992	Merrill Lynch
Petroleos Mexicanos (Pemex)	Notes	9 7/8	US$40	Jun 78	1993	Merrill Lynch
Petroleos Mexicanos (Pemex)	Notes	9 7/8	US$10	Jun 78	1993	Merrill Lynch
Petroleos Mexicanos (Pemex)	**Notes**	**11.43**	**US$100**	**Aug 90**	**1995**	**Paine Webber**
Petroleos Mexicanos (Pemex) 1981 Drilling Rig	Lease Financing	15	US$21	Mar 81	1992-97	Goldman/Citibank
Sunbelt Enterprises	Guaranteed Notes	11	US$150	Oct 89	1991	BCO Nac. de Mexico/ **Citibank**
Telmex	**Unsecured Notes**	**12 1/4**	**US$150**	**Jul 90**	**1992**	**JP Morgan**
Telmex	**Notes**	**11**	**US$335**	**Apr 90**	**1995**	**Citibank**
Telmex	**Notes**	**8.9**	**US$570**	**Dec 90**	**1995**	**Citibank**
United Mexican States	**Bonds**	**9 1/2**	**US$40**	**Jan 91**	**2000**	**Merrill Lynch**
Panama						
Republic of Panama	Guaranteed Notes	4.8 %	US$3	1958	1993	Citibank
Republic of Panama	Guaranteed Notes	3	US$2	1950	1996	Citibank
Republic of Panama	Guaranteed Notes	4 1/2	US$5	1962	2001	Chase Investment
Philippines						
Philippine Airlines, Inc.	Lease Financing	7.56 %	US$23	Oct 87	1992	SAL
Philippine Airlines, Inc.	Lease Financing	12 1/2	US$34	Sep 83	1995	Citibank
Philippine Airlines, Inc.	Lease Financing	8.1	US$27	Dec 87	1995	SAL
Poland						
LOT Polish Airlines	Lease Financing	LIBOR + 1%	US$210	Apr 89	2001	Citibank
Venezuela						
Tytan Securities/SIDETUR Steel	**Bonds**	**LIBOR + 1 3/8%**	**US$60**	**Dec 90**	**1996**	**Citibank**

Japan Private Placements

Issuer	Type	Coupon	Size	Placement Date	Maturity	Arranger
Algeria						
Banque de L'Agriculture et du Developement Rural	Shibosai	6.4%	¥8,700	Jul 88	1995	Fuji Bank
Banque Exterieure d'Algerie	Shibosai	6.8	¥10,000	Nov 89	1994	IBJ
Banque Exterieure d'Algerie	Shibosai	6.6	¥10,000	Oct 88	1995	IBJ
Banque Nationale d'Algerie	Shibosai	6 1/2	¥8,000	Mar 88	1993	Nomura
Banque Nationale d'Algerie	Shibosai	6.4	¥8,000	Apr 88	1995	Nikko Securities
Credit Populaire d'Algerie	Shibosai	6.4	¥8,000	May 88	1995	NKK
Argentina						
Yacimientos Petroliferos Fiscales	Shibosai	8.8%	¥10,000	May 81	1993	NA

Developing Country Bonds Outstanding Maturing August 1991 and Beyond (Currencies in Millions) (Continued)

Japan Private Placements (Continued)

Issuer	Type	Coupon	Size	Placement Date	Maturity	Arranger
Brazil						
Companhia Vale do Rio Doce	Shibosai	9 1/2%	¥5,000	Oct 82	1992	Nomura
Usiminas Siderurgicas de Minas Gerais SA	Shibosai	9	¥10,000	Feb 82	1992	Bank of Tokyo
Varig	Lease Financing	10.11	US$150	Sep 89	2004	Nissho Iwai Corp.
Bulgaria						
Bulgarian Foreign Trade Bank	Shibosai	5.7%	¥10,000	Nov 88	1998	Bank of Tokyo
Bulgarian Foreign Trade Bank	Shibosai	5.9	¥6,000	Oct 89	1999	IBJ
Bulgarian Foreign Trade Bank	Private MT Bonds	5.8	¥10,000	Mar 89	1999	Nikko Securities
Mineral Bank of Bulgaria	Private Bonds	5.8	¥5,000	Jun 89	1996	IBJ
Chile						
Republic of Chile	NA	7.4%	¥10,000	1979	1991	Daiwa
Colombia						
Republic of Colombia	Shibosai	LIBOR + 1 1/10%	¥6,000	Jul 86	1994	IBJ
Hungary						
National Bank of Hungary	Shibosai	7.9%	¥10,000	1984	1991	LTCB
National Bank of Hungary	Shibosai	7.6	¥10,000	Mar 85	1992	LTCB
National Bank of Hungary	Shibosai	5.7	¥20,000	Feb 87	1997	Daiwa
National Bank of Hungary	Shibosai	5.9	¥30,000	Oct 88	1998	Daiwa
India						
Industrial Dev. Bank of India	Bonds	5.7%	¥20,000	Oct 89	1999	Daiwa
Oil and Natural Gas Commission	**Bonds**	**8 1/2**	**¥30,000**	**Dec 90**	**2000**	**Nikko Securities**
Mexico						
Petroleos Mexicanos (Pemex)	Shibosai	8.8%	¥5,000	Jul 82	1992	Daiwa
Petroleos Mexicanos (Pemex)	Shibosai	7 1/2	¥10,000	Oct 85	1992	IBJ
Panama						
Republic of Panama	Shibosai	8.9%	¥5,000	1983	1993	Yamaichi
Republic of Panama	Shibosai	7.6	¥8,000	Jan 79	1994	Bank of Tokyo
Philippines						
Devel. Bank of the Philippines	Shibosai	7 1/2%	¥10,000	Apr 79	1995	NA
Uruguay						
Republic of Uruguay	Shibosai	6.7%	¥3,750	Aug 89	1994	Nikko Securities
Yugoslavia						
Jugobanka Udruzena Banka	NA	NA	¥10,000	1979	1994	NA

* * *

APPENDIX C

Selected Information Sources on Developing Countries and the Developing Country Sovereign Bond Market

International Monetary Fund (IMF) Publications (available from the IMF, Washington, DC)

- *Balance of Payments Statistics* (monthly)
- *Balance of Payments Statistics Yearbook* (annual)
- *Annual Report on Exchange Arrangements & Exchange Restrictions* (annual)
- *Government Finance Statistics Yearbook* (annual)
- *IMF Survey* (biweekly)—Newsletter outlining IMF activities and proposals under discussion, as well as analyzing major economic trends.
- *International Capital Markets: Developments and Prospects* (annual, most recent edition April 1989). World Economic and Financial Surveys.
- *International Financial Statistics* (monthly)
- *International Financial Statistics Yearbook* (annual)
- *World Economic Outlook* (annual, most recent edition April 1989), World Economic and Financial Surveys.

World Bank Publications (available from the World Bank, Washington, DC)

- *Finance & Development* (quarterly)—A quarterly publication of the IMF and the World Bank that outlines economic reforms in developing countries and IMF and World Bank initiatives.
- *Policy, Research, and External Affairs Working Papers* (periodic)—Issued periodically to disseminate the findings of work in progress of World Bank staff.
- *Quarterly Review on Financial Flows to Developing Countries.* Debt and International Division (quarterly)—Includes analysis and statistics regarding capital flows to developing countries.
- *Transition: the Newsletter About Reforming Economies* (monthly)—Regular newsletter published by the World Bank's Socialist Economies Unit. Describes economic trends in countries moving from a socialist to a market economy, and highlights new books and working papers completed by World Bank staff.
- *Trends in Developing Economies* (annual)—Statistical series describing recent economic performance and trends in almost 100 developing countries drawn from the World Bank's internal data base and economic analyses of its member countries.
- *Trends in Private Investment in Developing Countries* (annual)—Economic data on investment trends in 40 developing countries.
- *World Bank News* (weekly)—Newsletter outlining loans and programs approved by the World Bank, as well as new initiatives for developing countries.

- *World Debt Tables: External Debt of Developing Countries*, volumes I and II, (annual, most recent edition December 1989).
- *World Development Report* (annual)—Includes World Development Indicators annex, providing selected social and economic data for more than 100 countries.

Bank for International Settlements (BIS) Publications (available from the BIS, Basle, Switzerland)

- *Bank for International Settlements Annual Report* (annual, most recent edition June 1989)—Includes economic and financial data on developing countries drawn from BIS database.
- *International Banking and Financial Market Developments* (published periodically)—Includes extensive data on reporting banks exposure to developing countries drawn from BIS database.
- *Statistics on External Indebtedness*, published jointly by the BIS and the Organization for Economic Cooperation and Development (OECD)—Includes bank and trade-related nonbank external claims on individual borrowing countries.

Other Publications

- *Asian Development Outlook*, Asian Development Bank, Manila, the Philippines (annual)—Includes economic information and assessments of Asian counties.
- *Comparative Country Statistics*, the Institute of International Finance, Inc., Washington, DC (semiannual, most recent edition November 1989)—A compendium of selected historical time series data from the country data bases that accompany IIF country reports and updates.
- *Country Exposure Lending Survey*, Statistical Release from the Federal Financial Institutions Examination Council, published by the Federal Reserve System—Includes breakdown of developing country external indebtedness and commercial bank exposure.
- *Economic and Social Development in Latin America*, Inter-American Development Bank, Washington, DC (annual, most recent edition September 1989)—Includes economic information and assessments of Latin American countries.
- *Economic Commission for Latin America and the Caribbean* (annual country overviews)—Publishes annual economic overview of economies in Latin America and the Caribbean.
- *The Economist Intelligence Unit*, Business International, London (annual country profiles and quarterly country reports)—Publishes economic and political analyses for developing countries in Latin America, Asia, the Middle East, and Africa.
- *Foreign Broadcast Information Service* (daily)—A U.S. government daily publication that contains current news and information from local newspapers,

journals, and radio broadcasts translated into English from Latin American, Eastern European, and the Near Eastern and South Asian countries.

- *The IFR Global Financing Directory,* IFR Publishing Ltd., London (annual)–Compiles all international borrowings by country for the year.
- *The World Bank Watch,* American Banker, New York, (weekly)–Reports development bank activities in Latin America, Asia, Africa, and the Middle East.
- *World Markets Reports,* DRI/McGraw-Hill, (semiannual)–Research reports on 53 countries, analyzing major economic and political issues. The reports contain economic data projections for ten years and provide historical data as well.

Selected Newsletters

- *International Financing Review,* IFR Publishing Ltd., London (weekly)–Includes section on developing country bond issuance.
- *LDC Debt Report: An American Banker Newsletter on Developing-Country Debt,* American Banker, New York (weekly).
- *Swaps: the Newsletter of New Financial Instruments,* the Intrados Group, Washington, D.C. (monthly)–Often includes features on developing country debt markets.

Africa

- *Africa Analysis,* London (biweekly)–Bulletin on financial political trends in Africa.
- *Financial Journal: Association of African Central Banks,* African Centre for Monetary Studies, Abijan, Cote d'Ivoire (quarterly)–Covers financial sector performance in Africa.

Asia

- *Asian Development Review,* Asian Development Bank, Manila, Philippines (quarterly)–Quarterly studies of Asian and Pacific economic issues.
- *Far Eastern Economic Review,* Hong Kong (weekly)–Weekly coverage of the Asian economies.

Brazil

- *Brazil Watch,* Orbis Publications, Ltd., Washington, D.C. (biweekly)–Reports on political, economic, and business events in Brazil.
- *Inside Brazil,* Goes, Piquet & Lobo/Contact Marketing International, Inc., Washington, D.C. (monthly)–Political risk analysis on Brazil.
- *Gazeta Mercantil* (English Edition weekly)–Covers Brazilian economy.

Eastern Europe

- *PlanEcon Report: Developments in the Economies of the Soviet Union and Eastern Europe,* PlanEcon, Inc. Washington, D.C.

- *Report on Eastern Europe* (weekly)–A publication of the RFE/RI Research Institute on current East European Affairs.
- *Report on the USSR* (weekly)–Research reports on the USSR and the Baltic States published by the RFE/RL Research Institute.

Latin America

- *Lagniappe Letter: Biweekly Report of Issues Affecting Business in Latin America,* Latin American Information Services, Inc., New York, (biweekly).
- *Lagniappe Quarterly Monitor,* Latin American Information Services, Inc., New York (quarterly).
- *Latin America Monthly Economic Report,* The WEFA Group, Bala Cynwyd, PA (monthly).
- *Latin Finance,* Latin American Financial Publications (monthly)–Covers major developments in the financial markets of Latin America.

Mexico

- Economic Report on Mexico, Economic Analysis for Company Planning, Mexico City (monthly)–Covers economic developments in Mexico.
- *El Financiera,* Mexico City (weekly)–Weekly international edition is published in English and summarizes daily news reports from Mexico's major financial newspaper.
- *The Mexican Economy: A Monthly Report,* Centro de Analisis e Investigacion Economica, A.C., Mexico (monthly).
- *Mexico's Financial and Stock Markets: Information and Analysis,* Banco Nacional de Mexico, Mexico City (weekly)–Analyzes the stock market and provides financial indicators on domestic instruments.
- *Mexico Services: A Publication of International Reports,* IBC Publications, New York (biweekly)–Covers Mexico's political and economic situations.

North Africa and the Middle East

- *Maghreb: Algeria, Libya, Mauritania, Morocco & Tunisia,* Middle East Economic Digest, London (quarterly)–Quarterly report on political developments, economic environments, and business update on Maghreb countries.
- *Middle East Economic Digest,* Middle East Business Weekly, London (weekly)–Weekly coverage of economic and political events in the Middle East.

Venezuela

- *Venezuela's Economy: Facts and Trends,* MetroEconomica, Caracas, Venezuela (monthly)–Outlines important facts and trends in the Venezuelan economy.
- *Veneconomy: An In-Depth Review of the Venezuelan Economy,* (monthly), VenEconomia, C.A., Caracas, Venezuela–Covers the Venezuelan economy, politics, international relations, and developments in the petroleum sector.

General Political Information

Two examples of the range of reference material available on the political systems of countries are:

- *Political Handbook of the World,* CSA Publications, State University of New York at Binghamton, Binghamton, NY (annual).
- *The Statesman's Yearbook: Statistical and Historical Annual of the States of the World,* St. Martin's Press, New York, NY (annual).

Chapter Seventeen

The Emergence of the Latin American Debt Market*

by Michael Pettis
Director
Emerging Countries Capital Markets
First Boston Corporation

The year 1990 marked a watershed in the secondary market for restructured Latin American bank debt. Following years of steady and seemingly permanent price decline, the market turned dramatically around during 1990 to show consistent and broad-based price gains throughout the year and up to the present. This turnaround reflects as much a change in the dynamics of the market as it does an actual change in economic expectations for Latin American borrowers.

From the early days in the development of the secondary market, in 1984–1985, when prices existed mostly as rough indications of relative value, to the end of 1989, by which time a fairly large cash market had developed with good liquidity and tight spreads, prices declined very steadily and with little variation. The price decline is illustrated by the behavior of the CS-First Boston Latin American Index, which is a weighted average of the prices of the benchmark debt of the five most actively traded countries—Mexico, Brazil, Venezuela, Argentina, and Chile (see Figure 17.1). From the beginning of 1986 to the end of 1989, the Index declined from a price of 72.17 to 30.59 (the Index is quoted as a percent of the face value of the debt).

* This chapter is based on an article that appeared in *Euroweek*, March 8, 1991.

Figure 17.1—FBC Latin American Index (from December 31, 1985 to July 31, 1992)

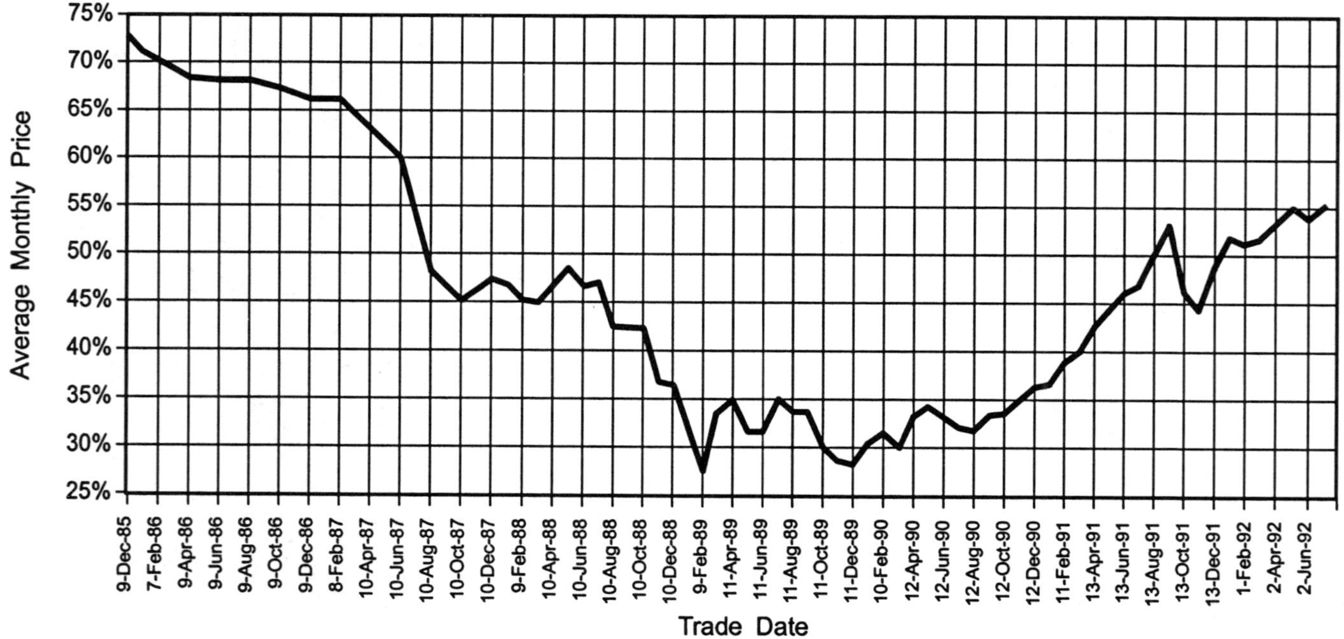

Within the general decline, the Index showed a significant price drop for each of the four years, and for all but three of the sixteen quarters:

Year	*Year-End Index*	*Annual Price Change*
1986	66.21	-8.1%
1987	48.55	-26.8
1988	38.01	-21.6
1989	30.59	-19.5

We should note that investors who had purchased a basket of debt during any of these years would not have fared quite as badly as the Index would suggest, since most of the debt paid interest regularly and, particularly as prices declined, the interest carry component was very high.

The Index bottomed out at 28.89 in February 1989, just before Mexico announced an agreement with the bank steering committee under the "Brady" plan. The announcement caused a rush of optimism among traders and creditor banks, and prices quickly shot up dramatically; but, by year end, much of the gain was given up and the Index showed a minimal 5.9% net improvement from the year's low.

PRICE CHANGES IN 1990 AND 1991

For 1990 the Index tells a radically different story that represents a significant break in market behavior. Each quarter shows an improvement in the Index, with three of the four quarters showing very large price increases:

Quarter	*Quarter-End Index*	*Quarterly Price Change*
1990 Q1	32.82	+ 7.3%
1990 Q2	35.57	+ 8.4
1990 Q3	35.93	+ 1.0
1990 Q4	38.29	+ 6.6
Total	–	+ 25.2

During 1991, the price gains accelerated further as, on the one hand, Mexico, Venezuela, and Chile raced to integrate themselves more fully into the world capital markets and, on the other hand, a combination of investors' desire to catch the "next" Mexico and the generally good noises coming primarily from Argentina brought the speculative countries (Brazil and Argentina) sharply up. During the last quarter, a combination of bad news in Brazil and excessive leveraging on the part of speculators brought Brazil crashing down, and the general ensuing decline brought the Index down in a sharp correction. The Index for the first three quarters of 1991 grew by over 43% to 54.78, but declined in the fourth quarter for a net gain for the year of just over 13%:

Quarter	*Quarter-End Index*	*Quarterly Price Change*
1991 Q1	43.17	+ 12.7%
1991 Q2	48.56	+ 12.5
1991 Q3	54.78	+ 12.8
1991 Q4	48.91	- 10.7
Total	–	+ 13.13

Once again we should note that the returns for investors who had purchased paper at the beginning of the year would have been on average higher than the change indicated in the Index because of the extremely high interest carry on the servicing assets (Mexico, Venezuela, and Chile paid interest fully and Argentina partially).

For example, a buyer of Mexico could have purchased Mexican Par Bonds (the benchmark debt) at the beginning of 1990 for a price of 36.00 and could have sold it at 44.75 at the end of the year. Besides the 24.3% capital gain, the investor would have also received a coupon of 6.25% on the face value of the debt, for a total annual return of 43.4%. If he had held the paper to the end of 1991, he could have sold it for 59.63 for an additional annualized return of 62.4%.

A buyer of Venezuela, the other favorite for yield investors, would have earned, similarly, a very hefty 63.2% between principal increase and interest income over 1990, and an additional annualized 60.6% through the end of 1991. Even Chile, whose price had never declined as much as those of other countries and consequently had a lower current yield and less room for capital appreciation, showed a solid 28.3% return to investors over 1990 and a very substantial 47.0% annualized for 1991.

For the more speculative investor who was willing to gamble on a nonservicing asset, the story is only marginally different. On the one hand, large-scale buying of Argentine debt for the privatization program knocked prices up by 65.3% (plus irregular bits and pieces of interest) in 1990, and euphoria over a perceived turnaround in the economy contributed an additional gain of 75.9% through the end of

September 1991. On the other hand, Brazil increased by only 2.1% in 1990, but jumped back on track in 1991 with an 18.3% gain. (Owners of Brazilian and Argentine debt were able to keep the accrued unpaid interest, which generally trades in the market at a premium to principal, so that total returns would have actually been substantially higher.)

Finally, the Index continued its strong growth in 1992 by growing 6.4% during the first quarter, to 52.03, and 2.6% during the second quarter, to 53.40. On an annual basis this represents 19.2% capital appreciation (which, of course, does not include the significant interest component of total returns) for the first two quarters of 1992. This growth occurred in spite of a significant fall in Venezuelan debt prices because of coup attempts in February 1992 and November 1992 and a tremendous amount of volatility in Brazil brought about by a Brady agreement amid corruption charges aimed at the president.

FACTORS AFFECTING PRICES

The sudden reversal in the pricing trends probably reflects two factors: the changed strategy of the creditor banks who had been the big sellers, and the increased interest on the part of new investors. The importance to the market of the creditor banks' strategies reflects, of course, their position as the predominant holders of debt in the market—in fact they were virtually the only holders of any importance for most of the period of the "debt crisis."

This meant that until 1990–1991, the price of most restructuring country debt had primarily reflected the selling, or "dumping," decisions of creditor banks. These decisions were and are more likely to have been caused by market pressures among the creditor banks—e.g., levels of reserves, the pressure to exit Latin America, net profit for the year—then perceptions of the countries' economic prospects.

Interestingly enough, during this period traders knew that price changes in each of the countries were far more closely correlated with the general price index than with any other factor, even though the economic prospects of the various countries varied widely from country to country. This would suggest that the factors affecting prices have been in the past not country-specific so much as general-market-specific, and, in fact, as we note above, it has been conditions affecting the *creditor banks* that have influenced prices for all debt.

Since 1990, however, fewer of the remaining creditors seem to have been as determined to dump their Latin American exposure as they had been in the past. This is partly because many of the smaller, less committed creditor banks are wholly or partially out of Latin America, and partly because many of the larger banks no longer see their exposure in these countries (particularly in Mexico and Chile) as being as much of a problem as it had once been. In fact recently, and perhaps a bit prematurely, a number of large banks have suggested that by its tenth anniversary, in August 1992, the debt crisis will have finally been over. These claims followed the Brady restructuring of Brazil, the last of the big borrowers to reach a "Brady" agreement with creditor banks.

This new reluctance to dump paper probably reflects three factors. First, and unfortunately for the creditors, within the hierarchy of bank loan problem areas Latin American exposure no longer enjoys the primacy it once had, as other problems areas—such as commercial real estate loans and highly leveraged transactions—become increasingly visible. By turning management and shareholder attention elsewhere, this has relieved the "dump-at-any-cost" mentality that had afflicted the attitude towards Latin American exposure.

The second factor is the increasing differentiation on the part of creditors among types of obligors within Latin America, with certain obligors enjoying a much higher degree of confidence, reflected in their gradual return to the voluntary capital markets. In the past, the strategy of the most aggressive bank sellers reflected a general revulsion towards all Latin American credits, with a concomitant desire to sell any asset at any price that could be absorbed by reserve levels. Over the past two years there seems to have developed a belated recognition that many borrowers have real and in fact very probable repayment prospects and that there is a yield above which these assets should not be sold. Nonetheless, it is worth noting that there continue to be some fairly substantial pricing inefficiencies in the market.

Third, and most importantly, there is a growing—although still cautious—optimism that certain countries in Latin America are finally in a position to grow out of their loan problems. Of course, it is not clear that the debt crisis is over, but there is a feeling that, subject to certain conditions—the U.S. pulling out of a recession, stability in commodity prices, and, most importantly, continuation of the domestic liberalization and growth policies that certain governments have been pursuing—these countries will gradually be in a position to manage and grow out of their external debt.

EMERGENCE OF NEW INVESTORS

Accompanying this "sellers' exhaustion" and equally significant in its effect on the market has been the role of investors. Over the past two years debt traders have seen nontraditional investors become an increasingly important, although still small, part of the market. It is worth noting that the tremendous growth in liquidity that the market has experienced has done much to ease one of the major concerns that investors have had in the past—i.e., the inability to execute buy or sell decisions quickly and efficiently.

Since 1990–1991, foreign investors, largely U.S. and European nonbank institutions and European retail buyers, have started purchasing selectively either bonds that were created out of the debt restructurings (e.g., the "Brady" bonds) or the new issue bonds. U.S. institutions have largely been buyers of the former assets which tend to be long term, extremely liquid, and often have enhancements, such as U.S. Treasury collateral backing the principal.

This inflow of foreign capital (which has been directed at equity even more than debt) has generated a great deal of comment in the market and in the press. However, we would stress that the total inflow of foreign capital is probably much smaller than the noise around it would suggest, and that most investors are still evaluating the risks and prospects of fixed income investments in Latin America.

It should be noted that the price increases have affected nearly all the debt obligations of Latin American borrowers regardless of quality. It is not clear that these price increases are always justified. On the one hand, the very illiquid markets for obligations of the smaller "marginal" countries have seen tremendous price increases reflecting a speculative frenzy—led primarily by Latin retail buyers and certain market players, glutted by two very profitable years—and their prices probably exceed any rational repayment expectations. On the other hand, for the higher quality assets—obligations of Mexico, Venezuela, Chile, Uruguay, and certain "blue chip" corporates in any of the major countries—the yields continue to exceed the risk and most sophisticated market participants expect a continuing but more gradual strengthening of prices.

Because of the brutal problems faced by Latin American debtors and their bankers through most of the 1980s, there has been a real reluctance on the part of many bankers and investors to differentiate and evaluate the types of risks on separate instruments. Clearly, many borrowers in the late 1970s and early 1980s were fundamentally unsound and should not have had such easy access to the international credit markets. But an important factor in the crisis and one which affected all borrowers was the sudden and near total drying up of liquidity upon Mexico's August 1982 announcement that it would not be able to meet upcoming principal payments. The inability of Latin American borrowers to refinance existing debt probably forced many of them into unnecessary restructurings.

Since borrowers have had almost no access to the credit markets, a withdrawal of new lending to the region is, ironically, no longer as big a problem, and consequently one of the most serious problems facing several major borrowers has been, in its own way, resolved. Furthermore, the withdrawal of liquidity ensured that the grinding restructuring that certain countries underwent, most notably Mexico and Chile, included a significant amount of debt reduction, and several institutions in these countries have emerged with clean balance sheets and a large and unutilized debt support capacity.

That is not to say that the external debt of a country does not weigh on any individual borrower, and all Latin American borrowers have heavy external debt burdens. But for certain of these countries the burden has become manageable and there is clearly a strong political commitment to remaining within the international capital markets, particularly as local economies are poised for such strong growth and as capital flows back, largely in the form of equity. It is for this reason that value investors and the more sophisticated traders continue to see very strong upside potential in the "blue chip" debt instruments whose yields, although low by recent Latin American standards, are still extremely high by the standards of equivalent risk elsewhere.

NEW CORPORATE BOND ISSUES

The large number and great variety of U.S. Dollar bond issues from various sovereign and corporate borrowers in Mexico, Venezuela, Argentina, Brazil, Chile, and Uruguay has opened up one of the more interesting investment opportunities. The market has distinguished pretty strongly between sovereign and corporate issues on a price basis given the strong retail preference for sovereign issues. As a result, corporates trade at spreads to the sovereign of anywhere from 75–100 basis points for the best corporate credits to 100–200 basis points for less well-known but still strong credits.

This spread reflects primarily the significantly smaller universe of investors in corporate credits, since, on a risk basis, most investors agree that the main risk for investors in Latin American corporates is the sovereign risk. Some sophisticated investors would even argue, in fact, that certain prime corporates are better credits than the sovereign entity. They point to the willingness of certain obligors during the 1980s, for example, to skirt local foreign exchange rules in order to pay creditors on time during periods in which the local central bank had prohibited the repayment of foreign currency obligations.

As U.S. institutional investors become increasingly bigger players in the Latin American markets, their greater willingness to evaluate credit risk and structured transactions will probably bring yields on corporate credits more in line with sovereign yields, and we should see, along with a further narrowing of spreads on sovereign paper, an additional narrowing of spreads between sovereign and corporate paper.

CONCLUSION

The mood among investors is, as it should be, cautious. In spite of all the recent publicity, investors are not yet charging back into Latin America in a big enough way to resolve long-term repayment risk on all the external debt. Even though the huge price increases recently shown by the Latin American debt and equity markets have been attributed largely to the inflow of foreign capital, it should be noted that the growth in foreign investment has been rapid only in relation to its very low base. Now that Chile has finally received an investment grade rating from S&P, there are very strong expectations that Mexico will soon get investment grade ratings from one of the two major agencies and, should that happen, the capital inflows into these two countries should become much larger.

We expect that the two trends causing the price increase—the reduced pressure among creditor banks to sell, and the increased buying by true investors—will continue through the next few years, particularly the latter trend, although we would expect that at some point investors will discriminate more carefully among types of assets. The current yields on the Mexican and Venezuelan "Brady" bonds as well as on the new issue capital markets instruments continue to be extremely high and very attractive relative to the risk. Venezuela in particular, because of the aborted coup attempts in February and November, and in spite of the strongest economic fundamentals in Latin America, is trading at excessively high yields. With the increased liquidity and the greater confidence in growth prospects for certain of the Latin American economies, investors will probably continue to buy into the market, and prices for the higher-quality assets should continue to rise in the near term until their yields approximate those for equivalent BBB or BBB+ instruments.

Table 17.1—Prices of Benchmark Debt for Major Latin American Countries—December 30, 1991

Country	*Bid*	*Offer*	*Coupon*	*Maturity*
Mexico	59 1/2	59 3/4	6 1/4	2019
Brazil	28 1/4	28 5/8	L + 13/16	NA
Venezuela	66 3/4	67	6 3/4	2020
Argentina	35 3/8	35 5/8	L + 13/16	NA
Chile	90 1/4	91 1/2	L + 13/16	2005

SECTION TWO:

HIGH YIELD MORTGAGE-BACKED SECURITIES

Chapter Eighteen

CMO Residuals*

by Adrian Katz
Vincent Pica
Rick Villaume
Prudential Securities

In 1992, the CMO/REMIC new issuance market experienced a record year with issuance at the $280 billion mark. This year, volume of new deals appears to be off to a record once again, running at an annualized rate of $300 billion. Each deal includes a residual.

These instruments can be extremely complex. Without appropriate analytical insights and support, particularly in hedging, this opportunity can result in unanticipated fluctuations in value and outright losses. The insights expressed herein are intended to add some of that necessary clarity and insight.

A thorough comprehension of the cash-flow dynamics allows the investor to either utilize a residual for the purpose of hedging or to build a stable portfolio of securities. Whatever this application, there is no doubt that a complete understanding of residuals is a definite advantage to the investor.

Thus, we intend to address the following issues—where do residuals come from? what types of residuals are available? and what impacts their value? In addition, we will discuss hedging considerations, risk-based capital requirements, accounting issues and phantom-income and phantom-loss implications.

WHAT IS A RESIDUAL?

The word "residual" aptly describes the investment as it is comprised of the remaining cash flows from the underlying mortgages after all other cash flows are securitized into either a bond or a pass-through security. In essence, a residual's cash flow is comprised of the difference between the cash flows of the collateralizing assets and the collateralized obligations. For certain residuals, reinvestment income and servicing fees are also components of the cash flows. Residuals can take the form of scheduled principal and interest-bearing securities or of cash flows with neither a defined coupon nor any principal. The amount of cash flow can vary tremendously from very small to even being the largest component of a deal. The legal characteristics of the offering can be as simple as a government agency security with a REMIC (Real Estate Mortgage Investment Conduit) tax election or as complex as an Owner Trust equity private placement. Residual cash-flow features can span the entire performance spectrum; they can be either bullish or bearish in nature or can act as either a long or short straddle. The multitude of available performance characteristics is a function of client-requested design, economic realities, i.e., the shape of the yield curve, and changes in the tax, accounting, and regulatory environment.

History of the Residual Market

The first CMO was issued in 1983 by FHLMC as a debt obligation collateralized by a designated pool of FHLMC mortgage pass-through certificates. The collateral remained an asset on FHLMC's balance sheet while the fully cash-flow-supported bond obligations remained a liability. A necessary outgrowth of this structure was the equity component (otherwise known as the residual). The tax treatment of residuals as equity implied that, in a rather illiquid manner, the only method for investing in residuals was through the creation or purchase of an issuing vehicle. For tax benefits, many of the early issuers were builder conduits, with only a few precocious investors creating arbitrage subsidiaries. These conduits or subsidiaries required up-front capital investments for such expenses as legal, accounting, and SEC filing fees. Since residuals were integral components of the deals, the awkward and expensive legal treatment significantly impaired the early growth of CMO issuance and residual liquidity.

In 1985, Wall Street, in conjunction with legal counsel, created a "better mousetrap" with the introduction of the Owner Trust residual structure. This structure allowed for the sale of equity partnerships in a residual. The immediate effect was the proliferation of Wall Street subsidiaries establishing registration shelves with the SEC to become CMO issuers. The innovation permitted the investor in a residual to be decoupled from the bond-issuance business. Further, the residual could now be purchased in percentages deemed small enough to eliminate accounting concerns over on-balance-sheet recognition. Typically, the ownership percentage was understood to be less than 50%, in order to maintain the off-balance sheet treatment. The residual investor base was now expanded to include investors with no special knowledge of bond origination and investors who required the off-balance-sheet treatment.

Probably the most significant development in the cash-flow engineering of residuals occurred in 1986 with the introduction of the floating-rate bond class. Up until 1986, the residual cash flows were comprised of either fixed-coupon spread or principal (invariably in the form of over-collateralization). The residual's investment dynamics therefore were either bullish or bearish, with the dominant influence being the prepayment rate on the underlying mortgages securing the deal. The introduction of the floating-rate class and the natural leftover effect of inverse floating-rate cash flows allowed the residual characteristics to vary with more subtlety. It was now possible to design a residual with characteristics previously external to the mortgage product securing the deal, such as the inclusion of LIBOR as an index for some of a deal's coupons. Furthermore, the effects of prepayments (usually influenced by long rates) now could be combined with the effects of coupon adjustments (usually influenced by short rates).

The enactment of the REMIC tax law in 1986 significantly improved the previously clumsy legal structures by removing many of the potential economic disadvantages associated with prior regulations. Essentially, REMIC allowed for the creation of fast pay/slow pay, multiclass pass-throughs whose mortgage cash flows would be passed through to investors with no equity retained by the issuer. Thus, in most cases, the transaction would be accounted for by the issuer as a sale of assets for tax purposes and taxed at the investor level. For financial accounting purposes, the issuer can treat the transaction as either a sale of assets or as a financing. In sum, REMICs reduce inefficiencies, increase flexibility and enable more issuers to enjoy the economic benefits of off-balance-sheet, multi-class mortgage financing.

Under REMIC, residuals can be structured so that they are sold as rated, SEC-registered bonds with no restrictions on transferability, financial statement consolidation concerns, or contingent liability for expenses. There would be numerous enhancements to and simplifications of the REMIC laws through subsequent Technical Corrections Bills providing further flexibility to issuers and investors. The more flexible and efficient treatment of residuals under REMIC helped to significantly increase the investor base—and in turn helped to create a more liquid and more active residual market. The tax implications associated with residuals are discussed later in this chapter.

In 1986, another significant cash-flow-engineering development occurred with the introduction of PAC (Planned Amortization Class) bonds. This method of cash-flow separation allowed for classes to be designed with more or less prepayment stability, and this flexibility implied the ability to design long-straddle or short-straddle investments. Not only could residuals now be influenced by long and short interest rates, but also could react with substantial variation with respect to anticipated changes in interest-rate volatility.

The inversion of the Treasury yield curve in 1988 and the economic reality that accompanied it provided the stimuli for more stable performing residuals. As floating-rate classes became too expensive to include in deals, residuals were less able to offer inverse-floater characteristics. Even bearish, fixed-coupon spread was not easily created as a flat yield curve suggested that all classes of deals include the same coupon, which was typically the same as the underlying collateral coupon. By 1989, this trend had in fact stimulated the formation of residuals with insignificant cash-flow value, sometimes called *de minimus* residuals.

Residual Investment Characteristics

By now we have indicated that a kaleidoscope of residuals exist. Here, the various types of residuals currently available are categorized and explained. Specific hedging techniques as they apply to different residual types are explained later in this chapter.

Bear residuals. The first residuals were comprised primarily of coupon spread, i.e., the differential between the higher coupon on the underlying mortgage collateral and the lower coupon on the outstanding obligation. For example, if mortgages with a net coupon of 10% secured a single-class obligation with a coupon of 9%, the cash-flow difference available to be passed through to the residual would be 1%. Since the balance on which the amount of interest due varies with prepayments, some discussion of prepayments is appropriate.[1]

Homeowners are less inclined to prepay their mortgages if the prevailing interest-rate environment is higher than the rate on their obligation. Conversely, in a lower-rate environment, a homeowner is more likely to prepay a mortgage in order to refinance at a lower cost. This suggests that in a higher-rate environment the effect of slower prepayments would cause more cash to be paid to the residual holder since the coupon is based on a higher outstanding principal balance. Conversely, when rates are falling, the probability is that the outstanding principal balance will decline more rapidly due to an increase in prepayments, hence generating less coupon payments and inherently less cash flow to the residual investor.

Investments that perform well in rising-rate environments are considered to be bearish. The degree of bearishness is determined by the coupon on the underlying collateral relative to current market rates and the structure. The most bearish investments typically are those with anticipated short durations. Short-duration investments have the potential to extend the most, ultimately creating higher returns as more cash flow is returned to the investor over a longer period of time. Coupon cash flows from Companion classes, volatile bonds themselves, tend to increase the bearish behavior of a residual. Conversely, coupon cash flows from PAC classes naturally tend to stabilize the performance. In addition, residuals from higher-coupon underlying cash flows tend to be more volatile as a function of more volatile prepayment behavior. This in turn causes the bearish residuals from such collateral to be even more accentuated. Bearish residuals can act as excellent hedging tools for a fixed-income portfolio or for a balance sheet whose combined assets have a longer duration than its liabilities (see Figure 18.1).

Bull residuals. Since interest spread is what leads to the creation of bearish residuals, it is not surprising that a residual comprised only of principal cash flows is considered to be bullish. As the principal of a mortgage is returned in full (at par), the issue most affecting a bullish residual comprised only of principal is the timing of the return of the

---

1 *See* Lakhbir Hayre, Kenneth Lauterbach, and Cyrus Mohebbi, "Mortgage Pass-Through Securities," in Frank J. Fabozzi (ed.) *Advances and Innovations in the Bond and Mortgage Markets* (Chicago, IL: Probus Publishing, 1989), and Lakhbir and Cyrus Mohebbi, *Prepayment Behavior of 15-Year Pass-Through Securities,* (New York, N.Y.: Financial Strategies Group, Prudential Securities Incorporated, May 1989).

Figure 18.1—Typical Bearish Residual Return Profile

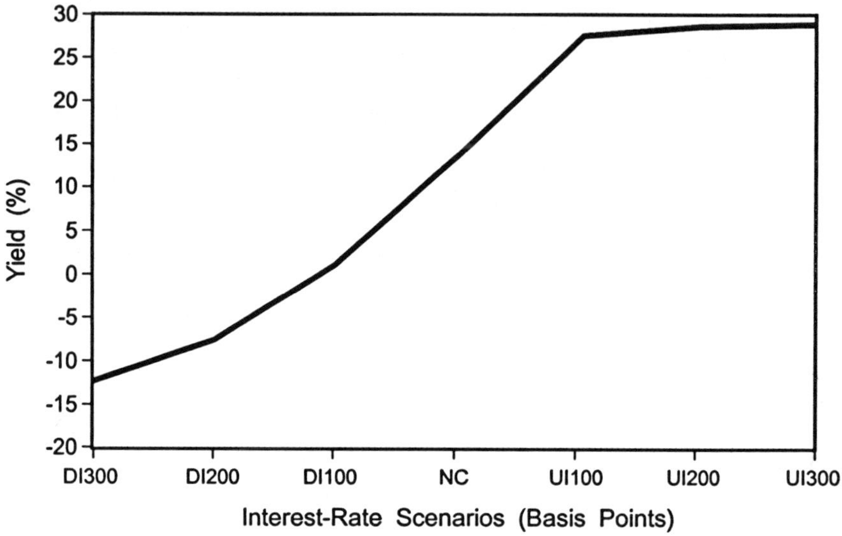

principal. Therefore, higher prepayment rates, which are experienced in declining interest-rate environments, positively influence the performance of bullish residuals. Conversely, an increase in rates causes underperformance (see Figure 18.2). Residual "principal" can be created by overcollateralization (more mortgages than bonds) or by passing excess cash flows forward to pay down bond principal (i.e., acceleration) and creating overcollateralization over time. This "principal" is typically returned once the bonds have matured.

Bullish investments can be more or less leveraged based on the structure from which they are carved and the coupon on the underlying collateral. Generally speaking, longer-duration principal cash flows are more volatile as they are purchased at a greater discount price to par and thus have the greatest upside potential when they are returned at par sooner than anticipated. Further, principal cash flows that are derived from Companion bonds within structures containing PAC bonds tend to be more bullish. This effect can be attributed to the added volatility implicit in these structures, which increases the possibility of tremendous upswings in value in the event of increased prepayments. By contrast, PAC principal cash flows stabilize the residual

Figure 18.2—Typical Bullish Residual Return Profile

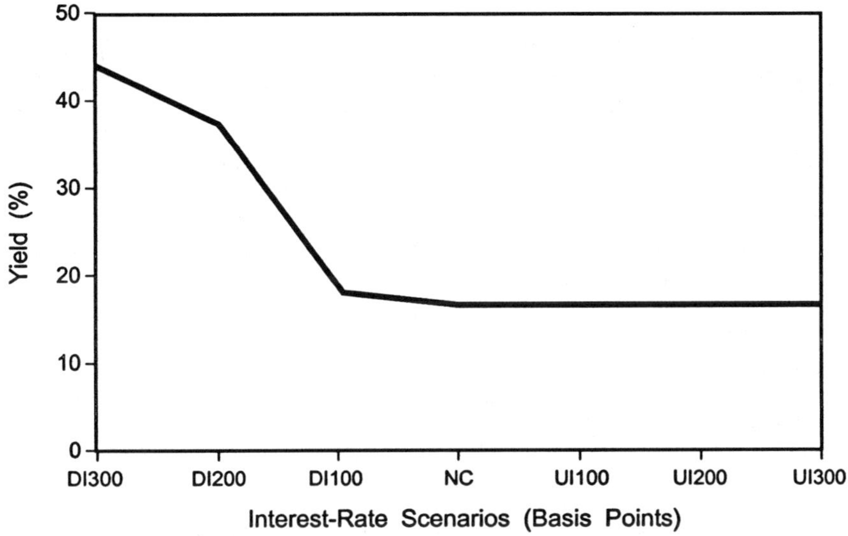

fluctuations. The uses of bullish residuals in fixed-income portfolio management range from lengthening the effective duration of a portfolio that is inadequately positioned for a rally to providing a hedge to a mortgage servicer.[2]

Humped residuals (a.k.a. Short straddles). Residuals derived from structures that contain floating-rate classes may vary significantly due to such factors as the coupon on the underlying collateral, the size of the floating-rate component as a percentage of the deal, the position of the floater in the deal, the floating-rate index and the absolute level of the floating-rate cap relative to the current coupon. In most cases, there is a common cash-flow characteristic, which is evident when sce-

[2] For details on hedging mortgage servicing, see Adrian Katz, Vincent Pica, and Michael Sternberg, *Strategies for Mortgage Bankers in a Bullish Environment,* Financial Strategies Group, Prudential Securities Incorporated, May 29, 1989 and Adrian Katz, Vincent Pica, and Michael Sternberg, *Strategies for Traders and Investors in a Bullish Environment,* Financial Strategies Group, Prudential Securities Incorporated, June 14, 1989.

nario analysis reveals that the residual tends to underperform when interest rates vary from the initial environment. This behavior is a function of the combined effect of changes in prepayments and the coupon adjustments.

In a rising interest-rate environment, the amount of interest-rate spread declines while, at the same time, prepayments decline. Therefore, the remaining spread is outstanding for a longer period of time. These influences may be offsetting. As rates rise sufficiently for the floating-rate class(es) to approach its (their) coupon cap, the residual cash flow typically is curtailed and hence the residual's performance is undermined. When interest rates decline, the coupon spread increases and prepayments accelerate; thus the amount of time during which the spread is outstanding is abbreviated. If rates decline sufficiently for prepayments to be almost instantaneous, the residual cash flow becomes insignificant and the residual will underperform. These so-called "humped" residuals (so named because of their return profiles in declining and rising rate scenarios, see Figure 18.3) are therefore not well suited for an investor anticipating a volatile environment. In contrast, investors who foresee a market stall will be well rewarded by the higher base-case yields associated with humped residuals.

Figure 18.3—Typical Humped Residual Return Profile

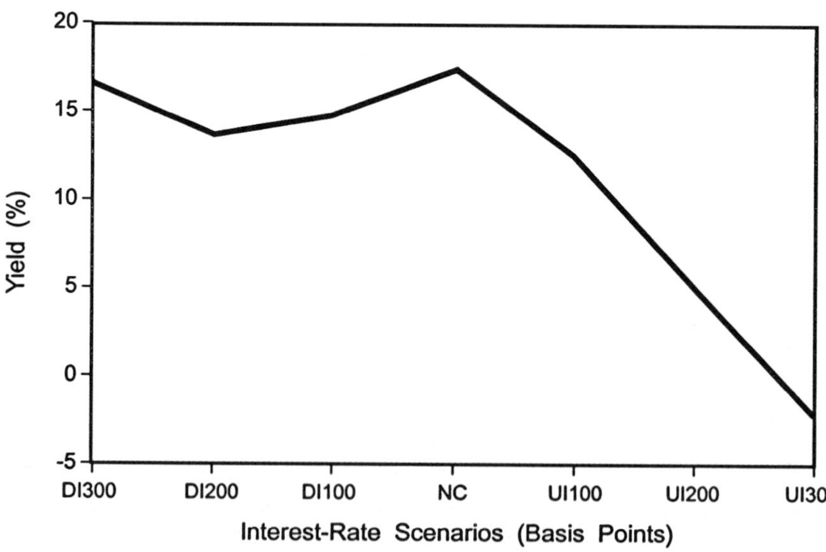

A further subtlety relating to the shape of the yield curve should be noted here. Yield-curve movements seldom occur in parallel and the implications of a steepening or inverting yield curve to these humped residuals are critical. First, keep in mind that floating-rate coupons are indexed off a short interest rate and that prepayments typically are triggered by changes in long interest rates. In an environment in which long rates are increasing and short rates are declining, humped residuals experience an increase in available coupon spread and a longer time period over which the spread is received. Hence, the steepening is doubly beneficial.

However, the opposite holds true when the yield curve is inverted and, in fact, the effect is doubly disadvantageous. Any serious attempt to hedge this type of short-straddle residual should not only address the question of volatility but also the potential fluctuations in the shape of the yield curve. Due to these implied vulnerabilities and the range of cash-flow fluctuations, these residuals are the most volatile generically. (The coupling of very high base-case yields and sharp declines in value outside the base case should come as no surprise to the reader.) The majority of residuals being offered by the thrift industry through liquidations fall into the humped residual category.

Smile bonds (a.k.a. Long straddles). Mortgage securities, by their nature, are "buy/writes" consisting of a long-bond component (scheduled payments by the homeowner) and a short-call component (the prepayment option held by the homeowner). Therefore, with mortgage securities as the collateral for CMO structures with multiple classes and a residual, it is fairly difficult to design a long-straddle residual and very few exist. Residuals with superior performance in highly volatile environments invariably consist of short-duration interest spread and long-duration principal. The compromise for the Smile bond residual investor is that the anticipated yield for the base-case scenario (no interest-rate change) tends to be below Treasuries.[3] See Figure 18.4 for a typical Smile-bond return profile.

Stable residuals. There is no rule that requires residuals to be complex or volatile. Indeed, when a residual is comprised of PAC cash flows, the residual is more stable than the underlying collateral and actually could be designated the most stable class in the entire deal

[3] For details on smile bonds, see Howard Chin, Alan Galishoff, and Vincent Pica, *Structured Portfolio Trades: Unruliness Begets Opportunity*, Financial Strategies Group, Prudential Securities Incorporated, October 25, 1989.

Figure 18.4—Typical Smile Bond Return Profile

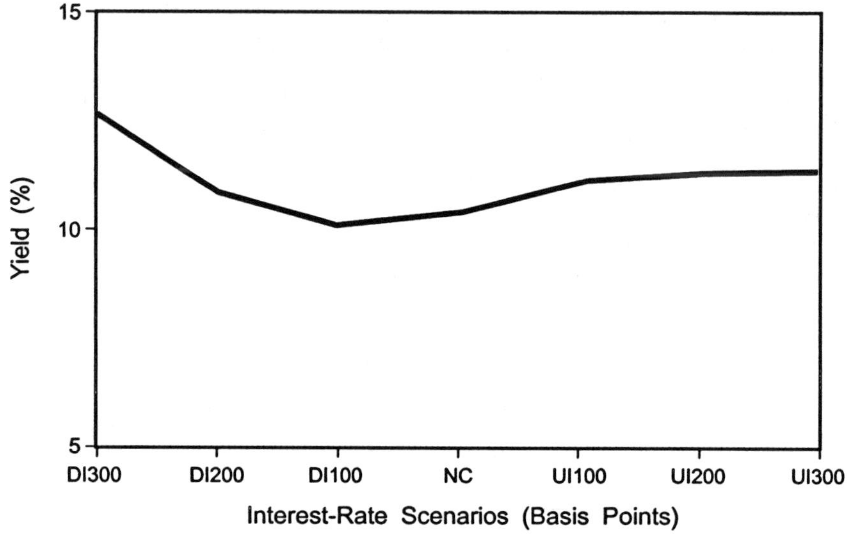

Figure 18.5—Typical Stable Residual Return Profile

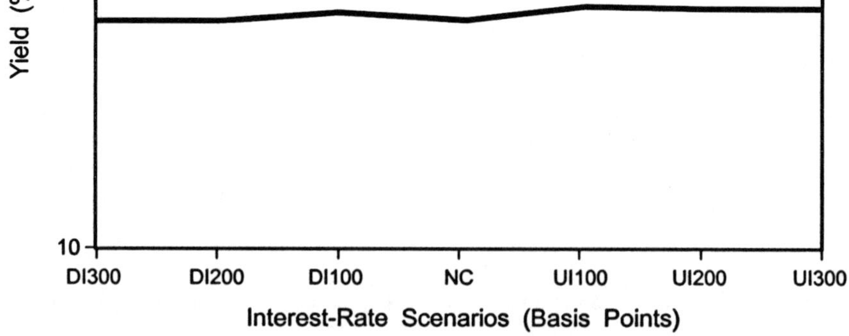

(see Figure 18.5). In many structures, the residual is a class carved from a regular PAC component and may even pay in parallel with such a PAC. Not surprisingly, stable residual investments of this type offer purchasing opportunities to a very broad spectrum of investors.

De Minimus residuals. As shown later in this paper, the residual class of a REMIC bears the tax liability of the entire REMIC. Non-economic, or *de minimus* residuals, receive little or no cash flow. Given minimal (or no) economic value, these instruments then become a tax strategy unto themselves. An investor can use these instruments to create or modify an existing tax strategy.

This type of residual is typically sold with a zero or "negative" price, i.e., the investor receives cash at settlement. The investor then reinvests this money in securities that, on an after-tax basis, are expected to generate enough cash to pay the tax liabilities of the REMIC (recalling that all taxable income from a *de minimus* residual is non-shelterable). After the "income period" of the REMIC, the investor can then use the losses created by the REMIC to offset other sources of income. In short, the investor is "buying" these tax losses in the future.

THOUGHTS ON HEDGING RESIDUALS

As could be inferred from our above comments, residuals can be divided into two basic groups—those that allow the investor to take a position on the direction of future interest rates and those that allow the investor to take a position on interest-rate volatility. Bearish and bullish residuals essentially take a position on the direction of rates. Humped (short-straddle) residuals appeal to investors who expect interest rates to remain generally the same, i.e., low volatility. Long straddles and stable residuals typically appeal to investors who expect at least some degree of interest-rate volatility. Hedging against adverse interest-rate moves is fairly straightforward—take the opposite position for the amount of expected risk (i.e., the chance of rates reversing). Hedging residuals based on a volatility position is more complex.[4]

---

[4] The analyses for all securities/hedges discussed in this section were generated using the Prudential Securities Structured Portfolio/Synthetic Security (SP/SS) System. All results are stated on a pre-tax basis. SP/SS total returns are the "all-in" percent return on an investment assuming complete reinvestment of all interim cash flows at the assumed reinvestment rate. In all cases the analysis was done based on immediate parallel shifts of the yield curve by the appropriate amount.

Bearish Residuals

As mentioned in the previous section, bearish residuals tend to perform better in rising-rate environments. The obvious hedge for this type of residual is a bullish security with similar underlying prepayment characteristics. For those wishing to add to their residual portfolio, bullish residuals of similar collateral are an obvious hedge. For the investor concerned about using additional residuals to hedge a current position, leveraged PO classes provide good protection. With the large variety of PAC structures being created, there are numerous opportunities to obtain Companion or Targeted-Amortization Class (TAC) POs that are custom designed to provide the necessary cash-flow "kick" in declining interest-rate environments without the tax implications of some bullish residuals. The investor who purchases a bearish residual as an investment rather than as a hedging instrument has implicitly taken a position on the direction of future rates. Duration-matched hedges in this scenario do not make economic sense. Instead, the investor should use expectation-weighted matching; for example, if the investor believes that there is a 20% change of rates reversing and the total exposure is $10 million, then approximately $2 million in bullish securities should be added to the portfolio (all other things, such as leverage and yield sensitivity, being equal). See Figure 18.6 for a return profile of this hedge.

Bullish Residuals

Since bullish residuals tend to perform better in declining-rate environments, the obvious hedge is a bearish security using similar underlying collateral. A typical nonresidual hedge for this type of residual is a TAC IO, generally purchased at a very low yield, that has some call protection but little, if any, extension protection. The lengthening of the TAC IO's duration in rising-rate environments provides for a yield pick up, making the TAC IO a good hedge for bullish residuals. See Figure 18.7 for a return profile of this hedge. The purchase of a bullish residual for investment purposes indicates that the investor has an opinion on the direction of future interest rates. Again, investors must consider the probability of interest rates reversing direction before any hedging program is established.

Humped Residuals (Short Straddles)

Humped residuals are volatility plays—the investor believes that there will be little or no interest-rate change and no prepayment change

Figure 18.6—Performance Characteristics of a Bearish Residual and a Super PO Hedge

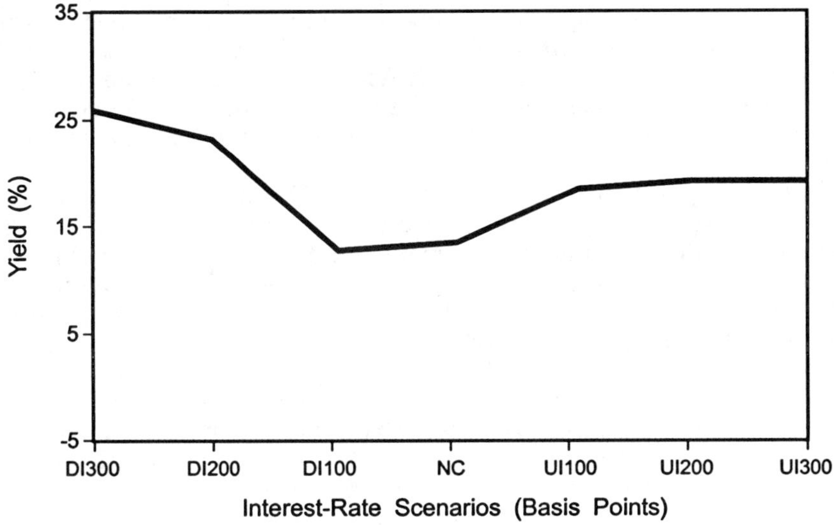

Figure 18.7—Performance Characteristics of a Bullish Residual and an IO Hedge

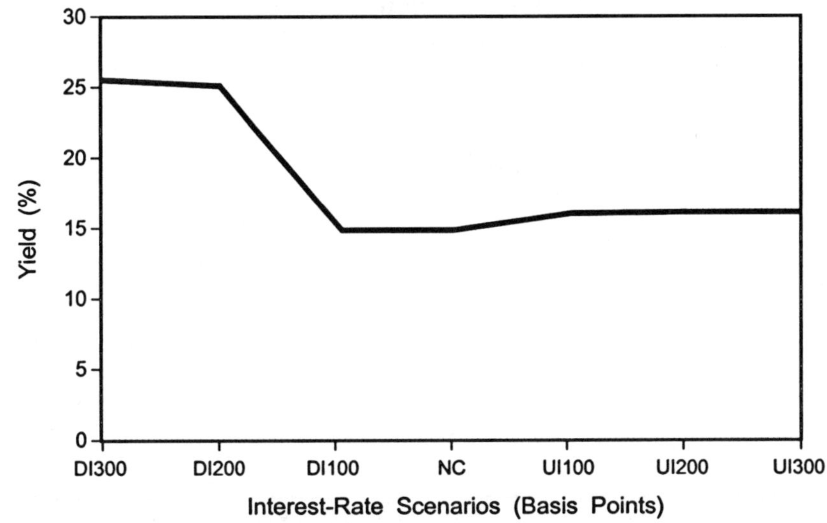

from current levels. These residuals are effectively short positions on both short-term and long-term rates. Decreases in short-term rates (and the floating-rate coupons based on these rates) typically are offset by increases in prepayments (assuming parallel shifts in the yield curve). Decreases in prepayment speeds are usually offset by increases in short-term rates (again, using parallel shifts for example purposes). When factors such as nonparallel shifts and inversions in the yield curve are added to the equation, you have an instrument that is a challenge to hedge.

At any point in time, the holder of a humped residual is at the no-interest-rate-change point in Figure 18.8. The curve may slope differently in different rate environments (and may even turn bullish or bearish), but generally has the characteristic hump shape. While the investor may believe that interest rates will remain close to where they are now (i.e., low/no volatility), he probably has an opinion as to the most likely direction of future rates.

If short-term rates rise and the corresponding decrease in coupon spread causes a less negative effect than changes in prepayments (in parallel shifts, one would expect a benefit), then there is little benefit in hedging against prepayment risk since the additional cost of hedg-

Figure 18.8—Performance Characteristics of a Humped Residual

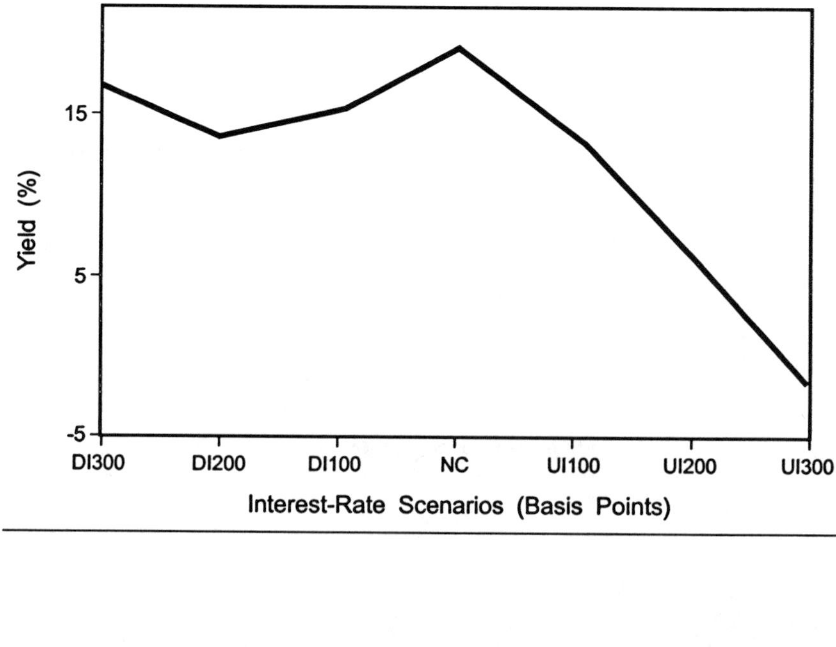

ing would result in little or no gain. Conversely, if the holder expects long-term rates to decrease (prepayments to increase) and the residual is more sensitive to increases in prepayments than decreases in short-term rates, then there is little benefit in hedging short-term-rate risk. In brief, the investor must consider the following three questions:

- Which rate, long or short, is expected to move the most (or cause the most harm)?
- In which direction is the rate expected to move?
- How long is this rate change expected to affect the residual?

When these questions are answered, a hedging program that fits the investor's expectations can be established.

Working Through an Example

To answer the questions above, assume that short rates will rise, while long rates will remain more or less stable. In addition, assume that the change will last for two months (similar to year-end changes in LIBOR). The dollar amount of the floating-rate classes in the underlying CMO is the amount of short-term-rate exposure that must be hedged, e.g., a $300 million CMO with $150 million in floating-rate class(es) has $150 million in short-term-rate exposure. To hedge the entire amount of exposure, $150 million in LIBOR caps must be purchased, with an expiration date approximating the expected time period to be hedged. As the floating-rate classes prepay, the hedge needs to be rolled off on a 1:1 basis, e.g., if, in month one, $5 million in the floating-rate class pays off, then $5 million of the hedge needs to be rolled off. Ideally, the gain (loss) on the hedge should approximate the loss (gain) in cash flows on the residual. See Figure 18.9 for a return profile of this 1:1 hedge.

This strategy of matching hedging to expected changes in interest rates requires constant monitoring of the residual and hedge instruments. A month-by-month adjustment in hedge positions must be undertaken, as well as a constant review of short-term and long-term interest-rate expectations.

This example illustrates the hedging of short-term expected cash flows. For longer-term hedging, the investor should use something closer to duration matching. Smile bonds or stable residuals with durations similar to that of the humped residual can be used.

Figure 18.9—Performance Characteristics of a Humped Residual with a One-Year LIBOR Cap Hedge

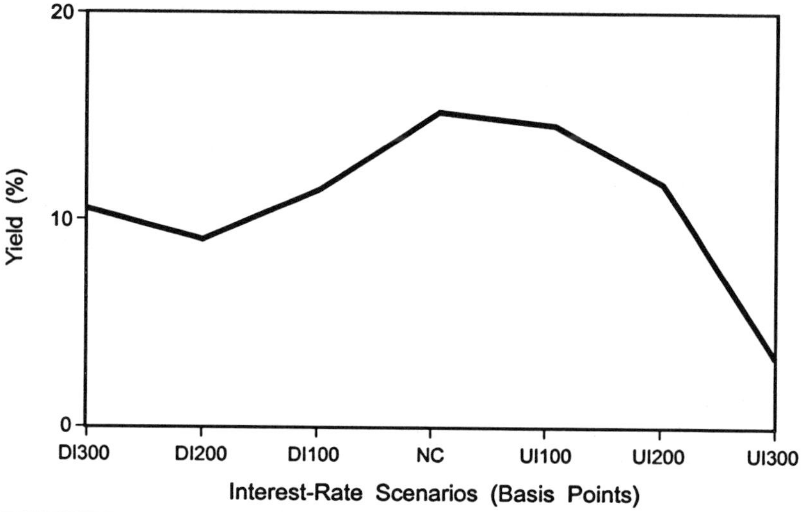

Stable Residuals and Smile Bonds (Long Straddles)

Stable residuals and Smile bonds are also volatility plays—they presume that there will be high levels of interest-rate volatility but that its direction will not be easy to discern. These residuals, by their nature, tend to sell at lower yields than other types. Since stable/long-straddle residuals have flat (stable) to smile-shaped (long-straddle) return profiles, hedging them against interest-rate movement is not beneficial; they are a hedge themselves. The primary use of these residuals is to pick up yield outside the base case, which makes them a good match for humped residuals. For both bearish and bullish residuals, stable residuals and Smile bonds provide some protection by lessening declines in adverse-rate environments.

RISK-BASED CAPITAL CONSIDERATIONS

Banks

Residuals fall within the 100% risk-weight basket for banks under their risk-based capital standards. In meeting its risk-based capital requirements, a bank must hold capital equal to 8% times 100% of the residual value. Relative to other securities, this is five times the amount required for an equivalent amount of FNMA and FHLMC pass-throughs (20% risk weight) and the same as for an equivalent amount of IO/PO strips (100% risk weight).

Thrifts

Residuals fall within the 100% risk-weight basket for thrifts under their risk-based capital standards. Thrifts must hold 8%[5] of 100% of the residual value in capital. The Office of Thrift Supervision has indicated that residuals may be moved to a lower risk-weight category when an interest-rate-risk component of capital is introduced. Thus, the interest-rate-risk calculation will be used to determine the capital required based on the interest-rate-related volatility separately from capital required for credit risk. Residuals that reduce the overall volatility of a thrift's market value of portfolio equity (the present value of all asset cash flows less the present value of all liability cash flows plus the present value of all off-balance-sheet cash inflows less outflows) could potentially lower the capital required for interest-rate risk. If the reduction of capital for interest-rate risk exceeded the marginal capital required for residual credit risk, the overall risk-based capital required could be reduced.

Both banks and thrifts can benefit by maximizing the return on capital generated by the assets they hold. In purchasing assets, they should consider the spread-to-funding generated given the capital allocation. This will continue to be a consideration, particularly for capital-constrained institutions in light of their other existing investment criteria.

GAAP AND TAX ACCOUNTING FOR RESIDUALS

GAAP income for REMIC residuals may be calculated according to the Statement of Financial Accounting Standards No. 91 (SFAS 91) method.

The Emerging Issues Task Force (EITF) of the Financial Accounting Standards Board (FASB) discussed a method of accounting for non-equity CMO investments on December 14, 1989. It was determined during these discussions that CMOs that were carried as long-term

[5] This requirement was phased in. The actual requirement was 6.4% until 12/30/90; 7.2% from 12/31/90 until 12/31/92 and 8% after 12/31/92.

investments would be considered to be nonequity if the investor had little or no control of the cash distribution from the CMO structure. Securitized residuals (i.e., bond form) are considered to fall into this category.

SFAS 91 details the appropriate method for income recognition. Specifically, SFAS 91 states that income should be calculated by applying the "interest method" using a yield that is recalculated for every period in which the remaining projected cash distributions will differ from those previously projected. This will occur whenever the prepayment assumptions for future cash flows are changed or the current distribution differs from that last projected. The original yield is calculated by using the purchase price and the residual cash flow at the pricing speed. When a distribution occurs that is other than that projected, a new yield is calculated by using the actual distributions to date, the new projected distributions and the original purchase price. The yield is then used to compute a new carrying value of the residual by discounting the new set of future cash flows at this rate to the current accounting date. When the carrying value of the residual is changed, a corresponding adjustment should be made to income for that period. If this new yield is less than zero, the investment is subject to an *impairment test.*

If the residual is an equity interest in an Owner Trust, the appropriate accounting method is determined by the percentage owned. Ownership of greater than 50% of the residual may require full consolidation of assets and liabilities with adjustments made for minority residual interests. Investors with ownership of less than 50% but greater than 20% may be able to use the equity method, or SFAS 91. With the equity method, an investor reports the pro-rata share of GAAP earnings, reported by the issuer, corresponding to the percentage owned. Investors with ownership of less than 20% in an Owner Trust may not use the equity method. The EITF is considering a proposal that would recommend the use of the SFAS 91 method for all residuals that are considered to be nonequity CMO investments. This would include all securitized residuals and equity interests of less than 50% in Owner Trusts.

Taxable income on residuals is computed under a different method than SFAS 91. Taxable income is computed by taking the excess collateral and reinvestment income over the REMIC regular interest deductions, expenses and ongoing fees. If the regular-interest expense relative to the outstanding bond principal amount increases over time, there will be less relative expense at the beginning with greater relative expense toward the end. This increase will occur if shorter-maturity regular interests have lower yields than longer-maturity ones. This is typically the case in a normal yield-curve environment. This results in phantom income followed by phantom losses. The excess taxable income over economic income is referred to as phantom income. The sum of all phantom income and phantom losses will equal zero and the total taxable income will be equal to the total GAAP income over the life of the residual.

Phantom Income and Phantom Losses of Residuals

What is phantom income? Simply stated, phantom income is created when taxable income exceeds economic income (GAAP income). How is this phantom income created? From the standpoint of the Trust that owns the collateral supporting a REMIC transaction, the collateral is an asset and the payments received are income. Conversely, the bonds outstanding are liabilities and the payments due to the bond holders are expenses. In a positive yield-curve environment, phantom income is created when these deductible weighted-average expenses are deferred through the tranching of the collateral into bonds with different yields and maturities. The creation of phantom income is increased if the collateral going into the Trust is "bought-in" below par. The IRS treats this market discount as if it were an Original-Issue Discount and thus it must be accreted into income. In addition, certain types of bonds, such as Z-bonds, also increase phantom income due to the accrual feature. Usually, however, the majority of phantom income/loss is created through timing and yield mismatches between the assets and the liabilities of the Trust. In the later years, when earlier tranches have been retired, the relationship between the assets and the liabilities flip-flops such that phantom losses are created when economic income exceeds taxable income. (For many investors, phantom losses are desirable since they shelter cash flow that otherwise would be taxed.) These phantom amounts always net out to zero at maturity, or in other words, taxes are due only on the *true* economic income of the residual over the entire life of the residual.

Of additional interest and of perhaps dominating import given the volatility that is extant in the fixed-income marketplace, the actual accounting for phantom income and phantom losses is dominated by *prepayments*. Specifically, if the entire deal pays down because of prepayments accelerating through the pricing speed (thus retiring early tranches very quickly and long tranches commensurately early), the amount of phantom income/phantom losses will be dramatically lower than projected at pricing. This is due to the foreshortening of the timing disparities between the assets (the collateral) and the liabilities (the bonds). In the case of a powerful rally after pricing, the difference between the *projected* phantom income and the *actual* phantom income can be dramatically in favor of the residual holder. In contrast, if there is a dramatic market decline, this will cause the timing disparities between the assets and the liabilities to be outstanding longer. This results in actual phantom income exceeding the pricing projections. It is a function of the nature of mortgages, however, that this is not a symmetrical relationship. Mortgage collateral that is going into a REMIC deal generally has a weighted-average maturity that is not *dramatically* shorter than its original maturity. Thus, it cannot get that much longer. This is why not as much additional phantom income is created in a market decline as is destroyed in a rally. In short, a mortgage can get prepaid tomorrow but there isn't any chance that homeowners will pay one more month than they are required to!

Excess Inclusions/Unrelated Business Taxable Income

While not by any means an exhaustive discussion of the causes of phantom income, the above text does present an accurate picture of the major components of phantom income. Of more interest to sophisticated investors would be the economic effect of phantom income on the yield of a residual held in portfolio. The economic effect is the reduction of the effective after-tax yield during the early years of the CMO; caused by the present value of the taxes being paid on phantom income exceeding the present value of the tax savings due to phantom losses.

With very limited but important exceptions, all residual income, including phantom income, is always subject to tax because such income is treated as an excess-inclusion item. The "excess-inclusion amount" is the amount of interest income generated by the residual that is greater than 120% of the *Federal Long-Term Rate.*[6] If the residual is held by a tax-exempt entity such as a pension plan or any entity that is only taxed on its Unrelated Business Taxable Income (UBTI), phantom income will be treated as UBTI.

As far as exceptions go, there are few and what follows is a general, not detailed, description of them.

---

[6] By statute, the Federal Long-Term Rate is defined as the average of the current yields on U.S. Treasury obligations that have a remaining term to maturity of greater than nine years. The IRS computes this figure and publishes it monthly.

- **First,** if a residual does not have significant value, all income from a residual is treated as excess inclusion. Significant value generally is regarded as being at least 2% of the value of the REMIC. Thus, ultra-small residuals are always part of the excess-inclusion base.
- **Second,** thrift institutions are exempt from the rule that prohibits excess inclusions from being offset by unrelated losses. In addition, qualified subsidiaries[7] of the thrift can be consolidated for tax purposes with respect to offsetting losses of the thrift against excess inclusions realized by the qualified subsidiary.
- **Third,** Real Estate Investment Trusts (REITs) and Registered Investment Companies (RICs) can offset excess-inclusion income with a dividends-paid deduction. The excess-inclusion taxation issue is passed along to the shareholders.

SUMMARY

At this time, there exists an incredible variety of residuals; it is hoped the above abbreviated history of their issuance will help the investor understand the breadth of choices available and the inherent complexities. Of course, we anticipate that the future of the residual market is likely to be an improvement on the past with respect to flexibility, creativity, and liquidity.

[7] A qualified subsidiary is one whose stock and substantially all of its indebtedness is owned by the thrift. The qualified subsidiary also must be operated and organized for the express and exclusive purpose of operating one or more REMICs.

Chapter Nineteen

Stripped Mortgage-Backed Securities

by Lakhbir Hayre
Errol Mustafa
Vincent Pica
Prudential Securities

INTRODUCTION

As the mortgage pass-through market has matured, a number of derivative mortgage products have been introduced to appeal to different investors of the fixed-income market. In 1983, FHLMC launched the collateralized Mortgage Obligation (CMO) structure that enabled issuers to tailor-make mortgage securities according to investor coupon, maturity, and prepayment-risk specifications.[1] In July 1986, FNMA introduced a new addition to the mortgage security product line—Stripped Mortgage-Backed Securities (SMBSs). By redistributing portions of the interest and/or principal cash flows from a pool of mortgage loans to two or more SMBSs, FNMA developed a new class of mortgage

[1] For more information regarding CMOs, please see *CMO Primer*, Lakhbir Hayre and Lisa A. Pendergast, Financial Strategies Group, Prudential Securities, July 1987 and *Floating-Rate CMOs*, Lakhbir Hayre, Financial Strategies Group, Prudential Securities, September 1987.

securities that enabled investors to take strong market positions on expected movements in prepayment and interest rates.

SMBSs are highly sensitive to changes in prevailing interest and prepayment rates and tend to display asymmetric returns. SMBS certificates that are allocated large proportions or all of the underlying principal cash flows tend to display very attractive **bullish** return profiles. As market rates drop and prepayments on the underlying collateral increase, the return of these SMBSs will be greatly enhanced since principal cash flows will be returned earlier than expected. Conversely, SMBSs that are entitled to a large percentage or all of the interest cash flows have very appealing **bearish** return characteristics since greater amounts of interest cash flows are generated when prepayments of principal decrease (typically when market rates increase).

STRUCTURE OF THE PAPER

This chapter is divided into three sections:

- The first section provides an overview of the SMBS market and discusses the various types of SMBSs.
- The second section examines the investment characteristics of SMBSs. A review of the fundamentals of mortgage cash flows is first presented, followed by an investigation of the price, OAS, effective duration, and convexity characteristics of SMBSs.
- The third section describes various SMBS application and the use of SMBSs in portfolio hedging strategies.

OVERVIEW OF THE STRIPPED MORTGAGE-BACKED SECURITIES (SMBS) MARKET

Size of the SMBS Market

The SMBS market has grown substantially since the introduction of the first SMBS in July 1986 (see Figure 19.1). In total, an estimated $81.1 billion SMBSs in 306 issues have come to market as of March 1993. FNMA has been the predominant issuer of SMBSs. The remainder of new SMBSs have been issued by private concerns and FHLMC.

Figure 19.1—Issuance of SMBSs
July 1986 through March 1993

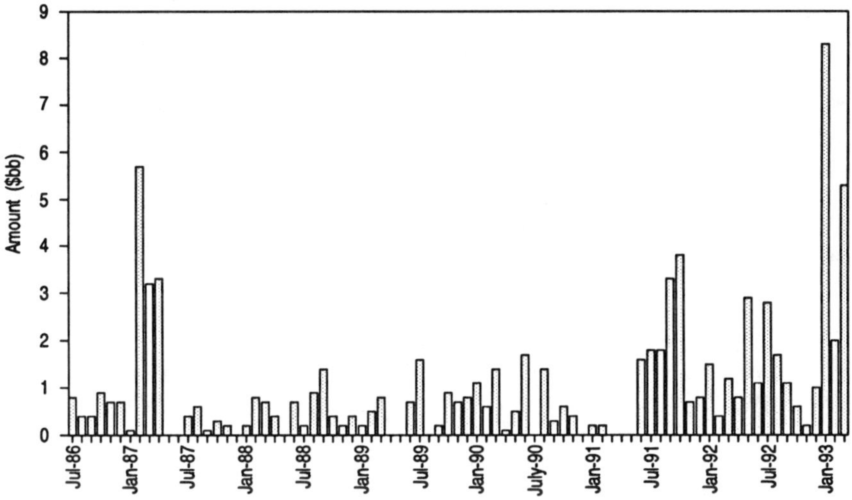

Note: Issuance figures includes FNMA, FHLMC and private issuance of IOs/POs and synthetic discount-coupon/premium-coupon securities.
Source: Prudential Securities, FSG Mortgage Security Data Base.

Types of SMBSs

Strip securities exist in various forms. The first and earliest type of mortgage strip securities are called **synthetic-coupon pass-through securities.** Synthetic-coupon pass-throughs receive fixed proportions of the principal *and* interest cash flow from a pool of underlying mortgage loans. Synthetic-coupon pass-throughs were introduced by FNMA in mid-1986 through its "Alphabet" Strip Program. **IOs and POs**, the second and most common type of strip security, were introduced by FNMA in January 1987. IOs and POs received, respectively, only the interest or only the principal cash flow from the underlying mortgage collateral. More recently, a third type of strip security, the **CMO strip**, has become popular among issuers and investors. As implied by their name, CMO strips are tranches within a CMO issue that receive only principal cash flows or have synthetically high coupon rates.

Development of the SMBS Market

The first mortgage strips—FNMA SMBS "alphabet" strip securities. FNMA pioneered the first stripped mortgage security in July 1986 through its newly created SMBS Program. For each issue of SMBS Series A through L, FNMA pooled existing FHA/VA and GPM mortgage loans that had been held in its portfolio and issued two SMBS pass-through certificates representing ownership interests in proportions of the interest and principal cash flows from the underlying mortgage loan pool. Alphabet strips were subsequently called synthetic discount- and premium-coupon securities since the coupon rate of the alphabet strip was quoted as a percentage of the total principal balance of the issue.[2] In total, 12 alphabet strip deals were issued by FNMA in 1986 totaling $2.9 billion.

The FNMA SMBS trust program and IOs and POs. The successive and current FNMA strip program, the SMBS Trust Program begun in 1987, provides a vehicle through which deal managers (e.g., investment banks) can swap FNMA pass-throughs for FNMA SMBS Trust certificates. In the swapping process, eligible FNMA pass-through securities submitted by the deal manager are consolidated by FNMA into one FNMA Megapool Trust. In return, FNMA distributes to the deal manager two similarly denominated SMBS certificates evidencing ownership in the requested proportions of that FNMA Megapool Trust's principal and interest cash flows.[3]

To date, the majority of FNMA SMBS Trusts have contained IO and PO securities. IOs and POs represent the most leveraged means of capturing the asymmetric performance characteristics of the two cash-flow components of mortgage securities. Recently, however, the SMBS market has witnessed a resurgence in synthetic-coupon security issuance (see FNMA Trust 66, 68, and 72). Although IOs and POs can be com-

---

2 For example, a strip that receives 75% interest and 50% principal of the cash flow from a FNMA 10% would be a synthetic 15% coupon security since the 7.50% coupon is expressed as 100% of principal (i.e., 7.50% coupon/50% principal = 15.00% coupon/100% principal). By the same logic, a strip security from a FNMA 10% that receives 50% interest and 1% principal would be a 5,000% coupon security.

3 FNMA tightly restricts the type of collateral that can be placed in Trust. For example, all mortgage securities must have the same prefix (be of the same loan type) and be within certain WAC and WAM ranges to correspond with preliminary pricing. Moreover, the minimum initial principal balance of each SMBS Trust must be $200 million.

bined in different ratios to create synthetic-coupon securities, some investors have shown a preference for one-certificate synthetic securities due to their bookkeeping ease.

To promote liquidity in the SMBS Market, all FNMA SMBS certificates (except FNMA SMBS Series L) have a unique conversion feature that enables like-denominations of both classes of a FNMA SMBS issue or Trust to be exchanged on the book-entry system of the Federal Reserve Banks for like-denominations of FNMA MBS certificates or Megapool certificates. The Federal Reserve generally charges an administration fee for this service. Any converted FNMA MBS certificate or Megapool certificate is subsequently **not** exchangeable for SMBS certificates. *Because of the potential for profitable arbitrages, the aggregate price of the two classes of any same FNMA issue or Trust tend to be slightly higher than the price of a comparable-coupon and remaining-term FNMA pass-through certificate.* Appendix A details those FNMA SMBS issues that have been recombined and the dollar amount of the SMBS issue (in original face) that has been exchanged for MBS certificates.

All FNMA SMBS pass-throughs (alphabets and Trusts) have the same payment structure, payment delays, and FNMA guarantee as regular FNMA pass-throughs. Payment histories and other relevant information can be obtained by referencing the pool number of the Megapool Trust. As of March 1993, 205 FNMA SMBS Trust deals have come to market, totaling approximately $54.6 billion.

Private issuance. Investment firms began to issue private-label SMBSs in late 1986. To date, it is estimated that 34 private-label SMBS issues totaling approximately $6.9 billion have been brought to market. Many of these private-label SMBSs were issued through REMIC structures. Since one class of a REMIC issue must be designated the residual interest, the super-premium coupon class of many of these private-label SMBSs is often the residual interest of the REMIC deal. Unlike investing in FNMA SMBSs, investors who purchase these residual securities are responsible for the tax consequences of the entire REMIC issue.

Recent Developments in the SMBS Market

A number of recent developments have occurred in the SMBS market that should further enhance its depth and efficiency. Among them are:

PO-collateralized CMOs. Profitable arbitrage opportunities have led to the recent introduction of CMO securities collateralized by POs. PO-collateralized CMOs allocate the cash flow from underlying PO securities between several CMO tranches with different maturities and payment patterns. *The potential for profitable arbitrages with PO securities has enhanced the efficiency of the SMBS market by effectively placing a floor on the price potential of POs and a price ceiling on corresponding IOs in a given market environment.* To date, 124 PO-collateralized CMOs totaling approximately $50.8 billion have been issued by FNMA and private issuers.

CMO strip securities. Strip securities are increasingly included in CMO issues as regular-interest (non-residual) CMO tranches. CMO strip securities that pay only principal or large proportions of interest cash flows (relative to principal cash flows) over the underlying mortgage collateral's life are termed PO securities and "high-interest" securities,[4] respectively, and tend to have performance characteristics similar to FNMA SMBSs. Other types of CMO strip securities receive initial and on-going collateral principal or interest cash flows after other classes in the CMO issue are retired or have been paid. These types of strip CMO securities are structured as PO or "high-interest" PACs, TACs, or Super-POs and perform differently from FNMA SMBSs.[5]

FHLMC stripped giant program. FHLMC has also become a participant in the SMBS market. In October 1989, FHLMC announced its Stripped Giant Mortgage Participation Certificate Program. As of March 1993, FHLMC had issued 34 FHLMC Giant PO and IO PCs totaling approximately $10.1 billion.

FHLMC's Stripped Giant Program is similar to FNMA's swap SMBS Trust Program. Deal managers submit FHLMC PCs to FHLMC; FHLMC, in turn, aggregates these PCs into Giant pools and issues Strip Giant PCs representing desired proportions of principal and interest to the deal manager. All FHLMC Strip PCs have the same payment structure, payment delays and payment guarantee as regular FHLMC PCs. Like FNMA SMBSs, FHLMC Giant Strip IOs and POs have a conversion feature that allows them to be exchanged for similarly denominated FHLMC PCs. Characteristics of each FHLMC Giant Strip issue can be

---

4 Since regular interests of a CMO issue currently must have a notional principal balance to qualify for REMIC tax status, true IO CMO securities do not exist. Typically, 99.5% of the initial value of a high-interest security is comprised of interest cash flows and .5% is comprise of principal.

5 For a description of CMO security types, please see *Guide to the CMO Marketplace,* Lisa Pendergast and Lakhbir Hayre, Financial Strategies Group, January 1993.

referenced by their pool number. 30-year and 15 year FHLMC IO securities are identified by the FHLMC prefix 90 and 92, respectively, while 30-year and 15-year PO or synthetic securities have 80 and 82 prefixes, respectively.

FHLMC Gold MACs Program

GNMA collateral for FNMA SMBSs. In 1990 FNMA began to issue SMBSs collateralized by GNMA pass-through certificates. Since the beginning of 1990, FNMA has issued 50 trusts that have had underlying GNMA collateral. The increased availability of GNMA SMBSs has further broadened the investor base of SMBSs, enhance the liquidity of the SMBS market and increase the number of hedging alternatives available to GNMA investors.

Buyers of SMBSs

The asymmetric returns of SMBSs appeal to a broad variety of investors. SMBSs can be used effectively to hedge interest-rate and prepayment exposure of other types of mortgage securities, such as CMO residuals and premium-coupon mortgage pass-through securities. SMBSs also can be combined with other fixed-income securities such as U.S. Treasuries and mortgage securities to enhance the total return of the portfolio in varying interest-rate scenarios. Insurance companies and pension funds with conservative duration-matching needs frequently use SMBSs as a method of tailoring their investment portfolio to meet the duration of liabilities and thus minimize interest-rate risk.

SMBSs are used by various types of investors to accomplish their investment objectives. Insurance companies, pension funds, money-managers and other total rate-of-return accounts use SMBSs to improve the return of their fixed-income portfolios. PO securities, which tend to have long durations, enable pension funds to more effectively manage the duration of their portfolios. Thrift institutions and mortgage bankers often use PO securities to hedge their servicing portfolios or use IO securities as a substitute for servicing income.[6]

---

[6] According to the applicable risk-based capital guidelines, strip securities that are backed by agency (FNMA, FHLMC and GNMA) pass-through securities (agency-issue or private-label issue) are in the 100% risk-based category for thrift institutions and commercial banks.

INVESTMENT CHARACTERISTICS

SMBSs enable investors to capture the performance characteristics of the principal or interest components of the cash flows of mortgage pass-through securities. These individual components display contrasting responses to changes in market rates and prepayment rates. Principal-only (PO) SMBSs are bullish instruments, outperforming mortgage pass-throughs in declining interest-rate environments. Interest-only (IO) SMBSs are bearish investments that can be used as a hedge against rising interest rates.

Variation of Interest and Principal Components with Prepayments

The cash flows that an MBS investor receives each month consist of principal and interest payments from a large group of home owners. The proportion of principal and interest in the total payment varies depending on the prepayment level of the mortgage pool. Figure 19.2 illustrates these cash flows for a $1 million 30-year FNMA current coupon pass-through security at various PSA prepayment speeds.

The top portion of Figure 19.2 shows the interest component and the lower portion shows the principal component of the monthly cash flows. Since the interest is proportional to the outstanding balance, the top part of Figure 19.2 also can be viewed as showing the decline in the mortgage balance at the various prepayment speeds.

At a zero prepayment level, the interest and principal cash flows in Figure 19.2 compose a normal amortization schedule. In the earlier months of the security's life, the cash flows primarily contain interest payments. This occurs because interest payments are calculated based on the outstanding principal balance remaining on the mortgage loans at the beginning of each month. As the mortgage loans amortize, the cash flows increasingly reflect the payment of principal. Towards the end of the security's life, principal payments make up the bulk of the cash flows.

Prepayments of principal significantly alter the principal and interest cash flows received by the mortgage pass-through investor. Home owners who prepay all or part of their mortgage loans return more principal to the investor in the earlier years of the mortgage security. All else being equal, an increase in prepayments has two effects:

1. The time remaining until return of principal is reduced as shown in Figure 19.2. At 100% PSA, the average life of the principal

Figure 19.2—Interest and Principal for a FNMA Pass-Through at Various Prepayment Speeds

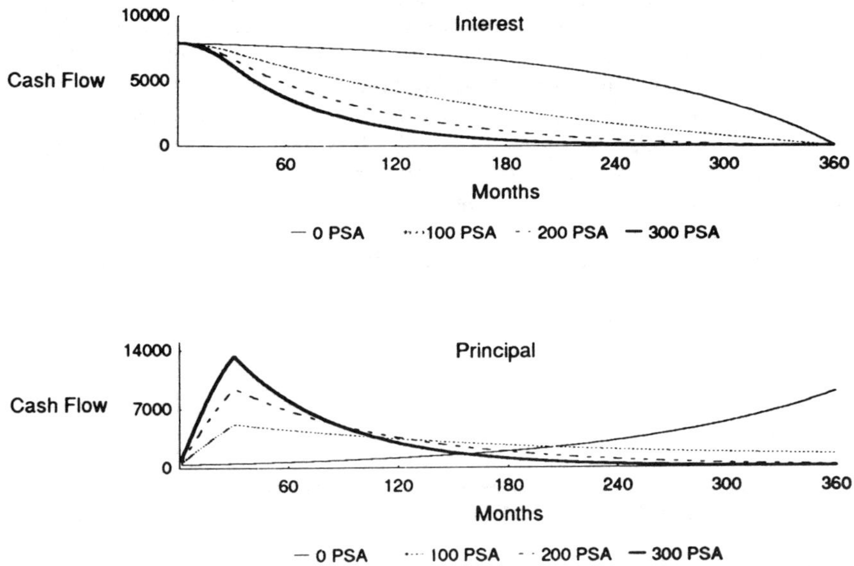

cash flows is 12.4 years while at faster speeds of 200% PSA and 300% PSA, principal is returned in average time periods of 8.2 years and 6 years, respectively.

2. The total amount of interest cash flows is reduced, which also is illustrated in Figure 19.2. This occurs because interest payments are calculated based on the amount of principal outstanding at the beginning of each month and higher prepayment levels reduce the amount of principal outstanding.

Effect of prepayment changes on value. A mortgage pass-through represents the combined value of the interest and principal cash flows. The effects of prepayments on the present value of each of these components tend to offset each other. Increases in prepayments reduce the time remaining until repayment of principal. The sooner the principal is repaid, the higher the present value of the principal. Conversely, since increasing levels of prepayments reduce interest cash flows, the value of the interest decreases.

Thus, the interest and principal cash flows individually are much more sensitive to prepayment changes than the combined mortgage pass-through. This is illustrated in Figure 19.3, which shows the present values of the principal and interest components of a FNMA current coupon pass-through at various prepayment levels.

The greater sensitivity of IOs and POs to prepayment changes is further illustrated in Figure 19.4, which shows the realized yields to maturity (or internal rates of return) for a typical IO and PO and for the underlying collateral for given purchase prices.

The IO and PO reflect sharply contrasting responses to prepayment changes; the IO's yield falls sharply as prepayments increase, while the PO's yield falls sharply as prepayments decrease. The yield of the underlying collateral is, on the other hand, relatively stable since it is assumed to be priced close to par.

Figure 19.3—Present Values of Principal and Interest Components of Cash Flows at Various Prepayment Speeds

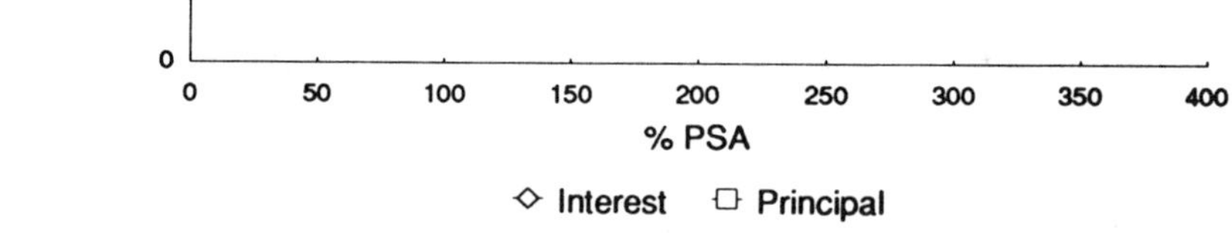

Figure 19.4—Realized Yields to Maturity for a Current Coupon IO and PO and the underlying Collateral at Various Prepayment Speeds

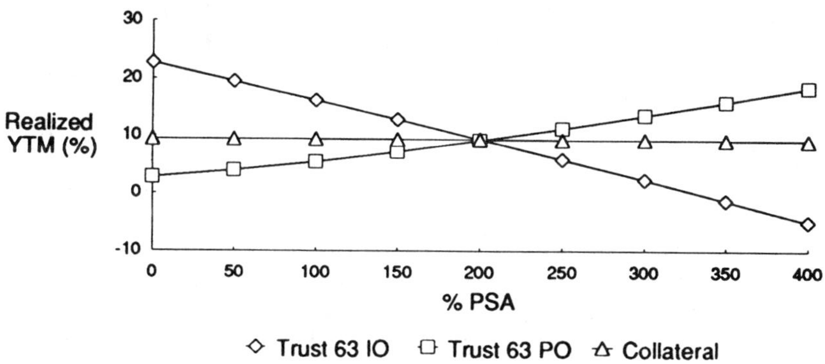

Price performance of SMBSs. The discussion above indicates that prepayment speeds are by far the most important determinant of the value of an SMBS. Since the price response of an SMBS to interest-rate changes is determined, to a large extent, by how the collateral's prepayment speed is affected by the interest-rate changes, we will start with a discussion of mortgage-prepayment behavior.

The prepayment S-curve. The prepayment speed of an MBS is a function of the security's characteristics (such as coupon and age), interest rates, and other economic and demographic variables.[7] While detailed prepayment projections generally require an econometric model, the investor can obtain some insight into the likely behavior of an SMBS by examining the spread between the collateral's gross coupon and current mortgage rates.

[7] See *Prepayment Models and Methodologies*, Lakhbir S. Hayre, Kenneth Lauterbach and Cyrus Mohebbi, Financial Strategies Group, Prudential Securities Inc., February 1988.

This spread is generally the most important variable in determining prepayment speeds. With respect to this spread, prepayment speeds have an "S" shape; speeds are fairly flat for discount coupons (when the spread is negative and prepayments are caused mainly by housing turnover), start increasing when the spread becomes positive, surge rapidly until the spread is several hundred basis points and then level off when the security is a high premium. At this point, there is already substantial economic incentive for mortgage holders to refinance and further increases in the spread lead to only marginal increases in refinancing activity. This S-curve is illustrated in Figure 19.5, which shows projected longterm prepayments for current coupon collateral for specified changes in mortgage rates.

In the remainder of this section, we make repeated references to Figure 19.5, as the performance of an SMBS can be explained to a large extent by the position of its collateral on the prepayment S-curve.[8]

Projected price behavior. Figure 19.6 gives projected price paths for a current coupon IO and PO for parallel interest-rate shifts.[9]

The projected price behavior of the SMBSs as interest rates change can be explained largely by the prepayment S-curve in Figure 19.5.

---

8 However, the investor would note that not all aspects of prepayment behavior are explained by the spread between the coupon and the mortgage rate.

The projected prepayments shown in Figure 19.5 are long-term **averages**. Month-to-month prepayment rates vary (for example, due to seasonality) even if mortgage rates do not change.

If a substantial and sustained decline in mortgage rates occurs, then mortgage holders exposed to refinancing incentives for the first time initially exhibit a sharp increase in prepayments. This gradually decreases as the home owners most anxious and able to refinance do so. This non-interest-rate related decline in the prepayment speeds of premium coupons usually is referred to as "burnout." The projected speeds shown in the declining-rate scenarios are the averages of the high early speeds and lower later speeds.

For seasoned coupons that have experienced a heavy refinancing period, burnout implies that prepayments may be less responsive to declines in interest rates. This applies to the majority of premium coupons currently outstanding.

The age effect on prepayments is well known. Prepayment speeds are low for new mortgages and increase gradually until the mortgages are two to three years old, after which the age is less important. This means that, other things being equal, an IO is worth more if it is collateralized by new FNMA 9s, for example, than by seasoned FNMA 9s.

9 The prices are calculated to give an option-adjusted spread (OAS) of 100 basis points in all cases. A discussion of OAS analysis is given in the next section. Note that if it is also priced at an OAS of 100 basis points, the collateral price is just the sum of the IO and PO prices.

Figure 19.5—Projected Prepayments for Current Coupon FNMA Collateral

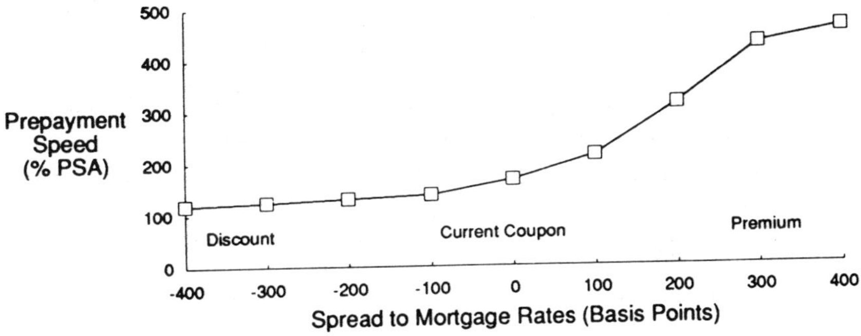

Figure 19.6—Projected Prices for a Current Coupon FNMA IO and PO

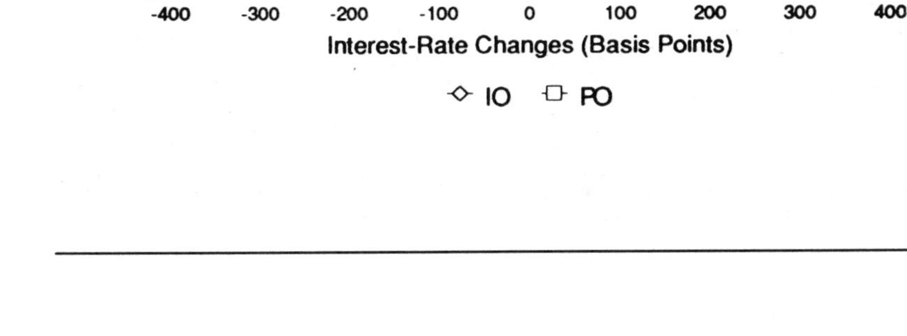

- As rates drop from current levels, the collateral begins to experience sharp increases in prepayments. Compounded by lower discount rates, this causes substantial price appreciation for the PO. For the IO, however, the higher prepayments outweigh the lower discount rates and the net result is a price decline.
- If rates drop by several hundred basis points, the collateral becomes a high-premium coupon and prepayments plateau. The rates of price appreciation of the PO and price depreciation of the IO both decrease. Eventually the IO's price starts to increase, as the effect of lower discount rates start to outweigh the effect of marginal increases in prepayments.
- If rates rise, the slower prepayments and higher discount rates combine to cause a steep drop in the price of the PO. The IO is aided initially by the slower prepayments, giving the IO negative duration, but eventually prepayments plateau on the lower side of the prepayment S-curve and the IO's price begins to decrease.

Effective duration and convexity. Figure 19.6 indicates that for current or low-premium collateral, POs tend to have large, positive effective durations while IOs have large, negative effective durations.[10]

The effective durations in Figure 19.7 reflect the price paths in Figure 19.6:

---

[10] Effective duration is a measure of the proportional price change if interest rates change by a small amount. Let *PRICE*(0) be the current price of a security. Let *PRICE* (Δ) be the price if interest rates increase by a small amount Δ and PRICE (- Δ) be the price if interest rates decrease by a small amount Δ. Then

$$\text{Effective Duration} = \frac{\text{PRICE }(-\Delta) - \text{PRICE }(\Delta)}{\text{PRICE }(0) \times 2\,\Delta} \times 100$$

This formula is straightforward; we take the total price change (the difference in the new prices), divide by the interest-rate change (2Δ), and, since we want a proportional price change, divide by the initial price (the 100 is a scaling factor).

To obtain the projected prices and durations, we have, for simplicity, assumed parallel shifts in interest rates. In practice, of course, rates do not move in parallel (typically, short-term rates tend to be more volatile than long rates). However, using nonparallel yield-curve shifts raises questions which, while interesting, are best left for another book. For example, suppose the yield curve shifts such that short rates move twice as much as long rates, and we compute the corresponding price change. The effective duration will be twice as large if we compare the price change against the change in short rates (i.e., Δ = change in short rates) as opposed to comparing the price change against the change in long rates (i.e., Δ = change in long rates).

Figure 19.7—Effective Durations of a Current Coupon FNMA IO and PO

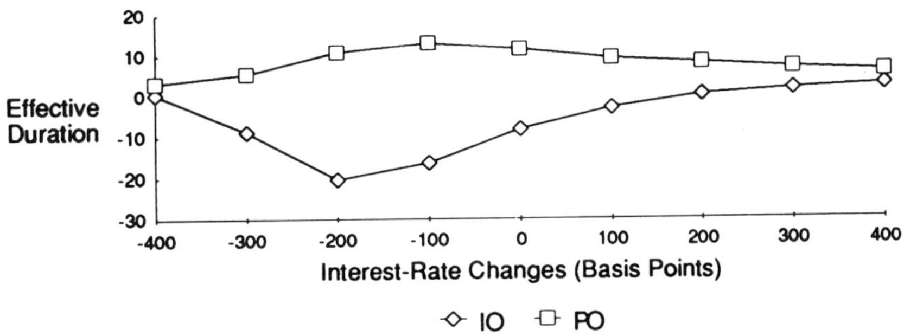

- For the PO, as rates decline, the effective duration initially increases, reflecting its rapid price appreciation as prepayments surge. Note that this is in complete contrast to traditional measures such as Macaulay or modified duration, which, reflecting the shortening maturity of the PO, would actually decrease. As rates continue to drop, the PO's effective duration levels off and then decreases, reflecting both a leveling off of prepayments and the fact that, to calculate the effective duration, we are dividing by an increasing price. If rates increase, the PO's duration decreases but remains positive.
- For the IO, the effective duration is initially negative and decreases rapidly as rates drop, before eventually increasing and becoming positive after prepayments plateau. If rates increase, the duration increases and eventually becomes positive.

Convexity measures the rate of change of duration and is useful in indicating whether the trend in price change is likely to accelerate or decelerate. It is calculated by comparing the price change if interest

Figure 19.8—Convexities of a Current Coupon IO and PO

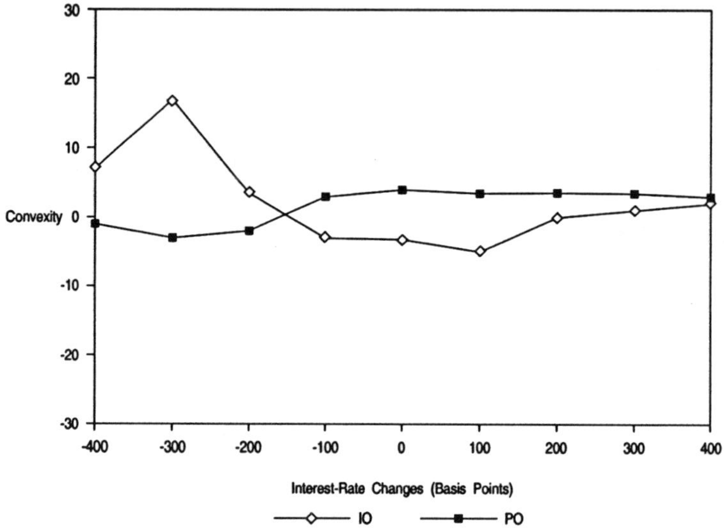

rates decrease with the price change if rates increase.[11] Figure 19.8 shows the convexities obtained using the projected prices in Figure 19.6.

Comparing Figure 19.8 with Figures 19.6 and 19.7 shows that the convexity indicates how the duration is changing. When the duration is increasing (as in the case of the PO when rates begin to decline from the initial value), the convexity is positive, and when the duration is decreasing, the convexity is negative. For example, the IO's convexity is initially negative but begins to increase after rates fall by more than

---

[11] Convexity is calculated by comparing the price changes if rates move up or down by small amounts. Let

$\Delta P^+ = PRICE(0) - PRICE(\Delta)$

$\Delta P^- = PRICE(-\Delta) - PRICE(0)$

where ΔP^+ *and* ΔP^- *are the price changes if rates increase or decrease by* Δ, respectively. Then

$$\text{Convexity} = \frac{\Delta P^- - \Delta P^+}{\text{PRICE}(0) \times \Delta \times \Delta} \times 100$$

100 basis points; although the duration is still negative at –200 basis points, the positive convexity indicates that the duration is increasing. The peak in the convexity of the IO at a change of –300 basis points indicates that the ***rate*** of increase in its duration is greatest at this point as shown in Figure 19.7; the slope of the IO's duration curve is higher from –200 to –300 than from –300 to –400.

In summary, the prepayment S-Curve implies that for SMBSs collateralized by:

- **Current or discount pass-throughs**, the PO has substantial upside potential and little downside risk, while the converse is true for IOs;
- **Low premiums**, there is somewhat comparable upside potential and downside risk;
- **High premiums** (including the majority of SMBSs issued to date), the PO has little upside potential and significant downside risk while the reverse is true for IOs.

Pricing of SMBSs and Option-Adjusted Spreads

The strong dependence of SMBS cash flows on future prepayment rates, combined with the typically asymmetric response of prepayments to interest-rate changes, make traditional measures of return such as yield to maturity of limited usefulness in analyzing or pricing SMBSs. The most common method of pricing SMBSs is with OASs. OAS analysis uses probabilistic methods to evaluate the security over the full range of interest-rate paths that may occur over its term. The impact of prepayment variations on the security's cash flows is factored into the analysis. The OAS is the resulting average spread over Treasuries provided by the security.[12] It gives a long-term average value of the security assuming a market-neutral viewpoint on interest rates.

Table 19.1 shows the use of OAS analysis for FNMA Trust 215 and FNMA Trust 6 and the underlying pass-through collateral. In each case, the price is chosen to give an OAS of 100 basis points at a 15% annual volatility of short-term interest rates. Also shown are the yields to maturity and standard spreads over the WAL Treasury at these prices using a projected prepayment speed.

[12] More detailed descriptions of the OAS and how it is calculated may be found in *An OAS Primer*, Lakhbir S. Hayre, Financial Strategies Group, Prudential Securities Inc., July 1989, and *Stochastic Valuation of Debt Securities*, Lakhbir S. Hayre and Kenneth Lauterbach, Financial Strategies Group, Prudential Securities Inc., September 1988.

Table 19.1—OAS Analysis of SMBSs

		Price	YTM	WAL	SPD/Tsy.	OAS @ Vol. 0%	OAS @ Vol. 15%	Opt. Cost
FNMA Trust 215	PO	61-30+	6.25	9.0	35	30	100	-70
FN 7% Coll.	IO	38-11	8.39	9.0	248	280	100	180
WAM 29-09 Years	PT	100-10	6.70	9.0	108	114	100	14
Proj. PAS: 156%								
FNMA Trust 6	PO	82-18+	6.29	3.4	182	138	100	38
FN 9% Coll.	IO	24-05	7.05	3.4	257	72	100	28
WAM 22-04 Years	PT	106-21	6.50	3.4	201	120	100	20
Proj. PSA: 413%								

Note: PT stands for pass-through; projected prepayment speeds are obtained from the Prudential Securities Prepayment Model; and the option cost is the difference in OASs at short-rate volatilities of 0% and 15% per annum. Analysis based on yield curve from close on March 30, 1993.

The OAS at a 0% volatility when mortgage rates stay at current levels, is typically close to the standard Treasury spread in a flat yield curve environment. The difference between the OASs at 0% and 15% volatilities, which we label the ***option cost***, is a measure of the impact of prepayment variations on a security for the given level of interest-rate volatility. The option cost, to a large extent, does not depend on the pricing level or the absolute level of prepayment projections (although it does depend on the slope, or response, of prepayment projections to interest-rate changes). Hence, the option cost is a measure of the intrinsic effect of likely interest-rate changes on an SMBS.

Before discussing the option costs in Table 19.1, note that, in general, interest-rate and prepayment variations have two effects on an MBS:

1. For any callable security, being called in a low interest-rate environment typically has an adverse effect, since a dollar of principal of the security in general would be worth more than the price at which it is being returned. (An exception is a mortgage prepayment resulting from housing turnover, when the call could be uneconomic from the call-holder's point of view.) To put it another way, the principal that is being returned typically has to be reinvested at yields lower than that provided by the existing security.
2. For MBSs priced at a discount or a premium, changes in prepayments result in the discount or premium being received sooner

or later than anticipated. This may mitigate or reinforce the call effect discussed in (1).

In general, the first effect is much more important than the second; however, for certain deep-discount securities, such as POs, the second effect may at times outweigh the first. The net result of the two effects depends on the position of the collateral on the prepayment curve shown in Figure 19.5.

- FNMA Trust 215, shown in Table 19.1, illustrates the characteristics typical of SMBSs collateralized by current or discount coupons. For discount or current-coupon collateral, prepayments are unlikely to fall significantly but could increase dramatically if there is a substantial decrease in interest rates. This asymmetry means that the PO is, on average, likely to gain significantly from variations in prepayment speeds. The option cost for the PO is usually negative, i.e., the PO *gains* from interest-rate volatility indicating that the benefits of faster return of principal outweigh the generic negative effects of being called in low interest-rate environments. On the other hand, the underlying collateral tends to have a positive (but usually small in the case of discount collateral) option cost; the negative effects of being called when rates are low outweigh the benefits of faster return of principal. Finally, the IO typically has a large positive option cost; the asymmetric nature of likely prepayment changes, discussed above, means that the IO gains little if interest rates increase (since prepayments will not decrease significantly), while a substantial decline in rates is likely to lead to a surge in prepayments and a drop in interest cash flows.
- FNMA Trust 6 is representative of most outstanding SMBSs, which currently have premium collateral. For **premium** collateral, there is, generally speaking, potential for both increases and decreases in prepayments, and the net effect of prepayment variations will depend on the particular coupon and prevailing mortgage rates. Seasoned premiums, for example, will not have potential for substantial increases in speeds and, hence, FNMA Trust 6 PO has a positive option cost. The collateral has a positive option cost for the same reasons. The IO has a negative option indicating that the beneficial effect of prepayment variations outweighs call effects for this security.

The importance of likely variations in prepayments makes the standard yield to maturity of very little relevance in pricing SMBSs and therefore, they tend to be priced (as in Table 19.1) on an OAS basis.

HEDGING APPLICATIONS

Hedging Prepayment Risk and Interest-Rate Risk

The much higher price sensitivity and yield sensitivity of IOs and POs to changes in interest rates and prepayments compared with non-stripped mortgage pass-throughs have been discussed in the preceding section. It is natural, therefore, to consider whether a portfolio of several mortgage pass-through securities can be hedged adequately for short-term holding periods against changes in prepayments or interest rates with a small but highly price-sensitive position in either IOs or POs. Before discussing details of how such a hedge works in practice, it is important to consider the relationship between prepayment risk and interest-rate risk.

Prepayment risk for a security is defined as the price sensitivity of the security to changes in the rate at which unscheduled principal is prepaid. All other factors that may affect price, in particular interest-rate movements, are held constant in order to isolate prepayment risk. The much greater price sensitivities of IOs and POs to changes in prepayments compared with mortgage pass-throughs were discussed in the previous section and illustrated in Figure 19.3.

A second component of price sensitivity, referred to as interest-rate risk, arises from changes in interest rates over a given holding period. Shifts in prevailing interest rates have a direct impact on the present values of a security's cash flows and, hence, its price. In addition, changes in interest rates affect projected prepayment rates (see Investment Characteristics section) which, in turn, have a bearing on the security price. Thus, shifts in interest rates affect price both directly and indirectly (via changes in prepayments).

Mechanics of a Hedge

In the previous section, two risks that are relevant to hedging MBSs—changes in interest rates and prepayments—were described. In this section, the issue of quantifying the degree of hedging is addressed.

In hedging a portfolio of securities against a particular risk, the investor must be willing to sacrifice some portion of his potential profit (in favorable market environments) in order to reduce the variation in portfolio performance across a wide range of market environments. The investor also must consider how long the portfolio will be held before either closing out or rehedging the position. This holding period could vary from one day for an interest-rate-sensitive portfolio in a volatile market to perhaps a month or two in a more stable environment. For short holding periods, the market value of the hedge position at the end of the period is the measure of portfolio performance used in this section. An investor who wishes to evaluate a hedge on this basis must then decide:

1. The range of interest-rate (or prepayment) changes to hedge against. For example, for a one-month holding period, the investor may wish to hedge the market value of the portfolio only against gradual interest-rate moves of between +200 basis points and –200 basis points in the yield on six-month Treasuries.[13] In general, a greater variance in market value is implied by a wider range of interest-rate or prepayment changes.
2. The spread in market value of the portfolio that is considered to be acceptable. The extreme case is to hedge so that there is no change in market value across the range chosen in (1). In practice, a small variation of a few percent in market value may be acceptable.

The calculation of the market value of a hedged portfolio is done using an "average" OAS for each security in the portfolio, as described in the Investment Characteristics section earlier. Two specific examples that illustrate the unique hedging characteristics of SMBSs are discussed later.

Hedging Characteristics of IOs and POs

One reason for the attractiveness of IOs and POs as instruments for hedging MBS portfolios is that they have much higher (absolute) effective durations than mortgage pass-throughs (see Figure 19.7, for example). This implies a much greater price sensitivity to changes in interest rates. An investor who wishes to reduce the price sensitivity of a portfolio to changes in interest rates can achieve this by establishing a

---

[13] Assuming a normal distribution for relative interest-rate changes, an initial interest rate of 8% and a volatility of 15%, there is a probability of approximately two-thirds that interest rates will change by no more than 35 basis points over the course of a month. Although unlikely, interest-rate moves of up to 200 basis points within a short period have occurred in recent years, e.g., following October 19, 1987.

small position in the appropriate SMBS. (The market value of the SMBS need only be a small fraction of the market value of the portfolio.) The large negative durations of IOs make these securities appropriate for hedging portfolios with an overall positive duration; POs may be used for hedging portfolios with an overall negative duration. In each case, the hedged portfolio exhibits a lower (absolute) effective duration than the unhedged portfolio. Table 19.2 illustrates the effect of an IO and a PO on reducing the effective duration of two MBS portfolios.

Table 19.2—Matching Effective Duration with SMBSs

Portfolio 1*: GNMA 7 and FNMA Trust 215 IO								
IO Market Value ($mm)	0	10	20	30	41	60	80	100
GNMA 8 Market Value ($mm)	100	90	80	70	59	40	20	0
Effective Duration of Portfolio	7.0	5.3	3.6	1.9	0.0	-3.2	-6.6	-10.0
Portfolio 2*: FNMA 8 Servicing Portfolio and FNMA Trust 215 PO								
PO Market Value ($mm)	0	10	20	40	50	65	80	100
Servicing Portfolio Market Value ($mm)	100	90	80	60	50	35	20	0
Effective Duration of Portfolio	-28.6	-24.2	-19.8	-11.0	-6.7	-0.1	6.5	15.3

* Total market value of portfolio is $100 mm.

Note: The servicing portfolio of FNMA 8% pass-through collateral receives a gross coupon of 75 basis points.

The first portfolio matches the large negative duration of the Trust 215 IO with the positive duration of a GNMA 7% pass-through. A combination of approximately $41 million market value of the IO with $59 million market value of the GNMA pass-through has an overall effective duration of close to zero, and should show little price sensitivity to small changes in interest rates. The second portfolio combines the Trust 215 PO with a servicing portfolio of FNMA 8% pass-throughs as collateral (from which the servicer receives a gross coupon of 75 basis points). The servicing portfolio exhibits the features of an IO, e.g., large negative effective duration for low-premium collateral and as such is a bearish security. The combination of $35 million market value of the servicing portfolio with $65 million of the PO has an overall effective duration of close to zero. For both portfolios in Table 19.2, variations in the mixture of the appropriate SMBS results in a synthetic security that exhibits either bullish, bearish or neutral price characteristics (as measured by overall effective duration).

Additional points in favor of using SMBSs for hedging include:

- The market for SMBSs has become increasingly liquid as more investors take advantage of the characteristics offered by these securities. Increased liquidity facilitates the use of SMBSs for particular hedging purposes, since the appropriate SMBS or combination of SMBSs is more easily assembled in a liquid market. In a less liquid market, the limited availability of certain SMBSs would restrict the type of portfolio that can be hedged. One particular concern in an illiquid environment would be a mismatch between some of the factors affecting prepayment characteristics of the portfolio under consideration and those of the available SMBSs.[14]
- Prepayment risk for mortgage pass-throughs is best hedged with mortgage instruments such as SMBSs since Treasuries, by their very nature, have no prepayment sensitivity.

Hedging Portfolio Market Value

Figures 19.9 and 19.10 illustrate the sensitivity of the market value of the Trust 215 IO/GNMA 7 synthetic security and the Trust 215 PO/FNMA Servicing Portfolio synthetic security to sudden parallel shifts in the yield curve. The holding period is one month in each case and the initial market value of each portfolio is $100 million.

The total market value of each portfolio is shown for various interest-rate scenarios and for different proportions of the hedging security (SMBS). The least variation in total market value, i.e., the flattest profile, for interest-rate shifts of –200 basis points to +200 basis points is obtained when approximately $20 million of the GNMA/IO combination is invested in the Trust 215 IO and $60 million of the FNMA Servicing Portfolio/PO combination is invested in the Trust 215 PO. These amounts result in a low or zero overall effective duration for each of these portfolios in the NC case (see Table 19.2). This is hardly surprising, since a portfolio with a zero effective duration (and small convexity) in the NC base case should have a flat-market value profile for small (i.e., local) changes in interest rates.

[14] One such factor is the geographical origin of the mortgages underlying the security.

Figure 19.9—Market Value of FNMA Trust 215 IO/GNMA 7 Synthetic Security

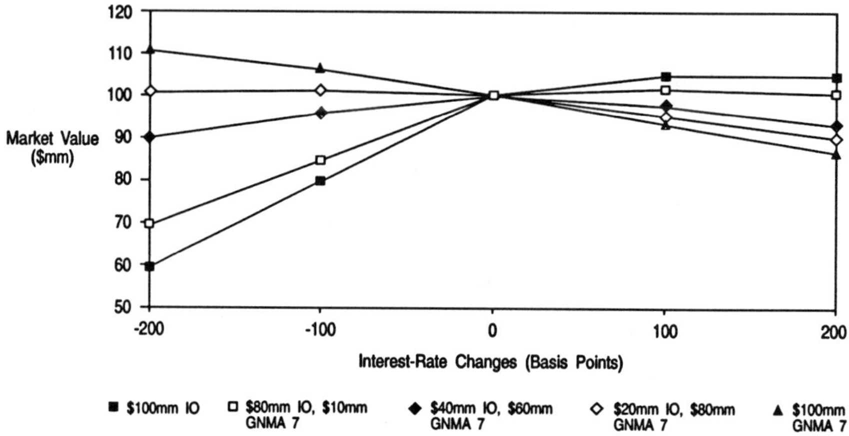

Figure 19.10—Market Value of FNMA Trust 215 PO/FNMA 8 Servicing Portfolio Synthetic Security

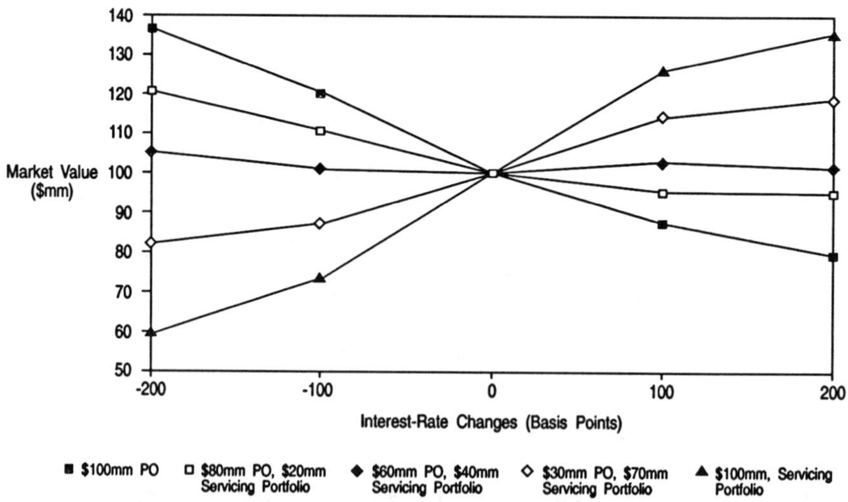

Summary

POs and IOs offer the investor the opportunity to hedge a portfolio of MBSs against interest-rate and prepayment risk for short-term holding periods. In addition, an investor can choose to adjust the proportion of the SMBS hedge in the portfolio according to his perception of market direction. The resulting customized portfolio would then offer optimal performance in a market environment that adheres to investor expectations.

APPENDIX[15]

LIQUIDITY, PRICE EXECUTION, AND COMPLEXITY CONSIDERATIONS OF MORTGAGE DERIVATIVE SECURITIES

Many investors fear the derivative markets. Looking back, there were sound reasons for such concerns. As a surrogate for the entire derivative market, let's focus on the IO/PO market as a case in point. In their infancies, new businesses often suffer from wide bid-offer spreads. IOs and POs were no exception. All market participants may recall the huge losses suffered by Merrill Lynch, one of Wall Street's largest derivative trading areas, in the Spring of 1987. However, in the intervening years, liquidity has slowly but steadily grown. For example, 1988 saw 24 FNMA SMBS Trusts come to market for a total market value of $5.6 billion. Total issuance as of March 1993 exceeds $80 billion.

Investor concerns should center around three issues: liquidity, price execution, and complexity. In reverse order, let's review some of the salient points that investors should consider in each regard.

Complexity

In reality, a simple conventional MBS security is already a structured trade. The holder is long a Treasury bond and short an in-the-money call. In trader's parlance, the investor has put on a "buy/write" posi-

[15] The following is a partial reprint from *The Optimal Portfolio System—Targeting Horizon Total Returns under Varying Interest-Rate Scenarios,* Evdokia Adamidou, Yosi Ben-Dov, Lisa Pendergast and Vincent Pica, Financial Strategies Group, Prudential Securities Inc., February 20, 1990.

tion. In the absence of any additional information, the investor is increasing yield without sacrificing credit quality via the sale of a call option to another investor (the option holder or mortgagee).

A structured trade is very similar. By creating a portfolio of mortgage securities and mortgage derivatives, the investor has, as in the Treasury example above, the opportunity to "leg out" of strategies as the component pieces react differently to market-setting forces. Specifically, the investor can take profits and/or limit losses because the component pieces are visible and divisible. This flexibility is directly analogous to the opportunities available to the "buy/write" investor.

Of significant benefit to investors is that structured mortgage-security trades do not present the investor with the "all-or-none" situation with which the "buy/write" investor is faced. For example, if the Treasury option holder exercises the right to call the bonds from the investor, it is "all-or-none." The entire call is exercised and the investor delivers the bond to the option holder in exchange for, as an example, a payment of par. With mortgages, bond factors "call" (pay down) some fraction of the position away from the investor at par. Depending on the purchase price, this is either good news or bad news. For the sake of this point, let's assume that this is bad news. But while we agree that it is bad, we still own some fraction of our original position. Thus, we have the opportunity to take a point of view about the future: Was last month an aberration? Will it get better? Will it get worse? This degree of flexibility is extremely difficult to duplicate in other fixed-income markets.

Price Execution

The marketplace is an efficient arbiter of value when two factors are in place: the rules of engagement are known and sufficient visibility among market makers is extant. Both factors are now in place in the IO/PO marketplace.

- **Rules of Engagement.** Sophisticated investors have known for some time of FNMA's ability to issue SMBS transactions. The fee that FNMA charges the underwriter is between 1/8 and 1/4 point. Hence, before making a decision to underwrite an SMBS transaction for FNMA, there must be sufficient spread, offer-to-offer, between the component parts (the collateral and the derivatives) for the underwriter to pay FNMA, his lawyers and accountants and still leave some spread to compensate the underwriter for positioning risk and the cost of carry. Since each underwriter has different risk profiles and different sources of financing, there is no hard and fast number to quote as a Street-wide triggering point. However, given the liquidity that the Street itself sees within the community, it wouldn't take a spread disparity of much more than 5/8ths or so to induce a major market maker to step in and underwrite an SMBS transaction. This arbitrage sets the upper boundary for the derivative market.

On the recombination side, if the sum of the bids for the IOs and POs are less than the bid-side price of the collateral itself, major market makers have the ability to recombine the pieces in portfolio at a lower price than the collateral. Buy low, sell high. Thus, the lower boundary is established.

- **Visibility.** Most sophisticated investors have access to the same market quotation services that are available on the trading desks of the major market makers. Telerate has long maintained several pages (23000–23004) of information on the prices of IOs and POs. Recently, Telerate has worked with the dealer community to expand the number of market makers who provide information to the service. (Prudential Securities Inc. is one such firm.)

  In addition, prepayment predictions are available on Telerate (starting on page 40850). Since derivatives have powerful reactions to changes in prepayments, this visibility provides the sophisticated investor the opportunity to make informed decisions about value. Thus, no monopoly on pricing is possible. In both cases, visibility clearly begets efficiency.

Liquidity

As we pointed out earlier, since their inception in 1986, over $80 billion SMBSs have been issued. Prudential Securities Inc., has underwritten over $6 billion itself over this period. While no one is suggesting throwing caution to the wind, it is (positively) surprising to many investors when the absolute size of the market is inspected.

Chapter Twenty

Subordinate Mortgage-Backed Securities

by William F. Wallace,
Managing Director
Stephen H. D'Antonio,
Vice President
Randall C. Hoffman,
Vice President
Morgan Stanley & Co.

INTRODUCTION

Insurers are constantly looking for higher-yielding assets. One asset class that offers these higher yields is the subordinated class of AAA/AA-rated mortgage pass-through securities. These securities, often referred to as "B" pieces, currently have spreads of approximately 300 to 500 basis points over the Treasury curve and are prepayment buffered. In addition, their credit risks are measurable and, with proper diversification, may be small in comparison to other high-yielding securities. The credit risk profiles of B pieces can be improved further through the use of Letters of Credit (LOCs), the creation of "C" pieces, first loss insurance or other credit-enhancement techniques. These enhancements, however, will reduce the yields offered.

These securities are generally well-suited to interest-sensitive life insurance liabilities. With the choices of Cost of Funds Index (COFI), one-year Constant Maturity Treasury (CMT) or fixed-rate issues, portfolios with high correlations to Single Premium Deferred Annuity (SPDA), Flexible Premium Deferred Annuity (FPDA), and Universal Life (UL) reset rates can be created.

ORIGINATION AND SECURITIZATION PROCESS

AAA/AA mortgage pass-throughs are created when a mortgage originator pools its nonconforming mortgage loans for sale into the secondary market. Since these mortgage loans are primarily nonconforming due to size or documentation, they cannot be sold to the traditional agency issuers (i.e., GNMA, FNMA, FHLMC). They must instead be pooled and sold under the originator's name. With no agency backing, Moody's and S&P require that some form of credit enhancement exist for these pools to receive a AAA or AA rating.

In the past, four methods of achieving credit enhancement for these mortgage loans have been used. In order of 1990 size of issuance, these methods are:

- Senior/subordinated structure
- Pool insurance
- Letter of credit
- Parent guarantee

In 1990, just over 50% of the private pass-through productions were senior/subordinated structures (see Figure 20.1). We expect that in the future this percentage will increase to the levels of 1988–1989, which was roughly two-thirds of the market.

In a senior/subordinated pass-through structure, monthly payments of principal and interest are passed through to the investors in a predetermined order of priority. At time of issue, the subordinated, or class B, holders generally represent 6% to 10% of the outstanding balance but bear the full risk of losses from the entire pool. In this fashion, the B piece is providing the credit protection for the senior piece. In turn, the B piece is buffered from prepayments by the senior piece. To achieve this, most AAA/AA mortgages allocate all prepayments from the underlying collateral to the senior piece until it is paid off or for the first 10 years, whichever occurs first. Beginning in Year 11, prepayments are allocated in increasing percentages to the B piece until it is

Figure 20.1—Private Pass-Through Production by Type of Credit Enhancement

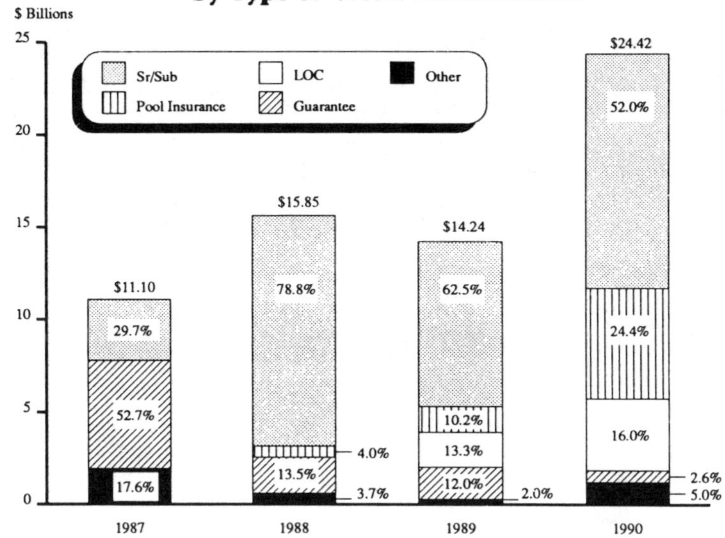

Source: Inside Mortgage Capital Markets

receiving its full prorated share of prepayment in Year 15.[1] This structure, along with the discount price, keeps the prepayment costs small.

B pieces have been issued with ratings from AAA to BBB, however the majority are not rated but carry shadow noninvestment grade ratings.

CREDIT RISK

The risk in B pieces derives from the negative leverage of owning 6% to 10% of the mortgage collateral while bearing 100% of the risk of loss. Therefore, it is important to find ways of both subjectively evaluating the quality of the underlying mortgages and quantitatively esti-

1 This structure is generally true of adjustable-rate B pieces. Fixed-rate B piece structures are similar, but the allocation of prepayments will generally begin in Year 6.

mating their default costs. The following are some of the most important factors in assessing the underlying quality.

Loan-to-Value Ratio (LTV)

The LTV is the original dollar amount of the mortgage loan divided by the original market value of the property. This ratio has been a very good indicator of default risk. In Figure 20.2 we see that there are non-linear increases in the default risk as the LTVs rise. For this reason, it is as important to know the distribution of the LTVs in the issue as it is to know the weighted-average LTVs.

Figure 20.2—FNMA Default Experience 30-Year Fixed-Rate Texas Loans

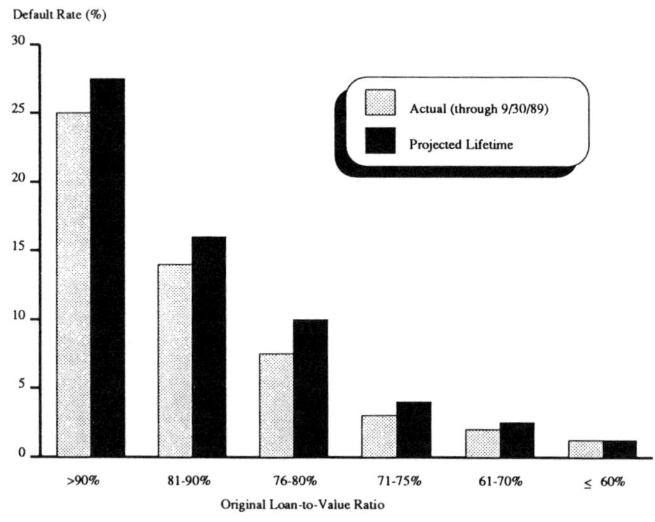

Source: FNMA

Seasoning

The age of a pool of mortgages has been found to have an impact on the pool's default rate. We see in Figure 20.3 that defaults, on average, begin at very low levels, peak in Year 5, and are by S&P's estimates 95% complete by Year 7.

Figure 20.3—Annual Default Rates
1973–1989 Mortgages Nationwide (Covered by PMI)

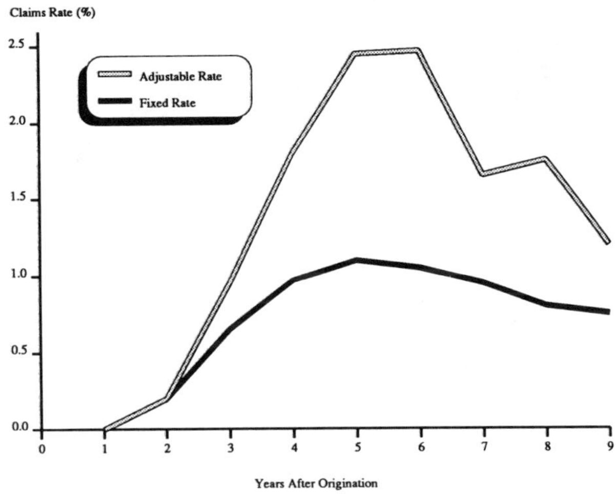

Source: Moody's Annual Report of the Private Mortgage Insurance Industry

Mortgage Type

Is the mortgage a fixed rate, ARM, negative amortization ARM or graduated payment mortgage (GPM)? Most investors believe that ARMs have had a higher default rate than fixed-rate mortgages. However, if we disaggregate the ARM category into fully amortizable ARMs and negative amortization ARMs (including GPMs and GEMs) we find that most of the additional risk is coming from the negative amortization ARMs written between 1980 and 1983 (see Figure 20.4). Since 1983, ARMs, including negative amortization ARMs, have shown default rates nearly equivalent to those of fixed-rate loans.

Underwriting Standards

These standards are the amount of documentation and verification required for the borrower to receive its mortgage. Full documentation requires:

- Application by borrower
- Verification of employment
- Verification of income

Figure 20.4—Annual Default Rates
1973–1989 Mortgages Nationwide (Covered by PMI)

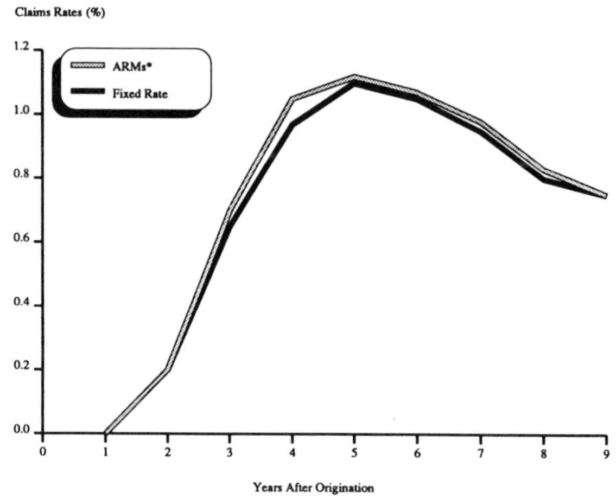

* Excluding 1980–1983 negative amortization ARMs
Source: Moody's Annual Report of the Private Mortgage Insurance Industry

- Verification of down payment
- Source of down payment
- Credit checks
- Settlement statement on sale of previous home
- Appraisal

Any loan origination in which less documentation is required is considered a *low-documentation* loan. Most AAA/AA mortgage pass-through issues contain these low-documentation loans. These loans are not inherently bad, however they do carry higher risks then full-documentation loans. Therefore, it is important to understand which underwriting procedures were omitted. As an example, loans with low LTVs may be good quality low-documentation loans.

Property Type and Purpose

Is the loan secured by an owner-occupied single-family dwelling or a rental condominium? Single-family and owner-occupied dwellings traditionally have the lowest default rates.

Property Location

Geographic diversification is important. A location with high economic diversity will be less susceptible to single industry recessions than a town or state with one major industry. In addition, the state and local laws will affect the ability of the servicer to foreclose as well as the foreclosure costs involved.

Underwriter/Servicer

Know your issuer! Not all issuers/servicers have had the same loss experiences on residential mortgage loans. The experiences of three prime pool issuers/servicers are presented in Table 20.1.

We will now lay out a framework for quantitatively estimating the cost of defaults. To do this we examine the sources of loss in these securities and review the historical data for these components in both Texas (as a presumed worst case) and the nation as a whole.

Foreclosure Rate

The foreclosure rate is the percentage of the outstanding balance of mortgage loans for which the subject property is under foreclosure (see Figure 20.5). National foreclosure rates for the period 1980–1990 averaged 0.16% per quarter, apparently peaking in early 1990 at approximately 0.21%. The experience in Texas during this same period saw lower foreclosure rates than the national averages through 1984 but experienced a dramatic rise thereafter. Rates peaked on a quarterly basis at 0.65% in the third quarter of 1986. The worst one-year period encompassed the second half of 1986 and the first half of 1987 at 2.16%.

Property Value Declines

These are the percentage declines in the market values of the properties versus the values at times of origination (see Figure 20.6). On a nationwide basis, during the last 10 years housing prices have grown at an average annual rate of 4.5%.

The experience in Texas has clearly been worse. Using 1983 as a base (the start of the Houston decline), a diversified portfolio of Texas mortgage loans showed a total market value decline of 5% as of the first quarter of 1988, with Houston showing a 25% market value decline. As of the third quarter of 1990, the same diversified Texas portfolio was off 3%, with Houston again the only loss of the group at 15%. It is important to note that this period includes the full peak and

Table 20.1—Delinquencies, Foreclosures and Loss Experiences for Select Mortgage Issuers

	The Travelers Mortgage Services			
	1987	*1988*	*1989*	*1990*
Loan Portfolio ($MM)	3,898	5,620	9,067	12,220
Delinquency (%)	1.11	1.00	1.38	2.82
Foreclosure (%)	0.20	0.23	0.14	0.19
Loss (%)*	0.01	0.06	0.04	0.05
	Western Federal Savings & Loan Association			
	1987	*1988*	*1989*	*1990*
Loan Portfolio ($MM)	3,443	4,815	8,051	9,128
Delinquency (%)	1.10	0.41	1.57	1.97
Foreclosure (%)	0.01	0.005	0.005	0.267
Loss (%)*	0.0002	0.089	0.0079	NA
	Marine Midland Mortgage, Inc.			
	1987	*1988*	*1989*	*1990*
Loan Portfolio ($MM)	2,678	4,916	11,998	14,678
Delinquency (%)	1.68	2.78	3.63	2.89
Foreclosure (%)	0.08	0.06	0.06	0.36
Loss (%)*	0.00	0.00	0.00	0.00

* Cumulative losses for total originations

Source: Morgan Stanley

trough in the Houston market, and that for both periods, Houston was the only city among the Texas cities shown whose property values were below their 1983 values. The Houston experience again points out the importance of diversification.

Implied Loss Severity

Implied loss severity is the percentage of the original mortgage loan that may be lost in a default situation. It is calculated from the LTVs,

Figure 20.5—Texas Foreclosure Rates versus National Foreclosure Rates for 1–4 Family Residential Mortgages 1980–1990

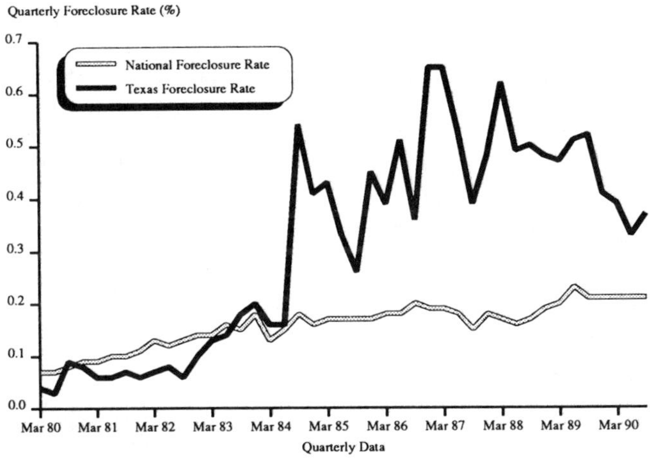

Source: Mortgage Bankers Association of America Delinquency Survey–Historical Series

Figure 20.6—National versus Texas Home Sales Price Indices 1980 Base

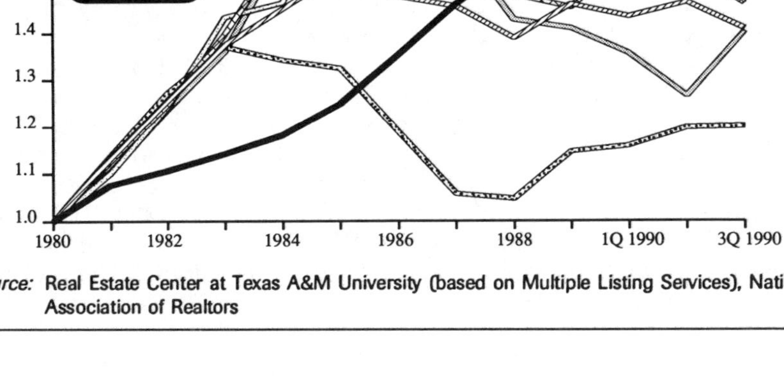

Source: Real Estate Center at Texas A&M University (based on Multiple Listing Services), National Association of Realtors

property value declines, foregone interest, and foreclosure costs, as shown in Table 20.2. This analysis assumes an 80% LTV and 7.5% of the loan balance for foreclosure costs. Lower LTVs decrease the loss severity, higher ones increase it.

Table 20.2—Implied Loss Severity Calculation

	Property Value Decline	
	30%	*15%*
Initial Home Value ($)	100	100
Property Value Decline ($)	(30)	(15)
Foregone Interest (One Year) ($)	(8)	(8)
Foreclosure Costs ($)	(6)	(6)
Net Realized Property Value ($)	56	71
Original Mortgage Amount (80% LTV) ($)	(80)	(80)
Loss ($)	(24)	(9)
Implied Loss Severity (%)*	30	11

* Loss ÷ Original Mortgage Amount = Implied Loss Severity

Source: Morgan Stanley

Utilizing the Formula

Credit Risk = Foreclosure Rate × Implied Loss Severity

We can create a matrix for estimating the yearly cost in basis points of default/credit risk for an entire pool of collateral. The matrix presented in Table 20.3 assumes 80% of LTVs with a variety of property value declines and foreclosure rates.

Since the subordinated class bears the full risk of loss on the mortgage loans, the numbers shown in Table 20.3 must now be used to calculate the cost of defaults to the subordinated class. The model that we have developed allocates the principal, interest, and prepayments generated by the mortgage loan collateral to the senior and subordinated tranches according to their predetermined schedules. The model then utilizes the credit risk from Table 20.3 to determine the net cash flows and post-default yield received by the subordinated class. In this

Table 20.3—Effect of Foreclosures on Entire Structure's Yield (Percent per Year)

		Texas			
Property Value Declines (%)		30.00	15.00	10.00	6.00
Implied Loss Severity (%)		30.00	11.25	5.00	0.00
Foreclosure Rate (%)					
Worst Experience	2.16	0.65	0.24	0.11	0.00
10-Year Average	1.28	0.38	0.14	0.06	0.00
5-Year Average	1.86	0.56	0.21	0.09	0.00
1-Year Average	1.83	0.55	0.21	0.09	0.00
Best Experience	0.24	0.07	0.03	0.01	0.00
		Nationwide			
Property Value Declines (%)		30.00	15.00	10.00	6.00
Implied Loss Severity (%)		30.00	11.25	5.00	0.00
Foreclosure Rate (%)					
Worst Experience	0.88	0.26	0.10	0.04	0.00
10-Year Average	0.61	0.18	0.07	0.03	0.00
5-Year Average	0.73	0.22	0.08	0.04	0.00
1-Year Average	0.84	0.25	0.09	0.04	0.00
Best Experience	0.16	0.05	0.02	0.01	0.00

Source: Morgan Stanley

fashion, the effects of leverage and the reduction of principal and future interest flows are modeled correctly.[2]

To estimate the default risk of B pieces we have utilized a generic AAA/AA ARM structure with the B piece equal to 8% of the initial collateral. No credit enhancement is assumed on the B piece. Additionally, no prepayments go to the subordinated class until after Year 10 and then they go to the subordinated piece in an increasing, predetermined share. At inception, the mortgage loans are required to be cur-

[2] The model will *overstate* the credit risk because we have assumed that defaults continue for the entire 30 years and we have not reduced the loss severity as principal repayments (both scheduled and prepaid) that reduce the LTVs with time.

Table 20.4—Effect of Default Experience on Subordinated Tranche's Yield

Default Experience (%)			*Cost of Default (bp)*
Year 1	*Year 2*	*Years 3–30*	*Effect on B Piece per Year*
0	0	0	0
0	0.08	0.08	40 (Best estimate)
0	0.10	0.10	50
0	0.10	0.25	84
0	0.25	0.06	84
0	0.25	0.10	93
0	0.25	0.25	129
0	0.55	0.55	307 (Houston experience)

Source: Morgan Stanley

rent and can have had only one 30-day delinquency in the preceding 12 months. Because the loans are current at issue and we have assumed the loss of one year's interest in the implied loss severity numbers, we further assume that no defaults take place in the first year.

Table 20.4 presents the default costs to the subordinated piece of different default experiences for the entire collateral. As an example of how the table works, most real estate market estimates point to potential foreclosure rates of 0.75% and market values bottoming 15% below initial home values. We can take these estimates into Table 20.3 (across the five-year nationwide average foreclosure rate row, and down the 15% property value decline column) to arrive at a default experience rate of 0.08%. We then input this 0.08% experience into the model for Years 2 through 30 and arrive at our best estimate default cost of 40 basis points per year.

If we use more severe estimates for foreclosure rates and/or property value declines to arrive at default experiences for the entire pool of 0.10 and 0.25, we would see expected yield reductions due to a default of between 50 and 129 basis points for the B piece. A Texas-type scenario would cost approximately 307 basis points. It is important to note once again that these numbers are based upon 80% LTVs and 8% ownership of collateral initially. Reduction of the initial LTVs

Figure 20.7—Universal Life versus COFI ARMs

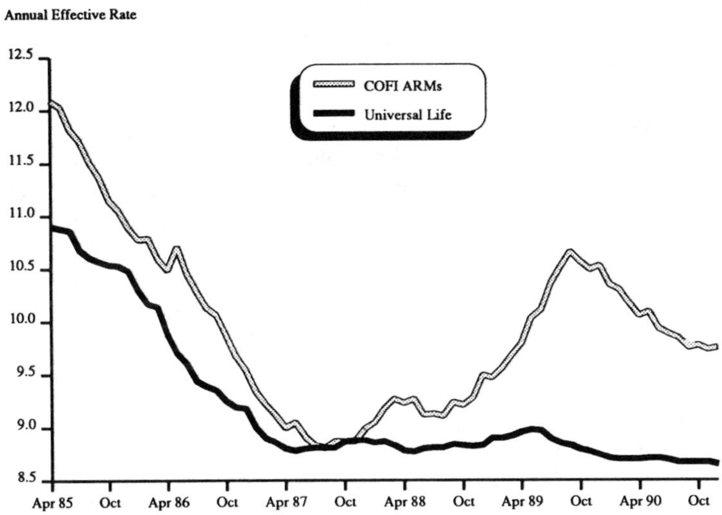

Source: Morgan Stanley

would improve these numbers; a decrease in the initial senior/subordinated leverage would decrease default costs.

CORRELATION TO SPDA, FPDA, AND UL RATES

It has been shown in earlier studies that a high correlation exists between the 11th District COFI and UL crediting rates.[3] Figure 20.7 shows that this high correlation remains in effect.[4] These high correlations also exist between SPDA/FPDA reset rates and one-year CMT rates, and these correlations provide an opportunity to construct portfolios that are sensitive to crediting rate needs.

[3] For more information see the Morgan Stanley publication *Investing for Interest-Sensitive Insurance Products: Adjustable Rate Mortgages*, April 1989.

[4] It has been hypothesized that the divergence seen between September 1988 and September 1990 is due to the weaker savings and loan institutions bidding up the Cost of Funds Index; then the Index declined as these pressures subsided.

AN SPDA EXAMPLE

For most interest-sensitive portfolios, portfolio managers are forced to go too long in duration in order to achieve their yield targets. This duration mismatch translates into both parallel and nonparallel risks. The parallel risk arises when rates rise, but the portfolio rate does not rise quickly enough to keep policyholders from lapsing. The nonparallel risk comes in the form of a change in the rates used for resetting the crediting rate without a corresponding change in the portfolio rate. One-year CMT-based B pieces, with their high yields and short durations, help reduce this disintermediation risk.

As an example, we will use a generic new issue SPDA. The insurer guarantees the current three-year Treasury rate to the policyholder for a period of three years. After the initial period, the rate resets annually to the one-year Treasury rate. There is a surrender penalty of 7%, which declines by 1% per year.

Expenses and other product features lead to an "all-in cost" for the SPDA of 74 basis points above Treasuries. This 74 basis point spread is known as the "required spread"[5] and includes the cost of the interest-sensitive withdrawal feature that is part of any SPDA liability.

The price-sensitivity duration (otherwise known in investment literature as "option-adjusted" or "effective duration") of the generic product is 3.1 years. We now construct and test two portfolios. Both portfolios will be duration-matched, without regard to a profit target. Table 20.5 shows a traditional asset mix for this type of product, emphasizing noncallable corporates. Table 20.6 includes a small position in one-year CMT B pieces to examine what benefits can accrue from the inclusion of this asset.

The portfolio shown in Table 20.6 has several advantages:

- Higher expected profitability
- Lower credit risk with no giveup in yield or OAS
- Average rating of AA3 versus A3 for the portfolio in Table 20.5
- Diversification of risk away from the junk market

---

[5] A more detailed discussion of the required spread concept can be found in the Morgan Stanley publication *The Excess Spread Approach to Pricing and Designing the SPDA*, December 1989. The required spread is the spread that equates the present value of the liability and expense cash flows to the market value of assets. Liability cash flows are generated along a carefully constructed set of interest rate paths so that all the interest-sensitive characteristics of the product are recognized.

Table 20.5—Portfolio 1

	Yield (%)	OAS (bp)	OAD (Yrs.)	Credit Risk (bp)
95% 3-4 Year Noncallable Bonds*	8.45	110	3.1	35
5% Top-Tier High Yield	12.00	450	3.4	200
Weighted Average	*8.63*	*127*	*3.1*	*43*
Credit Risk		43		
Credit-Adjusted OAS		84		

	Change in Interest Rates					
	-200 bp	*-100 bp*	*0*	*+100 bp*	*+200 bp*	*+300 bp*
Market Value ($ Thousands)	994	964	935	907	881	855
Earned Spread on Assets (bp/year)	84	84	84	84	84	84
Required Spread on Assets (bp/year)	82	76	74	75	76	79
Expected Profit (bp/year)	2	8	10	9	8	5

* This portion of the portfolio is composed of A/BBB noncallable corporates, clean CMO tranches, and asset-backed securities.

Source: Morgan Stanley

- 50% of the portfolio resets at the same frequency and against the same index as the renewal crediting rate.

These advantages are available because the high yields on the B piece allow the use of agency securities and a larger floating-rate component. This short component in turn allows us to extend the duration of the balance of the portfolio and thus pick up the 70 basis point yield curve advantage between three and seven years.

Table 20.6—Portfolio 2

	Yield (%)	*OAS (bp)*	*OAD (Yrs.)*	*Credit Risk (bp)*
46% One-Year CMT Agency ARMs	7.70	90	0.4	5
5% One-Year CMT B Piece	10.35	375	0.5	125
46% 7-10 Year Noncallable Bonds*	9.15	115	5.9	35
3% Top-Tier High Yield	12.00	450	3.4	200
Weighted Average	*8.63*	*127*	*3.1*	*30*
Credit Risk		30		
Credit-Adjusted OAS		97		

	Change in Interest Rates					
	-200 bp	*-100 bp*	*0*	*+100 bp*	*+200 bp*	*+300 bp*
Market Value ($ Thousands)	995	964	935	908	882	851
Earned Spread on Assets (bp/year)	97	97	97	97	97	97
Required Spread on Assets (bp/year)	81	76	74	74	75	84
Expected Profit (bp/year)	16	21	23	23	22	13

* This portion of the portfolio is composed of A/BBB noncallable corporates, clean CMO tranches, and asset-backed securities.

Source: Morgan Stanley

SUMMARY

Opportunities exist to use B pieces effectively in insurance company portfolios. The credit risk in the subordinated pieces of AAA/AA mortgage securities is measurable and, depending upon one's outlook for real estate values, likely small or very small. The nominal yield spreads on these securities are high, and credit enhancement is available for investors desiring an investment grade rating or a further reduction of default risk.

Chapter Twenty-One

Subordinate Credit Card Certificates

by William F. Wallace
Managing Director
Kenneth J. Bock
Vice President
Richard J. Watson
Vice President
Kimberly L. Hirschman
Associate
Morgan Stanley & Co.

SUMMARY

The increased popularity of credit cards in the United States during the past several years has led to a related rise in term credit card securitization as a means of funding for credit card issuers. Pressure on banks to achieve and/or maintain higher capital ratios, as well as to obtain the funding flexibility provided to both banks and retailers, has caused a greater volume of credit card securities to be issued. As securitization techniques have become more sophisticated and cost efficient, various methods of credit enhancement for investor certificates have been developed. This publication will focus on the senior/subordinate method and, in particular, describe the credit and cash flow timing profile of subordinate classes. While each subordinate class has unique structural characteristics, which are described in its prospectus or offering memorandum, substantial similarities exist that can simplify investment decisions for potential investors.

Given the current market environment, we believe that even at AA or A levels of credit support, significant loss protection exists for subordinate class investors. A breakeven analysis indicates that a combination of lengthy deterioration in a portfolio's excess spread and a severe slowdown in payment rates would be required before available credit support is exhausted. As a result, these subordinate class securities represent truly attractive instruments that can provide good value in today's market.

STRUCTURAL CONSIDERATIONS

Overview of Revolving Trust

The sale of more than $63.5 billion in publicly offered credit card securities has been made possible through the development and evolution of the credit card trust structure. In a credit card securitization, credit card accounts and the receivables that periodically arise in these accounts are sold to a trust, which funds the purchase of the receivables through the issuance of investor certificates. As the principal is paid on the receivables, the cash proceeds are reinvested in new receivables that are generated from the same or other accounts in the trust. This revolving process can be structured to continue for as long as the seller of the receivables desires, as long as the portfolio generates enough yield to support periodic losses, servicing costs, trust expenses, and certificate interest costs. If this excess spread becomes negative, the revolving period stops and all principal is utilized as received to pay the remaining certificate balance. The accelerated principal repayment is analogous to converting the structure to a pass-through. The revolving process is similar to an ongoing business, which is permitted to operate only if positive cash flow is generated (see Figure 21.1).

Amortization Events (Triggers)

The rating agencies require a receivables pool to begin to self-liquidate upon the occurrence of an event that is perceived to create material credit risk to investors (an Amortization Event, or Trigger). The following are examples of Amortization Events:

- The inability of the trust to be self-supporting, as indicated by a negative excess spread

Figure 21.1—Understanding Credit Card Subordinate Certificates Calculation of Excess Spread During Revolving Period

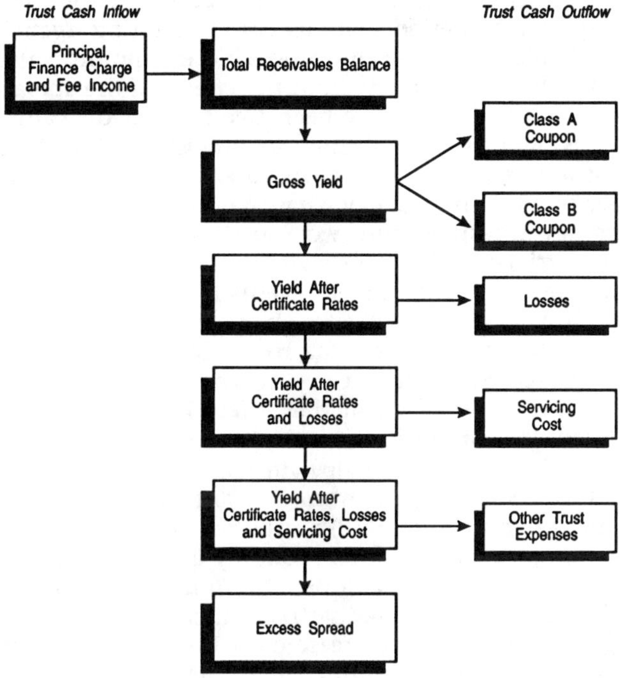

Source: Morgan Stanley

- An increase in losses to a certain percentage level, usually calculated on a three-month moving average
- A reduction in the amount still available from the Subordinate Amount (i.e., the dollar amount of credit enhancement)
- A reduction in the principal payment rate below a certain level
- The failure of the seller to add additional accounts to the pool when the Seller Interest falls below a minimum threshold of 7%–25% of the pool balance
- A material disruption in the ongoing business of the seller/servicer, as indicated by a receivership of bankruptcy filing
- A change in the legal characterization of the trust, such as qualifying as an investment company

- Other events, such as a breach of warranty or failure of the seller to make payments.

Once an early Amortization Event occurs, a Rapid Amortization principal repayment period commences. The rating agencies want a portfolio to liquidate as quickly as possible to minimize the potential damage to the Investor Interest from the effects of the actual Trigger or Amortization Event. There have been five term credit card issues that have hit early Amortization Events. In August 1988, a Republic Bank Delaware issue was redeemed after its parent went into receivership. In the summer of 1991, two Chevy Chase Savings Bank issues hit a three-month loss rate threshold and two Southeast Bank issues hit negative excess spread triggers. The Southeast Bank Credit Card Trusts 1990A and 1990B announced that payout events for each occurred at the end of June and July 1991, respectively. The payout event was the result of the average yield less losses on the receivables falling below the level required to cover transaction carrying costs, including the coupon, servicing fee and letter of credit (LOC) fee. The overall trust portfolio yield declined in combination with increased losses. For example, losses on 1990A moved from 4.46% in January 1991 to 6.83% in June 1991; losses on 1990B moved from 3.68% to 6.87% during the same period. Standard and Poor's (S&P) attributed some of this increased loss experience to a weakened Florida economy and a dramatic increase in collection personnel turnover during the fourth quarter of 1990. The Southeast Bank issues illustrate that rapid increases in losses can trigger repayment if yield does not increase or at least remain constant. However, the rating agencies confirmed that the existing cash flow from the receivables plus the LOC available to cover principal and interest shortfalls would continue to provide a AAA level of investor protection from principal losses, even though early principal repayment began as a result of an excess spread trigger. This phase is critical for subordinate class investors in senior/subordinate structures since it is the only time that a claim may be made by senior class investors on the subordinate principal cash flows.

RISKS TO SUBORDINATE CLASS INVESTORS

The subordinate class investors will not incur losses as long as there is credit support available to them. As a result, the key determinants of the magnitude of potential losses to subordinate class investors are:

- The portfolio payment rate subsequent to the Amortization Event
- The probability and potential severity of the portfolio's negative excess spread during the Amortization Period
- The ability of structural features and credit enhancement to absorb losses

Pool Payment Rate

Payment rates are a function of both the minimum payment terms of the credit card issuer and the number of cardholders who actually revolve balances and incur finance charges (revolvers) versus those who pay in full every month (convenience users). The payment rates of selected major issuers are shown in Table 21.1.

Table 21.1—Selected Average Monthly Credit Card Payment Rates* In Percent

Issuer	*1989*	*1990*	*1991*
Citicorp	13.36	12.78	12.48
Discover Card	12.84	13.37	13.66
First Chicago	13.87	14.51	14.09
MBNA America Bank	14.86	14.55	13.94
Norwest	12.80	13.69	13.14
Sears	7.90	7.28	7.10

* Total payment rates include payments by cardholders of principal and interest.

Source: Most recent 1991 prospectus for each of the above issuers, Moody's, S&P

The payment rate, defined as the monthly collections on the credit card accounts as a percentage of the receivables outstanding, has a significant impact on the allocation of losses from the receivables pool between the Investor Interest and Seller Interest. The faster investors are paid down, the lower their pro rata shares of losses on the pool will be in absolute terms. The rating agencies focus their analyses on the principal component of monthly collections, since it is this principal that will be used to fully pay down first the senior class portion, then the subordinate class portion, of the Investor Interest. As payment rates decline, there is a greater risk that the credit enhancement will be tapped to cover losses.

The purchase rate, defined as the amount of new cardholder charges available to be purchased or contributed to the trust, will affect the overall balance of the pool. Fluctuations in the purchase rate are caused by various economic and marketing factors. During recessions, for instance, when consumer credit demand is low, purchase rates tend to decline and credit card issuers often experience little or no growth in receivables balances. Purchase rates increase to reflect seasonal demand, especially at the end of the year during the Christmas shopping season, as well as in response to marketing programs initiated by credit card issuers (e.g., frequent flier mileage programs and programs that allow cardholders to select catalog merchandise depending upon their credit activity, etc.). If the purchase rate is lower than the payment rate, the receivables balance in the pool will drop, which could trigger an Amortization Event if the seller does not add new accounts to the trust. A continued low purchase rate subsequent to an Amortization Event could cause the Amortization Period to extend. Statistics have shown that a low purchase rate is not an immediate consequence of the recession, as demonstrated by VISA International's disclosure that charge volume was up by 16% in the second quarter of 1991 over the second quarter of 1990. Figure 21.2 indicates the relatively low likelihood of a cyclical decline in receivables balances as a consequence of the increasing trend in revolving consumer debt.

Negative Excess Spread

Negative excess spread can result from various factors such as a flawed business strategy, (e.g., poorly defined target market), poor credit underwriting standards, recessionary pressures (e.g., personal bankruptcy filings), and a competitive squeeze on finance charge income, fees and interchange. For example, some credit card issuers target customers with large revolving balances and are comfortable with the higher loss potential for this type of borrower. Other issuers may target higher-quality borrowers who pay off balances more quickly and therefore do not generate either yields or losses but generate significant interchange income. Investors should evaluate the likelihood, if any, of a prolonged simultaneous deterioration in both yields and losses. Representative recent yields and losses are shown in Table 21.2.

Credit Enhancement

The general motivation for an issuer of credit card-backed securities to use a senior/subordinate structure as opposed to a stand-alone LOC is to improve the pricing of the senior class of the Investor Interest. In-

Figure 21.2—Growth in Revolving Consumer Credit 1985–September 1991

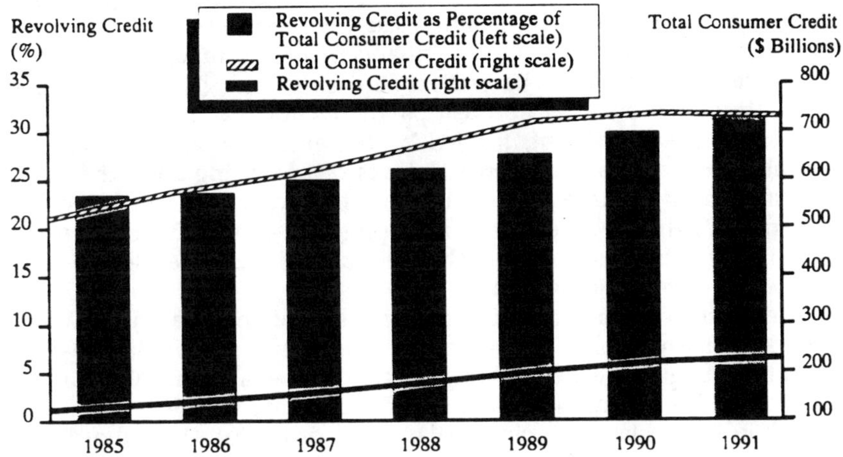

Source: Federal Reserve's G.19 statistical release of Consumer Installment Credit

Table 21.2—Selected Yield and Loss Statistics In Percent

Issuer	*Gross Yield*	*Losses*
Citicorp	20.05	6.59
Discover Card	18.41	4.29
MBNA America Bank	18.61	3.21
Norwest	20.34	3.99
Sears	18.21	3.44

Source: Most recent 1991 prospectus for each of the above issuers, Moody's, S&P

vestors have been concerned by the event/third-party risk of an Aaa/AAA-rated LOC provider and are attracted to the downgrade protection provided by both the senior/subordinate and cash collateral account structures. The introduction of the cash collateral account as credit enhancement in the spring of 1991 was well-received by investors and may also provide attractive economics to issuers as a method of credit enhancement.

The senior/subordinate structure normally involves multiple layers of credit protection to benefit the various parties involved in the transaction, beginning with the senior class investor's protection via the subordinate class. External credit enhancement, normally in the form of a partial LOC or cash collateral account large enough to achieve a A or AA rating, is provided to protect payments due the subordinate class investor. A spread account, funded by the excess of the yield on the receivables less coupon payments to investors, servicing and other trust expenses, builds up to a stated cap amount and is available solely for the benefit of the credit enhancement provider. Free cash flows on the entire Investor Interest, not just the subordinate class, are used to fund or replenish the spread account.

The level of credit enhancement and size of the subordinate class depend upon the desired rating for the senior and subordinate classes. The rating agencies generally require that either a cash collateral account or an LOC from an A-rated or higher bank cover 54% to 70% of the subordinate class principal balance in order for the subordinate class to qualify for an A rating. On the other hand, the first Discover Card subordinate class to be sold publicly in July 1991 was rated Aa1/AA and had a reserve account (a cash collateral spread account funded initially by a deposit from the seller/servicer and maintained at a given level by deposits from excess spread as necessary) that was initially 102.5% of the subordinate class balance. However, the more recent Discover Card 1991C and 1991D transactions in October 1991 featured an A2/A-rated subordinate class with a reserve account that initially covered 69.8% of the Class B principal but could build to 77% under certain circumstances.

To receive a subordinate class rating, the rating agencies employ a credit sizing methodology. The level of credit enhancement on the subordinate class is calculated as if the entire Investor Interest (senior and subordinate classes combined) was rated A or AA, as applicable. The subordinate class is then sized to obtain a AAA rating for the senior class. The rating agencies also determine the expiration date for the credit enhancement, which allows for a severe slowdown in the pool's payment and purchase rates in a stress scenario. This date will extend beyond the expected final payment date on the Class B certificates.

CASE STUDIES: CITIBANK AND DISCOVER CARD STRUCTURES

While all of the subordinate classes sold to date (Citibank, Colonial National Bank, Discover Card, Household, and Signet) provide significant credit protection against all but the most severely adverse performances, structural differences can create significant timing differences of cash flows to investors should a stress case scenario actually occur. These timing differences can result in quicker or slower repayment of the subordinate class principal. A detailed matrix of cash flow priorities for each structure is included in Appendix 1 to this chapter.

Although the detailed cash flows of each particular issue are complex, the sequence and priority of payment is generally a three-step process.

Step 1

If the senior class required amount (generally defined as certificate interest, servicing fee and charged-off principal including interest on past due certificate interest) exceeds the senior class finance charge collections and reinvestment income, the subordinate class collections (finance charges, principal or both, depending on the structure) are used to cover the deficiency. Subordinate class interest is paid from subordinate class and senior class excess finance charge collections.

Step 2

If subordinate class principal collections are applied to the senior class required amount or a shortfall still exists, the subordinate class ownership percentage shifts downward. Ownership percentage can be reinstated through future excess finance charge collections. Principal payments not used to pay the senior class required amount are used to pay senior class principal.

Step 3

Subordinate class interest shortfalls and unreimbursed ownership percentage shifts are reimbursed from excess finance charge collections and credit enhancement (timing varies depending on the structure).

We have selected the A2/A-rated Discover Card structure issued in October 1991 and the A2/A-rated Citibank structure for comparison.

The Citibank model was selected because of the relatively large volume issued. The Discover Card issue was selected because it has a different cash flow sequence than the Citibank structure. Table 21.3 provides an overview of the investor protection features of each issue.

Table 21.3—Summary of Credit Enhancement Features Discover Card and Citibank Subordinate Classes

	Discover Card	*Citibank*	*Comments*
• Rating	A2/A	A2/A	-
• Amount of Class B Credit Enhancement	69.8% initial 77% maximum	63.5%*	-
• Type of Credit Enhancement	Reserve (Cash Collateral) Account	Cash Collateral Account; Letter of Credit	-
• Class A Fully Paid Prior to Class B Principal Payout	Yes	Yes	Protects Class A
• Class B Interest Shifts if Significant Class A Shortfall	Yes	Yes	Protects Class A
• Fixing of Investor Principal Allocation as of End of Revolving Period	Yes	Yes	Protects Classes A and B
• Maximization of Investor Finance Charge Allocation as of End of Revolving Period	Yes	No	Protects Classes A and B
• Subordinate Amount Increases in Certain Events	Yes	No	Protects Classes A and B
• Subordination of Servicing	No	Yes	Protects Classes A and B
• Use of Excess Servicing to Reimburse Class B	At All Times	At All Times	Protects Classes A and B
• Use of Credit Enhancement to Reimburse Class B	Yes	Yes	Protects Class B
• Credit Enhancement Balance Does Not Decline in Proportion to Investor Interest**	Yes	Yes	Protects Class B

* Approximate; varies slightly from issue to issue.

** As compared to traditional securitization in which the credit enhancement generally declines in absolute terms as the pool principal balance amortizes.

Source: Morgan Stanley

Breakeven Analysis

To illustrate how unlikely the scenarios must be in order for the subordinate class investor to lose principal, we calculated breakeven scenarios by lowering finance charge rates 9 percentage points below current and historical finance charge yields for each structure (e.g., from 18%

to 9% annually for the Discover Card and from 20% to 11% for Citibank), by assuming purchase rates equal to payment rates and by using current market financing rates. Summary model results are included in Appendix 2. We then determined the combination of the monthly principal payment and annualized principal loss rates required for the subordinate class investor to just avoid losing principal. The actual Discover Card and Citibank credit enhancement structures were used (see Table 21.4).

Table 21.4—Breakeven Loss Rate
In Percent

Principal Payment Rate	*Discover Card*	*Citibank*
2	6.6	5.2
4	9.4	8.5
6	12.1	11.6
8	14.8	14.7
10	17.4	17.7

Source: Morgan Stanley

Both structures can withstand severe deterioration in yields, losses, and payment rates before subordinate class investors would lose principal. For example, the principal payment rates in Table 21.4 can decline to as low as 2% (9–10 percentage points below historical averages) and only at loss rates higher than 6.6% for Discover Card and 5.2% for Citibank would a subordinate class investor lose principal.

For example, the Discover Card, at a yield of 12% and a principal payment rate of 8.7%, as indicated by Point A in Figure 21.3, would require a loss experience greater than 20% before a subordinate class investor would sustain losses. As shown in Figure 21.3, actual loss performance reported for 1989, 1990, and 1991 was 3.3%, 3.9%, and 4.3%, respectively, far below the principal loss threshold.

At higher payment rates, the Citibank structure can withstand slightly higher losses since the subordinate class credit enhancement (e.g., either the LOC or cash collateral account) cannot be drawn upon to reimburse subordinate class investors for senior class losses that had caused a subordinate class draw in prior periods until the senior class has been fully paid.

Figure 21.3—Subordinate Class Principal Loss Frontier Discover Card Trust 1991C

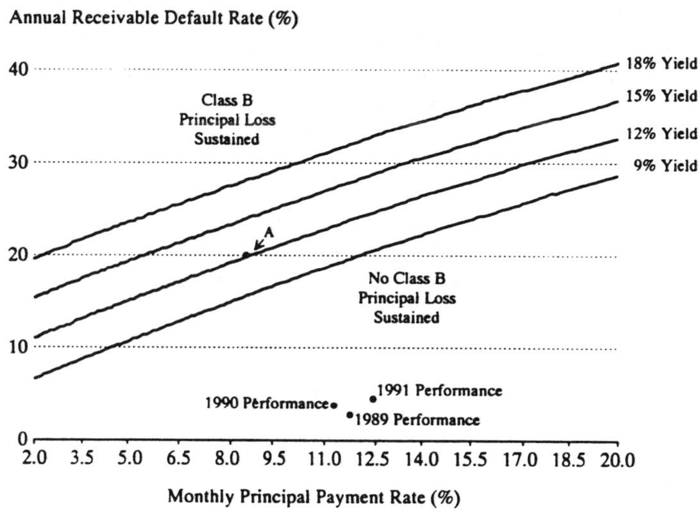

Source: Morgan Stanley

Credit enhancement is accessed sooner in the Discover Card structure. Consequently, slightly lower subordinate class credit enhancement remains in the Discover Card structure to absorb subordinate class losses. On the other hand, the Discover Card structure performs slightly better at slower payment rates. See Appendix 1 for a detailed comparison of cash flow priorities in each structure.

Figures 21.3 and 21.4 illustrate the subordinate class principal loss frontiers (each modeling stress scenarios with differing yield assumptions). Investors should note that the results as illustrated in Appendix 2 are affected by:

- Absolute level of yield and losses
- Mix of yield, losses, coupon, and servicing fee that determines excess spread (e.g., greater losses will result in faster prepayments, assuming all other factors are held constant)
- Principal payment rate
- Ratio of Investor Interest to receivables balance at the time of the Amortization Event

Figure 21.4—Subordinate Class Principal Loss Frontier Standard Credit Card Master Trust 1

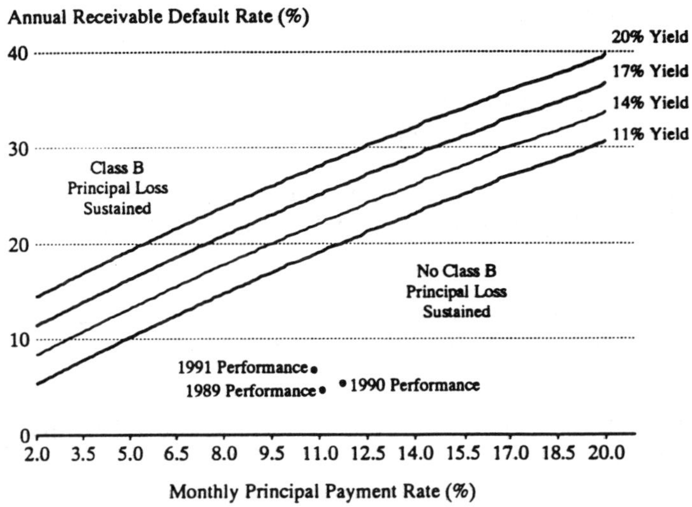

Source: Morgan Stanley

- Subordinate class as a percentage of senior class
- Credit enhancement as a percentage of subordinate class balance
- Credit enhancement expiration date
- Cause of the Amortization Event (e.g., bankruptcy)
- Purchase rate versus payment rate.

CONCLUSION

Subordinate classes of credit card securitizations are structured to provide a significant level of protection in all but the most severely stressed scenarios for losses and payment rates. Investors willing to take the time to understand the structural protection afforded in the various subordinate securities available will be rewarded with attractive yields. Morgan Stanley would be pleased to discuss the mechanics of each issue in more detail with interested investors. For further information, please contact Kenneth J. Bock at (212) 296-6450; Richard J. Watson at (212) 296-6544; or Kimberly L. Hirschman at (212) 296-6446.

Glossary

Total Receivables Balance: Total balance of all receivables in the pool sold to the trust.

Investor Interest: Predetermined dollar amount of the Total Receivables Balance (e.g., $500 million). Comprised of Senior Class (Class A) and Subordinate Class (Class B).

Seller Interest: Portion of Total Receivables Balance necessary to absorb daily volatility. Calculated as the Total Receivables Balance minus the Investor Interest.

Gross Yield: Sum of annual percentage rate, annual, late, and over-limit fees, cash advance fees and interchange income (merchant discount).

Certificate Rate: Coupon on both the senior and subordinate classes of the Investor Interest.

Losses: Actual net losses (after recoveries, if applicable).

Servicing Cost: Compensation to the servicer for the cost of providing customer service and collections personnel excluding marketing expenses. Generally 2% to 2.5% per year.

Other Trust Expenses: Credit support, trustee, accounting, and other ongoing expenses.

Excess Spread: Gross Yield less Certificate Rates, Losses, Servicing Costs, and Other Trust Expenses.

Appendix 1

SOURCES AND USES OF FUNDS MATRICES

Figures 21.5, 21.6, 21.7, and 21.8 illustrate the sources and uses of funds in order of application for the Discover Trust 1991C, 1991D, and Standard Credit Card Master Trust. The examples of how to use these charts (Figures 21.5 and 21.6) should assist the reader in understanding how to compare the cash flows of these securities. The examples that follow illustrate the Discover Card model.

Figure 21.5—Sources of Funds

	Class A Interest	Class A Defaults	Class A Servicing New Old	Class A Balance Reduction Reinstatements	Class B Interest	Class B Defaults	Class B Servicing New Old	Class B Balance Reduction Reinstatements	Regular Investor Principal Payments	Cash Collateral Account Deposits
Class B Finance Charges	1	3	2		4	7	6 5			8

The Source of Funds (vertical axis) is applied or used in the following order for the purpose described along the horizontal axis.

Source: Class B Finance Charges are applied in order to:

1. Class A Interest
2. Unpaid Prior Period (Old) Class A Servicing
3. Class A Defaults
4. Class B Interest
5. Unpaid Prior Period (Old) Class B Servicing
6. Current Period (New) Class B Servicing
7. Class B Defaults
8. Cash Collateral Account Deposit

Note: For example, Class B Interest only has a claim on any remaining Class B Finance Charges after Class B Finance Charges have been used to fully pay Class A Interest, "Old" (past due) Class A Servicing and Class A Defaults.

Source: Morgan Stanley

Figure 21.6—Use of Funds

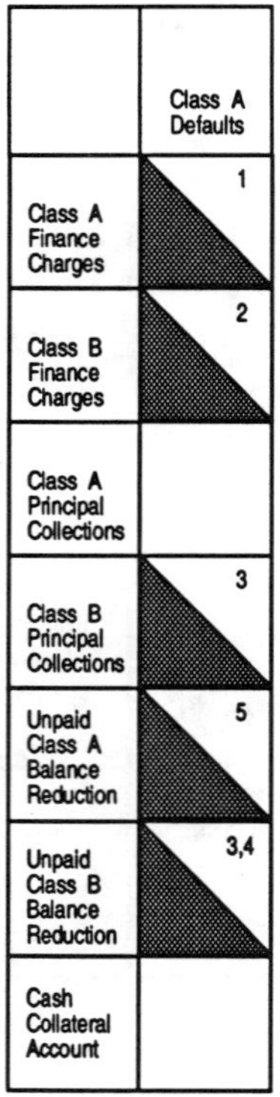

The Uses of Funds (horizontal axis) draws upon the sources (vertical axis) in the following order:

Use: Class A Defaults are drawn in order from:

1. Class A Finance Charges
2. Class B Finance Charges
3. Class B Principal Collections

3,4. Unpaid Class B Balance Reduction

5. Unpaid Class A Balance Reduction

Note: For example, Class B Principal Collections are third in line to be used to cover Class A Defaults after Class A Finance Charges and Class B Finance Charges have either been depleted during the distribution period or were originally unavailable.

Source: Morgan Stanley

Figure 21.7—Discover Card Trust 1991C and 1991D Cash Flow Priority Schedule

Uses of Funds

Sources of Funds	Class A Interest	Class A Defaults	Class A Servicing New	Class A Servicing Old	Class A Balance Reduction Reinstate-ments	Class B Interest	Class B Defaults	Class B Servicing New	Class B Servicing Old	Class B Balance Reduction Reinstate-ments	Regular Investor Principal Payments	Cash Collateral Account Deposits
Class A Finance Charges	1 / 1	1 / 4	1 / 3	1 / 2		2 / 5	2 / 7		2 / 6			1 / 8
Class B Finance Charges	2 / 1	2 / 3		2 / 2		1 / 4	1 / 7	1 / 6	1 / 5			2 / 8
Class A Principal Collections											1 / 1	
Class B Principal Collections	3 / 1	3 / 3		3 / 2							2 / 4	
Unpaid Class A Balance Reduction		5 / 1										
Unpaid Class B Balance Reduction	3 / 1	3,4 / 2					3 / 3					
Cash Collateral Account						3 / 1	4 / 3		3 / 2	1 / 4		

Note: The numbers in the upper right corners of the boxes indicate the order uses listed along the top draw upon the sources listed down the left side. The numbers in the lower left corners of the boxes indicate the order the sources listed on the left are applied to the uses listed along the top.

Source: Morgan Stanley

Figure 21.8—Standard Credit Card Master Trust Cash Flow Priority Schedule

Uses of Funds

Sources of Funds	Class A Interest	Class A Defaults	Class A Servicing	Class A Balance Reduction Reinstate-ments	Class B Interest	Class B Defaults	Class B Servicing	Class B Balance Reduction Reinstate-ments	Regular Investor Principal Payments	Cash Collateral Account Deposits
Class A Finance Charges	1 \ 1	2 \ 1	3 \ 1	4 \ 1	5 \ 2	6 \ 1		7 \ 1		8 \ 1
Class B Finance Charges	3 \ 2	4 \ 2		5 \ 2	1 \ 1	6 \ 2	2 \ 1	7 \ 2		8 \ 2
Class A Principal Collections									1 \ 1	
Class B Principal Collections	1 \ 3	2 \ 3							3 \ 2	
Unpaid Class A Balance Reduction		1 \ 5								
Unpaid Class B Balance Reduction	1 \ 3	2 \ 3,4				3 \ 3				
Cash Collateral Account					1 \ 3	2 \ 4		3 \ 3		

Note: The numbers in the upper right corners of the boxes indicate the order uses listed along the top draw upon the sources listed down the left side. The numbers in the lower left corners of the boxes indicate the order the sources listed on the left are applied to the uses listed along the top.

Source: Morgan Stanley

Appendix 2

SUMMARY FINANCIAL MODEL CASH FLOWS

Table 21.5—Summary Credit Card Certificate Cash Flows
Discover Card

505,474,592	Initial Pool Principal Balance	9.00%	Annual Finance Charge Collection Rate	8.96	Class A Average Life
350,000,000	Initial Class A Investor Balance	5.00%	Monthly Principal Collection Rate	18	Class A Final Maturity
35,000,000	Initial Class B Investor Balance	10.00%	Annual Net Charge-Off Rate	0	Class A Principal Loss
24,440,000	Initial Credit Enhancement Amount	1	Charge-Off Starting Period	19.08	Class B Average Life
26,950,000	Maximum Credit Enhancement Amount	2.00%	Servicing Fee	20	Class B Final Maturity
35,000,000	Available Subordinate Amount	0.00%	Reinvestment Rate	0	Class B Principal Loss
8.000%	Class A Pass-Through Rate			9.88	Investor Average Life
8.375%	Class B Pass-Through Rate				

			Class A Percentage			Class B Percentage										
Period	Principal Receivable	Seller Balance	Fin	Prin	Net C/O	Fin	Prin	Net C/O	Class A Investor Balance	Class B Investor Balance	Class A Investor Charged-Off Amount	Total Principal Paid to Class A	Class B Investor Charged-Off Amount	Class B Principal Losses Reserve Draw	Total Principal Paid to Class B	Reserve Account Amount
0	505,474,592	120,474,592							350,000,000	35,000,000						
1	482,172,720	119,470,637	69.24	69.24	69.24	6.92	6.92%	6.92	327,702,083	35,000,000	2,916,667	22,297,917	2,964,063	2,964,063	0	24,440,000
2	459,218,053	118,475,048	72.59	69.24	67.96	7.26	6.92%	7.26	305,743,004	35,000,000	2,730,851	21,959,079	2,762,205	2,762,205	0	21,247,708
3	436,600,411	117,487,756	76.22	69.24	66.58	7.62	6.92%	7.62	284,112,654	35,000,000	2,547,858	21,630,350	2,576,213	2,576,213	0	18,182,899
4	414,309,808	116,508,592	80.16	69.24	65.07	8.02	6.92%	8.02	262,801,116	35,000,000	2,367,605	21,311,538	2,398,960	2,398,960	0	15,301,083
5	392,336,445	115,537,786	84.48	69.24	63.43	8.45	6.92%	8.45	241,798,659	35,000,000	2,190,009	21,002,457	1,958,729	1,958,729	0	12,599,519
6	370,670,704	114,574,971	89.21	69.24	61.63	8.92	6.92%	8.92	221,095,733	35,000,000	2,014,989	20,702,926	1,458,207	1,458,207	0	10,338,186
7	349,303,147	113,620,180	94.42	69.24	59.65	5.58	6.92%	9.44	200,682,968	35,000,000	1,842,464	20,415,766	1,219,732	1,219,732	0	8,577,375
8	328,224,507	112,673,345	100.00	69.24	57.45	0.00	6.92%	10.02	180,551,163	35,000,000	1,672,358	20,131,805	1,038,441	1,038,441	0	7,055,038
9	307,425,688	111,734,400	100.00	69.24	55.01	0.00	6.92%	10.66	160,691,288	35,000,000	1,504,593	19,859,875	859,683	859,683	0	5,713,994
10	286,897,756	110,803,280	100.00	69.24	52.27	0.00	6.92%	11.38	141,094,476	35,000,000	1,339,094	19,596,812	683,376	683,376	0	4,551,706
11	286,631,940	109,879,920	100.00	69.24	49.18	0.00	6.92%	12.20	121,752,020	35,000,000	1,175,787	19,342,456	509,439	509,439	0	3,565,726
12	246,619,623	108,964,254	100.00	69.24	45.66	0.00	6.92%	13.13	102,655,369	35,000,000	1,014,600	19,096,651	337,792	337,792	0	2,753,683
13	226,852,342	108,056,218	100.00	69.24	41.62	0.00	6.92%	14.19	83,796,124	35,000,000	855,461	18,859,245	291,667	291,667	0	2,113,287
14	207,321,783	107,155,750	100.00	69.24	36.94	0.00	6.92%	15.43	65,166,033	35,000,000	698,301	18,630,091	291,667	291,667	0	1,642,326
15	188,019,773	106,262,785	100.00	69.24	31.43	0.00	6.92%	16.88	46,756,988	35,000,000	543,050	18,409,045	291,667	196,749	0	1,338,668
16	168,938,283	105,377,262	100.00	69.24	24.87	0.00	6.92%	18.62	28,561,021	35,000,000	389,642	18,195,967	291,667	0	0	1,141,919
17	150,069,420	104,499,118	100.00	69.24	16.91	0.00	6.92%	20.72	10,570,302	35,000,000	238,009	17,990,720	291,667	0	0	1,166,762
18	131,405,422	103,628,292	100.00	69.24	7.04	0.00	6.92%	23.32	0	27,777,130	88,086	10,570,302	291,667	0	7,222,870	1,352,953
19	112,938,661	102,764,723	100.00	69.24	0.00	0.00	6.92%	21.14	0	10,173,938	0	0	231,476	0	17,603,192	1,698,651
20	101,908,350	101,908,350	100.00	69.24	0.00	0.00	6.92%	9.01	0	0	0	0	84,783	0	10,173,938	2,204,347

Source: Morgan Stanley

Table 21.6—Summary Credit Card Certificate Cash Flows
Standard Credit Card Master Trust 1

700,000,000	Initial Principal Receivables Amount	11.000%	Finance Charge Collection Rate	9.64	Class A Average Life
500,000,000	Initial Class A Investor Balance	5.000%	Monthly Principal Collection Rate	19	Class A Final Maturity
62,000,000	Initial Class B Investor Balance	10.000%	Annual Net Default Rate	0	Class A Principal Loss
39,340,000	Initial Credit Enhancement Amount	1	Default Starting Period	19.39	Class B Average Life
39,340,000	Maximum Credit Enhancement Amount	2.000%	Servicing Fee	20	Class B Final Maturity
8.250%	Class A Pass-Through Rate	0.000%	Reinvestment Rate	0	Class B Principal Loss
8.470%	Class B Pass-Through Rate			10.72	Investor Average Life

Period	Principal Receivable	Seller Balance	Investor Principal Collection	Class A Fin Charge/ Default	Class B Fin Charge/ Default	Class A Invested Amount	Class B Unpaid Principal Balance	Class A Default Amount	Total Class A Principal Payment	Class B Default Amount	Class B Principal Loss Draw	Total Class B Principal Payment	Cash Collateral Account Amount
0	700,000,000	138,000,000				500,000,000	62,000,000						39,340,000
1	665,784,167	136,333,333	80.29%	71.43%	8.86%	471,003,881	62,000,000	4,166,667	28,996,119	516,667	0	0	39,340,000
2	632,115,289	134,710,164	80.29%	70.74%	8.78%	442,305,509	62,000,000	3,925,032	28,698,372	487,058	0	0	39,314,921
3	598,958,160	133,128,416	80.29%	69.97%	8.72%	413,902,215	62,000,000	3,685,879	28,403,294	459,163	0	0	39,266,216
4	566,385,686	131,586,058	80.29%	69.10%	8.67%	385,791,352	62,000,000	3,449,185	28,110,863	432,954	0	0	39,195,312
5	534,308,885	130,081,105	80.29%	68.11%	8.65%	357,970,296	62,000,000	3,214,928	27,821,055	408,402	0	0	39,103,612
6	502,746,884	128,611,617	80.29%	67.00%	8.66%	330,436,448	62,000,000	2,983,086	27,533,848	385,479	0	0	38,992,496
7	471,691,922	127,175,697	80.29%	65.73%	8.69%	303,187,229	62,000,000	2,753,637	27,249,219	364,157	0	0	38,863,320
8	441,136,343	125,771,491	80.29%	64.28%	8.76%	276,220,085	62,000,000	2,526,560	26,967,145	344,408	0	0	38,717,417
9	411,072,600	124,397,189	80.29%	62.62%	8.87%	249,532,481	62,000,000	2,301,834	26,687,604	326,206	0	0	38,556,098
10	381,493,248	123,051,021	80.29%	60.70%	9.04%	223,121,907	62,000,000	2,079,437	26,410,574	309,524	0	0	38,380,648
11	352,390,947	121,731,260	80.29%	58.49%	9.26%	196,985,874	62,000,000	1,859,349	26,136,033	294,336	0	0	38,192,334
12	323,758,460	120,436,218	80.29%	55.90%	9.56%	171,121,915	62,000,000	1,641,549	25,863,959	280,615	0	0	37,992,398
13	295,588,651	119,164,247	80.29%	52.85%	9.95%	145,527,584	62,000,000	1,426,016	25,594,331	268,336	0	0	37,782,062
14	267,874,481	117,913,738	80.29%	49.23%	10.45%	120,200,457	62,000,000	1,212,730	25,327,127	257,474	0	0	37,562,526
15	240,609,013	116,683,121	80.29%	44.87%	11.11%	95,138,130	62,000,000	1,001,670	25,062,327	248,002	0	0	37,334,967
16	213,785,405	115,470,864	80.29%	39.54%	11.96%	70,338,222	62,000,000	792,818	24,799,908	239,898	0	0	37,100,544
17	187,396,910	114,275,470	80.29%	32.90%	13.09%	45,798,371	62,000,000	586,152	24,539,851	233,136	0	0	36,860,394
18	161,436,879	113,095,483	80.29%	24.44%	14.58%	21,516,236	62,000,000	381,653	24,282,135	227,692	0	0	36,615,632
19	135,898,753	111,929,477	80.29%	13.33%	16.62%	0	23,969,276	179,302	21,516,236	223,543	35,520,221	2,510,503	847,135
20	110,796,988	110,796,988	80.29%	0.00%	17.64%	0	0	0	0	199,744	190,989	23,778,287	405,433

Source: Morgan Stanley

Index

D

E

F

G

H

J

L

M

N

O

P

R

S

About the Publisher

PROBUS PUBLISHING COMPANY

Probus Publishing Company fills the informational needs of today's business professional by publishing authoritative, quality books on timely and relevant topics, including:

- Investing
- Futures/Options Trading
- Banking
- Finance
- Marketing and Sales
- Manufacturing and Project Management
- Personal Finance, Real Estate, Insurance and Estate Planning
- Entrepreneurship
- Management

Probus books are available at quantity discounts when purchased for business, educational or sales promotional use. For more information, please call the Director, Corporate/Institutional Sales at 1-800-PROBUS-1, or write:

Director, Corporate/Institutional Sales
Probus Publishing Company
1925 N. Clybourn Avenue
Chicago, Illinois 60614
FAX (312) 868-6250